LAST MAN STANDING

LAST MAN STANDING

MORT SAHL

and the Birth of Modern Comedy

James Curtis

University Press of Mississippi / Jackson

Also by James Curtis

William Cameron Menzies: The Shape of Films to Come
Spencer Tracy: A Biography
W. C. Fields: A Biography
James Whale: A New World of Gods and Monsters
Between Flops: A Biography of Preston Sturges
The Creative Producer (editor)
Featured Player (editor)

www.upress.state.ms.us

The University Press of Mississippi is a member
of the Association of American University Presses.

First printing 2017
∞

Library of Congress Cataloging-in-Publication Data

Names: Curtis, James, 1953– author.
Title: Last man standing : Mort Sahl and the
birth of modern comedy / James Curtis.
Description: Jackson : University Press of Mississippi, 2017. |
Includes bibliographical references and index.
Identifiers: LCCN 2016043629 (print) | LCCN 2017004229 (ebook)
| ISBN   9781496809285 (hardback) | ISBN 9781496811998
(epub single) | ISBN   9781496812001 (epub institutional) |
ISBN 9781496812018 (pdf single) | ISBN 9781496812025 (pdf
institutional) Subjects: LCSH: Sahl, Mort. | Comedians—United
States—Biography. | BISAC: BIOGRAPHY & AUTOBIOGRAPHY /
Entertainment & Performing Arts. | PERFORMING   ARTS / Com-
edy. Classification: LCC PN2287.S22 C87 2017 (print) | LCC PN2287.
S22 (ebook) | DDC 792.7/6028092 [B] —dc23
LC record available at https://lccn.loc.gov/2016043629

British Library Cataloging-in-Publication Data available

In Memory of Robin Williams

I'll publish right or wrong:
Fools are my theme,
Let satire be my song.

—LORD BYRON

CONTENTS

CONTENTS

PART ONE

The Next President of the United States

1

I'M NOT GEARED
TO TOTAL ACCEPTANCE

A canopied entrance off Madison Avenue leads to one of New York's most intimate concert venues, a place where time has seemingly stood still for more than half a century. To the left of a small foyer is the Bemelmans Bar, its walls covered with fanciful scenes of Central Park as rendered by Ludwig Bemelmans, the celebrated author of *Madeline*. Jazzy standards fill the air, listeners scattered among nickel-trimmed tables and perched like placid crows at the black granite bar. It's as civilized a spot as exists on the Upper East Side of Manhattan, the sort of room where the conversations come accessorized with dry martinis and the gimlets are mixed with fresh lime.

Opposite the Bemelmans is a shrine to the art of cabaret, a performance space only slightly larger than a regulation racquetball court. Here is where musical acts as varied as Herb Alpert and Eartha Kitt have held forth, and where Bobby Short was seasonally featured for thirty-six years. On its walls are the murals of Marcel Vertès, the Academy Award–winning designer of *Moulin Rouge*, its blue-hued banquettes encircling a floor still dominated by a grand piano.

Although Short, whose portrait hangs just outside, liked to refer to himself as a saloon singer, the Café Carlyle has never been the province of comedians. When Woody Allen sits in with the Eddy Davis New Orleans Jazz Band, he sticks to his clarinet and never utters a word. So of all the people who could possibly be booked into this elegant little sanctuary on a Monday night, one of the most unlikely is the man who single-handedly made the stage safe for an open collar, a jazz artist who can neither sing nor play an instrument, a satirist so savage that *Time* once described him as "Will Rogers with fangs."

Seated at a table near the back, Mort Sahl doesn't appear nervous in the least. Clad in a red cashmere sweater, he is still strikingly handsome at age 86, the celestial nose suggesting the profile of a much younger man, the graying hair at once both combed and unruly. He chats comfortably as the room fills, quick to break into a grin as if some private absurdity has just caught his attention. Occasionally a stranger leans in to shake his hand; one man asks him to sign a copy of his book *Heartland* and tells him that he's been a fan for fifty years.

Among those taking their seats are James Wolcott, cultural critic and blogger for *Vanity Fair*; the comedian Mark Pitta; broadcast journalist John Hart; and the star's third wife, Kenslea, who has flown in from California expressly for the occasion. At 10:50, Dick Cavett makes his way to the riser as applause fills the room.

"Some years ago," he says by way of introduction, "a meteor shot across the comedy sky. My new friend Woody Allen and I went to see him at a place called Basin Street East in New York. Woody said, 'Wait until you see him. You will agree with me that everyone else should quit the business.' Here is a man who said: 'Ronald Reagan won because he ran against Jimmy Carter— and if he had run unopposed he would have lost.'

"Once at Basin Street a guy yelled out, 'Is that a Brooks Brothers sweater?' So Mort picked up the subject of Brooks Brothers and said, 'It's a strange store. They have no mirrors, but they will stand another customer in front of you.'

"That's a bit of a weird curve," he admitted over the appreciative laughter, "but I love weird curves . . .

"Ladies and gentlemen, the great Mort Sahl."

Prolonged applause as Sahl moves slowly toward the stage, his friend Lucy Mercer at his side, his balance uncertain after a 2008 stroke robbed him of the sight in one eye. "Thank you," he says when firmly in place, a pair of newspapers clutched in his right hand. "I want to tell you that Barack Obama has taken a reverse mortgage out on the White House."

The laugh builds as the thought sinks in.

"The old saying was that if anything happened to the president, the Secret Service had standing orders to shoot Joseph Biden . . ."

More laughter.

"This is not going to be a political show tonight. I'd like to talk about a couple of other subjects I know something about—men and women. Politics are getting harder because the Democrats don't know how to make their comeback. They're already apologizing for this guy and promising you Hillary Clinton. . . . She rose through the ranks—slept with the boss. Or *didn't* sleep with the boss. . . . Okay, Lady Macbeth."

Sizing up the room, he seems caught in a perpetual state of amusement. His blue eyes glow as if electrified. He flashes a gleaming set of teeth as would an animal on the verge of attack.

"I brought two papers for you tonight," he announces. "One is the *New York Times* because of the nature of the people who patronize this hotel, and one is the *Post*, which they hide behind it. The *Times*, as you know, is the last liberal paper in America. In other words, if there was a war between North Korea and Iran and they both used nuclear weapons, this is the way the *Times* would report it: NUCLEAR WAR! WORLD ENDS! And below the fold: WOMEN AND MINORITIES HIT HARDEST."

The show continues past midnight, Sahl drawing from an arsenal of material compiled over a span of sixty years and eleven presidencies. On stage he is uniquely alone; he has no writers, no peers in the narrow field of political satire. There is an easy authority in his voice, the kind that comes from the knowledge that all the public figures on whom he once cut his teeth have now passed from the scene. By sheer animal endurance he is the victor, the conquering hero, the last man standing in a field of giants. Toward the close of the evening he takes questions called to him from the audience and responds extemporaneously. In all, it would be a sterling performance for a man half his age.

It probably doesn't occur to anyone—other than, perhaps, the man himself—that in its dimensions and intimacies, the Café Carlyle isn't much different from the bohemian space in San Francisco where Mort Sahl began mixing hard news and comedy in 1953. North Beach, which extended from Chinatown to Fisherman's Wharf, was the section of town where the pizza parlors and steakhouses kept late hours and the clubs offered everything in the way of entertainment from striptease to opera. It was noisy, colorful, aromatic, a place where all cultures and ethnicities could comfortably mix. Slashing through the center of it all was Columbus Avenue, home to Lawrence Ferlinghetti's City Lights Bookstore; the Black Cat bar, which singer Maya Angelou recalled as "a meeting place for very elegant homosexuals"; a cellar place near the intersection of Columbus and Jackson called the Purple Onion; and, directly across the street from the Onion, down a flight of marble stairs, the hungry i.

There were no banquettes in the basement of the shabby old Sentinel Building, a copper-clad flatiron dating from 1907, but there was a grand piano, the entertainment policy having been strictly musical up until Sahl's debut. The room sat eighty-three on kitchen chairs and old school benches, but standing room could swell the capacity to a hundred or more on a good night. The cover charge, collected at the top of the steps, was twenty-five cents on weekdays, fifty on weekends.

The hungry i first opened its doors on September 9, 1950, as a membership club catering to artists and musicians. The founder was an enormous German-born impresario and sometime actor named Eric Nord, whose size brought him the sobriquet "Big Daddy." The name of the place was properly expressed in lower case, but the press rarely complied. "I started to paint 'hungry intellectual,' across the door," Nord would explain, "and ran out of space." The walls were bare concrete and the bar, at which the featured drink was mulled wine, was all of six feet in length.

Open until three in the morning, the club was a hit with students and the free-thinking denizens of Telegraph Hill. Nord stuck with it a year and some months, but after drawing a fifteen-day penalty for serving liquor to a minor, he sold the hungry i to one of his patrons for $800. "It was relaxed and funky," reasoned the buyer, a beret-wearing restaurateur named Enrico Banducci. A natural showman, Banducci formalized the entertainment calendar and made the hungry i something more than a mere hangout. A rug thrown on the concrete floor became the stage, its only dressing an apple crate on which the featured performer, a muscular folk singer named Stan Wilson, rested a foot while strumming his guitar. Lighting came from candles flickering atop a few low tables and the tips of countless cigarettes. "'European' was the adjective people always used to describe it," said Donald Pippin, who played the piano there five nights a week. "In the warm glow, it was not hard to imagine oneself in Paris or the dream city of one's choice."

On the evening of December 22, 1953, a slight, diffident man took the stage in a brown suit salvaged from the traveling wardrobe of the Stan Kenton band. The newspaper he held in his hands wasn't merely a prop; his cues, typed out on index cards, were stapled to its inside pages. There is no record of what he said, nor precisely how long he was on, but by all accounts he went over big. Don Steele, who was there in his capacity as entertainment columnist for the *Oakland Tribune*, recalled that "like all pure genius" Mort Sahl was as clever that first night as he would later be as an established headliner. If Steele sensed that Sahl had jammed the room with friends,

UC students intent on laughing at practically anything the young comedian said, he never let on.

The job at the hungry i was the result of an awkward audition that had taken place a couple of weeks earlier. The pitch was made by Larry Tucker, a pal from Los Angeles who had appointed himself Mort's manager for the occasion.* Witnessing the performance were Enrico, his manager Barry Drew, and Stan Wilson. The man Tucker placed before them was pallid and underfed, a five o'clock shadow suggesting he may have spent the night under a car. Banducci didn't think much of his brief set with the exception of one joke. At a crowded press conference, President Eisenhower, who had always resisted taking a public stand against Joseph McCarthy, strongly endorsed Secretary of State John Foster Dulles' characterization of the senator as "arrogant, blustering, and domineering." Without mentioning McCarthy by name, the president added: "The easiest thing to do with great power is to abuse it—to use it in excess."

Taking the cue, Sahl recalled his army days and the design of the famed Eisenhower field jacket, praising the flaps that prevented its button front and breast pockets from catching on equipment and describing its "multi-directional zippers" in elaborate detail. "You have zippers over here you can put your pencils in . . . and a zipper here you can open for your cigarettes and cigars. . . . And you had a big zipper here and you reached in and you pulled out all your maps . . ." He then suggested that the army, having been called a "communist bastion" by McCarthy, could redesign the Ike jacket to become a McCarthy jacket by adding a flap "which buttons over the mouth." The senator, he observed, "doesn't question what you say so much as your right to say it."

Edward R. Murrow's famous takedown of McCarthy on *See It Now* was still three months in the future. There had been no frontal assaults from the dominant TV comedians of the day—Groucho Marx, Milton Berle, Jackie Gleason—and Bob Hope's infrequent cracks almost came across as friendly. Nightclub comics were even more circumspect than the media variety, always wary of turning a drinking crowd hostile. "The rest of Mort's audition was terrible," Banducci said, "but that joke killed me."

---

* A hanger-on at the time, Larry Tucker (1934–2001) would be remembered by Enrico Banducci as "a big fat kid." Later, while running a club in New York called Upstairs at the Downstairs, Tucker met a struggling comic named Paul Mazursky. Together, they wrote for Danny Kaye and developed the *Monkees* TV series. They also wrote the films *I Love You, Alice B. Toklas* and *Bob & Carol & Ted & Alice*, the latter of which Mazursky directed.

Not quite knowing what to do with the guy, Banducci took him next door and staked him to a meal. "You look like you are starving," he said, "and even if you never work, here's twenty dollars." When he learned that singer Dorothy Baker, the supporting act on the bill with Wilson, wanted to spend Christmas in Los Angeles with lyricist Jack Brooks, Banducci offered Sahl $75 to take the week. For a man just a few dollars short of vagrancy, it was a windfall. That first Tuesday night performance doubtless included the McCarthy joke, but Mort remembers another political jape that may actually have been his first: "Every time the Russians throw an American in jail," went the observation, "*we* throw an American in jail to show them they can't get away with it!"

In all, there wasn't a lot of political content. "It was women and behavior and trying to get along in the system," Mort says. "It was sort of random." And without the help of his student claque, the rest of the week didn't go as well. "It was horrible. That was when the hungry i sold only beer and wine, and the pre-liquor license stratum threw things—peanuts, water glasses, bottle caps." The only other comic in town that week was the manic Pinky Lee, who was playing to packed houses at Bimbo's 365 Club. "Enrico wanted to fire me," said Mort, "but he was too kindhearted. At the end of the third week, I broke the sound barrier and I was in."

Dorothy Baker, who eventually married Jack Brooks, never returned to the hungry i. Her permanent absence forced Enrico Banducci to do what he could to put Mort Sahl across. "I didn't care for nightclubs," Banducci said. "I detested those kinds of nightclubs where girls came out and danced and sang and a stupid comic would come out and say stupid jokes. I wanted a place where a lot of expression went on." He liked the sophisticated stuff in Mort's act; there just wasn't enough of it. "It was new to hear him talk about political situations. That was new in entertainment. They weren't even doing it in New York yet."

With his dislike of traditional nightclub comedians, Banducci urged Sahl to look as nontraditional as his material. "Enrico said, 'Take the tie off.' Then he said, 'Take the coat off.' And then I said to myself: Who would ruminate on this? A graduate student. In those days the preppy thing was in. That's where the sweater came from—the sweater and loafers. It was easier for them to process it from a guy that wasn't dressed up." The change of clothes was only the start; the new jokes had to be smarter, snappier. "I hid behind the material," Mort admits. "I felt naked up there." The audience, he found, wanted to be as smart as the man on stage. "They wanted to be on the level of the material—but not always. They can be very, very savage. In the beginning I just wanted them to laugh, but they were pretty resistant. Enrico would start the laughter over the P.A. system." Banducci impressed him as an old-world character, a man who saw life through the eyes of an artist. "He seemed like a guy from another country—singing opera, playing the violin. He was the greatest chef. He was a guy with flair. He had the flamboyance to create things."

Just as he was breaking through, Sahl had his first taste of public notice with an item in Herb Caen's *Examiner* column: "Herbert Hoover and his fellow high-collarites will be shocked to learn that Mort Sahl, new comic at the Hungry I, is doing a Sahlacious routine called 'Palo Alto, City of Sin.' Must be a different Palo Alto."

Caen had been writing about the city and its nightlife since 1938, and his column, as was frequently noted, was more widely read than the front page. The mention brought an immediate surge of interest in the unconventional comedian opening for Stan Wilson, a circumstance that didn't sit well with the singer, a black postal employee from Oakland who mixed calypso with folk ballads and modestly billed himself as "one of America's greatest contributions to music." Wilson, says Mort, saw him as a threat: "He had the club all to himself. It was sold out every night. And he had the girls that liked him up there doing that Belafonte stuff. He let me know that he was the boss and he wanted to cut my time—but the audience was the constituency."

As word spread and the lines along Columbus grew, Banducci added shows—as many as five a night. Stan Wilson had his following, but now Mort Sahl was building one of his own. "I used to walk across the street to a Chinese restaurant and write jokes in a book," he says. "And I found out that's not the way to do it. But I never made that public because the people I considered my enemy were actors that improvised. I thought it was anti-intellectual, so I didn't want to do it. I was very much a puritan in that sense." Not yet knowing his onstage character, he had not yet found his voice. That, he acknowledges, took a long time. "When I dropped the memorized act and threw in the asides—the observations—that won people, but I was too intimidated to do it."

Commuting from Berkeley in a dilapidated Jaguar, Sahl occasionally had one of his pals from campus, an English major named John Whiting, along for the ride. "He never stopped talking," Whiting recalled in an essay:

On the way he'd pick up the evening *Examiner* from a newspaper dis-
penser and leave it folded on the seat beside him. He didn't look at it
until he went on stage, whereupon he opened it up and took off from a
headline like Charlie Parker chasing a fugitive melody. I'd sit through
the evening's shows wondering what he was going to say next—no
two were ever the same. Then we'd pile into the Jag and head back
across the bay to Kip's, an all-night hamburger joint on Bancroft just
below Telegraph. All the way back and into the morning, three A.M.
or later, he never stopped talking. His monolog was as seamless and
as endless as the Ring cycle, its familiar leitmotifs weaving in and out
of the structure—Ike, Nixon, Joe McCarthy, the FBI, the D.A.R. All
those uptight right-wingers who made the political, intellectual, and
artistic life in Fifties America a tightrope walk over an abyss became
larger-than-life caricatures on Mort's colorful canvas.

The night Mort Sahl made his debut at the hungry i, the most compel-
ling entertainment to be found in San Francisco was on display at the city's
jazz venues. Billie Holiday was winding up a two-week stand at the Downbeat, the Hangover Club was presenting the New Orleans blues singer Lizzie
Miles, and the Dave Brubeck Quartet, featuring a brilliant alto saxophonist
named Paul Desmond, was in residence at the tiny Blackhawk.

With the cover of *Time* in his immediate future, Brubeck was the most
exciting new artist on the American jazz scene, a curly-haired dynamo in
horn-rimmed glasses who had developed into an unlikely attraction on college campuses. When they weren't on the road, which was six months a year,
the quartet settled in at the Hawk, which served as home base and a sort of
conservatory for its own progressive brand of swing—austere, abstract, disciplined. A devoted family man with four children, Brubeck could otherwise
be found overseeing the construction of a new house, a hilltop structure of
glass and redwood overlooking the bay in Oakland.

Desmond, by contrast, was divorced, living at his parents' house in the
Twin Peaks district, and out on the scene most nights. "He got to know me
because I was in the public domain," said Mort. The two men, both equally
hip, became fast friends, and it was Desmond who brought Sahl to the
Blackhawk for the first time in January 1954. The Brubeck Quartet traded
in popular songs—standards and slightly musty relics rendered with crisp
musicianship and adventurous time signatures. ("Jazz styled 1980" is the
way the quartet billed itself.) Discovering Brubeck's piano work, with its

complex, classically-inspired harmonics and its pulsing climaxes, must have been a thrill, but it was the lightness and clarity of Desmond's lyrical solos that really blew Mort away. Paul Desmond, he decided, was a genius.

"He was with me every day," says Mort:

They worked at the Blackhawk, he and Brubeck. Then we'd go over to [my girlfriend] Sue's apartment and play records. It was beginning to become its own language. Desmond would say, for instance, that he fancied this girl, but her parents thought there was no security in being a musician. So he said, "This is the way her world ends—not with a whim but with a banker." That's the way it was going. He thought he was inspired by me—the idea that I could say the words. He said, "I can only say them through the reed." But he had no political structure.

On March 3, 1954—ten weeks into Sahl's association with the hungry i— Herb Caen ran an actual endorsement (of sorts) in his column: "Howzat again dept.: Mrs. Dorothy Kay of Southgate is a great fan of Mort Sahl, the bright new comic at the Hungry I. 'Give him a plug,' she implores in a letter. 'Why, he's so far ahead of other comedians it isn't even funny!'"

Caen would eventually meet Mrs. Dorothy Kay of Southgate, but what he wouldn't know until then was that she was actually Mrs. Dorothy Sahl of South Gate, wife of Harry Sahl and the mother of Mort. And although he obligingly ran the item, it took Mr. San Francisco another eight weeks to actually see the bright new comic in action. By then the "i" had moved to slightly more respectable quarters, the old location having flaunted the fire code by having exactly one exit that also happened to serve as its entrance. One carelessly tipped candle could have turned the place into a death trap. There was also the not inconsiderable matter of a huge uptick in business.

Around the corner, Enrico Banducci took a lease on the cellar of the old International Hotel, locating the new hungry i on the lower level of an abandoned restaurant. (By most accounts, the space was either a wine cellar or a Chinese gambling den.) A scheme of emergency exits allowed him to more than double the capacity of the old room, but the space was woefully undeveloped. Mort continued to work the "i" on Columbus, sprinting over between sets to check on the boss, who was busy sandblasting the walls and building his own mahogany bar. "I used to finish the show and bring the money in the cigar box from the small club, so that he could go ahead and pay for his building materials in the new club," Mort recalled. "I'd go in there in the middle of the night with coffee and donuts from Sai Yon's restaurant in Chinatown to keep the guy going."

The building was constructed the same year as the Sentinel, but unlike the Beaux-Arts showplace at Columbus and Kearny, the I-Hotel (as it was locally known) was a conventional affair of red brick and concrete. The advantage it offered was space, and so by necessity Banducci embraced its natural aesthetics. "I said, 'What's the wall going to be?' Mort remembers, indicating the place where the performer would stand. "He had gone through to the bricks, and he said, 'Gonna leave it just like it is.' And everybody copied that." Once they relocated, the two men observed a different dynamic at play. "The first thing we found was that nobody would listen to me standing on the floor. So we added a nine-inch riser. Then a sound system, which makes them feel less loud—*them*—so they aren't on an equal footing with the performer. Then the black paint [on the walls] and the tables. And the light is outside where you line up; all the business is done outside. When they come in there it's like a theater; it was perfect. Then I'd jump up on stage and act like I'm carefree—the illusion of theatre."

Herb Caen's visit to the new venue was reported in the April 23 edition of the *Examiner*. "Vast basement, decorated in formula off-beat style with mobiles and concrete abstractions," he summarized. "Mobiles not moving, on account no air. People not moving, on account no room." Caen surveyed the local color and moved on, returning later that evening to catch the new comedian he had plugged but never seen. What he observed on stage was "a lean, bristly young man wearing an open-throated shirt and a sweater and carrying a rolled-up newspaper whose contents he occasionally commented on. He talked, in blinding bursts of speed, about cable cars and cops and raids and politicians—much in the manner, it seemed to me, of a jazz musician playing a chorus: toying with phrases, following the melody and suddenly losing it, trying for high notes that he sometime splattered."

Used to the mainstream acts that routinely passed through the city, Herb Caen immediately responded to someone as fresh and original as Mort Sahl: "He very funny. Discusses everything from the difficulty of necking in Jaguars ('The front seats are divided with a gear shift between. They figure you're rich enough to own a Jag, you must have an apartment') to the reason [used car dealer] Horsetrader Ed was sent to prison. ('They caught him selling a sports car to somebody who doesn't live in Sausalito.') I don't know where Mr. Sahl came from, but I'm glad he's here."

Herb Caen's endorsement solidified Mort Sahl's position as the Bay Area's hottest new act. When Stan Wilson took an open-ended engagement in Reno, briefly ceding the top spot on the bill to the Mississippi-born cabaret singer Billie Haywood, it suddenly became clear it was Sahl who was driving new attendance at the hungry i. "I observed people you do not see in nighteries on the average," wrote Don Steele. "A sort of professorly looking congregation who seem to have free-wheeling senses of humor. Mort's comedy material is pretty advanced stuff and is based on some fairly controversial characters and situations. By advanced, I mean he uses terms right out of college sociology classes. He dresses in contemporary campus style—wags the evening paper all through his act, although it has no bearing on what he is talking about. If you are alert for new trends in public entertainment and can laugh—Mort is quite a guy."

The new business model at the hungry i called for a full-service kitchen offering buck'n'quarter dinners from 6 P.M. It was Banducci's notion that the entertainment policy would take care of itself, but patrons would need to know that he wasn't just laying out cold cuts anymore. For the first time, he bought display advertising in the *Chronicle* and the *Examiner*, thrusting the "i" into the mainstream of San Francisco nightlife. He hired an experienced food manager to oversee the dining operations, while personally assuming responsibility for the showroom and the policies that governed it. Gone were the old wooden benches, replaced by canvas garden chairs arrayed in a semicircle fanning out from the stage. Instituting a sense of what he called "quietude," Banducci demanded absolute silence from the audience when an act was on—no change rattling, no forks clanking, no small talk or whispering, no standing or otherwise obscuring the view of others. And no drinks were to be served while a performer was on stage.

"The room was so quiet, Mort could take the lingering pause—it was a great room for comics—and you could *feel* it, the buildup," Banducci said. "You could hear a pin drop in the whole damn room. Then he'd whap ya, and the whole room would just break up. That's the only way it should be." In time, the place would become known for ejecting more "butter and eggers" than any other establishment on the West Coast. "I managed the club—managed it really strict—for the artist," he said.

Boorish customers weren't the only hazard of a broader following. "Enrico," Mort says, "had a coterie of Jewish friends from Los Angeles who kept saying, 'Get rid of him—he's a communist.'" Fortunately, Banducci loved all the political content and defiantly stood his ground. "As our club was literally subterranean, guys would come by and yell, 'Communists,' and other epithets, and would roll our garbage cans down from the sidewalk, down the steps, and through the door, and the momentum would make them lethal. Guys would wait upstairs to beat me up after work, and Enrico would walk out with me and take them on." As Banducci said, "We were putting down McCarthy at the time, and you just didn't *do* that then. You not only didn't put Eisenhower down then, you didn't *dare* put down McCarthy." Soon, Herb Caen was stopping in every night after dinner to marvel at the obsessive quality of the comic's delivery. "Everybody thought it was too thoughtful, too reflective," says Mort. "My father said, 'You don't have any timing.' And then I began to make my own rules and I got a very manic style in which I didn't want to wait for them not to laugh. It was too embarrassing. I just kept going."

In mid-June, *Your Show of Shows* producer Max Liebman brought Sahl to Los Angeles to audition for one of Liebman's NBC TV spectaculars. A few days after that, a stringer for *Variety* caught the act at the hungry i and filed what amounted to its first formal review. The critic, whose *Variety* handle was "Rafe," covered the two musical acts, folksinger Josh White (Stan Wilson's mentor) and an elegant balladeer named John Hawker, before turning his attention to the club's resident satirist. "Comic Mort Sahl, who is kicking up quite a storm locally, is a natural click in front of an intelligent audience, with frequent barbed political and psychological quips. A monologist who works with no props other than the daily papers, he is glib, sharp, and effective in this setting." Although he thought the thirty-minute set overlong, Rafe conceded the audience ate it up, and that Sahl could have remained on stage even longer. "His mind is basically so hip to the frailties of modern civilization that he should be able to broaden his material to please a less sophisticated audience."

It was taken for granted that not everyone laughing at Mort Sahl understood what he was talking about. "It was his own Mort Sahlian technique; go along, go along, go along, and then whack," said Enrico Banducci. "See, it was not smart not to laugh because he'd use a lot of big words. So people would wind up laughing and not know what they were laughing at." Sahl's impact, he suggested, depended more on his passing as an audience's idea of what an intellectual looked and sounded like than what he actually said. "I could listen to him all night," said Luba Sharoff, the proprietor's wife, admiringly, "and not learn a thing."

Sahl's ascendancy coincided with an entertainment boom in San Francisco, the biggest the city had seen in years. The national touring company of *The King and I* was breaking all records at the War Memorial Opera House, Nat King Cole was likewise setting a new house standard at the Fairmont Hotel, and *This Is Cinerama* was playing to capacity crowds in its twenty-second week at the Orpheum. The Italian Village nightclub was selling out with Mel Tormé and Frances Langford on the bill, but the clamor for live acts was particularly evident in the city's smaller rooms, traditionally the hardest to fill. Count Basie set a new Saturday night record at the Downbeat Club that was promptly demolished by Duke Ellington, while Erroll Garner was packing the Blackhawk at the edge of the Tenderloin district. Everyone, it seemed, was fleeing summer TV reruns and rediscovering the joys of live performance. And it was at precisely that moment that Mort Sahl chose to leave town.

2

I KNEW WE WERE IN TROUBLE

The first real test of Mort Sahl's appeal outside of San Francisco came in August 1954, when he traveled to Chicago for a two-week booking at the Black Orchid, a swank Gold Coast cabaret. Three months earlier, a comedian named Paul Gray had caught the act at the hungry i and liked what he heard. Gray next went into the Orchid, opening for singer-songwriter Gertrude Niesen, who, along with her husband, Al Greenfield, owned the club. Gray made the recommendation, and the resulting engagement paired Sahl with the Piafesque torch singer Felicia Sanders. Management expected the North Beach comic to wear a tuxedo, completely missing the point of the act. "The new outfit was always gray slacks, black loafers, white socks, white shirt, red sweater," says Mort. "The idea was to have a bright color that would stand out on stage."

After being advised that he had no class, Sahl was told that he could keep the sweater but that he would have to enter and leave the club through the kitchen so as not to flout the dress code—and that he would have to spend his time between shows in the alley. The first night did not go well; Sahl was heckled throughout by Earl "Madman" Muntz, a flamboyant TV and automobile manufacturer based in Evanston. Says Mort, "I was preceded on the show by Dr. Arthur Ellen, who was a hypnotist. He had hypnotized Muntz's wife, whose back had been broken, and she started walking under his spell. So Muntz was there to support him. I walked out after him, and nobody laughed. So I said, 'You can bring them out of it now.' That's how it happened."

According to Herb Caen, Muntz's badgering "made Mort so mad that between acts he wrote a long, needling routine about Muntz, which he performed for his second show and absolutely fractured the customers. All except Muntz, who went to the boss and demanded that Mort be fired."

Columnist and TV personality Irv Kupcinet, in his book *Kup's Chicago*, maintains that Sahl *was* fired after a few performances "because Greenfield insisted that he wear a coat and tie." In his book *Heartland*, Mort himself says that he quit. But Caen's column had him there a week into the engagement, and at the end of two weeks Will Leonard led his *Chicago Tribune* column with a ringing endorsement: "He talks up a conversational gale, wildly imaginative, wackily witty, sophisticatedly corny. He pitches to the intelligentsia, but dresses like a Bughouse Square orator in a rumpled sweater, an open collar shirt, and a haircut and shave that need redoing. Rambling along in all directions, he comments on everything under the moon, and if he thinks he's beginning to bore the patrons, he simply drops the subject and takes up another one."

On the whole, the expedition to Chicago was a qualified success. "I had a fair engagement there," Mort concludes. "Just *fair*." Back home in San Francisco, he was hailed as a returning warrior, having taken a smart new sensibility eastward and spread the word like a disheveled Paul Revere. "Mort Sahl is back," heralded Don Steele, who told his readers he had never enjoyed a better evening of entertainment. Enrico Banducci likewise celebrated his star comic's reappearance by awarding him his own radio show over KGO, the local ABC affiliate, to go along with his perch at the hungry i.

Mort had previously subbed for Don Sherwood, the morning man at KSFO, but otherwise had no experience in broadcasting. Banducci grandly underwrote the weekly half hour, which aired Tuesdays at midnight, but wisely left the format to the whims of its extemporaneous host. ("Sometimes don't even mention the hungry i," Mort was instructed.) Playing just one record, Sahl riffed on politics, psychology, college life, and jazz to such an extent the audience, even at the hip hour of midnight, had to work hard to keep up. On the first show, in fact, he was halfway through an interview with guest Woody Herman when the bandleader stopped to exclaim, "Does anybody out there know what we're talking about?" Two weeks in, the decision was made to cut the show to fifteen minutes and expand it to five nights a week, Sunday through Thursday. Stan Wilson returned to the hungry i in September and found that he was now sharing the bill equally with Enrico's upstart comedian. And since Banducci was advertising in the *Chronicle*, the paper's nightlife columnist, Harold "The Owl" Schaefer, was finally permitted to take notice. "Speaking of the 'i,'" he blurbed, "if you haven't seen Mort Sahl there yet, you're missing San Francisco's—if not the country's—freshest young comedian."

Inspired by the broadening media exposure, Herb Caen made Sahl something of a protégé, preparing him for bigger things while establishing a degree of personal ownership. "We got very tight," Mort says. "Herb started taking me to Brooks Brothers, and taking me to the Cadillac dealer to get a convertible. . . . And he started taking me around to all the social engagements." Caen exhibited an almost perverse pride in the resulting makeover, which he showcased in an item for his column: "Mort Sahl, the Hungry I's comic, shocking his avant-garde admirers by blossoming out in white shirts, neckties, and sports jackets (instead of his usual sweater and jeans) and flashing around town in a Cadvertible." The urgent campaign to turn him into a sort of Barbary Coast dandy came in advance of Mort's first New York booking, an opportunity he couldn't afford to squander. And while going from homeless to headliner in nine months would turn anyone's head, the events leading up to his departure for the Big Apple would make it appear as if a swell-headed neophyte was getting run out of town.

First there was a careless ad lib made about the coeds on the Berkeley campus during a rally held prior to the Cal-Oklahoma football game. At a particularly rowdy moment in the proceedings, Sahl suggested the girls at a notorious "maison" weren't so much different from those in the local sorority houses "except that *they* have a purpose." The incident made the papers, and the fallout was evident when Sahl found himself banned from campus, costing him a gig with the Cal Tjader Quintet. Then he cut off Larry Tucker, the young man who, according to Enrico Banducci, "stayed with him, took care of him when he was sick, and fed him. But then when Mort got to thinking he could get along without Larry, he told him to go to hell."

Mort doesn't remember it that way.

I could always mesmerize people talking, so Larry liked to talk to me. He would drive down from L.A. to South Gate, where I was, and talk to me at night. So when I came to San Francisco, he came with me. He wasn't really an act, so Enrico put him on the light board and had him announce the acts. . . . Larry and I split up because I came into the club in the afternoon and Milt Kamen was on the stage doing an impression of me—which was uncomplimentary to say the least— and Larry was urging him on. Kamen was talking fast about politics and Larry said, "Don't forget to pick your nose . . . and don't forget to pass gas." Crude, you know? I always had a very puritanical thing about that. And I still do. I believe people are vulgar because they are not clever. So they did all that not knowing I was there, and I stopped talking to him. . . . I took a vacation from Larry, and I never put it back together with him. I was very dramatic about things at times like that. I thought it was disloyal because I had broken a door down. I thought they admired me for it, but far from it.

Hypersensitive and hotheaded, Mort Sahl had a hair-trigger temper that upped the tension level in any room he entered. "I liked Mort—he was so intelligent," Banducci said, "but he was very intense. You had to be careful what you said to him." Mort and Enrico stopped speaking altogether, and Herb Caen's column of November 17 made it official: "Our town's hottest young saloon comic" had left the previous day to play an engagement at New York's famed Blue Angel. "And if he comes back, it won't be to the Hungry I. He and owner Enrico Banducci parted without speaking. In fact, Mort left without his paycheck, and that REALLY hurt."

The Blue Angel had a storied past, having served as a launching pad for such renowned entertainers as Pearl Bailey, Eartha Kitt, and Harry Belafonte. A typical bill in the mid-forties, which reportedly cost $400 a week, consisted of Yul Brenner, Evelyn Knight, and the Revuers, a cabaret troupe that counted Betty Comden, Adolph Green, and Judy Holliday among its members. Comedy, as with most New York cabaret bills, was limited to novelty singers and the occasional standup. Intimacy and Cold War hysteria discouraged topicality; the acts that flourished were affable and low key—Myron Cohen, Wally Cox, Orson Bean, who fashioned a eucalyptus tree of newspapers. The one great exception was the blustery Irwin Corey, an ersatz professor in a swallowtail coat who was the only true character comedian on the circuit.

Dark and formal, with pink leather banquettes, walls of gray velour, and a plump blue cherub clinging to a corner of the proscenium, the Angel didn't resemble a nightclub so much as a funeral parlor. At least management—Herbert Jacoby and the Village Vanguard's Max Gordon—knew what to expect even if the audience didn't. (Again it was Paul Gray who made the recommendation.) Mort Sahl made his New York debut on November 18, 1954, as part of an eclectic mix of performers. Headlining was pianist Dwight Fiske, long a darling of café society whose salty ditties were delivered with leering bravado. Opening the show was Broadway vocalist Susan Johnson, followed by "Black Theatre" puppeteer George La

Faye and his company. How Sahl would go over in this cramped little room was anyone's guess.

The first two weeks passed without notice, aside from a one-line acknowledgment in Walter Winchell's column. Fiske was the undisputed star of the show and old news to the press. It wasn't until he dropped off the bill in early December and was replaced by Jonathan Winters that the accent firmly shifted to comedy. Suddenly the Blue Angel merited attention. Winters had played the room before, a trade review in *Variety* noted, but Sahl was something entirely new and different. "His delivery—it reminds of the street-corner bookie who's just discovered books and wants to tell the world about them—virtually stuns the audience at first, but rapidly proceeds to panic the ringsiders. He heightens the sense of the offbeat by using the inflection of a semi-literate and the vocabulary of a Ph.D., and to this he applies some topical humor on a variety of such touchy subjects as McCarthy, widescreens, and [TV's Arthur] Godfrey. Completely unexpected delivery and some metaphorical non-sequiturs make Sahl a real comedy find."

Winters, in his set, impersonated a number of characters, both male and female. "They didn't get Jonathan right away either," says Mort, "because he was doing entire movies. When he did the western he did 'Big Boy' Williams and Edgar Buchanan. They didn't get all that. 'Get the women on back to the waterline—here come the Sioux!' And then he'd do the crack of the whip." Winters' Hollywood parody for his stand at the Angel was "Marine Diary," in which he assumed half a dozen voices and supplied all the sound effects. In other bits he was a British explorer, an old lady, and a gas station attendant.

Sahl clearly strengthened the bill at the Blue Angel, but he found that New York was essentially a closed shop when it came to comedians. "One of my lingering disappointments when I got into it was that there were no intellectuals among the Jews," he says. "They were just a bunch of guys who felt superior, unjustifiably, because they were on the inside of the tribe. But they weren't—they just outnumbered everybody. In Yiddish it's called *prost*: unrefined, not reaching for anything." Not having worked the Catskills was an advantage—Mort came from no tradition and had no imitators. "It was a blessing. Back there the limits were all self-imposed—who you've emulated, who you went to the track with. When I got back to New York, I went to Hanson's Drug Store at 57th Street and there they all were, all the embryonic comics with Jack Rollins. I asked him to manage me and he turned me down. He said, 'I've got a comedian already.' (That was Will Jordan.) They all predicted doom and gloom for me. 'No, people won't understand it.' So, of course, it meant that, in effect, I had a monopoly."

In his last two weeks at the Angel, Sahl was joined on the bill by actor John Carradine, who, in white tie and tails, did readings from the likes of Abraham Lincoln, Lewis Carroll, and Edgar Allan Poe. (Abel Green, the editor of *Variety*, thought the combination "a shade on the cerebral side.") The club had a communal dressing room for the men, small and dingy, and Mort usually made himself scarce between performances. "He came in, did his act, and left," said comedienne Pat Carroll, who was also in the show. "He was very busy at the time because he was frighteningly popular."

While still in New York, he made plans to move to the Purple Onion upon his return to San Francisco. In late December, *Variety* reported the husband-wife vocal team of Jackie Cain and Roy Kral would open at the Onion on January 14, "to be on the same bill with Mort Sahl, now at the Blue Angel." The move, however, would have been a step back in terms of capacity as well as earning power, and the managing Rockwell family was more comfortable with exotic musical acts like Maya Angelou and her mentor, a world-weary chanteuse named Jorie Remus. Enrico Banducci had used the latter weeks of 1954 to add a restaurant wing to the new "i" with plans to expand the kitchen and give the after-two dining spots a run for their money. He and his controversial new comic needed each other, and so when Mort Sahl did in fact return to North Beach on January 18, 1955, it was once again to the brick-lined basement known as the hungry i.

Whenever somebody important came to town, Herb Caen would take them to see Mort's act, which in Caen's mind was akin to showing them Coit Tower or the Golden Gate Bridge. One night he brought Eddie Cantor into the club, another night Danny Kaye was with him. Cantor was so impressed he recommended Sahl to some agents who determined—predictably—that he wasn't commercial. "They wanted me to write gags for their regulars—something they call 'picking your brains.' I said, 'No thanks. Pick on someone else.'"

Now the media began to close in. In February, Sahl became the subject of his first profile, a two-page cover story in the *Chronicle*'s Sunday magazine. In March, the fashion weekly *Harper's Bazaar* flew a photographer in from New York to shoot a spread. That same month he was offered a contract by CBS vice president Harry Ackerman, who underscored the importance of "young potential" by offering fifty-two week contracts "whenever we see talent worthy of future stardom." The contract Ackerman offered Sahl was for a far more tentative thirteen weeks, delivered to the storeroom of the hungry i by the network's director of business affairs, Phil Feldman. The two men sat on cases of scotch going over the forty-eight-page document and initialing the riders, but Feldman was dubious. "Well, you're pretty intellectual," he said. "I am a graduate of the Harvard Business School myself, but I don't know if an audience will accept you."

Again, says Mort, it was all Herb Caen's doing. "Herb took Ackerman to dinner, got him drunk, brought him in. 'Why don't you sign him?' And then he signs me and turns me over to these guys [Bernie Gould and Paul Harrison]. They keep flying me in on the off day, which at the hungry i was Monday. So I fly into L.A. or Burbank, see the smog, and go to CBS. Bob Crosby had *Club 15* for Campbell's Soup and I'd do the warm-up. Then those two guys—two Jewish guys—you know, they're teams, with the cashmere sweaters and the loafers—said, 'Nobody's gonna understand this.' And I knew we were in trouble." Upon joining CBS, Sahl found himself part of an unlikely stable of talent that included radio artists Barbara Ruick and Gale Gordon, comic Bob Sweeney, actor Steve Dunne, and a local sketch comedian named Johnny Carson.

Meanwhile, business at the "i" was better than ever, Mort having finally attained top billing over Stan Wilson, who had shown himself unable to consistently fill the 265-seat showroom on his own. In the lounge, the Vince Guaraldi Trio, in the days long before Guaraldi's fame from the *Peanuts* TV specials, held forth on Fridays and Saturdays. "One Saturday night we had a thousand paid admissions," Banducci proudly told the *Chronicle*'s Jim Walls, putting an affectionate arm around Mort. "And they said my boy isn't commercial." A female fan pushed forward. "Oh, Mr. Sahl, you were just wonderful," she gushed. "Just wonderful." Sahl stepped back as if deflecting the praise. "Please," he said, "I'm not geared to total acceptance."

As a snapshot of a work in progress, the *Chronicle* article, titled "Out in Left Field," is valuable. Sahl is painted as "mournfully happy" with rubbery features, his outfit of the evening a sweater vest, his shirtsleeves rolled in a rumpled approximation of a campus lecturer. "As he gets going his eyes light up, his arms poke and toss like hayforks, and the audience is fooled for a moment into thinking that his wild monologue is really a two-way conversation." No longer is the rolled newspaper just a prop; Sahl opens it, gestures with it, whacks it to shreds during the course of his act. "What I like to do is a jazz solo in words—an improvisation on a theme," he explains.

"The old jokes just disappeared. My material is a patchwork of old and new ad libs."

A selection of jokes demonstrates the churn of the old and new. The Cold War line about matching the Russians prisoner for prisoner is there, while the supposed title of Arthur Godfrey's autobiography (*It's No Fun Being God*) is not. "[Developer and Fairmont Hotel owner] Ben Swig listened to everything I had to say," Mort said in a comment that would play only in San Francisco. "When I got through, he made me an offer for the land I was standing on." He riffed on American cars, high fidelity ("I have a record of a man eating celery—you'd swear he was eating celery right in the room"), the Richmond–San Rafael bridge, the military. He anticipated the rap on cops a decade early, telling the audience they had an authoritarian complex: "They try to establish psychological dominance by putting their foot on your bumper. If you're in a sports car, they put their foot on your chest."

A tipsy young woman comes up to him after the show. "You know, Mr. Sahl, I understand you," she says, "but I wonder how many others do." A pained look crosses his face. "A ten-year-old girl told me that in New York," he confides to Walls. "I guess that's what they mean when they say I'm not commercial." A man approaches, a chronic back-slapper with a paunch and a sly wink. "Very funny, Mort, but I know what kind of politics you're peddling out there." Again to Walls: "Get him. He thinks I'm a college radical. That's because no one jokes about politics anymore and they can't figure out what I am. It's a funny thing—most of the complaints about me come from recanted leftists."

Mort Sahl hit his stride that spring at the hungry i, but the reconciliation with Enrico Banducci, heartfelt as it was, wouldn't last. At CBS there was talk of a summer series, a replacement for Arthur Godfrey's Wednesday night variety show in which Mort would be paired with singer Frankie Laine. In June, comedian George Gobel caught the act with his manager Dave O'Malley. Lonesome George was just about the hottest name in television, with a top-rated NBC series and an Emmy for Outstanding New Personality. O'Malley saw in Mort "a latter day Julius Tannen" (a famed vaudeville monologist) and sought him out between sets. "He said, 'I'll be your manager and you'll go with MCA,'" as Mort remembers it. "And I went over there. I met [Lew] Wasserman, and I met [agent] Pat Kelley (who wound up with George Roy Hill). But Wasserman was already looking ahead; he had the Catholics represented by Catholics, the gay guys represented by gay guys. . . . He was very respectful of me. He never said, 'Don't say this' and

'Don't say that.' He was like, 'Your turf is your own.' Very charming guy; the same when I wasn't working than when I was."

Sahl passively assumed the prestige of being O'Malley's only other client, but from Banducci's perspective he was throwing his weight around, the corrosive effect of all that head-turning attention after twenty-seven years of near-poverty. "Enrico fired the doorman, Frank Werber," Mort recalls. "Frank took the Kingston Trio out of there, managed them, went on record and became a millionaire. But he fired him. I said, 'Don't do that. He can't make his rent.' He said, 'I'm running this club.' So I appointed myself, erroneously, as John L. Lewis. I said, 'I'm walking out of here. You've got to give him his job back.' And I left the club. I thought I was representing mankind when I was really overstepping myself."

He made plans to return to Los Angeles, where O'Malley was based and where CBS had its West Coast headquarters. Still, he hadn't the slightest idea what his future—presumably in TV—would involve or exactly when it would begin. Breaking camp, he proposed to his longtime girlfriend, Susan Babior, who at the age of twenty-one was an undergraduate at Berkeley. On June 24, 1955, Herb Caen put out word that the couple would be married in Marin, when in fact they would be wed the next morning at Caen's own home in Pacific Heights with only the columnist and his wife Sally in attendance. They all went to breakfast at the Lochinvar Room of the Mark Hopkins Hotel; then, loading the Cadillac with their relatively few possessions, the newlyweds took off for L.A., the only work on the horizon a concert in Carmel where Mort would perform before the largest audience he had ever faced.

"Jazz at Sunset" was an annual event promoted by disc jockey Jimmy Lyons, so named because it took place at the Sunset Auditorium, a neo-Gothic assembly hall on the campus of Carmel's Sunset School. Used to intimate rooms, Mort had no idea how he would go over in a place that seated over seven hundred people. Could he manage the same conspiratorial conversation he achieved at the hungry i? Or would he be lost in the relative vastness of the place, an impatient crowd waiting to hear the Dave Brubeck Quartet and not some anxious young comic whose name was virtually unknown on the Monterey Peninsula?

The ads in the *Peninsula Herald* trumpeted Brubeck's name in 36-point type, marking his third appearance in the area under Lyons' sponsorship.

("Dave Brubeck is God," the saying went, "and Jimmy Lyons is his prophet.") Sahl, in the subordinate position, was billed as a great new comic discovery "direct from the 'hungry i' in S.F. for his first concert appearance." The Sunday night performance began at 8:30, and in a nod to Sahl's obscurity the quartet went on first, bracketing his appearance both fore and aft, kicking off the first set with an aggressive reading of "Gone with the Wind" that put Paul Desmond front and center. Expansive versions of "Jeepers Creepers," "Little Girl Blue," and "Take the A Train" followed, while at the back of the room an engineer from Fantasy Records captured it all on tape.

By the time Jimmy Lyons introduced Mort to the audience, the room had warmed considerably and the man in the pullover sweater quickly shattered any notions of what a supporting act looked or sounded like. Accorded a friendly welcome, he was off, quickly finding his groove in the subject of an upcoming hardware expo. "The Do-It-Yourself Show will be here in the Sunset Auditorium a week from tonight," he began, nervously anchored to the standing mic at the center of the stage. "In our wake the Do-It-Yourself Show is coming in, and there are going to be all kinds of booths in which you'll learn to make modern coffee tables by taking doors off hinges and planing [them] off, and painting them with three coats of primer, rat-gray primer, and you take the door and put it on four bricks and make a modern coffee table out of it. That kind of thing? And if your wife doesn't like it, and she likes French Provincial, she can put it on *eight* bricks. . . ."

And so began an unscripted tour of a sizzling mind, a relentless cascade of words and images delivered with the rhythmic precision of a jazz soloist, nimbly hooking one observational topic to the next like an anxious party guest with a seemingly endless line of patter. "The UN has met in San Francisco," he announced, holding the bulldog edition of the *Chronicle* aloft. "Sixty member nations got together, and now we have fifty-eight more enemies." He skewered the local newspapers, touched briefly upon the subject of police corruption, made a laugh line out of the city of Gilroy, the self-proclaimed garlic capital of the world. Sometimes the thoughts failed to connect, the points missing their mark, but the crowd laughed anyway, happy to be along for the ride, applauding sometimes, willingly seduced by the illusion of a hip, fun-loving intellectual. With the satirist's gift for spinning reality to its logical extreme, he settled for a moment on the hi-fi craze and the prevalence of sound effects albums that exploited the two-channel stereophonic effect.

A lot of people have gone out of their skulls, especially up around San Francisco, as you know, on high fidelity, and guys are going into hock, further out than with cars or anything, just out of their minds, you know, like for Thorens arms and Lincoln changers, and the Swedish cactus needle that comes from Oslo—you know about this?—trying to get a big sound. So you have all these bugs living around you, especially up in Marin County–and I'm talking about Marin when it was *really* Marin. That is to say, before the toll on the bridge came down. See, it came down from forty cents to thirty cents and we started getting *all* kinds of people. . . . There are degrees in our society—I don't want you to think that there are snobs or anything, but there are degrees. You may have noticed it if any of you were at the Pebble Beach races and you saw the guys who raced and wore *blazers*. They wore blue blazers, gold buttons with jewelers rouge on 'em, and a crest up here with little ducks on it, you know, and a green cross for safety, and then they have kind of a mortar and pestle like when you make Caesar salads, and a big hub cap, and over the top it says: The Pebble Beach Rod Gun Yachting Tennis and Discrimination Club . . .

Now he had them, racing along in a percussive game of free association, the stimulus of one subject giving way to another, the laugh lines hitting their marks amid all the baroque setups, the crowd hooting and applauding and eager for more.

So this fellow who lived next to me was one of the high fidelity bugs— he calls himself an *audiophile*, you know? And they have license plates on the bottom of the speaker and all that kind of thing. Kind of a weirdo, and a lot of people didn't dig him because he kind of bugged communal living. He'd turn on the set and all the lights in the neighborhood would get *dim*. You know one of those guys? So he went on to greater heights, in which he got this large speaker, and it was kind of hard to get. He wanted to get a Thorens speaker but they're kind of expensive—they cost seven hundred and fifty bucks. So he decided to get the biggest speaker he could, and he took his family and he moved them into the garage. He's using the house as a speaker . . .

He went on to commend the people of Monterey and Carmel for not looking like the characters in John Steinbeck's books. The '55 Jaguars were out, he announced, noting that brakes on these "weapons of prestige" were now being offered as an option. Briefly, he returned to the UN conference at the Fairmont Hotel, proposed to give a book review of *The Yalta Papers*, and then, reminded of the Fairmont, began to describe an item in the Sunday *Chronicle* ("on page three of the newsy part") about a recent hold-up attempt, which would go on to become one of the classics of his repertoire.

It tells about these fellows who are three veterans, sort of maladjusted you know, and they tried to rob the Fairmont Hotel . . . and these guys are an example of *bad* people versus *good* college people—there are no grays in between here—because the guy who stemmed the robbery was a good college person who was working up there, and he had a Ph.D. in English, which he had just got, and he was working as a night relief clerk at the Fairmont. You know, about ninety-five cents an hour, but it's tremendous experience, and if you're a writer there's all kinds of wonderful impressions you can get there. So he's working there, wearing one of those terrific jackets from DuPont that you can rinse out and take on the next shift. So these fellows came in while all this UN stuff was going on. They came inside, and they figured that in all the noise they could rob the Fairmont. And they had a fantastic plan; it's amazing the lengths people will go to not to work in our society. They figured out that they will rob the Fairmont and live in the hotel the rest of their lives on the money, you know that kind of thing? So they walked in, and they had sawed-off shotguns and tear gas shells under the left arm, you know, under the sleeve—great plan. And the clerk was there, and he thought they were going to register for a room. So he put down a card and said, 'Can I help you gentlemen?' They had it all figured out—no noise and don't awaken any of the guards. There was a lot of security because of the UN thing, so they took out ballpoint pens, you know, and they wrote to him on the registration. Instead of what they're taking, what room and where they're from, they wrote down THIS IS A HOLD UP. GIVE US ALL THE MONEY IN THE SAFE. And then it said, direct quote, it said: IF YOU ACT NORMAL YOU WON'T GET HURT. They wrote that in the note, and they put it under the cage. So he read it and, of course, being a college person it presented kind of a challenge to him. So he thought about it. He even forgot about the guns, and he turned it over and he wrote a rebuttal to them with his own pen. He wrote back and he said: ACT NORMAL? DEFINE YOUR TERMS.

The note goes back and forth several times, with the college man eventually marking it for spelling errors and the vets making off with $5,000 in pennies. They're apprehended when they try to buy a Cadillac with the money and the salesman gets suspicious. "Why wouldn't he? Who pays cash for a car these days?"

In all, he was before the audience for more than an hour, and as the set drew to a close there was a palpable sense that he had caught fire that night, that he was, after eighteen months of honing his style, ready for the biggest rooms, the toughest crowds. "So—it's been real good to talk to you," he told them, "and I guess Jimmy will be coming back now, and I'm gonna come out front and we'll rub elbows, okay? Okay, we'll see you later." And with that he left the stage to an ovation almost as loud and appreciative as the one Brubeck and his men would draw at the end of the evening.

The unsigned review in Monday's *Peninsula Herald* was uncommonly perceptive, noting how Sahl's wit was "strikingly comparable" to Brubeck's playing. "Both of them leave the standard melody as soon as possible, improvising freely, with frequent quotes from something familiar, on which new fantasies are based, and all this with gestures. Both performances are difficult to describe, although each complemented the other, making a very smooth package out of what would seem to be an incongruous pairing."

What Mort Sahl didn't know as he and his wife Sue left town the following morning, off to conquer Los Angeles and points beyond, was that he had not only proven the viability of his act in a concert setting, sustaining a solo performance that would tax the most experienced of comedians, but that he had also made recording history—something he wouldn't fully realize for decades.

3

I DISCOVERED I HAD TO TALK

Mort's father, Harry Sahl (née Soloducko), was born in New York in 1891, one of nine sons of Russian immigrants who eventually relocated to Stamford. Harry had artistic ambitions in what was otherwise a merchant-class family, and stenographic skills he could use to get work in the arts. In Connecticut, he served briefly as secretary for sculptor Gutzon Borglum, the future creator of the presidential monument at Mt. Rushmore, and for journalist-lecturer Irving Bacheller. By 1917 he was in Washington, D.C., working as a stenographer for the Department of Agriculture. Following a hitch in the Army, from which he emerged with heart and lung ailments, he settled in Los Angeles, where he may have tried seeking work in the movie industry.

Harry began writing plays, usually under the pseudonym Herschel Mindav Sahl, and after moving to Denver to study drama in the spring of 1920, flooded the Copyright Office with submissions. Titles like *The Light*, *The Pool of Life*, *The Call*, and *The Zero Hour* displayed a gift for dialogue and a weakness for structure. He wrote a novel, *The Heart of the Condor*, and in 1922 won a $500 prize in a scenario contest sponsored by the *Chicago Daily News*. The win may have inspired him to return to Los Angeles, but by 1925 he was working as a customs clerk, not a screenwriter, and living in a small apartment building in Hollywood. Discouraged, and with one failed marriage already behind him, Harry, at age 33, took out an ad in a magazine: *Is there still a woman out there who would like to meet a dreamer?* And up in Montreal, apparently there was. Dorothy Schwartz, 23, was both charmed and intrigued by Harry's unconventional appeal. "She came down on the train," Mort says, "and they were married in seventy-two hours." A Los Angeles County marriage license was issued on October 8, 1925. Two days later, she and Harry were married in Beverly Hills by Ernest R. Trattner, Rabbi of Temple Emanu-El. Witnesses were Dorothy's father, Benjamin Schwartz, who was stopping at the Hotel Palomar, and Morris W. Sahl, one of Harry's brothers, who owned and operated a hat shop in South Pasadena.

Not much is known about the early days of the marriage. Harry was thin and rugged-looking and at least a foot taller than Dot (or "Dora" as she was known to her family). She was from real means, bright and outgoing, an optimist where Harry could be dour and reserved. "He was estranged from all of his brothers," Mort says. "They were all merchants, and they made fun of the fact that he was a poet. He never kept in touch with them. He thought they were materialistic, and he didn't think they were capable of dreaming. Little did he know there'd be a whole country full of people who can't dream."

Five months into the marriage, Dorothy made a triumphant trip home to visit her parents and siblings, the details of which were covered in the pages of the *Canadian Jewish Review*. In October 1926 she returned once again, this time with Harry in celebration of their first wedding anniversary. She was already pregnant, although she may not yet have realized it, and within a few months the Sahls had relocated to a comfortable apartment in Outremont, a tiny residential city just north of downtown Montreal. Ben, her father, helped set Harry up in a cigar store on Bernard Avenue, one of the city's tonier shopping districts, and life, by the spring of 1927, was good. On the morning of May 11, Dorothy gave birth to a son, weighing seven-and-a-half pounds, at the Maternity Pavilion of the Royal Victoria Hospital. He was given the name Morton Lyon Sahl.

"He owned Montreal," Mort says of his maternal grandfather, whose fondness for bourbon and cigars carried him into his late nineties. "He started a bottling works, and then he started buying real estate. They didn't get into the United States. They got out of Rumania and got into Canada. He taught himself law; he was his own lawyer for all of these amalgamations. They had a huge house up on the hill." Lean and tall, Benjamin Schwartz was a commanding presence at family gatherings, especially to an impressionable three-year-old. "There was an uncle, and they always had dinner on Sundays. It was a lot of fun. Very European—a sense of noise and music and kids. And they're not talking, the old folks: 'Tell her I'm ready for my coffee.' 'He's ready for his coffee.' 'Tell him to get it himself.' I *do* remember that."

Mort was a kinetic child, with bright blue eyes and an unruly head of hair. Aggressively verbal, he would listen to adult conversations and play them back, embracing unfamiliar words and then using them freely. When her son became famous, Dorothy Sahl liked to tell interviewers that he was talking at seven months. "I used to stand by the radio and repeat what I heard," he says. "I think when we were in Montreal everybody probably made a big fuss over it because it was an extended family."

Harry Sahl's cigar business remained at its original location through 1929, then moved up the block to a shared space with a barber. It survived the great economic upheaval but just barely, and closed, as did a lot of retail businesses, in 1931. With the job market bleak, Harry moved his family to Washington, D.C., where he landed work as a typist with the Veterans Administration. They survived the worst of the Depression in Brookland, a poor residential neighborhood where Mort discovered custard and started grammar school in 1932. Franklin Roosevelt had just been sworn in as the new president. "At dinner my father would read to me what FDR had to say. 'Well, I see that Mister Big has decided . . .'"

The Sahls moved frequently in the latter half of the decade—Los Angeles, Mackinaw, Chattanooga, Los Angeles again. Socialization was difficult; a bright, friendly child grew into a sullen, introverted youngster, quiet and solitary. "All I knew was we kept moving. I'd go to another place and make friends and have to leave and I'd have no friends. You don't put that in capital letters—I mean I'm not a modern kid in a modern movie. You just know how you feel." They finally settled in the Westlake district of Los Angeles, a furnished apartment where Mort, once again, had no real space of his own. "There probably should have been more kids, because I had no one to talk to. It's like not having a union, you know? I didn't have my own bedroom; they'd fold out the couch. And so when they had people over, they'd talk after dinner. Somebody would say, 'Does that make into a bed?' And I'd say I had a little brother 'cause I was embarrassed. But I was going crazy. Looking to escape, I used to go to the library and hang around school afterwards. And then finally you meet some guys who have something in common with you."

Three miles to the east was downtown Los Angeles, and Mort Sahl, at age eleven, had the run of the town. "I used to go down on Main Street, and the Salvation Army kept those movies open on skid row. They were a nickel, and they ran like three movies. So it could be anything—a western with Tom Keene and then *His Girl Friday*. I used to go in there and stay in there all day." The theaters on South Main were disreputable little cousins to the big movie palaces two blocks to the west on South Broadway, three-hundred seat grind houses with names like Art, Banner, The Muse, Optic. Mort's ideal of America was formed during these impressionable years when American films adhered to the dictates of the Production Code, which ensured that crime was always punished, married couples occupied separate beds, and heroism was the norm for people of high moral standing. Crooked politicians were brought down by the citizenry, and the foundations of a great democracy were always held in reverence and awe. Spurred by changes in the national mood brought about by the New Deal and prodded by the Catholic Legion of Decency, Hollywood, in the words of historian Robert Sklar, "directed its enormous powers of persuasion to preserving the basic moral, social, and economic tenets of traditional American culture."

Absorbing these values subliminally, hour after hour, a young boy couldn't help but embrace them, celebrate them, aspire to them. "It was easier than trying to get my father's attention," Mort says today. "To him, character was everything." Harry Sahl never gave up on his dream of becoming a writer. By day, he worked as a clerk for the Department of Justice. At night, he would distance himself after dinner, retreating into his own insular little world. "He was very secretive with me. He used to write at the kitchen table. He had an Army footlocker, and he'd lock up everything after he wrote. It said: HARRY SAHL PERSONAL. And he said to me when I told him I wanted to be a writer, 'Don't tell your ideas to anybody, because they'll laugh.' That's one of the earliest things he ever said to me." Harry took his son to foreign films. "My father thought that American pictures were awful. He took me on a streetcar way down into downtown L.A. to 9th and Grand to go to those old movies where the manager, before he started the reel he'd go out with a Flit gun. My father liked that. He liked *Grand Illusion*—that kind of stuff. I didn't understand any of it at the beginning."

On school days, Mort would take the streetcar west along 3rd Street to Vermont, walking north past the massive Palomar Ballroom, ground zero for the swing era, a billboard for a mobster-like silhouette sticking in his memory, a rod protruding from the menacing figure like a machine gun. YOU ASKED FOR IT! the image warned, and over succeeding days painters added details until the apparent gangster was revealed to be Benny Goodman and his clarinet. At Virgil Junior High School, where Indiana-born Jane Peters had begun her transformation into Carole Lombard some twenty years earlier, he met two boys who took drama courses and seemed destined for careers in show business. One, Ed Penney, fancied himself another Orson Welles. The other, Dick Crenna, walked across the street to the KFI studios one day and got on as a regular on a radio show called *Boy Scout Jamboree*. Crenna later suggested that Mort Sahl had been antiauthoritarian since the age of ten—his authority figures being defined as his father, the school principal, and sometimes even the president. "Mort never told me he wanted a better world; he just said he wanted a cowboy suit. If his mother had gotten him a cowboy suit, then maybe Nixon wouldn't have been attacked by him for twenty years."

Mort had aspirations beyond a cowboy suit, but he lacked Ed Penney's moxie and Crenna's essential gift for mimicry. He recalled they were forever writing "plays, sketches, and radio programs" but that Crenna was the only one of the three who ever landed any work.

> My old man said, "It's all fixed. They put their relatives in those jobs. You can't ever be part of that." So I would go up to the radio studios— CBS at Sunset and Gower and NBC on Vine-and wait for extra tickets. Then I would go in, and they'd read the script and drop the pages on the floor. When the audience came out, I'd grab all the pages and bring them home. I made a rim velocity mic out of wood, and I had a girl next door to me going to Woodbury art school and she made up NBC and CBS to put on it. Then I used to read the scripts. I saw Burns and Allen with the Artie Shaw band, Groucho [Marx] and *The Circle* with Ronald Colman and Madeline Carroll, and that began to draw me.

As if to seal the deal, Frank Capra's *Mr. Smith Goes to Washington* went citywide in late 1939, and in it Mort found what was for him the most perfect of all Hollywood fables. *Mr. Smith* was shrewdly analogous to the cheap westerns he consumed by the hour in the grind boxes along Main Street. Jefferson Smith, the naive young deputy, comes to town and is expected to play along with the power elite. Full of civic pride and high ideals, it slowly dawns on him that the black hats are in charge and that the system is rigged. An insider throws in with him—Saunders, the jaded secretary who bucks him up. The showdown, as intense as any shootout, comes in the famous filibuster scene, where Jeff goes up against Boss Jim Taylor's stooges and a decisive role is played by the President of the Senate in the person of Harry Carey—one of the movies' original cowboy stars.

"*Mr. Smith* is easy to decode," Mort says today:

> It made me cry because I realized what they've done to the country. Then it's not that country, that that could happen. In a secondary sense, the girl is a total cynic and has given up love. And she rediscovers love as an option because she sees a heroic guy. So it gives us a reason to be heroic; there's a reward out there. And look at what

they can get away with in that script. Remember when his mother calls and says, "Jeff's message isn't getting out there. They're beating up the boys, Clarissa." And she hangs up and she says, "She called me Clarissa." If they can convince you that the rich guy is gonna lose—I mean, Edward Arnold always loses. Jimmy Stewart defeats the mob. It's a real affirmation of America. And I like the idea that there's a real paternal figure up there who will help him—Harry Carey.

Furloughed from the Justice Department, Harry Sahl reported just thirty weeks of employment for the year 1939, representing less than $1,500 in income. ("We were always poor," Mort laments.) Not long after the Palomar went up in flames in a spectacular conflagration that lit up the night sky, Harry landed a clerk's position in Honolulu and moved his family there in March 1940. "When we got there, it was ninety-five percent Japanese," Mort remembers. "It was all Japanese businessmen running it. They owned it already; they just never stressed it. It was like being in Tokyo. Then there was an Army post every three blocks. Schofield Barracks—it was subsidized by the War Department. The streetcars were open, kind of like cable cars, and we'd go to school without paying—we'd just get on. Every kid had a Swiss Army knife and would cut off a pineapple or a mango and eat it for lunch."

They remained in Hawaii just long enough for Mort to finish the eighth grade—scarcely two months—then Harry, shocked at the cost of living, returned them to Los Angeles aboard the SS *Monterey*. Settling his wife and son in yet another one-bedroom apartment, he went to work for the U.S. Maritime Commission while Mort waited out the summer watching movies, going to radio shows, and devouring library books on the roof of the Dorothy Mae apartments. "When we came back," he remembers, "I walked over to RKO, walked alongside the studio, and then up to Sunset Boulevard, and I said to myself, audibly, 'Mort Sahl, Hollywood welcomes you back!' And then I went over to [what became] the Huntington Hartford and saw the *Lux Radio Theater*."

Walking the two-mile distance to the Central Library from his new home at Sunset and Figueroa, Mort would stock up on military history, heraldry, the heroic stuff of the movies he consumed. ("I'd use both my father's card and my card to get twelve books.") He read everything he could find on Major General Smedley Butler, America's most-decorated Marine and the outspoken author of *War is a Racket*. Gripping six books under each arm, he'd walk back by way of Grand Avenue, passing Grand Central Market, the city's largest display of perishables, and Angel's Flight, a funicular that ferried passengers up and down Bunker Hill for a nickel. At the age of 13, he graduated to the plush theaters along Broadway, particularly the Orpheum and the Million Dollar, both of which offered vaudeville along with their double features. "I used to go into the movies and sit through them three times; wouldn't come out, just stay there," he says. "My mother would give me a dime to get in and a dime for candy."

Mort entered high school in September 1940, treading the two miles to the Belmont campus atop L.A.'s Crown Hill, a site that afforded students a commanding view of the surrounding city. He found the relative freedom of ninth grade a mixed blessing. "I liked those teachers that drew me out, like the music teacher. I was introverted in those days because I had no money. I couldn't go to any events. I worked in the cafeteria to get my lunch." He endured the anonymity of Belmont, reputedly the largest school in California, until the Japanese hit Pearl Harbor on December 7, 1941. "When the attack came, I was in the Million Dollar Theatre at Third and Broadway. [Singer-songwriter] Gene Austin came out on the stage and said, 'I've just gotten word that they attacked us, but we're going to whip 'em!' and everybody cheered."

Outside the theater, people milled in the streets and traffic came to a halt. At Pershing Square, four blocks away, more than a thousand bystanders listened to radio bulletins piped through a loudspeaker. In Little Tokyo, which was placed off limits to automobiles and surrounded by a cordon of police, Japanese Consul Kenji Nakauchi allowed as how he was "quite sorry." Having just witnessed a Monogram comedy called *Top Sergeant Mulligan*, in which two guys mistakenly volunteer for the Army, Mort tried to enlist in the Marine Corps. He was fourteen years old.

"I did some very crazy things," he admits. "I joined the ROTC and I got to be a captain." The modest battalion at Belmont, which dated from 1920, suddenly swelled to 140 underage boys eager to go to war. "I was locked into that movie thing—when the boys come back again. I excelled in the ROTC, and I could barely pay for my uniform. No natural gifts, just going back again and again, no matter how hard it hurt. And when a picture came out like *To the Shores of Tripoli*—John Payne and Randolph Scott—I must have seen it forty-two times." Inspired by the Technicolor training sequences in the 20th Century-Fox release, he memorized the film's drill scene and recreated it at school. "I practically lived in uniform," he said. "I guess it gave me a purpose."

The ROTC, he found, conferred a certain cachet on campus. "I got access to the rifle range, and finally worked up the nerve to say to a girl, 'Would you like me to teach you to shoot?' Which would mean you could recline there, and you could touch her shoulder. But I was scared to death. I didn't think I had anything to offer; I could barely get a pair of pants and a tee-shirt together in the morning. I couldn't take her home and entertain her. And I never had enough money to take her anywhere. So I was pretty well inhibited." In time he won a marksmanship trophy and captured the American Legion's Americanism award. One Sunday he walked to the Hollywood Canteen in his ROTC uniform and got in. He caught glimpses of John Garfield and Ida Lupino before he was thrown out.

The Sahl family moved to a duplex in Silver Lake, Harry having taken a job as secretary to Burbank Police Chief Elmer Adams. ("The cops were told that if anybody worked for Lockheed or Disney or Warners they should let them go," Mort remembers.) Rents were too high in Burbank and the family had no car, so Harry used his municipal connections to get hired on at South Gate, where Firestone Tire and Rubber and a General Motors assembly plant were the city's principal employers. "When they moved, I was fifteen miles from all my pals in the ROTC," Mort says. "The high school was in the next block, but I didn't know anybody. And they didn't have any money for an ROTC. Because it was wartime, I got a teacher to start a branch of the California State Militia, and I went to an Army-Navy store and got some stuff and tried to train guys. I was desperately searching for that movie identity."

Frustrated, he managed to enlist at fifteen, leaving a note for his mother on the kitchen table. "I was torn and nuts and futureless. I lied about my age and registered for the draft, so they weren't so strenuous about their standards. They sent me to Fort MacArthur [in San Pedro], and I was going to basic training in Texas, but my mother came and got me." Faced with another year at South Gate, he transferred back to Belmont and took to hitchhiking to school. "In those days, servicemen were all hitchhiking, so I'd put on my ROTC uniform and hitchhike to the high school. People thought I was in the service. My mother used to press those military creases into my shirt, and I'd lean back against my seat in class so that the creases wouldn't go out. I'd wrap myself around the ROTC and being a hero. I thought girls were going to write to me when I went overseas. I'd be a paratrooper and I'd have jump boots and I'd have my wings."

In his senior year, Cadet First Lieutenant Morton L. Sahl was made Cadet Captain and assumed command of A Company, which had won the banner in the All-City Federal Inspection, placing ahead of Belmont's B Company by a margin of twenty-two points. He also went to work on the school newspaper, the *Belmont Sentinel*, where the newly arrived journalism teacher, Frances Hov, made him a columnist. "She was great," he says of Miss Hov. "Ethel Barrymore—a real nurturer. She had her eye out for anybody that broke the rules. Instead of saying I was a misfit, she gave me a place to *be* a misfit." The column became his first taste of public comment, a place for poking innocent fun at his peers. Beginning with the first issue of the spring semester, he collected elliptical items and boldface names under the general heading "Saga of Sad Sack Sahl," emerging as the Walter Winchell of the Hilltoppers, a sixteen-year-old iconoclast observing life on Planet Belmont "through a ten-cent telescope from the side pocket of table three."

Mort didn't attend his own graduation, partly due to a lack of interest. "I just didn't think I could afford any fantasies," he says. "I couldn't go to the military ball; I couldn't afford the ticket. And I wasn't in the yearbook with a picture. I didn't have any money. And my parents weren't involved; they weren't like parents are now who are always on your back. My parents were never at the school." At age seventeen he had nowhere to go, nothing to do. "I went to see this admiral who commanded the Naval Reserve [Training Center] in Chavez Ravine about going to Annapolis. I was trying to keep my father at bay. His idea was: Go into the service. Have a career. And I had not yet realized that they didn't want me." Rebuffed, he tried enlisting in the Army, giving his birth year as 1926. This time the hitch was aborted in Georgia when his true age became known. Returned to South Gate, he faced the discouraging prospect of entering adulthood while sleeping on a couch.

"I had a very barren existence. I worked on getting an appointment to West Point from Congressman Clyde Doyle. Then I got very impatient and enlisted. I really wanted to go away and win my wings and have a girl write to me. If you had said to me: 'Well, that's okay from eighteen to twenty, but what are your plans?' Didn't have a plan. I had a plan of the stereotype of heroics and romance." Having finally turned eighteen, he joined the Army Air Corps on December 17, 1945. Roosevelt was dead, the war was over, and the term of enlistment was for a single year. "I thought America could cure the fever. I believed those guys driving around occupied Berlin. And then, of course, they needed an enemy and the Russians were handy."

It all started out well enough. He took basic training at Williams Field, outside of Phoenix, and drew front gate duty as an MP. "It was really hard. I had to stand on a box and wear white gloves and bring the cars in. I loved all that. I had eighteen pairs of white gloves; they were always clean and I really inhabited that part. I liked all that ritualistic stuff—and I hoped that the girls were going to like that we did." He was sent to Alaska as a flight engineer, to the Aleutian Islands at first, and then to Elmendorf Field, Anchorage, where he learned to operate a portable oxygen generator. "When I was in the Army I did a couple of camp shows. The shows were a preview of what the act was going to be. When I got on, I kidded the officers. I walked a very dangerous line."

A nemesis emerged in the person of Colonel Leslie Mulzer, who was commander of the 93rd Air Depot Group. "It was disillusioning," Mort said of his time under Mulzer's command:

> It was unjust. There was a great deal of favoritism. I put out a newspaper up there, *Poop from the Group*. The Colonel called me in and said to me, "You're causing dissension, but this could be a unifying weapon of morale. I'm trying to defend this country from communists." So he said he'd give me the paper full time if I would write about sports and stuff, and I refused. It was the beginning of a familiar pattern.
>
> When they bumped the guys up to corporal, I was off the list because I offended somebody. I sat on my bunk and I was hanging up my shirt and I twisted the coat hanger. I remember I twisted it into my hand, and I didn't notice because I was so furious. Mulzer had made his driver a master sergeant, and so I wrote in the paper that the table of organization for officers was written on cheap rubber, not paper. Mulzer said, "I know you're a communist" and he put me on KP. That's when I gave up the service as a career. I said, "This is like everything else."

Sahl spent eighty-three consecutive days cleaning pots, shoveling coffee, and generally helping to feed 7,000 men. "If I had gone to West Point and been part of the military establishment myself, it would have been okay. But a few months under the heel of authority killed it for me. I could never have been an officer after that." Discharged, he emerged from the service, as *The New Yorker*'s Robert Rice would later suggest, with "a strong desire to tell the world what was wrong with it."

With his mustering-out pay, Sahl bought himself some freedom in the form of an old flathead Ford—a three-window Model A coupe "chopped, with the frame zeed in and a suicide front end." Home, he found, hadn't grown any more welcoming in his absence, nor had it gotten any closer to Los Angeles and the jazz clubs he was in the process of discovering. "I worked in a gas station in South Gate," he remembers. "Union 76. Clean the lube rack, wipe the windshield. I worked in Huntington Park at J.J. Newberry's. Stock boy. Sixteen dollars a week, raised to nineteen." Such unprecedented industry failed to impress his father, who fretted he would have no future, no viable way of supporting himself. "I used to hang around at the clubs and come in at five in the morning and go to bed. He wanted me to get up in the morning and shave and put on a tie and go out and conquer Mt. Everest."

Mostly to placate the old man, Mort enrolled at Compton Junior College, where his earliest classes began at eleven and where he could work on the campus paper. At home, he listened to the radio, sampling what his mother was tuned to as she went about her housework. Initially devoted to humorist Fred Allen, he discovered ABC's Henry Morgan and became part of a cult that *Liberty* magazine described as "an astonishing collection ranging from professional humorists and show people to clergymen, children, taxi drivers, and an admiring clique in an insane asylum." Morgan's irreverence, particularly toward his sponsor, was like nothing else on the air, a weekly high-wire act devoted to savaging the hand that fed him. Morgan pointed the way to a new fearlessness in verbal comedy, but it was the sly conversational tone of Herb Shriner, who did fifteen minutes nightly on CBS, that really stayed with him. Shriner was so unpolished as to be subversive, a Hoosier philosopher often likened to the late Will Rogers, but with a mordant wit Rogers seldom displayed.

Then, of course, there was the music. "I remember being fourteen and hearing the Stan Kenton band on the radio," Mort says, savoring that early memory of the merciless Kenton brass.

Then when I got up in the Aleutians on the aircraft radio I heard the band from the [Hollywood] Palladium, and I started seeking it out when I came home. I was nineteen, and I took a girl. She didn't like it, so I didn't take anybody after that. I just went, and I stayed all night. I stood by the piano not to lose my place. The band manager, George Morte, said, "Would you like to meet Stan?" I said, "God, yeah." So he said, "Wait until the intermission." I started perspiring, scared and everything. I walked up and he said, "Stan, this is Mort Sahl." And before I could say anything, Stan, who was six-five, put his hand on my head and said, "I know this guy. He comes every night."

Kenton, Mort says, meant everything to him as an artist. "It's way beyond any movie star. I was really in awe of him and the way he'd pull it together." Records, he remembers, cost forty cents apiece. "There were no CDs then, and I was saving up all month to go to see Kenton [live]. I'd buy a ticket to the Hollywood Bowl to see the concert. There was no way to duplicate the music, so I remembered it in geometrics—the way they'd go in and the way they'd come out, and they had a scale and they'd come down. I sort of saw it digitally, visually, so that I could play it back to myself, all those Bill Holman arrangements."

To fund his jazz habit, Mort got a job selling used cars. "I met a guy at Compton. He was working at a lot at 108th and Vermont, and brought me over there. When you bought a car there, you'd get a ticket to go to this furniture store and get a television set. (Television was very big in '49.) I tried selling cars; I wasn't very good at it. I was really on the ropes." At the age of twenty-one, he transferred to USC on the G.I. Bill, declaring a major in public administration. He was "sort of a C student" in college, far more interested in cars and music than classes in civil engineering. He applied for a campus job and was hired as chauffeur to Dr. Rufus von KleinSmid, the university's former president and chancellor for life, for which he was required to wear a cap and uniform.

Awarded his B.S. in 1950, Mort began work on an advanced degree but hated it. "I thought I was going to die in South Gate. But something in me wanted to climb the mountain. And it looked pretty formidable at that time. It's your hope that dies. Nothing physical dies; your hope dies." At twenty-three he wrote a novel "about a dreamer and a girl who turned him over because of it" and showed it to his English professor, a man called Aerol Arnold. "He was really cruel to me. He read it and said, 'There's nothing there.' So I swallowed my pride and said, 'Could you help me with some direction? To resurrect it?' He said, 'I'm afraid your inner poverty overcomes everything.' In front of the class . . ."

One day, an acquaintance named Paul Ullmann, whose chosen field was social work, asked him if he still liked jazz. The reason, it turned out, was that Ullmann had met a girl who was fond of it and he didn't know where to take her. "I will get you a date with her girl friend," he proposed, "then we can double date and you can take us to one of the jazz joints." That night at the Palladium, Mort went to a public phone between sets and called the girl Ullmann had met in order to "open liaison." Even though they talked for thirty minutes, she gave him the deep freeze. ("Barbara Walters on a cold day.") She was equally incommunicado the following night when they arrived to collect her. "I met her parents," said Mort. "It was kind of a dream California home—upper middle class, Jewish, two girls."

She warmed up on the drive down to Hermosa Beach, and Mort found himself in a closed conversation for the rest of the evening. "She was very smart. Funny. Witty," he says. "When I took her home I said, 'What college do you go to?' And she said, 'I'm in high school.' Susan Babior was all of sixteen. 'Hey,' I said, 'I'm not going to be seeing you. I'm twenty-three.' She said, 'So what? A lot of people are older than you are.' That's how she won the conversation. I found her kind of unforgettable. I came back to see her, and then the father was in the door. You know: Do you have a job? Do you have any plans? The mother was more conciliatory, but the father thought I was [Communist Party leader] Earl Browder pursuing his daughter. I had no prospects. I had a car that barely got there; I was always late and greasy because I had fixed it on the way."

He dropped out of graduate school after a run of tension with the dean of the School of Public Administration, Dr. Henry Reining, who gave him a D on a term paper. "It was about the founding of the Department of Defense and how you've really duplicated fascism. You have the Department of the Air Force, you're not eliminating anything; you're not streamlining the budget. He said to me, 'If you want to insult people for a living, I suggest you become a radio comedian.' And that guy quit SC and went to work for the World Bank in Turkey."

It was around this time that Sahl turned to writing as a form of expression, his unpublished novel an early attempt to put his thoughts, both sociological and political, into words. "I wanted to be a writer because my dad was a writer," he said. "I loved my dad. I wanted to be like him if I could." Not yet given to polemics, he wrote philosophical short stories and one-act plays after the fashion of George Bernard Shaw, one of his literary heroes. "I wrote four one-act plays that were produced in L.A.," he said in a 1957 interview with *The New Yorker*. "I wrote a novel and a lot of short stories. I even wrote an oratorio for Stan Kenton—a big, heavy, serious, epic thing for half a dozen actors and the full band. I bound it up nicely in a book and showed it to Stan, and he was stunned. I wrote eighteen sets of lyrics for some song one of his arrangers was doing. I used words like 'misanthrope,' and *he* was stunned."* But I had a very jealous attitude toward my writing. I sat on it. Then I discovered I had to *talk*."

---

* This was recorded as "Prologue (This is an Orchestra!)" and can be heard on the 1952 album *New Concepts of Artistry in Rhythm*. "I wrote the introduction of all the guys," Mort says. "And I illustrated it. I really got carried away when I believed it."

The first time Mort Sahl went on stage, it was for bandleader Horace Heidt. "He rejected me. But I was naive in those days. I believed in opportunity." He began using the name "Cal Southern" and affecting a tousled stance not unlike that of Herb Shriner. "My dad and I weren't agreeing about much. I used to drive down to those nightclubs on Western Avenue. I could get on if I knew the person who was singing. It was [June] Christy, who came off the band. Also Jay Johnson; he succeeded Christy with Kenton. If he worked in a club, I'd go on at intermission." In Los Angeles at 108th and Western, Sahl was regarded as if he were a creature from another planet. "I'd make some references to jazz and the music of the times, and it was a dismal failure. It wasn't in tempo to the music, and I wasn't confident. I had some observations, but they won't get unleashed until you become confident."

The tidal wave of indifference had a curious effect: New York, he decided, couldn't be any worse. "I wanted some kind of approval, and I wanted an audience. I also wanted to be a jazz musician, but I couldn't play." He traveled to Manhattan in the fall of 1952, determined to give show business his all. He found two women who were going there, and offered to drive to cover his share of the expenses. His father gave him $40. "I lived in a hotel on West 47th Street on eighteen dollars a week, which covered room, laundry, and loaves of day-old bread from the A&P," he remembers. "Auditioned all over town. I'd pick up the paper, because that's what Will Rogers would do. I'd do a kind of general commentary, but nobody was laughing. They said it was too intellectual. 'It belongs in the Village in a chi chi club.'"

One memorable afternoon was spent auditioning for cabaret impresario Julius Monk, who managed a claustrophobic little club on East 56th Street called Le Ruban Bleu. Mort tried out with a man who was asked by Monk what he did. "I'm an emcee," the man said. "I introduce people."

"Well," said Monk, who struck Mort as a double for actor Clifton Webb, "how can I see what you do?"

"I don't know," the man replied. "Do you have someone I can introduce?"

In no mood to like anyone that day, Monk gave thumbs down to both Mort Sahl and Jonathan Winters. "Too sophisticated," he complained, although he would eventually end up hiring Winters.

Returning to Los Angeles, Mort worked intermissions at the Palladium when Stan Kenton was in residence, boldly putting himself up in front of four thousand people. "They didn't want to do it," he recalls of the venue's management. "Stan had trouble getting me in the door to see him, but he was always receptive." The crowds, he found, were receptive as well, open, it would seem, to anything endorsed by the man whose music they idolized. "I went over fine, but L.A. is a weird town. I was ignored—by managers, by the press, by everybody. I had no more publicity the day I quit than the day I started, and I was right back in nowhere."

Through his boyhood friend Ed Penney, Mort began writing for a magazine published by the nonprofit Altruistic Artists Foundation called *The Arts*— initially as a columnist, then almost immediately as an associate editor. The first issue of 1953 carried a general critique of network television ("Manhattan Antenna"), the second a nuanced review of Kenton's recent stand at the Palladium. ("The dynamics of the orchestra have been watered down. I no longer felt as though the chief arranger's mother had been frightened by Stan's brass section. Every fifteen minutes found the maestro apologizing for jazz and promising dance music.") The publication, which would end its run with the March issue, led to Penney's founding of Theatre X, which heralded itself as "a new professional experimental group doing entirely new works by new writers, choreographers, and composers."

Despite its pretensions, the first offering from Theatre X was little more than an old-fashioned vaudeville featuring the Mitchell Choirboys, Jay Johnson, a folk singer named Dave Zeitlin, and Mort Sahl "direct from the Ruban Bleu in New York" as the master of ceremonies. ("Even though they thought they were experimental," Mort says, "they were really quite traditional in the pieces they chose to do.") Encouraged to submit material, Sahl offered earnest one-acts about courts-martial, prison systems, and women not understanding men. "They were a bunch of misfits," he says of the company. "I tried to write for them, but they thought what I was writing was racy. I was writing Stan Kenton, who I sort of wrote as L. Ron Hubbard. A Kenton-like character, in other words, who was everybody's old man. I called it *The Old Man*, and he has this spell he casts over everybody. I wrote it as an outline and nobody liked it. Ed Penney didn't like it. It was too absolute for them. I had a serious case of Kenton worship."

Since the collapse of Theatre X came not long after Sue transferred from UCLA to Berkeley, Mort, with seemingly nothing to lose, followed her. They had a saying: "There's a lot of love in Berkeley." Which meant, in Mort's interpretation, that the citizens would listen to you if you had something to say. "I just staggered around Berkeley and people would buy me coffee. I didn't know what I was going to do." He audited courses, hung out in the libraries, mooched leftovers in a fast-food restaurant called Doggie Diner. "Real Bohemia," he said. "Guys living in packing cases, cars. No dorms, everybody lived with somebody else. We'd sit around in the joints all night. Somebody would get up and say he was going to Cuba. Somebody would say, 'Why?' 'Well, what else should I do? Sit here and drink coffee?' And nobody would see him again for a year."

Mort was living in the back of his car when Sue and her roommates took him in, allowing him to kip in the window seat of their North Street apartment. "They were very good to me. The girls all had fathers that were substantial, and I was floating around. Someone was always buying me dinner or making me dinner. And then one night I remember I saved up and I made dinner for the girls. And they all raved about how good it was, but you know how good it was with *me* cooking: 'At thirteen minutes after, start the potatoes. At fourteen minutes after . . .' I had it all written out like an engineering student."

One of the centers of campus nightlife was the White Log Tavern, the remnant of a chain of twenty-four-hour eateries on Bancroft Way. The menu had devolved to coffee and donuts, but the place was still open at all hours. "I would go in there and argue with the other radicals because I wasn't sleeping. Berkeley had three shifts of people who were forever talking politics in coffeehouses. There was a cadre of left-wing-oriented Jewish kids with fervor." The White Log became the place where Mort, in the words of poet Arnie Passman, "started calling out the McCarthy era," an event and location that Passman later suggested should be commemorated with a plaque.

"I was walking with Sue in Berkeley," Mort remembers,

and the ROTC was being dismissed. They said, "Dis MISSED!" and they pulled their ties down, put the caps in their pockets. I said, in the voice of a first sergeant in the Army, "What a piss poor lookin' outfit." And she said, "Well, they don't want to be there anyway." I said, "That's not the point. If you're going to soldier, you ought to soldier. And if you're going to protest, you ought to protest." Then I realized I was quoting James Jones; it was more of a homage. I needed to have some heroes too, so I managed to latch onto [Robert] Mitchum and [Burt] Lancaster, but also Jim Jones and Norman Mailer.

It was while in Berkeley that he awoke to the pain and nausea of what turned out to be appendicitis. "We had no money," he says.

It ruptured, and I kept taking Tums. Then finally we went up to the Herrick Hospital and they said $650 for an appendectomy. We had nothing. Sue was with me, and the doctor looked at me and he snapped his fingers and said, "Hey, were you in the service?" And the next thing I know I'm at the Oakland Veterans Hospital. And they take it out. As I go in, before they cut, the social worker says, "Do you have *any* means of income?" And so I dramatized that [in the act]. I say to her: "No! I'm an artist in America. Why don't you let me die?"

Actually, I had not qualified as an artist. I was sleeping on the window seat at Sue's apartment with two other girls. And I guess she had some kind of faith in me. We really loved each other, because I didn't show any signs of being anything. And her father hated me; I sounded like a Marxist.

Mort's recovery took weeks, time he used to contemplate his circumstances. "I was full of vague protest, but I was like the little dog in Sputnik. My yelps weren't heard." He told Sue that he was going to try his hand at being a comedian. "I didn't have the equipment," he wrote in *Heartland*. "I didn't have a tuxedo. You needed that in 1953, and a line of girls behind you."

Sue, he says, was the only true believer, the only one who really thought he could do it. "Why don't you try out in this club in San Francisco?" she suggested. "It's in North Beach, which is the bohemian area—which means a lot of Jewish people acting like Italians. Why don't you go to the hungry i? The audiences are all intellects, which means if they understand you, great, and if they don't they will never admit it because they will think it is whimsical humor."

She had, he later reported, a beatific smile on her face.

4

ARE THERE ANY GROUPS WE HAVEN'T OFFENDED?

When Susan Babior transferred to Berkeley in 1953, she vowed she'd never be back. She had told her father Abe, a grocer who settled his family in a neighborhood adjacent to the sprawling UCLA campus, that she needed a course that wasn't offered in Westwood. Two years later, when she married a man Abe always considered a bum, she didn't tell him directly, choosing instead to wire her mother. ("SILVER RING," she noted.) The news sent shockwaves through the family. Three days later, Sue was back in L.A. scouting for an apartment. "He thought I was a dreamer," Mort says of Abe Babior. "To his utter amazement, here I was in show business, or, as he put it, 'We never knew you'd become Mort Sahl.'"

Sue was a striking girl with light brown hair and big soulful eyes. "A very hip jazz chick," as her then-husband describes her. Their honeymoon consisted of seeing parents and old friends and being photographed by Bob Willoughby, who, having recently scored his first cover for *Life*, caught the young couple in a dreamy embrace. The only talk of work in those first weeks of married life came from Dave Brubeck, who liked the chemistry of the Sunset concert and proposed a series of dates on the fall college circuit. Mort fed the news to Herb Caen, who ran the item on July 5, 1955, adding that his correspondent was the proud author of a new do-it-yourself book, *How to Turn In Your Friends to the FBI for Fun and Profit*.

Nothing panned out in Los Angeles over that summer, and after providing "commentary" on the Berkeley campus for a crowded showcase of local talent called *Jazz: San Francisco*, Mort and Sue headed east in a new Austin-Healey, bound for New York and another stand at the Blue Angel. He opened on September 9 with the French-born vocalist Robert Clary topping the bill and comedienne Ceil Cabot kicking it off. To his delight, Sahl was preceded on stage by a powerful little package from Boston named Teddi King, whose set brought the room to a hypnotic silence and dazzled an inveterate jazz fan who thought he had heard them all. "Really magnificent singer," Mort says, noting her early passing at the age of forty-eight.

"We were staying at the Gramercy Park Hotel," Mort remembers, "and Sue and I were really in love. Those were great times." Audiences at the Angel were friendlier and more savvy than before, and the media seemed to be paying closer attention. "People were coming in like Popsie Whitaker from the *New Yorker*. New York kind of scared me, though. It was impersonal and you had to yell for cabs. I couldn't quite figure it out, but Sue was different. We'd find a place in the Village and eat Italian food."

It was in September that *Tonight!* host Steve Allen caught the act and was impressed by how "amateurish" it seemed. "The first time I saw Mort I wondered what he did for a living. He had none of that nightclub polish, he didn't wear a tuxedo. I wouldn't care if he wore a gunny sack, but that's indicative of his uniqueness. He had the newspaper rolled up under his arm, or just played with it, idling. He looked like some guy who stepped out of a history class for a minute and you couldn't tell if he was a member of the class or teaching the class. Very un-showbiz, and that was refreshing. It was one of the things I liked about him when I first saw him work."

Allen invited Sahl to appear on *Tonight!* which was telecast from the Hudson Theatre on West 44th Street. "He was on the stage," Mort remembers, "and I walked in and Herb Sargent and Stan Burns, the writers, met me in the lobby and asked me to run through the material. So I did it for them standing in the lobby. Herb said to me, 'Powerful.' And I went on and did it. I did a very unorthodox monologue for Steve out of the Blue Angel. They had taken away [physicist J. Robert] Oppenheimer's 'Q' clearance, and an FBI officer walks in and says, 'All right Dr. Oppenheimer, you're through. Turn in your brain.' No one laughed. Then I did 'Every time they throw an American in jail we throw an American in jail.' Nobody laughed. And six minutes in, it came like a dam bursting. But I was sweatin' bullets. I thought I was finished. It was just a strange language for them."

Allen carried similar memories of Mort's television debut, allowing as how they were "quite hazy around the edges" when he dredged them up for a 1989 interview. "There are some comedians," he said, "who immediately put an audience at ease just by showing up . . . but Mort, when he was young and fresh, didn't put an audience at ease. He made them suddenly think: Listen, what is this man saying? And that's great because he immediately had their attention, and then finally when, after four or five minutes, they felt they knew him, they could relax and laugh more heartily. But he did require more concentrated attention than the typical 'Lenny' or 'Jackie' comedian."

Steve Allen was more spontaneous than anyone in prime time, and *Tonight!* had an anarchistic quality in an otherwise over-scripted era. He loved to showcase new performers who were decidedly out of the norm, and he wasn't afraid to lock horns with squeamish programming executives. It was, he said, "very experimental, a canvas on which we could paint anything we wanted." In Mort, Allen saw an anticomedian, a sort of nightclub Marlon Brando who seemed to disdain not only the showbiz trappings of traditional standup, but even the jokes themselves. What was funny about Mort Sahl was his way of looking at things, how he caught the imagination as his targets withered.

A key result of the *Tonight!* appearance was Herb Sargent's fervent interest in this new style of comedy. Famously taciturn, Sargent was happy to let Mort do the talking, and he would frequently turn up at the Blue Angel to audit an act that was, by its very nature, in a constant state of flux. "Herbert Jacoby was very proper in Parisian suits," Mort remembers of the Angel's managing partner. "He'd walk around in the dark. He couldn't deal with you. He'd pretend to be a voice in the dark. 'I can't hear you.' That meant 'speak louder,' pretending it was spontaneous. So one night I said, 'I can't hear *you*.' Herb Sargent was in the audience, and Herb said: 'He said, I can't *pay* you.'"

Another writer on the network payroll caught the act in October 1955. But where Herb Sargent was an established figure, there to admire a man he considered a peer, nineteen-year-old Woody Allen was essentially an apprentice, a man at the very beginning of his career. "I was part of the writer-development program at NBC where they were developing—allegedly developing—young writers," he recalled. "The head of the program said, 'There's a guy at the Blue Angel called Mort Sahl, and we're high on him. We'd love you to go down and see him.'" Allen, who knew nothing about Sahl, was astonished by what he witnessed. "I loved everything he did, every word out of his mouth. There was nothing that he ever did or said, every inflection, every joke, every nuance, that I didn't think was brilliant. I mean, I just thought he was the greatest thing I ever saw." Here, he said, was a bright young intellectual whose comic observations were both literate and natural, a totally different animal from the Catskill-style comics that were so plentiful in New York. "He was nothing like them—he didn't speak like them and his subject matter was completely different." What was particularly impressive was how Sahl could merely suggest a topic and provoke laughter with a dangerous grin:

> It didn't occur to me until a long time after what a genuinely funny man he was, and how much of it he *made* funny. He could just come out on stage and say, "General Curtis LeMay, right?" No joke at all, and the entire audience would laugh. It was funny because there was something funny about him and his inflections. He completely hid the mechanics of performing. Comics used to say to me, "Why do you love this guy so much? He just comes out and talks. I can do that. I mean, everybody does that." And, of course, that wasn't the case at all. It seemed like he just came out and talked, but he was performing, and he was performing jokes, and maybe he was performing the same jokes night after night at shows, but it always seemed like fresh, totally off-the-cuff conversation due to his skill. All the nuances and inflections were very funny. It was like nothing I'd ever seen, and I've never seen anything like it after. It was an overwhelming experience.

In the eight months Mort Sahl spent away from the hungry i, Enrico Banducci brought in a succession of comedians—Dick Gautier, fresh from a four-year hitch in the navy, actress-comedienne Jane Dulo, Professor Irwin Corey. Gautier was popular and showed great promise, but it was Corey, imported from New York, who stayed the longest and did the most business. For a while Banducci even tried television with a weekly show called *From the hungry i*, thirty minutes of live remote over KOVR, a scrappy independent targeting the Sacramento market. The fissure between Banducci and Sahl was deep, and it fell to Enrico to make the conciliatory gesture of offering $1,000 a week to return Mort to the room he had inaugurated two years earlier. "I had overstepped myself," Mort acknowledges, "but he cursed at me in the worst terms, and I have a lot of trouble with that. He said some terrible things to me; I guess he thought I was too big for my britches, and I probably was." Mort and Sue took an apartment on Pacific Avenue, which, for a while, remained unfurnished apart from a double bed. "You can't stay mad at him," he said of Banducci. "It's like trying to stay mad at your parents. They always forgive you, even when it's their fault."

All three shows on that first night back, February 12, 1956, were sold out, the room packed solid at a dollar a head. Recycling virtually nothing from the Blue Angel, Sahl delivered the localized content audiences had come to expect, drawing a bead on the city's newest appointed official. "Police Chief Ahern says he's going to drive the hoods over to Oakland," he announced, flashing the *Chronicle*. "Mayor Christopher warned him not to use city cars." Linking that item to the upcoming Republican National Convention, he went on to say that the GOP was thinking of canceling out because "they heard Ahern was cleaning up the city." And from that he was spurred to declare the venerable San Francisco madam Mabel Malotte "the last leader of free enterprise" in the city.

"At the club here, I try to be sort of an oral columnist," he said in an interview with the *San Francisco News*. "I mean this town is big enough to accommodate a variety of entertainment, but still compact enough so that people know what I'm talking about. Generally, the act opens with a few topical stories, then one big story, then a few more topical single jokes, and before you know it, thirty minutes are up." The big story that evening was the trip back to California in the Austin-Healey: "I drove through this little gate, see, and a machine gives me a ticket and then I'm on the super-highway. It's 1,600 miles long, no curves, no cross streets, with a cement embankment twenty feet high on each side. Nothing to distract you—no clouds, no sun, the birds don't even fly over it. . . . When I get to the end I put the ticket in this machine and it punches $21.13. Friend of mine, only cost him $17.82. I get out of the car. Not another soul in sight, just this machine. I start to argue. 'What do you mean $21.13? This friend of mine—' This sign lights up: DO NOT CHALLENGE THE MACHINE. What can you do? I say, 'Take me to your leader.'"

Mort Sahl made his prime time TV debut on April 8, 1956, when he flew to Los Angeles to do seven vivid minutes on the *NBC Comedy Hour*, a new Sunday night showcase for young talent. Building his appearance around the story of the attempted holdup at the Fairmont Hotel, he was such a hit with the live audience—the show originated from the El Capitan Theatre in Hollywood—that the network offered him a return booking and a non-exclusive five-year contract, fueling rumors that he would be George Gobel's summer replacement.

Sahl's *Comedy Hour* triumph came after two years of being told by practically everyone the mass audience would never accept his smart new style of comedy. "The first thing I used to hear in San Francisco was, 'Well, only intellectuals will want to hear it.' Then after that it was, 'They don't want to hear it in the East.' Then, 'They don't want to hear it on TV.'" When Mort played the Blue Angel in 1955, he was thrilled to learn that NBC president Sylvester "Pat" Weaver was bringing the great radio comedian Fred Allen to see him. "It was kind of funny. Weaver said that I was the future. And I broke out in hives because Fred Allen was coming in, and Fred, to me, represented intellect. So he sits down, and when I finish he says, 'Nobody will get it. It's too intellectual. The guy has no future.' Weaver said, 'Fred, you're wrong. He's going to have anything he wants—whether or not he wants it.'"

The guest shot on NBC was also priceless publicity for the hungry i. "I had to warm up the studio audience for twenty minutes before the show to get them in a laughing mood," he told an audience at the "i" one night, "so I went out and told them the president was having the convention in San Francisco because of [champion golfer Ken] Venturi, and many people got up and left. Then I said that [Democratic presidential candidate] Adlai Stevenson had been called an intellectual by his adversaries, and other charges he didn't answer, and another group got up and left. Finally, there was only one man left in the studio, and I couldn't get to him until I insulted La Follette and the Bull Moose movement, and then he left—the last of the independents."

By the time of Mort's second appearance on the *Comedy Hour*, NBC had a biographical press release at the ready and Sahl was expanding the act at the hungry i beyond "the daily experiences of the average man" in anticipation of election season and the summer influx of Republican conventioneers. He did as many as five shows a night during the GOP convention, with delegates in dark business suits crowding in and giving the showroom the look of a chamber of commerce meeting. Telling them of a chance encounter with the vice president, he related how Nixon stretched out a hand and said, "I'm from California." He said he replied, "Well, there's not an awful lot you can dispute there, but you have given me something to think about." Concerning the self-important John Foster Dulles, a Cold War hardliner, he alleged a new foreign policy: "He flies now, we pay later."

One night a heckler called out from the audience, "Are you going to vote for Dick?"

"No," Sahl yelled back.

"Why not?"

"Because I'm a fascist."

When another heckler started in, Sahl was clearly perplexed. "I can't understand it," he said. "I've been watching the convention for four days and no one even moved."

Aside from the heaviest possible schedule at the club, Mort was also appearing daily on CBS' *Good Morning with Will Rogers Jr.*, a commitment that required him to be on the air live from the show's headquarters at the Mark Hopkins Hotel at 4:00 A.M. "I was young and strong and I kept on going," he says. "I thought you could change comedy. I didn't know if you could change the country—that was more problematic—but for a while I thought you could by example." Rogers' Chicago-based producer had nabbed him through his agents at MCA before NBC could decide on whether to use him for its own morning show, *Today*. Mort rode in on a fire truck—the producer's idea—at an hour when he was normally just getting to bed. "We were trying to act festive and happy," he said. "Television is never more false than when it's openly sincere."

Despite Sahl's best efforts, the presidential race of 1956 generated little political heat because the outcome was never seriously in doubt. ("Let's vote NO for president," he urged, "and keep the White House empty another four years.") The president's sketchy health aside, Gallup showed that seven out of ten Americans favored Eisenhower for re-election, even though the shifty Nixon was considered a liability. Certainly of all the major political figures on the scene, Richard Milhous Nixon was Sahl's most reliable punching bag, inspiring even Republicans to join in as he administered a well-deserved lambasting. Personally, Mort favored Stevenson, who was thoughtful, eloquent, and, most important, quick with a quip. "The real reason Eisenhower is running again," Stevenson said after the president declared for a second term, "is that he can't afford to retire to his farm at Gettysburg while [Ezra Taft] Benson [who liked to talk of the 'spiritual side' of farm prices] is Secretary of Agriculture." Instantly smitten, Mort began following the former governor of Illinois as never before.

Working the "i" six days a week, Sahl and Enrico Banducci grew closer than ever. "That was a great gang there," he says in retrospect, "all those Italians out on North Beach. I really found a family there. When the job was over, Enrico and I would drive to the T&D Theatre in Oakland—the last show was at two. We saw *The Harder They Fall* there. We'd go next door to get sandwiches from Larry's Pastrami Heaven and go into the balcony. I'd meet him before the show, I'd meet him on my days off, I'd go down and work the show a seventh day. He was really my family, you know. Then I introduced him to Desmond. Enrico thought the people running the Blackhawk were crazy. He thought he had a corner on purity there; he may have had. You know, he had people like [Walter] Cronkite and Isaac Stern coming to see him. And when he'd get mad, Enrico, when he couldn't reason with anybody, he'd take his violin and go through the club playing. There was nobody like him. Nobody."

When Mort was invited to play the Fairmont's Venetian Room, the city's classiest supper club, Enrico proudly displayed a poster plugging the appearance in the lobby of the hungry i. Once again, it was strongly suggested that Mort Sahl wear a suit and tie for the engagement. "It's funny—it got to be an issue." he says. "And I thought it ironic. The material never was an issue, and I thought that was where the fight was going to be." Though he ultimately had his way when it came to wardrobe, he seemed strangely out of place amid all the white linens and bald heads, the visiting firemen and their like who were not particularly hip to all the topical matters—both local and national—that made the act click. "Mort pulled his political punch lines because of election results," wrote Don Steele, who covered the opening, "and because he was obviously afraid of the room."

Then there was the matter of singer Monica Lewis, who closed the show and was more prominently featured in the ads. Herb Caen reported a tense early-morning confrontation between Sahl and Lewis' husband, agent Jennings Lang, "that could have reached the ugly stage." Mort, however, denies that billing played any part in the dispute. "Lang came up there to let me know—I'd just graduated from the hungry i—'These are the parameters, young man!' Enrico took a big table. It was election night, so Ben Swig, who owned the hotel, had a banquet for Stevenson, with waiters and everything, and, of course, Ike won, and there was no party. They were like pallbearers."

Once the booking at the Fairmont was fulfilled, Mort headed east for a five-week stand at Boston's Storyville. Named after the New Orleans sporting district that was considered the cradle of jazz, Storyville was a beautiful street-level space at the Copley Square Hotel that could seat up to four hundred banquet style. The club's compact proprietor, a concert promoter and record producer named George Wein, had been keen to book him for more than a year. Still, Mort was convinced that Wein, whom Paul Desmond dubbed "the fig from Newton," didn't like him. Greeted by *Boston Globe* columnist Ted Ashby, Sahl pulled up to the hotel in a gleaming new Karmann Ghia and wondered aloud where he could buy the late papers. (He estimated he spent $600 a year on newspapers, an expense more than justified when he came across an item like: "The Forty-Niners lost because of their inability to score.") The tiny sports car, he explained, was his part in helping West Germany recover. "I like the car because if I deflate the spare tire I can carry a clean shirt."

That first week at Storyville, he served as an added attraction on an extraordinary bill headed by Dinah Washington and featuring a young Japanese pianist named Toshiko Akiyoshi, then a student at the Berklee College of Music. Introduced as "the world's only working philosopher," Sahl made his way though a thicket of tables and onto the stage, where he began with the story of a guy from MIT who stole $18,000 because he felt rejected; ridiculed modern-day isolationists ("Let's pick up our water and get out of the canal"); and explained the credo of the new campus radical: "I am going to change the world . . . as soon as I get Dad's permission." That led into a long parody of campus poetry societies and a chaotic reading he said he attended at Stanford where Truman Capote doggedly explored the textures of the words "green grass," savoring the climatic line "long thin blades of green grass" until he fell out and was physically carried from the room, a victim of total artistic collapse. "The audience liked Mort," said a reviewer from the *Harvard Crimson*. "Those who didn't find him funny found him interesting."

As Sahl himself liked to say, "I always get attention, even if not laughs." The once-vibrant jazz scene in Boston was somewhat muted, with four clubs having closed in the previous three years, but there was still a jazz dentist everyone went to, and Father Norman J. O'Connor, S.J., the jazz priest, was still on the scene. "I got daggers from him from the beginning, I think, not because I strongly question organized religion, but who the Hell organizes it." Booked through the end of the year, Mort shared the bill with Gerry Mulligan's quartet, with cornetist "Wild Bill" Davison, with trombonist Vic Dickenson, and, during his last few days in town, with Teddi King. "The sophistication of an audience, any audience, is fantastically underestimated," he told the *Globe*'s Ashby. "I, of course, must definitely have a point of view, even though it be at times ludicrous. In the case of political comment, I first must establish that I have a right to say the things I do and, secondly, that the audience has a right to laugh. But I don't look too responsible. More like an observer."

Still under contract to NBC, Mort Sahl had planned to begin the year 1957 with an appearance on Perry Como's variety series, the network's top-rated show in a season otherwise dominated by CBS. He began rehearsals for the January 12 Como telecast, but almost immediately found himself mired in controversy. "Eisenhower's Secretary of Defense was Charley Wilson of General Motors," Mort recalls. "I said: 'They've got lawyers like other people got ants. . . . They may become vindictive and cut the government off with-out a cent.' They took issue with that." He was asked to drop the line from his act, but now every line he uttered was subject to scrutiny. "Perry Como traveled with a priest who passed on all the material—Father Bob. ('What do you think, Father Bob? That's pretty racy . . .') They not only dumped me, but they kept me in New York a week and didn't pay me. Not a nickel. And it was all over that antiseptic General Motors joke. He never apologized to me, didn't say goodbye to me. I said to MCA, 'Could you get my plane ticket to New York?' No. 'Como's too big a client.' Unbelievable."

Fortunately, there was work lined up in Chicago, Mort having been scouted in Boston by Oscar Marienthal, who with his brother George owned and operated Mister Kelly's, a popular club on a stretch of Rush Street known for its nightlife. Opening for Anita O'Day, idol Stan Kenton's origi-nal band canary, he took the city by storm, pulling some of the strongest business the club had yet seen. "It caught on," says Mort, "and they kept renewing me." But he was sensing something else in the air, the rumbling of a coming revolution that he himself had sparked.

The local entertainment scene was in transition, with jukeboxes bol-stering the softening jazz market and offbeat acts like calypso singers and comedians displacing old cabaret favorites. The durable Blue Note was dog-gedly sticking to an instrumental jazz policy, but the Gate of Horn, open less than a year, was offering folk singers in the tradition of the hungry i. A few miles north, a trio of actors known as the Commedia Players were doing nightly improvisations at a former speakeasy called the Argo Off-Beat Room. The "star" of that little group—though he was known only to follow-ers of the recently disbanded Compass Players—was a thirty-one-year-old actor named Shelley Berman.

Berman had trained at the Goodman Theatre, where a classmate had been the actress Geraldine Page. He was, she remembered, "just a wonder-ful, brilliant actor. Particularly in the Shakespeare." Having tried selling pots and pans, working as a dance instructor, and hacking in Los Angeles, Berman had gone to New York, where he played in stock and eventually sold some sketches to Steve Allen's *Tonight!* "Actors don't have anything tangible to sell," he reasoned. "Artists have paintings, authors have books. Actors can't produce sample cases. So I said to myself: 'Shelley, *write*.'" When he was recruited into the Compass in 1956, Berman thought he was on a career path to becoming a writer. His wife, Sarah, knew better and urged him to go back to Chicago. "You're an actor," she told him. "You've got to go there."

Inexperienced at improv, Berman caught on quickly. Yet he could never fully integrate and spent much of his performing time with actor Severn Darden. The two men developed an improvisation called "The Panhandler's Apprentice" that became an evergreen for the company, and eventually fellow players Mike Nichols and Elaine May invited Berman to work with them on their nights off. During their time together, Berman and May created two solid pieces, "The Driving Lesson" and, more significantly, "The Lost Dime," an exchange between a stranded driver and an officious telephone operator that evolved into one of Nichols and May's classic routines.

At one of the final performances of the Compass Players, someone in the audience yelled out during the suggestions period "The morning after the night before," and Berman had an inspiration. "I went back and said to Elaine, 'I have an idea about a guy who's carried on something dreadful at a party the previous night. You're going to tell me what I did, and my action will be to fight belief.' She said, 'I'm doing a thing with Mike.' So I decided, since I'd already done this phone thing, that I could go out and improvise another phone thing."

Berman's original phone thing was a routine he had performed during his one and only *Tonight!* appearance. In it, he was a man on the telephone desperately trying to advise various department store employees that there was a woman dangling from the ledge of a tenth-story window. Now Berman adopted the same technique as a way of performing a two-hander by himself, using his considerable skills as an actor to carry on both ends of the conversation. Dreadfully hungover and demanding of the Alka-Seltzer, "Don't fizz!" he dialed an imaginary phone and listened as his host recounted a humiliating litany of drunken acts he had apparently committed at a party the night before.

Shelley Berman formed the Commedia Players to replace the Compass at the Off-Beat Room in January 1957. "But pretty soon I was beginning to get a feeling of just being a comedian," he said. "I didn't know what that really meant." It was during his time with the Commedia that Berman first heard about Mort Sahl. "Somebody was talking about this guy who doesn't tell jokes but he tells funny. Politics was his thing and so I went to see him—and wow! It was nothing like I ever dreamed." To Berman, a nightclub comedian was Henny Youngman or Jack E. Leonard, maybe Joe E. Lewis, who seemed to predate everyone. "You were supposed to tell jokes! You were supposed to get up there and tell jokes! And this guy didn't know any damn jokes. What the hell was he doing? But he was making me laugh and the whole damn audience laugh, and he was doing very, very well. And therefore I hated his guts!"

Berman's nightly performances at the Off-Beat were spectacular feats of impromptu storytelling, but he could see no clear way of making himself viable as a single. "My God, I wasn't a comedian. I was an actor who had improvised a half-dozen routines. Nobody in nightclubs was doing anything like this." Yet here before him was a man in slacks and open collar on a small uncurtained stage, seemingly improvising his commentary with nothing more at hand than a copy of the *Chicago Tribune*. "Seeing Mort gave him the idea that, 'Hey, maybe there's a place for my kind of material too in the nightclub,'" said Sarah Berman.

"That was a city you could grow in," Mort says admiringly of the Chicago he once knew. With his three shows a night at Mister Kelly's, he was, in the words of Compass Players founder David Shepherd, "doing fine, holding court for a couple of hundred businessmen who loved to be mocked." He was already writing a monthly column for the New York–based magazine *Jazz Today*, contributing satirical reviews of books and records and random thoughts about the state of the art. And *Metronome* named him Entertainer of the Year for 1956 and again for 1957, proclaiming him "probably the most jazz-oriented, non-jazz performer" to grace the pages of the magazine's annual. Suddenly Mort Sahl seemed to be everywhere. When emcee Don Sherwood walked off NBC's *Club 60* just five days before the new afternoon show was to debut, it was Sahl who was tapped as Sherwood's temporary replacement, a gig that reportedly paid him $2,500 for the week.

"If his unbridled topical humor could be sufficiently housebroken for daily TV exposure, Sahl might well be the ingredient to give the venture its needed spark of individuality over the long pull," *Variety* commented. The initial broadcast didn't go well, the hour overwhelmed by an unnecessarily large orchestra, two house singers (one of whom was Mike Douglas), and a singing quartet called the Mello-Larks. Harriet Van Horne of the *New York World-Telegram and Sun* thought the result had "all the charm of a night at a bowling alley" but softened as the week progressed. "Young Mr. Sahl is what the trade calls a low-pressure comic. This, I gather, means that he is not convulsed by his own material, seems agreeably surprised if anybody else is."

Through NBC News correspondent John Chancellor, Sahl met Jane Warner Dick, a wealthy social and political activist, who in turn introduced him to Adlai Stevenson and his law partner William McCormick Blair. With

Stevenson it was love at first sight, wit and the nimble use of words forming a solid bond between them. "Stevenson would walk into the club and people would grab him and say, 'I voted for you, Governor,' and he would say, 'Yes, I met the other one recently too.'" Rumpled and wistful, the two-time presidential nominee was often described as everyone's favorite uncle, a meme that even Mort employed in the act. If Stan Kenton was a father figure to him, Adlai Stevenson became an uncle figure, the first politician he could really get behind since the death of Franklin Roosevelt.

A quick appearance for the Chicago Press Club put Sahl in front of the club's "Man of the Year," the New York–based columnist and TV host Ed Sullivan, who promptly wanted him for his weekly CBS broadcast. *Tribune* columnist Herb Lyon reported a long weekend of negotiations with NBC brass before he was cleared for a total of three Sullivan appearances. "In the last five years I've been discovered fifteen times," Mort told the *Tribune*'s John Fink, "and fourteen of those times I was discovered by Eddie Cantor." He went on to describe television as "the most exciting and frustrating" medium of all.

Serendipitous as it was, the Sullivan appearance on March 3, 1957, heralded the end of Sahl's time under Dave O'Malley's management, a two-year arrangement that ultimately suited neither man. "O'Malley had a certain timeline," Mort says, "and he didn't want me to get outside it. The timeline he saw was to work for a show on NBC and be safe. So he really didn't know what the hell I was doing. He was a nice guy, very able, very straight like a banker, but he was pretty busy with Gobel. He wanted me to stay on the back burner, but when the heat comes, it comes. You've got to move with it. . . . He wanted to keep me in abeyance there, so we parted company."

Among the businessmen and ad execs crowding the room at Mister Kelly's was a Chicago publishing tyro named Hugh Hefner, who was about the same age as Mort and had the same general ambitions to shake up the culture. Lean and restless, he came in late one night with his promotions director, Victor Lownes, and wanted to meet him. "I don't think he found it funny," Mort says of the act. "He saw that the people around him laughed, that I'd collected an audience." In Mort Sahl, Hefner saw the outward makings of what he called "the young urban man who appreciates the pleasures of an apartment, the sounds of hi-fi, the taste of a dry martini"—not necessarily the typical *Playboy* reader, but rather what the typical *Playboy* reader aspired to be. "He used to come in like every night," Mort says. "He used to wear a suit then—the young success. He had to see me, he had to know me, he had to go pub crawling with me, hear jazz with me."

Hefner told Mort how he had borrowed $500 from his mother to put out the first *Playboy* at the same time Mort was starting out at the hungry i. "And, like everybody I met in those years," Mort added, "he claimed to be my blood brother." Flattering the pretensions of his target market had paid off handsomely for Hefner. In three years, circulation had jumped from seventy thousand copies a month to well over a million. "The magazine has got to do what you do," he told Mort. "You make people feel hip. I don't think that they are. I want people to feel like playboys for the forty-five minutes they scan the magazine. With that, I'll be satisfied."

Hefner assigned entertainment writer Rolf Malcolm to develop a profile, which, under the title "A Real Free-Form Guy," ran in the magazine's June 1957 issue. Malcolm, who in 1955 had produced an admiring piece on singer-songwriter Tom Lehrer (". . . a shatterer of illusions, a mocker of traditions . . . that most feared of human fiends: a satirist"), was somewhat less impressed with Sahl's graduate-student persona than that of the wry college professor Lehrer actually was. Yet he commendably allowed the act to speak for itself, letting the lifestyle points so dear to Hefner's conception of the readership shine through. On stage at Mister Kelly's, Sahl is observed salting his lines with socio-psychological phrases like *father figure*, *value judgment*, and *group hostility*. Then he's off, riffing on the social significance of a movie poster.

"Outside the theater there's this picture of a girl about twenty-five feet high, and she has a towel around her from the Hilton Hotel chain. It's kind of like, you know, like good taste in panic . . . and she's got this kind of terror in her face, she looks real bugged, and her face is a social indictment of the entire insensitivity of society, you know, and, uh, there's this synthesis within her expression of a rejection of Old World thinking and yet a kind of, uh, dominance of this phony puritanical strain which makes our mores, you know. In other words, she's operating under the ostensible advantages of suffrage and, on the other hand, this phony double standard of morality. So, anyway, over her head there's an indictment of all of us and it says, '*You did it to her!*' Wonderful. I was standing there on the street digging this sign, and I noticed a lot of young men walking by had a look of communal guilt across their faces."

One sports car bug "has this car which was built around him—sheet metal pounded around his body. Luckily he has contemporary features." An

American auto he describes foresees the redundant safety features of forty years hence: "There's a new model out now—you can run it into a wall and not be hurt. That's because of the way the car is put together. First of all, it has these new Ivy seat belts. They're thin and they buckle in the back. Good taste. Then there's foam rubber, about six inches of foam rubber all over the dashboard, and dished steering wheel with a twenty-two-degree camber so it won't impale you on impact. And safety glass that breaks up into gelatinous cubes, with no sharp edges . . . So, in effect, if you'll just cool it as you come to the wall, light a cigarette and have faith, the car will realize the futility of what you're doing and what it will do . . . well, actually, it will sort of chicken out."

He touches on exposé magazines, statesmanship, religion, life as a graduate student, jazz LPs, cigarette ads. ("They have this rugged, masculine bit going. The ultimate will be an ape, smoking.") Revisiting the subject of the junior senator from Wisconsin, he says, "You've got to place McCarthy in proper perspective in your own life, because eventually you'll have to tell your kids about him—unless you want them to learn it on the street." On the nuances of integration, he notes that Eisenhower the previous fall had said that the problem should be approached *moderately*, while Stevenson had said it should be solved *gradually*. "Now if we could just hit a compromise between these two extremes . . ." Assessing Norman Rockwell, he describes "this magazine cover, and it shows this kid getting his first haircut, you know, and a dog is licking his hand and his mother is crying and it's Saturday night in the old hometown and people are dancing outside in the street and the Liberty Bell is ringing and, uh, did I miss anything?"

Sahl's debut at Mister Kelly's went so well that he was awarded $300 worth of General Motors stock as a bonus, and he was back in two weeks, this time opening for Billie Holiday. On stage, the legendary singer demonstrated an easy mastery of the room, a stark, almost ghostlike figure in a flowing white gown, but Mort would carry the backstage memory of "a lot of gin—all day. She was very depressed, downcast. . . . She was out of it. She couldn't make any contact with me at all, which is kind of funny because to Sue [who was a huge fan] that was the home office. But she didn't get to me." Holiday was followed into Mister Kelly's by actress-singer Josephine Premice, then by Sarah Vaughan, who was coming in for two weeks. With Vaughan's arrival it was arranged for Sahl to move over to the Blue Note, where, billed as a "conversationist in jazz," he spent three weeks as the first comedian in its ten-year history.

Shelley Berman was coming in regularly, bolstering his confidence and preparing to go out on his own. In April, he snared a solo spot at the Gate of Horn, where he became an unlikely programming quirk on a bill otherwise populated by Peggy Seeger, half-sister of folk balladeer Pete Seeger, and tenor Glenn Yarbrough. "It seems sort of funny to see a gent standing on this stage without a guitar or a banjo in his hands," Berman admitted to his bohemian audience, and although there were warm words from the *Tribune*'s Will Leonard, he would not remember the tiny club in the basement of the Rice Hotel with affection. "It was a restaurant, and it was trying to be something marvelous in Chicago," he said, "but it was just a bunch of bums sitting there."

Berman stayed after the last show at the Blue Note one night and worked up the nerve to introduce himself to Sahl, fully expecting to be regarded as a competitor. "I told him about the dump that I was in as a comedian, and he listened to me. I couldn't wait to talk to him about what he did, and he just opened up. He didn't have to, but he told me about the things he did and how he did them and why they worked out for him. . . . He said, 'If you're interested in doing comedy, you can watch what I'm doing at the dinner show.' And I watched. I didn't steal, but the ideas that he had and what he was doing were incredible. I really fell in love with him. That was it."

Subsequently, Sahl attended one of Berman's performances at the Gate of Horn and offered suggestions. "He said, 'You can do this, and what you should do is get an audition [at Mister Kelly's].' Now this guy is talking to me about an audition? And I am saying, 'You know that I'm going to be working against you?' But it wasn't a problem for him because he was so sure of himself. And I finally found a way to have an audition. There was a woman who told me that she'd like to be my agent. And me, I'm not sure I want an agent, but I do go for an audition and, son of a bitch, I'm doing okay! I get a lot of laughter. And all I did was listen to his advice."

The hungry i had maintained an all-music policy—as had the Blue Note, Mister Kelly's, and Storyville—until Mort opened it up. Now he faced the same challenge yet again in Los Angeles, where a local deejay and concert promoter named Gene Norman had taken control of the Interlude, an intimate showroom and cocktail lounge, and proposed to bring him in on a two-week "experiment" at $500 a week. In size, the room would approximate the original hungry i and, as with the "i," the core audience would be drawn from the surrounding neighborhoods. But where in San Francisco that meant

Chinatown, Fishermen's Wharf, and Russian Hill, the Interlude would draw from West Hollywood, Beverly Hills, and Laurel Canyon—the residential heart of the entertainment industry. "I had to build up my own network of places to play," Mort said, "because the others weren't available to me."

The club scene was one with which he was only too familiar. In 1952, prior to heading north to Berkeley, he had tried his luck at more than a few places where addressing the crowd meant getting heard over the general din of the room whenever the band took a break. The biggest venues in town were world famous—the Cocoanut Grove, the Palladium, Frank Sennes' Moulin Rouge, reputedly the largest theater-restaurant in the world. At the center of it all was a two-mile stretch of unincorporated land between the Los Angeles and Beverly Hills city limits that fell under the jurisdiction of the county sheriff's department. The Sunset Strip had a rich history of prostitution and gambling that made it a natural fit for W. R. "Billy" Wilkerson's Trocadero Café when it opened in 1934. The publisher of the *Hollywood Reporter*, Wilkerson wanted a place within easy reach of his readership, and at the height of its popularity the Troc was grossing $7,500 a night. He sold out in 1938, and eighteen months later opened Ciro's a few blocks east of the old location. The following year, a New York talent agent named Charles Morrison established the Mocambo at 8588 Sunset Boulevard and made it "society's newest rendezvous."

The Interlude and its big brother the Crescendo began life in 1946 as an upscale French restaurant called Chanteclair. Various managements came and went until 1954, when an experienced club man named Chuck Landis invited Gene Norman to be his partner in doing what no one else had ever done—make a go of the room that was now known as the Crescendo. Norman had what previous managements lacked—access to talent through his powerful radio pulpit and years of experience as a concert promoter. Instituting an all-jazz policy with a $1.50 cover and no minimum, he reopened the Crescendo with the versatile tenor Arthur Lee Simpkins and pianist Earl "Fatha" Hines and his band. The new operation was a solid hit from the beginning, and Norman followed his inaugural bill with the likes of Duke Ellington, George Shearing, Stan Kenton, and Billie Holiday. "Ciro's was down the street," he said, "and that was more like a boutique club. It was mostly a place to get dressed up and go for a social evening. Next door to me was the Mocambo, which was the same thing. At the beginning people would say, 'Go to the Crescendo? Well, no, *we'll* go to the Mocambo.' They can have the snob appeal. I was trying to play to the people."

Gene Norman and Chuck Landis parted ways at the end of 1956, and Norman's new Crescendo partners were Maynard Sloate and Joe Abrahams, the former proprietors of Strip City and its somewhat more respectable cousin, Jazz City. Norman and Sloate began sharing the programming duties at the Crescendo, and it was—to Sloate's surprise—Gene Norman's idea to hire comedian Lenny Bruce, who had worked at Strip City and was, by Norman's reckoning, totally unknown. "Of course, Lenny was my friend and I knew him very well," said Sloate. "We had been friends since I gave him his first job in L.A., so it was left up to me to get him." Bruce was still a work in progress who, when he first arrived from New York, was doing what Sloate characterized as "just a normal act" that leaned heavily on impressions and movie parodies. "So when he came to work at Strip City, he started doing more ad-libbing. Buddy Hackett got him a job writing for Leonard Goldstein on a movie Buddy Hackett was doing at Universal, and Lenny started writing more material for himself."

Accustomed to the raw edges of the burlesque circuit, Lenny Bruce knew he was an awkward fit for a big room like the Crescendo and worked hard at developing what Sloate considered "some really wonderful, classic routines." When Mort Sahl arrived upstairs on May 17, 1957, Lenny was sixteen weeks into a twenty-six-week contract as the Crescendo's house comedian, and Gene Norman had a serious case of buyer's remorse. "He used to say to me: 'Is he funny?'" Sloate chuckled, recalling his partner. "He could never understand his humor. Then Lenny would do things like: Gene would go into the kitchen, and Lenny would be on, and he'd say, 'Now everybody be quiet. Gene just went into the kitchen. When he comes out, let's give him a big hand.' Lenny was putting him on all the time."

Advertised as "America's most controversial comic fresh from a record-smashing Chicago engagement," Mort Sahl alternated on the stage of the Interlude with trumpeter Shorty Rogers, a leading figure in the West Coast jazz movement who, with his Giants, threatened to overpower the tiny space. Top billed, Sahl's forty-five-minute set covered a number of familiar topics—Dave Brubeck, hi-fi, Arthur Miller, evangelists, cops, the army, diplomacy. He denied the common charge that he was an intellectual: "In show business, if you have a library card you're an intellectual." He revealed a liking for Ku Klux Klan meetings ("I don't believe in 'em, but the ritual is so beautiful"), touched on the phenomenon of the *Mickey Mouse Club*, whose theme he described as "this very primitive, ritualistic tribute to this rodent," and got into personal career matters with the industry-savvy room. "I was with NBC for eighteen months," he told them, "but didn't do a show—they were trying to avoid over-exposure."

The word-of-mouth was quick and furious. "In the 60-some-odd hours since Mort Sahl opened at the Interlude on Friday night, a new cult has undoubtedly been formed in Los Angeles," is the way *Daily Variety* led its notice the following Monday. "The first genuine humorist to hit the nitery belt in a considerable period, he more than lives up to his advance billing from a lengthy stand at the hungry i in San Francisco and should easily become a prime local favorite." In side-by-side reviews in the trade, Lenny Bruce was described in less glowing terms, conceding he earned "chuckles" with bits on local newspapers and fan magazines while veering more to "off beat and sometimes macabre humor." Bruce's big finish was a bit about a singer with the Lawrence Welk show that enlisted saxman Marty Berman in the delicate task of blowing champagne bubbles through his horn, a scrubbed version of a drug-infused bit about Welk he had done in the strip clubs. "He was a riot," Mort said of Lenny's act, "and he wasn't dirty. That whole scatological thing came later. His attraction at first was his frankness."

Lenny Bruce was clearly fascinated by Mort Sahl, his relevance and topicality, and spent a lot of time studying his appeal. "The audience was there to see Mort," said Robert B. Weide, who made authoritative documentaries on both men, "and that made an impression on Lenny. He wanted mainstream success—Mort's success." Within days it was announced that Sahl would record an album at the Interlude for Gene Norman's Crescendo label. Four days after that, his weekly rate was tripled to $1,500 and he was held until June 16, when a commitment to the Blue Note would take him back to Chicago. Vocalist Jeri Southern came in on May 29, providing a more agreeable contrast to Sahl's iconoclastic nature, and the following week *Variety* reported the two were "busting all records" at the little Interlude. The irony wasn't lost on Mort: "When I came into Hollywood, it was as if Hollywood discovered me. But I was *from* there—a few miles away. I was really an L.A. kid."

In ways, Mort Sahl and Lenny Bruce were alike—Jewish, jazz inflected, reared on a steady diet of radio and movies. But where Lenny was a creature of the strip clubs who was still feeling his way into the mainstream, Mort was the mature artist Bruce longed to be, a guy in tune with his own rhythms and sensibilities. "Lenny was a product of [alto saxophonist] Joe Maini's imagination," said Mort, who had no real influence of his own. "The debt to the humor of jazz musicians in general—and Joe in particular—was never paid by the moviemakers/mythmakers. Lenny translated with maniacal fidelity Joe's comic viewpoint. Joe was the original."

Mort and Lenny became friends, but there was always an undercurrent of distrust between them. "God, I love you," Lenny would say to him, "but it's just as if we were in school. One person's going to get an A on the curve, and if there's a choice, I want it to be me, not you." Lenny, Mort remembered, "used to sit there and play sophomoric anti-authoritarian games. One night through the ventilator I heard him playing a prom—we had three or four hundred high school kids—and he had them chanting 'Lynch Mort Sahl.' Then he'd come upstairs to my club and order a drink and then say very loudly, "Let's see, ten cents for the cost of liquor, five cents for labor.' He'd itemize the bill and then start to yell, 'You are crooks, you are crooks.' If he could make people uncomfortable, he enjoyed it."

Unlike the Crescendo, the Interlude belonged to Gene Norman alone. He had no partners and disliked the scenes Lenny Bruce made in his austere little jewel of a room. "Gene Norman hated him," says Mort. "He said to me, 'The breach of taste here is something I don't want any part of.' So Gene was always kind of aloof, you know? Lenny had an old-fashioned Jewish thing—if you weren't convivial you were a sworn enemy. So he said, 'This guy's pretty strange. What is it with him?' I said, 'He's reserved. He's a contained guy.' Well, he wouldn't accept that. He didn't know how to process it. So he started attacking Gene from the stage. He said that when he went into the kitchen where the sides of beef were, Gene was embracing a side of beef. And Lenny said, 'What are you doing?' And reputedly Gene said, 'I'm resting! I'm resting!' Gene said to me, 'I can't sponsor this.' He was so offended."

Bruce had a live telephone wired into the sound system and would make crank calls from the stage of the Crescendo. "He would call the Maître d' at Ciro's," recalled Maynard Sloate, "and ask if he could rent a room where one of the members of the club might want to light the drapes . . . but they'd pay for them. He would call babysitters. He'd get the phone number from someone in the audience who had a babysitter, and he'd call the babysitter and do material with the babysitter. He would have unbelievably brilliant comedy calls to anybody."

Any lingering doubts about Mort Sahl's drawing power were firmly dispelled during his return engagement at the Blue Note, where previously he had been paired with such potent attractions as George Shearing and Mel Tormé. For his June 19 opening at the club, Frank Holzfeind abandoned any pretense of a balanced program and brought in Eli's Chosen Six as the supporting act. The all-white Yale ensemble played Dixieland—which Sahl detested—and with jazz in all forms on the commercial downslide it was left solely to the star attraction to fill the room. "The still durable Blue Note under Frank Holzfeind's hand does a generally heavyweight business with top band and combo names," *Variety* would report in a July assessment of the market, "but recent bookings of its first non-musical act, comic Mort Sahl, drew heavier crowds than co-billed musicians."

In Chicago, Mort continued his friendship with Hugh Hefner, who was carrying Rolf Malcolm's profile of him in the current *Playboy*. "In the beginning it was fashionable to accept me," Mort comments. "He liked me, and I was the flavor of the week." Having introduced him to his readers, Hefner now looked upon Mort as an advisor of sorts, perhaps even a contributor (as he was for *Jazz Today*). "He wanted me to come into the magazine and tell him about sports cars and hi-fidelity systems . . . and he would listen to my wisdom. Binoculars with a zoom, you know? He had a section every month on new inventions, and he wanted to present himself as well aware."

In time, Chicago would stand second only to Los Angeles as a market for the comedy of Mort Sahl. He didn't realize it yet, but he had already started to outgrow his association with San Francisco and the hungry i.

A watershed event took place when Sahl returned to the Interlude on July 1, 1957, an occurrence, given the circumstances, as unavoidable as an oncoming train at full throttle and only slightly less obvious. In the second year of their marriage, Mort and Sue Sahl had started to drift apart. She was a graduate student in psychology at San Francisco State College while he was a nightclub comedian who worked well past midnight and then hung out, the adrenaline still pumping, until dawn with pals like Herb Caen and Enrico Banducci. When he went off to Boston to play Storyville in November 1956, Sue, immersed in her studies, stayed home. Then Storyville led to Mister Kelly's, then Mister Kelly's to Ed Sullivan, the Blue Note, and, eventually, to the Interlude.

"Sue," Mort says, "got very tight with Sally Caen. Sally thought that Enrico was 'uncouth.' And she told Sue that I was no prize either. She encouraged her to divorce me. I liked Sally but she got mad at Herb, you know. There was no forgiving with that crowd. She was a tough customer; used to drive a Karmann Ghia. Very beautiful." He sensed the chill when he flew back from

Chicago. "I say, 'Can you pick me up?' Sue says, 'I've got a class.' I say, 'I'm a big hit back there.' And she says, 'I'm a person too.'"

In Malibu, Mort took an apartment from actress June Havoc (who only rented to people in the business) and proceeded to enjoy the considerable fruits of his labors. By one report he figured to make $75,000 that year and was tooling around town in a new Mercedes 300-SL. ("I was in court many times.") The club was miniscule, the heat oppressive, the cigarette smoke so thick it hung in the air like a permanent fog, burning his eyes and settling in his clothes. He would change sweaters after every show—as many as four or five changes a night—but could never completely rid himself of the smell. "I watched the fever come to the Strip as only it can with an audience when you crystallize what's been on their minds," he wrote in *Heartland*. "And in 1957 I was laying out for them everything they wanted to say about Eisenhower. The president was out to lunch. And it's easy to laugh at a guy like that."

Paul Newman and Joanne Woodward, both in town making pictures, came to the Interlude one night and formed an instant bond. Newman approached him outside the club and said, "Mr. Sahl, rarely have I heard a compendium of subjects so adequately covered as you did tonight." Jack Benny brought his daughter Joan. "I love your act," said Groucho Marx, "but it'll never go." Milton Berle took a paternal interest, as did Eddie Cantor ("Don't wear that red sweater. Wrong associations"). And Herb Caen flew down from San Francisco. "It was very exciting," said Gene Norman, who was used to radio and concert promotions and relatively new to the business of running a club. "Half the world's movie stars and political figures came to the Crescendo."

"It was mostly people in the business who went out at night," Mort says. "There were a lot of coffee houses along the Sunset Strip—there was Whisky a Go Go, and Max Lewin's place, the Renaissance—there were a bunch of them, and then the actors would come in there. Everyone was in a series, you know. [Steve] McQueen was there, Marlon used to come in, James Coburn, and then the heavyweights started to come in, like Gary Cooper and Benny and George Burns. They all got curious about it, you know? Berle, and then the people in the business. I found a lot of them, it's fair to say, were not that sophisticated. They talked to people who agreed with them all day. So I began to stretch their perceptions. Of course, the big thing I had then was that you worked every night. You could really become old friends with the material. Three shows a night."

A crew from the NBC newsmagazine *Outlook* arrived to film the act, the Interlude stifling on a hot summer evening, the people crowded in like cattle, their laughter and cigarettes the principal signs of life. Waitresses are bustling drinks, the minimalist off-white decor extending to the baby grand with which Mort shares the stage. The next morning they come to his apartment at Paradise Cove to shoot an interview, their subject somewhat subdued, having typically gotten to bed around five.

"I'm not the most tolerant guy in the world," he tells the interviewer, his friend John Chancellor. "I'm very intolerant. In fact, that's the basis of the act—the statement of a lone guy in rebellion. That's why people mistakenly call it negative. It's mainly me. I don't talk about the news; I'm a victim of the news. And it's all rebellion. It's rebellion against authority. Not all authority, but I am a loner. I'm the only guy in this business who went into a four-figure [weekly] salary without having an agent. I went five years without an agent or a manager. I'm completely at war with the elements." Asked about his material goals, he says, "I don't believe in the material situation because I haven't realized any of that. I don't own anything. I have a borrowed record player and a rented bed and that's it. I make a lot of money, but the money is a prestige weapon whereby you can make a lot of insensitive people accept work which otherwise they could not judge. You can take the initiative and get a lot of work performed that wouldn't be accepted otherwise. It's an index for them."

Chet Huntley, the host of *Outlook*, later told him that the worst thing about filming him was that he couldn't be edited. "You go on this endless cadence and there are no seams on which to cut," he said.

Mort nursed a fascination with actresses, the byproduct of his childhood obsession with the movies. Now he was seeing them nightly in his audiences and frequently talking to them. Many, like Marlene Dietrich, were of the generation he first knew as a kid. Women, he observed, seemed to react differently to the act than did men: "They first decide whether they like your looks, and after that whether they shall laugh at what you have to say." One night, a girl resembling the young Katharine Hepburn came to the Interlude on the arm of composer-arranger Pete Rugolo. She was seduced by the dark, bristling intellect on stage, a combustible intermingling of wit, testosterone, and raw manic energy. After the performance she went over to him. "That was fantastic," she said.

Phyllis Kirk had been in movies since 1949, first for Sam Goldwyn, later for M-G-M and Warner Bros. A former Conover model, she photographed beautifully and was even more striking in person, with reddish brown hair framing a hypnotic pair of blue eyes and, as Mort liked to put it, great cheekbones. Born Kirkegaard ("from a long line of Danish-American Lutheran ministers") she was about to turn thirty and had never been married. The previous year she had been linked to songwriter Lew Spence, who was inspired to write the melody and first line of "That Face" after seeing her across a crowded restaurant. "You're beautiful," he said after summoning the nerve to approach her. "Sit down," she replied. The song was recorded by Fred Astaire, but Spence and she never married. In a 1956 interview she was asked about the men in her life. "Lots of them," she responded. "Anyone serious?" came the follow up. "I take all men seriously," she said.

Normally, Phyllis Kirk lived in New York, but was in town shooting the new *Thin Man* TV series opposite Peter Lawford. (Rugolo had written the show's theme.) Though she went to work at thirteen, stretching her age and scarcely finishing high school, she was widely regarded as brainy for a movie actress and worked hard at it. "She is, beyond a doubt, one of the neatest overnight authorities ever to confound her elders," noted a 1951 magazine profile. Phyllis named her cat after Aldous Huxley, was open in her disdain for Lawford, whom she regarded as an "impossible snob," and liked it known that she dated neurosurgeons. "I prefer complicated types," she told Hedda Hopper. "A complex ego interests me."

The relationship began slowly, furtively, because Phyllis Kirk had a responsibility to stay out of the gossip columns and it was widely known that Mort Sahl was a married man. It soon gained in intensity, and before long she was mimicking his speech patterns in interviews. "You never think the girl you're taking out is just like you, from a poor home who got a job as an actress," observes Mort. "You think she was made in the lab." It all came out into the open one night when Mort was in bed with Sue and the phone rang. It was Phyllis. "That put the frost on everything," he says. Within days, Herb Caen was reporting that while Mort had "achieved exaltation" in Hollywood, Sue had moved out of their Pacific Heights apartment and into a place of her own on Telegraph Hill. The marriage, after twenty-seven months, was over.

Having played a total of eight weeks at the Interlude, Sahl moved downstairs on the occasion of Dave Brubeck's inaugural stand at the Crescendo, thus establishing the club, in the estimation of *Variety*, as Los Angeles' "real centre of avant garde entertainment" where before one hadn't really existed. "The Crescendo," says Mort, "you could get four hundred in if you stretched it, and upstairs maybe eighty—not too big." The larger room seemed to better suit him, and he wisely stayed away from material he had used upstairs. "Topicality of much of his material gets an added sharpness since, in Brubeck followers, he's working to a group more in line with his own tastes and ideas," wrote "Kap" in a trade review. "Thus many of his barbed political comments generate even more in this room."

Sahl took delight in the antics of Arkansas' segregationist governor Orval Faubus, who had submitted to a live interview with Mike Wallace. "I watched Governor Faubus on television tonight," he announced at a late show. "The networks have been giving him unequal time. Faubus has been on four times. President Eisenhower has been on only once. . . . There's a shortage of guest stars. They've been using Faubus a lot this season." Someone had suggested that if the president were really a man, he'd take the hand of one of the colored girls recruited to integrate Little Rock's Central High School and personally lead her past the white mob of protesters and into the building. "That's easy to say if you're not involved. But if you're in the administration, you have a lot of problems of policy—like whether or not to use an overlapping grip." Before dispensing with the subject he added: "I like Faubus, but I wouldn't want him to marry my sister."

In Washington, Mort noted that Secretary of State Dulles had called the United Nations "impotent"—a word popularized in the new 20th Century-Fox production of *The Sun Also Rises*. "He can use that word now, since Zanuck made that picture." He went on to illustrate how a genuine sports car enthusiast has to have his priorities straight: "When your car rolls and they come to get you out, you're supposed to say, 'Never mind me! Write to Munich for a grille!'"

The middle section of the act was devoted to a satire of airline disaster movies like *The High and the Mighty* or the more recent *Zero Hour!* At one point in the narrative, as the plane passes over New York City, a passenger has to be thrown overboard to lighten the load, and the criterion for survival is each passenger's relative value to society. "There was an awful fight between a disc jockey and a used car dealer as to who was going to go first." The nail-biting climax comes after both pilots have been disabled, leaving a stewardess to land the plane on instructions from the ground. "You can make it just as well as any of our pilots if you don't panic," the control tower assures her. "That's very well," she radios back, "but if I project myself into what is essentially a man's role, won't I have trouble adjusting when I'm back on the ground?"

There followed a few more thrusts at politicians and audiophiles and random items in the news ("The post office, according to Edward R. Murrow, loses three cents every time they handle a copy of *Life*. That's called Federal Aid to Education"). Then came the inevitable question that always wound up the act: "Are there any groups we haven't offended yet?"

The gig at the Crescendo gave Mort Sahl a more prominent profile in the entertainment industry. Jack Benny proposed him as a guest for Canadian singing star Gisele MacKenzie's new NBC variety series, which Benny was co-producing, but the sponsor's agency quickly nixed the idea. "They're afraid," Sahl told jazz journalist Nat Hentoff, "and unfocused fear is insane. I told one guy at an agency, 'You can't be afraid of *everything*.' 'But we are,' he said. It goes beneath that, though. These guys are part of the American tradition of the parasite. They appoint themselves the arbiter between the performer and the audience. Parasites are impotent, and so, characteristically, they declare that potency in television is impossible. And the artists go along with them."

In November, he traveled east to appear on the Jack Paar show, where jokes about Billy Graham were taboo due to a previous incident. Taking his cue, Sahl barreled into a critique of the evangelist's recently concluded New York crusade. "He obviously failed," he began. "Tennessee Williams is back." And then: "Like a lot of entertainers, he went into New York prematurely." Warming to the subject, he took on Graham's style at the pulpit:

You notice how he always looks up? He's very good at looking up, which even people in theology will admit is an assumption. It may be sideways. We don't *know*. I mean, we think it, right? He does that, and he always says to his audience, "'*Do you believe?*'" And the audiences always say—you know, they're very vociferous; they're kind of a cross between the Bonus March and Jazz at the Philharmonic. Anyway, he always says to them, "'*Do you believe?*'" And the audience always lays it on him. You know, like, "'*YOU KNOW IT!*'" Sure. And then a couple of minutes later he'll be into original sin or something, and all of a sudden he'll stop—you know, like they never said it—and he'll say, "'*Do you believe?*'" And then they lay it on him again. He does this all the time, you know. So he obviously is insecure in those areas.

According to Mort, Paar spent two hours backstage before the show demoralizing him by telling him not to be esoteric. "He said the audiences were made up of Rotarians. I was on nine and a half minutes being esoteric, and had to stop six times for applause."

While in New York, he played a guest spot at Max Gordon's Village Vanguard, where he was slipped in one night between Mike Nichols and Elaine May and "folk jazz" clarinetist Jimmy Giuffre and his trio. Nichols, for one, had seen Mort in Chicago and was puzzled by his partner's fascination with him. (In later years he would indicate a decided preference for Lenny Bruce.) Nevertheless, the stint resulted in a solid three-week booking at the Vanguard, which, combined with a return visit to the Paar show, was extended to four capacity weeks, one of which broke the club's twenty-two-year attendance record. Broadway columnist Dorothy Kilgallen proclaimed Sahl "the talk of show business" with most of the customers coming back "four and five times" to catch the act. Bill Blair stopped by, as did James Jones, Harvard psychiatrist Carl Binger, and Leonard Bernstein.

Praising his fearlessness, *Variety* noted a tendency for Sahl to "stick around too long," a failing that irked Nichols as well. "I was never a fan," he told columnist and critic Gerald Nachman, "and he never seemed funny to me. That was because we worked on the bill with him for a while and he was not generous, and that was what set in my head." Irwin Corey, who was once told that he stayed on too long at the Vanguard, claimed he clocked one of Sahl's sets at the club and that it timed out at an hour and ten minutes. "I was already losing discipline as a performer," Sahl admitted in the *New Yorker*. "I'd get going within the cadence of the audience's laughter, and sometimes I'd build for a solid thirty minutes and still never reach the core of what I wanted to say. I don't kid myself. I'm not a comedian. I don't build jokes around myself. There's too much to say about everything else, and nobody is saying it."

On his way back to the Coast, he stopped in Chicago to play off a commitment to the Marienthal brothers. "In Chicago the dates ran so long that they had apartments for rent—25 East Delaware. I'd go in there and get the place for a month, take my laundry to the corner. I never ran out of energy, it seemed. I carried the airline guide with me, and I had an I.A.T.A. card. I was looking to fall in love and beat the system." During his previous stands at Mister Kelly's, there had been nothing weightier to discuss than segregation and the hydrogen bomb. Now he worked intercontinental ballistic missiles, satellites, and space travel into the mix. Mister Kelly's had developed a reputation as a showcase for "cerebral comics" in the ten months since Mort's initial appearance, the leading example of this new wave in standup comedy being Shelley Berman. It was at Mort's urging that Berman auditioned for Oscar Marienthal, a gambit that lead to a four-week booking as an opener for Jackie Cain and Roy Kral. By October, Berman was appearing nightly at the Thunderbird Hotel in Las Vegas, and from there he jumped to the hungry i, where he would work out the remainder of the year.

"The agents all tried to make it competitive," says Mort, "but I was all for him. Why not? He was unique." The plain fact of the matter was that for all the strident criticism he frequently leveled at other comedians, Sahl didn't see any of them as competition. "He talked about political and social questions," said Steve Allen. "He talked about them in a very funny way, but in a way that made clear that these issues were important to him. They were not just something he thought: 'Ah, I'll get big laughs with that.' I don't think it mattered that much to him. He had the gift of being able to make others laugh, but he *cared* about what he was saying."

"So far as I know," said Mort,

I am the only political humorist, if that's the term, in nightclubs or on TV in this country. Some people have said that I'm in the Will Rogers tradition, but I've read all he's written—like the 1931 book *Sanity Is Where You Find It*—and there's a strong grain of anti-Semitism and Jim Crow there. Fred Allen would do topical jokes, but they were without a consistent point of view and were often without taste. Bob Hope also works in some political material, but his is the Lindy's attitude. It's like you're aware of [the Russian satellite] Sputnik and you're also aware Eddie [Fisher] married Debbie [Reynolds], but that's all. You're aware of being aware, but have no viewpoint on Sputnik in the context of our foreign relations, defense policy, and the like. There's really no one in my field to talk to, no gods to look toward, no stimulus from competition.

By December 1957 it was common knowledge that Mort was seeing Phyllis Kirk, TV's Nora Charles, and that it was finally okay to write about it. Chicago columnists, particularly Herb Lyon, reported on the long-distance calls Mort placed nightly to Phyllis in Hollywood, colleagues like Irwin Corey, Phil Foster, and Shecky Green bearing witness to the ritual. Interest intensified when Mort invited her to spend Christmas in the Windy City, nobody, up to then, having actually seen them together. In the aftermath of her visit he was seen sporting a bright red Yule sweater she had hand-knitted for him. A couple of weeks after that, both Lyon and Dorothy Kilgallen, among others, were reporting the demise of the relationship.

"Most of the time I was working," Mort explains. "I'd see her for an hour. She was in a series at Metro. She was down there at six in the morning and, with her, work always came first. . . . Then during the day I'd go down and hang around with [Paul] Newman at the studio. [Phyllis and I] went out a lot together. A lot of dinners at La Scala and all that. But I took it as far as it could go." Phyllis saw him as a project, someone to organize and manage. "The barber and where you're going to buy your clothes—but mostly for outward appearances. The question is: When everybody's gone and the party's over, who's there? Is she there? I don't know."

In February 1958 he was observed showing actress Jean Seberg around San Francisco. "I need the therapy of doing a lot of different things," he said at the time, "especially since discovering that I'm suffering from what Paul Desmond calls 'erosion of identity.' No personal life—that sort of jazz. When I finish my show, I buy all the newspapers and magazines and read till six in the morning."

5

YOU CAN'T DO BETTER THAN CAPACITY

Mort Sahl had been away from the hungry i for more than a year when Enrico Banducci redoubled efforts to get him back. The two men were far apart on the matter of price, however. Unlike Los Angeles, the San Francisco nightclub scene had split firmly into two distinct categories, square and hip, both troubled. The square spots were finding it tough going as the economy slipped into recession, Bimbo Giuntoli's 365 Club surviving through sharp cost accounting while the ornate Venetian Room was frantically rotating acts like Johnny Mathis and Liberace when it wasn't closed altogether. Along with the rising cost of name talent, club owners had to contend with a 20 percent cabaret tax (a relic of World War II) in addition to city and state sales taxes and the routine expenses of personnel. At the same time, growing competition from the casino showrooms in Lake Tahoe, Reno, and Las Vegas was siphoning off customers. "Unless I supply the public with the Mary Kaye Trio, or Four Freshmen, or June Christy every week," said George Andros, co-owner of Fack's II, a mainstream jazz club on Bush Street, "business depreciates tremendously."

For a while, the hip venues experimented with jazz-and-poetry recitals, but low overheads were their ultimate salvation, along with the so-called "egghead" acts that drew repeat business, notably Sahl, Tom Lehrer, and the Gateway Singers—favorites whose rates hadn't been driven beyond all reach by television. According to Herb Caen, Enrico was offering $1,500 a week, while Mort was seeking $2,250 against 50 percent of the gross. They finally arrived at an extraordinary accommodation: For the two weeks of Sahl's residency beginning January 26, 1958, Enrico would turn over *all* receipts, and his star comic would then rebate whatever he thought the proprietor deserved as his cut. Says Mort, "Enrico had a longtime bartender at the club named Marty Aborea, been with him a hundred years. He was down there, I walked in, and he said, 'Mr. Sahl! It's so great to be able to steal from you instead of Mr. Banducci.'"

For housing, Mort would occupy the Telegraph Hill apartment of his best friend, Paul Desmond, while the Brubeck quartet was abroad. This, Caen pointed out, would effectively make Mort a neighbor of his wife Sue, who had sued him for divorce and whose involvement with Desmond was now a matter of public record. In her complaint, Sue charged extreme cruelty and said that she figured $1,200 a month in alimony would be "reasonable." She said her husband had caused her "grievous mental suffering" that made living with him unbearable. A hearing took place in Superior Court on March 28, 1958. Mort wasn't present, but Sue testified that he had criticized her "in many ways," bickered constantly over trivial matters, and had nagged and embarrassed her in front of friends. Judge Harry J. Neubarth awarded her an uncontested interlocutory divorce decree and $900 a month alimony. An accompanying property settlement gave each party a sports car and an equal share of the holdings in four bank accounts, a sum which totaled $27,125 before taxes. The following day, Sue boarded a plane for Turkey, where she would join Desmond on his tour of Europe and the Near East.

"I think it takes me nine minutes to say what I have to say," Sahl told a reporter for United Press International, "and that's why I'm not on TV regularly. They tell me I can have nine minutes, and then cut me off after four. You just can't develop anything and get it across in that time." And to pioneering TV critic Steven H. Scheuer: "My idea of a TV booking that would make some sense is three or four shots on, say, the Steve Allen show, close enough together so that a comic could make friends with his audience. I don't think it's fair to go on other people's shows and in a few minutes be expected to make any kind of favorable lasting impression."

With no such bookings in sight, he began exploring other ways of extending his reach. He started recording twice-weekly commentaries for the NBC radio series *Nightline*, offending network brass by opening an early spot with: "Well, kids, if we're good today, General Sarnoff might like us, and if he likes us he'll go to Charles Van Doren [the network's biggest-winning contestant on the quiz show *Twenty-One*] and get us more money." He would soon contract to make his feature film debut, and was looking to conquer Broadway in the spring with a show called *The Next President*. "I was going to prove to them that you can be intelligent and you can hold an audience," he says.

But where *Nightline* put him in the homes of millions of listeners, it wasn't necessarily where Mort Sahl could be heard to best advantage. He was still a creature of the nightclub, and it was only before a live audience in a crowded room that he was likely to win new converts. Initially, he explored the possibility of cutting a new record of the act each month, a sort of news and lifestyle magazine for the ear that would go out on a subscription basis. Then Norman Granz, the founder of Verve, proposed adding him to the label, making him part of a roster of jazz artists that included Ella Fitzgerald, Billie Holiday, Dizzy Gillespie, and Anita O'Day. The contract with Verve was signed on January 20, 1958, and the recording of the first LP, which would carry the title *The Future Lies Ahead*, took place at the hungry i six days later.* "A chaotic performance, an anarchistic audience, and sixty-odd hours without sleep" is how Mort would succinctly describe the experience in the album's liner notes.

Comedy albums were not a new idea, and examples of the genre date back to the earliest days of commercial recording. *Cohen on the Telephone*, first issued in 1913, is widely cited as the first comedy record, although Cal Stewart, a vaudeville dialectician, was making brown wax cylinders for Edison as early as 1896. An album of Bob Hope radio performances flopped in 1945, as did 78s from Jack Benny, Fred Allen, and Edgar Bergen. It was the introduction of the long-playing record in 1948 that made challenging material more viable for home listening. Tom Lehrer entered the market in 1953 with a ten-inch record he produced himself, followed by Lord Buckley and Eddie "The Old Philosopher" Lawrence in 1955. All were studio recordings made without benefit of an audience, literal transcriptions neatly embalmed for posterity.

"What I do is improvise within a theme," Mort said, "and if the audience doesn't laugh, it's like playing *a cappella*. They cue me and provide my accompaniment. I often wander away from the theme and sometime violate the chord structure, but I usually come back and resolve it—and always I try to keep a beat." So when Verve engineers rolled tape on the night of January 26, capturing the essential exchange of energy that took place between Mort and his people, the brittle standard of studio perfection was shattered, and *The Future Lies Ahead* became the first modern comedy LP.

---

* Mort credits Senator William Knowland, publisher of the *Oakland Tribune*, with the title, evoking a line Knowland reportedly delivered on the Senate floor.

✧ ✧ ✧

Mort would remember nineteen-year-old Jean Seberg as a "great dame" who was, in his judgment, "too sane" for him. "It sounds facetious," he acknowledges, "but if someone wasn't crazy, I wasn't there." He introduced her to Paul Desmond, who decided she was too young for him, and then to Gene Norman, who said she lacked "specific gravity." (Seberg would marry François Moreuil, a French lawyer, within a few months.) When *The Future Lies Ahead* was released in March 1958, Mort's liner notes comprised eleven paragraphs, and nobody, with the exception of Herb Caen, noticed that the initial letters of those paragraphs, when read from top to bottom, spelled P-H-Y-L-L-I-S-K-I-R-K.

It wasn't that Phyllis was crazy, exactly, but it could be said that, like Mort, she had issues that could make her as difficult as she was appealing. "Her father deserted the family, left her mother with two girls," Mort remembers. "The mother worked graveyard at the hospital in Elizabeth, New Jersey. She really grew up suspicious of men.* And when she found somebody who could be trusted, she couldn't surrender." But then he admits: "I never gave anybody much of a chance. And I got mad awful easy. To be honest, my head was swimming with my accomplishments all the time. I had depression with great regularity."

Sahl had an endless reserve of energy and didn't seem to need much sleep. "I have an exclusive franchise on insomnia," he once said. "I drift through space and time, sleeping in patches of two or three hours. When the rest of the world's asleep, I drive to the beach. I go to all-night newsstands and magazine racks and buy an armload of everything in sight." Phyllis liked to say that he fed on crisis. Their splits were loud and frequent, their reconciliations intense. A recurring theme was his disillusionment with women, a product of years of watching idealized characters on the big screen and never quite realizing that no mortal woman was a match for Jean Arthur in a Frank Capra picture. "Bright chicks are a problem," he lamented in a *Holiday* profile, taking a subtle swipe at Phyllis. "This doesn't mean we're going to go out with dumb chicks; we're just going to suffer with the bright ones. You combine their body chemistry with their brightness and they're impossible to

---

* Megan Flax, Phyllis' younger sister, clarifies: "Our father was a sad alcoholic who had a lifetime illness. He had acute pancreatitis and ultimately had that removed, and it was just all downhill from that point on. It was not *Father Knows Best* because Father wasn't there. He may have been there physically, but not in person."

get through to." By "body chemistry," he meant what he called "the woman's gnat's-eye view of life" which he believed was native to all females. "Mort is gradually becoming more tolerant toward women," Phyllis commented, "which is, in view of his position, the only direction in which he could possibly go." His problem, she explained, was acceptance. "He's not accepted for what he is, and he hasn't yet learned to accept people for what they are."

In the weeks leading up to his divorce, Mort's friendship with Paul Desmond began to curdle, the strain of Desmond's affair with Sue too great to sustain it. ("She likes me better than she likes you," Desmond mused. "You like her better than you like me. And I probably like you better than I like her. Such is life.") Once, in the thick of it, Mort had given Paul a Rolex watch with the inscription: "To the Sound from the Fury." And when the Brubeck quartet toured small-town colleges under George Wein's management, he was sometimes along.

Desmond's attraction to his friends' wives was a pattern people noticed after his own divorce, which took place before Mort knew him. "He liked the married women," said a pal, the drummer Joe Dodge, "because then there wasn't any possibility of his getting roped into another marriage." On March 12, with Sue's plans apparent once the interlocutory decree was granted, Desmond began a long, chatty letter to Mort with the words: "Thought you should have at least one report from Europe before the lines of communication break down completely." Later, in an undated note to a friend in Florida, he wrote, "Am now settling quietly with a soft, bright, oddly vexing girl name of Sue, ex-wife of Mort Sahl, who used to be my best friend."

Mort's return to San Francisco was a big deal, played up in the press and noteworthy, in particular, to a twenty-two-year-old student at Hastings Law School named Lou Lotorto. Lou had caught one of Mort's performances at the hungry i just after his twenty-first birthday and was immediately transformed into the kind of fan who insistently drags others into the fold. When he learned through Herb Caen's column of the new January 1958 booking, he decided that merely attending a few performances wouldn't be enough to commemorate such an auspicious homecoming. "I started with the idea of having a social club," he said. "What the hell? I thought: This is a way to get girls."

Lotorto's name for the new club was the Sahl Cellar Shakers, and members at Hastings would distinguish themselves around campus with pullover sweaters and rolled newspapers. He even coined a club motto: Equal Discrimination for All. "I notified Herb Caen's office that this was going on, and that we were all going to Mort's opening night when he came back from the Interlude. I stretched the truth a bit and said that we had forty or fifty members, and at some point Mort intervened and had a section set aside for us. It was one of those things that got thrown out as sort of a lark, but there were a lot of people who admired Mort who said, 'If Lou's going to do it, then we'll go along with it.'"

The Shakers dutifully attended the first night festivities, Lotorto one of the few actually observing the self-imposed dress code. ("There weren't a lot of others who were as obnoxious as I was.") After the show Mort said to him, "Phyllis Kirk would like to be a member of the fan club." Lou was caught short: "We had nothing official—no charter, no nothing. But we decided we were going to have to do something. One of the guys with me, his wife was very artistic, good at calligraphy, and we did a charter. We burned parts of the charter to make it look official, and it said, 'I, Phyllis Kirk, being of questionably sane mind . . .' It was beautifully lettered, and we sent this charter to her and made her a member of the Sahl Cellar Shakers." Having cleared that hurdle, Lotorto decided that custom T-shirts were in order and asked Mort for a picture. "He said, 'I don't have anything with me. My mom and dad have everything.' So he gave me the phone number for Dot and Harry, and I connected with them."

Harry and Dorothy Sahl had an apartment on Cole Street, Mort having relocated them to San Francisco in 1955. "They were the dearest couple," said Lotorto. "I've always favored older people, so I told them what Mort said. 'We don't have anything. He's got it all in L.A. where he's living.' They were very sweet. Dot was fun, and she was a character. Mort was really doted upon by his mom, and I'm sure she let him know that he was God's gift to the world. She really adored him. Harry was a solemn kind of a guy; Mort used to moan about his dad being a sourpuss and closed off. I found out years later that he really wanted to be in show business and was a frustrated playwright. So he and I hit it off, and I managed to get through that solemnity. At that time he would moan a lot about Mort, which was typical—Mort never called, never wrote. So I kind of ended up as a surrogate son for Harry. He would come down when I was going to law school—Tuesday seemed to be the day. There was a little roast beef and turkey place right near Hastings, and he would come. We'd have lunch on Tuesday, and then we'd go to Schwab and Company where he would check out the stock reports and look at the tickertapes. We did that a lot."

After a while, Lou came to the realization that Mort didn't have any pictures anywhere—at least none he could lay his hands on. "One time I did visit him in his apartment in L.A.," he remembered. "It was just above the Strip, and we started to look for photos. It was just unbelievable. Everything was piled up, all the records, everywhere. It was pretty disheveled, so I never did get any pictures of him."

Before the chill settled in between them, Paul Desmond had introduced Mort to a man named Frank B. Nichols, who produced a CBS television series for the National Council of Churches called *Look Up and Live*. The show, broadcast Sunday mornings at 10:30, was aimed at secular viewers with a particular emphasis on teenagers and young adults; the Dave Brubeck Quartet made multiple appearances on a recurring segment called "The Theology of Jazz."

Nichols was a fan, having discovered Sahl in San Francisco, and was looking to move into bigger things. "Nichols wanted to be my manager," Mort remembers, "and he took all his savings and said, 'Let's go on Broadway and make a splash because nobody does what you do.' So I took Jimmy Giuffre in a jazz trio and I went on Broadway with the show." *The Next President* seemingly appeared out of nowhere, moving into the 600-seat Bijou Theatre on April 9, 1958, with little fanfare and almost no advance press. The title was drummer Chico Hamilton's idea, the show itself little more than the act in two parts, Mort Sahl bracketed by jazz and folk music as he was in the clubs. Giuffre and his men (trombonist Bob Brookmeyer, guitarist Jim Hall) ably furnished the jazz component, while the folk element was provided by a company of eight singers, coached by vocalese innovator Dave Lambert and featuring big band balladeer David Allen (later Allyn), folk singer Eric Darling, and twenty-one-year-old Mary Travers, later of Peter, Paul and Mary.

Directed by Frank Nichols, *The Next President* became an uneasy amalgam of conflicting sounds, a mess of obligatory packaging. Actress Mary Ure, appearing in husband John Osborne's *Look Back in Anger*, made Sahl rest in bed the day of his opening and sent flowers. Telegrams from well-wishers included one from Adlai Stevenson: GOOD LUCK TO THE NEXT PRESIDENT—AND I DO MEAN YOU.

On the first night, two numbers (one, incongruently, a folk spiritual titled "Cry Holy") preceded Mort's arrival on stage. He was followed by the Jimmy Giuffre 3 and more vocalizing in the folk idiom. The second part,

"A Brand New Attitude with the Same Old Prejudices," threw another four numbers at the audience before the star's reappearance. At a top of $5.75, more than a few theatergoers got the feeling they were watching a facsimile of the hungry i show at about twice the price of the real thing. "Mort was a genius in the show," said David Allyn, "but his material was too swift, too funny, and too close to the truth. There were no lavish sets. The backdrop was merely the theater's brick wall with its steam radiator hanging straight across the back of the stage."

As Mort later wrote in *Heartland*, "I broke every theatrical convention by sitting on the apron and talking to the audience without preparing material. Sold out every night. And got reasonably good reviews." The critics were indeed kinder than they might have been, heaping measured praise on the star while lamenting all the padding. "In *The Next President*," wrote John Chapman of the *New York Daily News*, "three things happen in the first act and they are all disarmingly pleasant. A good mixed chorus sings a couple of songs, Sahl talks wittily about current events but a little tiresomely about psychoanalysis. Three musicians called the Jimmy Giuffre 3 go to work very quietly on a number called 'The Train and the River.' The trouble with the show is that they do it all over again in the second half."

The Next President suffered in comparison to the other solo act on Broadway, the British character actress Joyce Grenfell in *Monologues and Songs*, a tighter, more theatrical offering housed two blocks away at the Lyceum. According to Sahl, it wasn't the lack of total acceptance on the part of the critics that killed the show, but rather a simple deficiency of cash flow.* "There was no lack of audience," he said, "but there was a lack of funds for operating capital. The audience was there, but the show was closing. There was no accounting for it." *The Next President* lasted all of ten days, a total of thirteen performances. "Mort was wonderful," said Phyllis Kirk, in town on *Thin Man* business, "but the show stinks. This show was *so* bad. Everyone was bugged. Red Buttons was there in the audience. I never saw a man weep the way Red did."

Suddenly, Sahl found himself in New York with nothing to do—a forced idleness he hadn't known in years. "Pie and coffee and three-thousand a week is no damned good," he groused to a writer from *Holiday*, his suite

---

* On April 16, *Variety* reported both Sahl and Grenfell as "holding their own," with *The Next President* scoring a gross of $4,875 for five performances, and *Monologues and Songs* hitting $8,088 in its first full week at the significantly larger Lyceum.

littered with dirty room service plates and glasses. "What I'm really hungry for is a rug on the floor and pictures on the wall, a girl and music. My god, how I miss my records." He took a quick booking on Jack Paar's *Tonight*, about the only work he could stir up on a moment's notice, lingered a few days, then followed Phyllis back to Los Angeles, where, bent on getting his life organized, she engineered his move from MCA to the William Morris Agency. "NBC didn't pick up my option," he rationalized. "Few NBC people knew that I was there, thanks to MCA."

The *Tonight* appearance drew the belated wrath of *New York Journal-American* TV critic (and noted McCarthy apologist) Jack O'Brian, who, under the headline MORT SAHL NO WILL ROGERS, ground out eight hundred words of loathing for a comic he had sampled but twice: "It's always a cinch Sahl will have something harshly impertinent to garble about Ike or Nixon or John Edgar Hoover, which Sahl likes to think proves courage. We do not mean just selecting such Washington folk as targets, for they are prominent and therefore open to all comment including humor and wit. . . . Our exception is that Mort Sahl essentially is a dissatisfied performing ego seeking expression in a field he cannot quite encompass."

O'Brian, whose idea of a modern comic was Jack Paar, equated controversy with subversion, topicality with witlessness. Sahl would make other enemies in the press—all conservatives in the short run—but the widely reviled O'Brian would be a particularly tenacious one. At least Sahl was in good company; among those O'Brian regularly attacked in the *Journal-American*: Ed Sullivan, Arthur Godfrey, Steve Allen, Chet Huntley, Jackie Gleason. "The list of entertainers who are consistently treated unfairly by O'Brian is long and imposing," Allen wrote that year in the *Village Voice*, "and, significantly enough, largely comprised of the biggest names in the business."

In a sense, then, Mort Sahl had arrived.

While Gene Norman worked to clear time at the Interlude, Sahl played a private dinner at Romanoff's for attorney Greg Bautzer and his wife, the actress Dana Wynter. (Mort remembers a line: "If Bautzer comes, can Wynter be far behind?") One of Bautzer's closest friends was producer Jerry Wald, and Wald was so taken with Mort's performance that he offered him a role in a movie he was preparing at 20th Century-Fox. Titled *Hell Raisers*, it was based on a novel called *The Big War* by Marine Corps veteran Anton Myer. To Philip Dunne, who was to direct the picture, the idea was a masterstroke of showmanship that could only broaden the film's appeal "especially among young people." Wald had screenwriter Edward Anhalt add a part for Sahl as one of the film's Marine platoon, leaving room for him to ad lib an approximation of what he might say on stage, but the plan didn't work. "In the end," said Dunne, "he and Anhalt sat down and wrote out specific lines, which included the best moment in the picture, when Mort, under heavy fire in a forward foxhole, picked up the field telephone and caroled, 'Good morning! World War II!'"

With the movie set to go before the cameras in July, Sahl began a four-week stand at the Interlude on June 6, 1958, appearing in rotation with the Modern Jazz Quartet. Taking the stage with an issue of General Motors stock in hand, he laid into Edsels, USC, and his old nemesis, former GM CEO Charles Wilson.

"A conservative Republican believes it shouldn't be done for the first time," he said on the distinctions of generational politics. "A modern Republican believes it should be done for the first time—but not now."

Vice President Nixon, he pointed out, "has been on the cover of every magazine except *True*." The best he could say about Eisenhower: "He kept us out of space." The Democrats, meanwhile, didn't have any plan at all. "They haven't even contacted an advertising agency."

On the recession: "They just made a movie at M-G-M called *The World, the Flesh and the Devil*. It's a story of the last eight people left on Earth . . . four of whom are unemployed."

On Billy Graham: "The first thing he said on his newest crusade was, 'I'm here to save San Francisco.' Which was a little presumptuous, I thought. Not that San Franciscans aren't approachable. But maybe he should have opened a restaurant."

On the mounting tensions between China and Formosa: "The Reds will invade Quemoy—if they can get past the American supplies on the beach." And on race relations: "We used to pick out minority groups and tolerate them."

On the latest recordings: "These records are real jazz. Notice how the solos are different each time you hear them?"

The summer season was in full swing and the competition around town was fierce: June Christy downstairs at the Crescendo, Rowan and Martin next door at the Mocambo, Don Rickles at Slate Brothers, Jimmie Rogers at the Moulin Rouge, Teresa Brewer at the Cocoanut Grove with Judy Garland scheduled to come in on July 23. Attendance was so heavy that Sahl was extended indefinitely, then moved into the Crescendo when the crowds kept growing. Opening July 15 with headliner Count Basie and singer-pianist Frances Faye, an overflow crowd packed the bar four deep, and at the end of the first show a line stretched from the captain's stand, spilling out onto the Sunset Strip and setting a new opening night record. Among the celebrity onlookers: Nat King Cole, Sammy Davis Jr., singer Billy Daniels.

The move into the Crescendo was for seven-and-a-half weeks, overlapping with the filming of the picture, which had been retitled *In Love and War*. As cast, the film became a showcase of sorts for what director Dunne called "the studio's bright young talents." Robert Wagner, Jeffrey Hunter, and Bradford Dillman were the three principal Marines of the story, while Hope Lange, Dana Wynter, Sheree North, and France Nuyen played the girls back home. "I think a lot of times [the lines I wrote] were out of context and maybe didn't fit," Sahl admits. "Sometimes they're kind of extraneous. And I also didn't know anything about acting. Sheree North wanted me fired: 'He doesn't study with anybody. He'll never get any better.' God, she was mean."

By August 1, Mort was filming the picture in the daytime, performing nineteen shows a week at the Crescendo, and still taping his twice-weekly commentaries for *Nightline*. Functioning, at best, on three hours of sleep a night, he managed to keep to the routine for seventeen punishing days before collapsing one morning at the Fox ranch in Malibu. Admitted to St. John's Hospital, he was put through a battery of tests by his physician, Dr. Robert Kositchek, who noted the yellowish cast to his skin and solemnly told the press, "We cannot rule out the possibility of infectious hepatitis." The doctor was appalled to learn that Mort had been sleeping an average of an hour a night. "I've never seen a man so exhausted," he said.

It wasn't hepatitis, Kositchek concluded, but rather mononucleosis— which could lead to hepatitis. Strict bed rest was ordered, and among Mort's visitors at the hospital were Phyllis Kirk, Jerry Wald, Marlon Brando, and actress Barbara Rush. Complications set in over the weekend, and he was heard to ask the Sisters, "How much time do we all have?" After two weeks of hospitalization, he was well enough to return to Fox for a day of retakes and additional scenes, but he still wasn't cleared for club work. A four-week engagement at Mister Kelly's had to be scratched, and comic Jimmie Komack took the gig.

Now at last home, jittery and restless, he visited the set of *The Thin Man*, an excursion that Phyllis, who was all business when she was working, had discouraged in the past. It was the first time Mort had ever been on the

M-G-M lot, and he was greeted warmly by Peter Lawford, the actor's personal manager, Milton Ebbins, and, on an adjacent stage, Frank Sinatra, who was shooting interiors for the Vincente Minnelli production of *Some Came Running*. "We're both rebels," Sinatra told him, and a volatile friendship was thus formed.

Saying he felt "beat, but back among the living," Mort emerged from his convalescence to emcee the final evening of the Monterey Jazz Festival, a three-day event that took place the first weekend of October 1958. The brainchild of Jimmy Lyons, the festival consisted of five overstuffed programs, opening with Louis Armstrong and continuing with Jimmy Giuffre, Cal Tjader, Dizzy Gillespie, the Modern Jazz Quartet, Billie Holiday, Harry James, Gerry Mulligan, and the Brubeck Quartet. The event put Sahl and Brubeck back together with Lyons just as Fantasy was releasing an unauthorized LP titled *Mort Sahl at Sunset*, drawn from recordings made in Carmel in 1955—tapes that Mort never knew existed. Leaving for Chicago to record his second album for Verve, he retained L.A. attorney Richard Mark to seek an injunction and sue for $50,000 in punitive damages. "How old is the material?" Mort asked rhetorically, responding to a question from Herb Caen. "Well, there are some very topical references to the Boston police strike."

Attorney Mark succeeded in getting the album withdrawn, which had the effect of making genuine collector's items of the few copies remaining. Predating *The Future Lies Ahead* by nearly three years, the recording itself would come to be regarded as historic.

Mort Sahl at Sunset was a tacit acknowledgment of the growth in Sahl's following, now broad enough to make the risk of a lawsuit worthwhile for the enterprising Weiss brothers of Fantasy Records. The show business establishment was slowly coming to recognize a younger, smarter audience, a direct result of the education benefits conferred in the Servicemen's Readjustment Act of 1944. With the end of World War II, college enrollments surged and publicly funded institutions were expanded to meet the demand. In 1946 there were 1.5 million veterans enrolled, up more than a million from the previous year. It was an audience Mort knew well because, having attended USC on the G.I. Bill, he was part of it. "I can't seriously think that somebody at the agency telling me what people want has anything to do with what people want," he said in a roundtable for *Esquire*. "And we've got a financial record to back that up in nightclubs. You can't do better than capacity. There *is* a market for comedy. So I mean we're not in trouble from that standpoint. People want to hear social criticism, but you can't be asked to divorce content from your material; in fact, you can't trust the person who asks you to do it."

His original audience was bohemian, small and exclusive, politically aware. Then young professionals discovered him, the white-collar vogue for jazz exposing him to a broader swath of the economic spectrum. Along the way, the Beats claimed him as one of their own, but, as Mort pointed out, their embrace was transitory. "The Beat Generation thrives on the fact that it is uncommon," he said. "Once they become common they are no longer Beat. Success will spoil the Beat Generation because it can't cope with it." Mort, of course, was never a Beat, but for a while the Beats made an appealing background for his grad student persona.

Gradually, he began to speak to the men who had served in the Second World War and, later, in Korea, guys who had known challenge and responsibility in the military, and who, after four years of college, attained a reasonable facsimile of the American dream—family, house, car, well-paying job—while nurturing the discontent of having sold out for the trappings of material success, the illusion of status. Sahl's political broadsides flattered their intellects, while his lifestyle commentaries indulged their dreams of escape, giving voice to the notion that most aspects of modern life celebrated the trivial. As Tom Rath, the protagonist of Sloan Wilson's 1955 novel *The Man in the Gray Flannel Suit*, dreams of writing on an application for a job in public relations: "The most significant fact about me is that I detest the United Broadcasting Corporation, with all its soap operas, commercials, and yammering studio audiences, and the only reason I'm willing to spend my life in such a ridiculous enterprise is that I want to buy a more expensive home and a better brand of gin."

Once Sahl had built a national audience for himself, painstakingly assembling it one city at a time, it became available to other modern comedians: Shelley Berman, Lenny Bruce, Jonathan Winters, Mike Nichols and Elaine May. Berman, in fact, joined *Nightline* in July 1958, as did Nichols and May, who became regulars on Wednesday nights. And when *The Future Lies Ahead* became a hit for Verve in the Spoken Word category, Sahl urged Berman to join the label, eventually delivering Winters as well. "I'm credited with a trend," he acknowledged. "I don't think you can label air currents in a vacuum. People were always capable of better than they have been offered. They've been so good to me, not because of what little I contribute, but because of general malnutrition."

✧ ✧ ✧

With the imminent release of *In Love and War*, Jerry Wald dispatched members of the cast and creative team to a host of foreign and domestic locales with the hope of stirring up interest in a rather staid and monotonous movie. Dana Wynter was sent to London, Hope Lange to Ireland, and Robert Wagner, accompanied by his wife, actress Natalie Wood, traveled to eight American cities, including New York. Sahl, already east for a quick appearance at Mister Kelly's, covered Chicago and Washington, D.C., before returning to Los Angeles, where he would open at the Crescendo on October 23, 1958. Still not fully recovered, he was slightly off his game, and the press detected familiar lines pertaining to the troubles of White House Chief of Staff Sherman Adams (who had been pressured to resign following a bribery scandal) and Billy Graham's crusade in an unyielding San Francisco. Fresher material covered such subjects as the Pentagon, Chiang Kai-Shek, and segregation. "I approve of H-bomb tests because we might get a clean bomb and the tests are good for morale," he said. "Besides, I'm not planning a large family anyway."

His slightly diminished state seemed to embolden hecklers, a rare phenomenon at a Sahl performance. "Some people have the impression performers are incapable of any sensitivity, and that when some loudmouth makes a crack they turn to water," he angrily said to one, breaking his usual policy of ignoring them. "Neither is true, buster, and I'm not going to interrupt the show, but when the lights go on I'll be over to see you." When the lights came up, the man had fled. "Didn't get them often," says Mort. "Who can say why? I pretty much had a target on my back. . . . I remember one night, a guy just kept it up. I said, 'When you going to quit, pal?' He said, 'Never. I'm gonna dog you to the end.' So I said, 'You can't stop me. But this isn't the first time you've failed in the dark, is it?' You know, if you start to trade punches with them, they've won. They'll never leave once they get the recognition. The club has to take them out."

When *In Love and War* opened citywide on October 29, Mort Sahl's name was nowhere to be found in the ads or on the posters. Phil Dunne, vacationing in La Quinta, took notice and called Jerry Wald for an explanation. "You won't believe this," Wald told him, "but the reason they refuse to use Mort's name is that there's nothing in his contract that requires them to give him billing. I tried to explain to them that it wasn't a question of contractual obligation, that we thought Mort's name would help us sell tickets, but they told me that it was against their policy to do anything they weren't legally obliged to do." Sahl's relationship with his new agency was off to a rocky start. ("Lenny Hirshan didn't do his homework," he says today.) It was too late to change the ads, even if the studio miraculously came to see the wisdom of Wald's argument. "So once more an arbitrary policy won a pyrrhic victory over common sense," Dunne concluded. "The presence in our picture of one of the most provocative personalities of the time continued to be officially classified as Top Secret."

Ironically, Sahl's appearance fifty-five minutes into the film is one of its few highlights, Anhalt's earnest screenplay otherwise being utterly devoid of humor. Approaching a shore landing under considerable fire, the platoon listens as Danny Krieger reads aloud from a booklet titled *Know Your Enemy*. ("You are entering a strange, alien, but fascinating country. Make friends, dress neatly, and smile.") As the company's token Jew, Sahl is offbeat and understated, a welcome relief from the routine characters driving the story, and he is genuinely missed when killed in battle twenty minutes later. Beaten into numbness by the monotony of it all, most reviewers gave *In Love and War* short shrift, the *New York Times'* Bosley Crowther dismissing it in just eight withering sentences.

Jerry Wald put Mort under personal contract, signaling his intent to cast him as a beatnik in his new picture, *The Best of Everything*. "Mort is brilliant, incisive in his wit, and churned by inner conflicts," the producer said. "He has all the attributes of a great comedy genius, including an incurably morose disposition and emotional instability." Mort returned the compliment in an interview with the Los Angeles *Mirror News*: "He is the only man I know in Hollywood who will answer his own telephone anytime you call him, even though a recording may sometimes take your call. When this happens, I just say that Mort Sahl called and that *this* is a recording."

After a shaky start, Mort was back filling the Crescendo twice nightly, three and sometimes four shows a night on weekends. The *New York Times* sent someone from its Sunday department to audit a couple of performances, observing how a spotlight picked him out on stage, his yellow cashmere sweater contrasting with the twinkling green and white lights of Los Angeles, picture windows on the back wall taking full advantage of the building's hillside perch. "Hello," he said, spotting a blond nightclub photographer working the room.

I see there's someone here from the FBI to photograph me. So we're all set. I have here a Republican paper from Los Angeles. But that's redundant. I haven't got too many jokes, just little lectures.

Before the last election, our illustrious Senator Knowland, or something like that, helped President Eisenhower to send over ninety million dollars to the Formosa beachhead. At the same time, the president vetoed the school bill over here—spenders, you know. Of course, before Chiang got his money, he had to promise he wouldn't use any of it for schools.

It's smoky here. Fallout. Anyway, onward.

I'm in the movies now, playing this marine. I get shot in the back— either the enemy was unethical or we were retreating. You have to interpret this for yourself. I'm dying, and in the background Johnny Mathis is singing. The chaplain bends over me and, if you look closely, he's wearing a Zen Buddhist emblem. I think Hollywood must have a grudge against the Japanese. They keep making the same movie again and again. You know, the one with the old newsreel shots of MacArthur walking through the water and getting his pants wet. I understand that he had planned to walk *on* the water but Truman interfered.

Right? Right! We're fully integrated in our talk tonight.

He mentioned poet-bohemians who sit on floors and "make friends" and who don't occupy mere rooms but rather "living areas." He caricatured a fifteen-year-old beatnik he encountered in a coffee house who declared, "The Western religions have failed me." He needled tough L.A. cops and revealed how he jammed their radar "by putting tinfoil in my hubcaps." There were no women in the Beat Generation, he said, "just girls who have broken with their parents for the evening." Those people driving around in $8,000 Dual-Ghias were not "just anybody—they're Beverly Hills doctors." And the best thing about psychoanalysts was that if you didn't make it with one, he'd refer you to a friend. "They call it rehabilitation referral motivation therapy, and we call it fee-splitting." He ended with the disclaimer that nothing he had said was factual, only truthful. "Are there any groups left that I haven't offended? Good. Next show I'll use the *Christian Science Monitor*. Now let's all join hands and sing folk songs."

His lengthy stay at the Crescendo, which would extend into January 1959, put him on the best of terms with impresario Gene Norman, whom he had grown to admire unreservedly. "Gene was like a genius," he says. "He had an IQ of about 300; he knew everything. And he knew a lot about jazz. Didn't know a lot about women. (Some of us deceive ourselves into thinking we do.) He was a radio guy. He was on KLAC. They had five disc jockeys— The Big Five. They controlled L.A. He was on from ten to midnight." An unprepossessing man of average height and build, Norman's fortune was his voice. "He had great pipes, and his pipes were always in shape. He took me to Dolores drive-in one night, and you know how you order through the speaker? 'Your order, please?' He said [clears throat] '*Good evening . . .*' Then he ordered. I never forgot that."

Gene Norman once named Oscar Wilde, Gustav Mahler, George Gershwin, and Duke Ellington as his heroes, but Ellington was the only one he got to know. He presented the great American composer and bandleader in concerts and on packaged tours for sixteen years, bringing him into the Crescendo as often as possible. "My secret as a concert promoter and a nightclub owner was packages," he once said. "I never presented one act. You always got an opening act, maybe a middle act, and then the headliner, usually comedy and jazz." Mort suggests that he had another secret: No books. "He watched everything. Didn't keep a lot of records. Lot of cash. He'd go to Europe and he'd say, 'If you need me I'll be staying at Brotha Slovenia because the record company owes me money there.' He was always cautious about the future."

Though Stan Kenton didn't quite rise to the level of personal hero in Gene Norman's pantheon, he was nevertheless revered as the father of West Coast Jazz, having gained fame at Balboa's Rendezvous Ballroom in the early 1940s. "Stan was the prophet," Norman said, "the man with the ideal; the evangelist who created the new conception of playing jazz. His music reflected his own enormous intensity. The brass was louder, the rhythm more pronounced. In the beginning, the whole approach was based on excitement." Gene Norman had been showcasing Kenton alumni for years—June Christy, Shorty Rogers, drummer Shelly Manne, alto saxophonist Charlie Mariano, trumpeter Stu Williamson, flutist Bud Shank— but had only landed the man himself a couple of times. So when he returned from a New York business trip with Kenton's agreement to come in December 19 with Mort holding into the New Year, it was a dream booking for all three men.

Mort loved Kenton. At six foot five, the bandleader towered over him, and whenever they met he would hoist Mort skyward and give him a kiss. Kenton's band, Mort was fond of saying, was the only one that screamed the blues. "With all the others there is a whispering of sadness, but he *screams* how unhappy he is. The brass is full pitch. And it's a sad song. He's the only guy. And he's also doing something else. He's saying, 'Listen to me.' He wasn't afraid of the volume." Like Dave Brubeck, Kenton was a controversial figure in American jazz, a fact he wryly acknowledged with a joke. "When a crowd likes us," he would say, "we can do no wrong. We're in the Crescendo, and a busboy drops a plate of dishes—and the audience applauds."

Paul Desmond once said to Mort, "I have this recurrent nightmare."

"What is it?"

"I'm the *second* alto in the Kenton band, and I have a lifetime contract."

Kenton, who was there, overheard the comment and turned around. "You know, you're a genius," he said to Desmond. "But I wish you'd play that goddamn thing so I could hear it."

The Kenton-Sahl combination was a winner for the Crescendo, adding a powerful draw to what was already a busy time of year. "We got hot," said Norman, whose only real competition that holiday season was Louis Prima and Keely Smith at the Moulin Rogue. Among those spotted in the Crescendo audience over the course of the two-week engagement: Ava Gardner, who became something of a regular, songwriter Bobby Troup and actress-singer Julie London (who were soon to be married), and Phyllis Kirk on the arm of Beverly Hills psychiatrist Dr. Frederick Hacker.

Mort Sahl spent the first months of 1959 working in television to no great effect. While he was still at the Crescendo, talks with ABC's Leonard Goldenson collapsed over Goldenson's plan to "start Sahl on our local station first, and if he makes good we'll put him on network." The predictable reaction at the Morris office: Mort Sahl was sufficiently established already and didn't need a local test run. After closing at the Crescendo, he filmed a cameo set at the club for the CBS series *Richard Diamond, Private Detective*—hardly a stretch since he was playing himself. (The previous November he had taped a similar appearance for the CBS series *Pursuit*, attempting to explain a series of bizarre murders with the aid of a book of Freud.) Then he guested on Eddie Fisher's NBC variety show, a subdued performance according to UPI's William Ewald: "Sahl seemed to be working under velvet censorship—his material lacked its usual bite." The highlight of the Fisher show came when the host, momentarily at a loss, asked Sahl to "say something funny." Mort looked into the camera and said, "Ezra Taft Benson." Miriam Nelson, the ex-wife of dancer Gene Nelson, was the show's choreographer. "She said, 'We're going to do *Paint Your Wagon.*' So I said, 'Please leave me out of this.' They never would; I never purported to have any chops. They did this big production number. '*Paint your wagon, come along . . .*' So I take the paint brush and I go past the wagon . . . over Eddie Fisher's pants."

Television, he lamented, "is Gimmick City. Dinah Shore comes on and says, 'Tonight we are saluting snow.' Perry Como keeps laughing and putting his tie back inside his coat and he's called 'Mr. Nice Guy.' They all seem to be dedicated to the proposition of killing time. It's considered an accolade for Perry when the fans say, 'He doesn't offend me.' That's a step ahead in this business. For what they are, the westerns do a better job. At least something happens in them."

In February he was given a dramatic part on CBS' *Playhouse 90*, a supporting role as a downhill actor in an original teleplay by J. P. Miller called "The Dingaling Girl." It was a prestigious assignment—Miller was the author of "The Rabbit Trap" and "Days of Wine and Roses"—and *Playhouse 90*, despite having switched from live broadcasts to videotape, was still TV's premiere dramatic showcase. Starring in the title role was Diane Varsi, making her TV debut after an Oscar-nominated turn in Jerry Wald's *Peyton Place*. The other principal cast members were Eddie Albert, Sam Jaffe, Harry Townes, Clu Gulager, and Edward Brophy.

"I'm snowed!" exclaimed Mort, who bailed on a hungry i booking with just forty-eight hours notice. "It's wild! Everyone runs around looking for motivation. Finally somebody says, 'The real issues are on the inside.' In one scene I say to Diane Varsi, 'See you later.' Then somebody shouts, 'He isn't the kind of a guy who says see you later.' Now I don't know what kind of a guy I am. 'Don't play it broad like you were in a nightclub,' the director says to me. Isn't that wild?" The director, Fielder Cook, had his hands full portraying Varsi and Albert's delicate marriage and little time left to work with the others. "I don't want to play myself in this," Mort said, smarting at the memory of his two previous assignments, "so I went to the writer to find out how he saw the character. I hate to use the word, but I'm filled with humility in this case. I want to learn about acting. I want direction."

The result wasn't terribly well received. "As for Mort Sahl's first performance in a straight acting part," hedged Cecil Smith in the *Los Angeles Times*, "let's say that he's still the funniest nightclub performer in the land." Stung, Mort signed up for Sanford Meisner's acting class at the urging of Joanne Woodward, who had studied under Meisner at the Neighborhood Playhouse. "I was hanging with Joanne and Paul every night," he says. "I was like their kid. When Sandy came here it was with a promise from Fox that if he would start a school for them they'd let him direct a picture. Joanne said, 'I want to go back to Sandy.' And Paul said, 'I'm an established star now. I can't show up in that class.' She said, 'I have to have a partner.' So I became the partner."

Others participating in Meisner's eight-week summer session: Mala Powers, Marge and Gower Champion, Diane (later Dyan) Cannon, and Phyllis Kirk (though she wasn't in the same class as Mort). Meisner, who, along with Lee Strasberg, Stella Adler, and Robert Lewis, was an original member of the Group Theater, preached the twin gospels of instinct and intuition. Acting, he maintained, was "the ability to live truthfully under imaginary circumstances." For an improvisational performer like Mort Sahl, who played off an audience the way good actors play off each other, Meisner's class should have been the key to a whole new career in movies and television. But Sahl, who could never get the feedback he craved from a camera lens and the stony faces of a crew, emerged from the class with little to show for it. "Sandy said to me, 'This isn't going to work. You have to find your character, and you've already found it.' He was pretty good—maybe the best acting teacher of them all."

When Mort first broached the idea of a comedy album, Shelley Berman was dubious. Eighteen months had passed since Berman's audition for Oscar Marienthal and his career had caught fire—at Mister Kelly's, the hungry i, the Blue Angel, in Las Vegas, and on TV with the likes of Jack Paar, Rosemary Clooney, and Ed Sullivan. "I kept saying, 'But everybody will know my material,'" Berman remembered. "He said, 'It won't happen like that. Just do it.' He almost, literally, tried to sell me on myself." As with Mort's own album, the Verve engineers captured a particularly lively night of performances at the hungry i. "It was all marvelous. I was just absolutely wild with the laughter I was getting." Berman had no involvement in the editing or the design of the album jacket. He didn't even choose its title: *Inside Shelley Berman*. "Mort said, 'It won't do a lot of business," Sarah Berman recalled. "You won't get rich on it, but you'll have a copy for your friends and relatives. It'll be nice to have.'"

Released in January 1959, *Inside Shelley Berman* was a phenomenal hit, the best-selling album in Verve's three-year history. ("Shelley Berman, if you like, helped subsidize [tenor saxophonist] Ben Webster," said Norman Granz.) Mort's second LP for Verve, *Mort Sahl 1960 or Look Forward in Anger*, came out the following month. Recorded at the Crescendo just after Christmas, it was technically superior to *The Future Lies Ahead* but not expected to sell on the scale of the Berman album. It had become widely accepted in the trade that Mort Sahl was, as *Variety* put it, "the darling of the eggheads" with a fan base "confined to a cult." Collectively, however, the three records inspired a trend in party-giving, where guests would gather around the hi-fi, drinks in hand, and enjoy an actual nightclub performance. "One day," said Shelley Berman, "I'm walking down Lexington Avenue in New York City, and somebody was saying, 'Well, what are you doing tonight?' 'Oh, we're doing Shelley Berman.' Honest to God. And who did it? Mort Sahl! All of a sudden, everybody knows my name."

Granz's success in the Spoken Word category didn't go unnoticed. As Verve expanded into readings by Jack Kerouac, Alice B. Toklas, and Evelyn Waugh, other labels rushed to sign nitery comics who could be recorded in their natural settings. In March, Mercury released the debut album of Mike Nichols and Elaine May, *Improvisations to Music*, and Fantasy followed with *The Sick Humor of Lenny Bruce*, a solo set recorded during an extended stay at Ann's 440 Club in San Francisco. By April, saloon owners were fretting that such albums would hurt the cabaret business, an LP like *Look Forward* costing about the same as the cover charge for a single performance and a couple of drinks.

As it turned out, the albums helped drive business—as did network television appearances on shows like Sullivan and Paar. More pressing was the bad rap the new comedy was getting from the "sick" label embraced and promulgated by Lenny Bruce. Unlike the others, Bruce welcomed the opportunity to shock his audience, carving out a place for himself as an iconoclast in overdrive. In 1958 he had starred in *A Wonderfully Sick Evening* at a tiny Hollywood space called the Attic Cabaret Theatre. And the cover of his *Sick Humor* album pictured him in a cemetery, reclining atop a grave, the remains of a picnic lunch scattered in the foreground. The press picked up on it, raising Bruce's profile to the point where he was commanding $1,750 a week. The *New York Times* steered clear of the word in a May profile, opting instead to describe him as "a sort of abstract-expressionist stand-up comedian." But two months later, *Time* went all in, coining the word "sicknic" and wantonly spraying it over an entire generation of comics. Sahl himself was branded "the original sicknic," while right alongside him in the "hierarchy of disease" was Jonathan Winters. "While these two once seemed more or less alone in their strange specialty, it is now clear that the virus has spread."

The magazine went on to gather Shelley Berman, Nichols and May ("who are barely sick at all," it was forced to acknowledge), and Bruce into the same general category. Short of Lenny's extremes were a host of other comedians "displaying varying degrees of sickness or satire." Among them: Tom Lehrer, Don Adams, and, by some people's lights, Irwin Corey.

"Lenny Bruce was part of the entertainment that we were involved in," said Berman, "but he was difficult for us because we were shaded by his shadow—and he was a dirty mouth. Lenny Bruce was a *filthy* mouth. That's what he did, and he did it well, but we were not in that groove. So we didn't want him with us."

It was *Time*'s lumping together of sickness and satire that Mort found egregious.

> The people who tell 'sick' jokes don't jab specific targets, just anything that will bleed. They're juvenile rebels at best. When a child is repressed by the authority of his parents and cannot make a rebuttal, he breaks everything in reach. It's the same with a generation enjoying technical advances but lacking a morality to control them. In satire, introducing a topic without comment is like learning a language but having nothing to say in it. For instance, if a comic's act is in trouble you can depend on him to mention the Diners Club. Why doesn't he say, instead, that the new Mobile Highly Efficient Strategic Army Corps can go to any spot on the earth with a machine gun and an American Express card?

Shortly before *Look Forward in Anger* hit the stores, the California Highway Patrol found a $5,000 check made out to Mort Sahl on the Hollywood Freeway. It was, it turned out, his advance for the album, which he had blithely tossed into the back seat of his open convertible—along with shoe polish, old newspapers, magazines, and the general detritus of a bachelor's lifestyle. "Whenever anybody paid me, because I had no help, no road manager, I'd stick it in the trunk," he explains. Every so often, he'd drive down to his bank in Beverly Hills, open the trunk, gather all the cash and miscellaneous checks into his arms, and carry them inside. "A guy made me go to the merchants' window—like I came from a business. I never thought of any of that stuff. Then Phyllis got me a business manager. I didn't know from nothin'. Desmond finally got me to join the Diners Club so we could take each other to dinner and deduct it. That was the only card there was back then."

✧ ✧ ✧

Shelley Berman landed a Las Vegas booking straight out of Mister Kelly's, but it took five years for the town to give Mort Sahl a chance. Considered too off-beat for Vegas audiences, Sahl found himself part of a package when finally paired with Gisele MacKenzie for a four-week booking at the Flamingo Hotel. On the supporting bill with a maniacal singing act called the Goofers, he felt awkward and out of place. "Gisele MacKenzie insisted I do twelve minutes," he says, "and I found that constricting." He cut everything down, and found that he could encapsulate a lot of it. "I talked to [Bob] Hope and he said, 'Just keep going.' She did too much time and I did not enough." The trades were skeptical, certain he would bomb with audiences used to the likes of Jimmy Durante and Joe E. Lewis, and who would soon be getting an early taste of Don Rickles. "I saw Sammy Davis at Vegas a couple of nights ago," said a Hollywood director, "and he got up there, rolled around the floor, jumped and sang until he socked those dice players between the eyes. Could Sahl do that?"

The verdict from *Variety*: "It's true that Sahl has a limited audience, but he'd be the last one to be bothered by this fact. Only the sharpies dig his comments (not jokes) about current events, but their laughter is contagious, causing the squares at least to pay closer attention and perhaps learn something. Sahl is an angry young man who's not really That Angry—he has a disarming smile, doesn't he? Sahl's turn boils down to the fact that he's intelligently funny—very funny—and his is the kind of act that is flexible enough to improve daily."

Sahl had just committed to another nine weeks at the Crescendo—at his, by then, established rate of $4,000 a week—when he learned from Jerry Wald that the producer had selected him as one of six emcees for the 1959 Academy Awards ceremony. Retaining Bob Hope and David Niven from the previous year's telecast, Wald added Sir Laurence Olivier, Jerry Lewis, and Tony Randall as hosts for the April 6 event.

"Jerry wanted tails—it was white tie and tails. The only two people who owned them were Niven and [Clark] Gable. They had their own. I went to Dedrick's on Melrose with Bill Holden and John Wayne. We were all over there together." Wayne had a bottle of Jack Daniel's with him. "Wayne said to me, 'You're a great kid, but you don't drink enough.' Bill Holden was charming and modest—charming to a fault. Wayne later said to me: 'I want to drink with a guy, and I won't ask him what he thinks. But they have to ask me. Then when I tell them, they go crazy.' He was really bewildered by it."

Coming off a month in Vegas, Sahl was rehearsing for the Oscars and anticipating his opening at the Crescendo when he again fell ill with mononucleosis. "My skin got kind of yellow and I fainted. I was with Dyan Cannon on the sidewalk in front of Martindale's bookstore, next to La Scala." To marshal his strength for the broadcast, Mort cancelled his Crescendo opening, and Gene Norman got June Christy and Nichols and May as last-minute substitutes. "I noticed one thing about Hope," Mort says. "Everybody was glad-handing everybody—in the worst Hollywood manner. He sat by himself and went over his material. And when they called him for blocking, he knew all the jokes.* I met Sophia Loren there. And Niven. And Gable. We got dressed over at the Plaza Hotel at Hollywood and Vine—it was right next to the Huntington Hartford—and then walked over to the Pantages. Dedrick's was going to give me a clip-on tie and Niven said, 'No!' Then he stood in front of me—didn't get behind me—and tied it for me. And it was perfectly even on both sides. He was everything he was supposed to be."

The show began at 7:30 with Wayne and Holden doing the introduction from the backstage press room. Out front, conductor Lionel Newman struck up the overture as cameras scanned the audience. Kirk Douglas and Burt Lancaster launched into a spirited song-and-dance routine, then Hope strode out to deliver his monologue. Leading with the most nominations were Metro's *Gigi* and Stanley Kramer's *The Defiant Ones*. Announcing the evening's five emcees, Hope singled out Mort as "the favorite comedian of nuclear physicists everywhere." He added: "Mort's backstage putting pearl studs in his sweater right now."

The awards got under way with Bette Davis and Anthony Quinn presenting the Oscar for Best Supporting Actor to Burl Ives for his performance in *Cat on a Hot Tin Roof*. The cascade of stars continued with Barbara Rush, Jacques Tati, Tony Curtis, Janet Leigh, Niven, Shelley Winters, June Allyson, Charlton Heston, Ernie Kovacs, Natalie Wood and Robert Wagner, most of the winners limiting themselves, as Wald had implored, to a simple thank you and a quick exit. Tony Randall pointedly noted that seven minutes had been cut from his remarks (which, he added, were hilarious). The editing and documentary awards were delivered, and then the nominated song performances

---

* Sahl was always open in his respect for Bob Hope. "If it weren't for him," he once said, "I wouldn't be here either."

began with an introduction by Sophia Loren and a visibly tipsy Dean Martin. Forty-eight minutes into the show, Martin returned to the stage. "At this juncture," he said, "may I introduce a young man who is breaking in his white tie, his tails, and his material at the same time, Mr. Mort Sahl."

The orchestra played him on with a few bars of "Let's Call the Whole Thing Off," and Sahl, acknowledging his formal wear, started by saying, "Well, we just lost the college crowd. All over American they're saying, 'Sell out!' But it's okay. Later, Sir Laurence will be out in the sweater for those of you who were waiting. . . . Now, I want to mention, first of all, I think recognition is due to Trans World Airlines—TWA as it's known at the corner—for flying the foreign personnel in and Miss Varsi out. Sterling Hayden took the boat—I checked all this before we started."

Diane Varsi had abruptly walked out on her Fox contract two weeks earlier saying, "Acting is destructive to me. I don't see any reason to be made miserable just because other people say I should go on with my career." There had been one reference to the twenty-year-old actress on the show already, and Mort suggested a category for the evening's best Diane Varsi joke. Keeping with the decidedly "insider" tone of the evening—NBC producer-director Alan Handley covered the show as a news event, not a spectacle staged expressly for home viewers—Sahl went on to skewer stage-trained actors who thought they were slumming when working in Hollywood.

> The first picture I worked on had all Actors Studio people in it—now, you may have some out front, and usually New York actors, and a lot of them have been out here between five and seven years on studio-secure contracts, but they don't want to give in to the town. So they usually live in hotels for five or seven years, and they rent cars, and they don't maintain long relationships. Most of them shop at night— we have two all-night markets here in Hollywood—and they walk in there at night and they usually shop in a very spartan fashion and buy something like instant coffee and Woolite—you know, for the socks— and Coke. This is for real. The checker always says, "Don't you want to buy more than one Coke? How about the six-pack?" And the actors always say, "Well, no, because I might be going back to New York."

The theater rocked with laughter as viewers in Kansas scratched their heads. "Right?" he called. "Right!

"So whenever you talk to them, they always say things like they think this is a phony town, you know, because they all have integrity. They're hard to talk to because these are bright guys—they've all been in analysis—and they say, 'Well, I think this is a phony town, but I'm tired of the theatre in New York because New York is a sterile town. I did stock in the Midwest and I know that's a cultural desert. And I had to leave my home in the South because I was suffocating as a person.' So there's not an awful lot I can say to that, like . . . 'Were you happy on the train?'"

The response this time was followed by applause. He updated his recession joke, replacing *The World, the Flesh and the Devil* with Kramer's *On the Beach*: "It's the story of the last eight people left on Earth . . . four of whom are out of work." And then the one political jape of the evening: "I just had one bulletin. I found out that President Truman was in the audience; he got four seats. Some of the younger actresses backstage only know Mr. Eisenhower, and I explained in terms of how I know him best: I was in the service under General MacArthur—that's the frame of reference . . ." A great, knowing rumble began to swell, followed again by applause. "As you'll recall, General MacArthur led us through the water . . ." And with considerable flourish he ended with the line about MacArthur planning to walk on the water until Truman interfered.

The eruption that came from that, along with even more applause, left the Republican minority in the room fuming and caused Dorothy Kilgallen to declare him the "blockbuster" of the evening "indicating that intellectual comedy is forging ahead." As Sahl led into the station break, having just held the stage, and the international viewing audience, for four and a half minutes, the show was running seven minutes short. There was less than an hour's worth of content left in the wings.

The highlight of the second half was an honorary award to Maurice Chevalier, who sang "Thank Heaven for Little Girls" in a memorable production number. Jack L. Warner was presented with the Irving G. Thalberg Memorial Award, and the major winners of the evening—director, actor, actress, picture—were announced by Gary Cooper, James Cagney, Irene Dunne, and Ingrid Bergman. It all came off without a hitch until the last of the record nine statuettes for *Gigi* was carried off by producer Arthur Freed. Suddenly, as Mitzi Gaynor started to sing "There's No Business Like Show Business" and all the presenters and hosts began to crowd up alongside her, the production team realized that the live broadcast, for the first and last time in the history of the Academy Awards, was a full twenty-two minutes short.

The Irving Berlin song seemed to go on interminably—a full three minutes—before Jerry Lewis waded to the center of it all with a hand mic and called for Lionel Newman to silence the orchestra. "And they said Dean and I wouldn't be on a stage together again," he cracked, bringing the biggest insider laugh of the evening. Given the stretch signal, he added: "We would like now to do three-hundred choruses of 'There's No Business Like Show Business.'" Impulsively, he grabbed the baton from conductor Newman, leading into yet another rendition of "Gigi" as the world's greatest assemblage of talent awkwardly stood around, utterly devoid of material. "Jerry," Mort remembers, "said, 'Everybody dance!' And who was I standing next to who would be my partner? Cyd Charisse. Who started yelling as loud as you could hear anybody, 'This guy can't dance!' I mean, I felt bad about it, but she was terrible, complaining to the director."

In rehearsal, the show was nine minutes short, but it was felt those minutes could easily be regained during performance. As ten cameras panned the theater and its backstage areas, an announcer read a recap of the categories and their winners. Finally, with fifteen minutes left to fill, the credits began to roll, and then the network, which was carrying the extravaganza on both television and radio, cut away from the commotion, putting a random sports film on to fill the remaining air time.

The $300,000 broadcast drew one of the largest television audiences in history, rivaled only by the World Series. The immediate Trendex rating put the figure at some twenty-nine million sets in the U.S. and Canada, with actual viewers numbering somewhere between forty and seventy million. Most reviewers cut Wald and the Academy plenty of slack because the show had been so good before it was a shambles. ("The show ended too soon simply because it went too smoothly," reasoned Cecil Smith of the *Los Angeles Times*.) There were only scattered objections to Jerry Lewis and his general lack of taste, and a small protest over Mort's comment about General MacArthur. "If Mort Sahl is a comedian," fumed seventy-three-year-old gossip columnist Hedda Hopper, "I'm an apprentice haircutter, but the beatniks adore him." Sahl was amused by her vehemence: "She called Tom Moore at ABC. 'You shouldn't put a guy like that on the air. He's not a loyal American.' I'd made a very innocuous joke about MacArthur—corny, actually. She was up at the American

Legion hall on Highland, holding those meetings on who should be put in the stocks and who shouldn't."*

John Crosby, in his syndicated column for the *New York Herald Tribune*, was unabashed in his celebration of the telecast, its suspense and star power, and its complete lack of commercials. "Mort Sahl was refreshingly funny," he wrote. "He was also the butt of the jokes from the other comics like Bob Hope and Jerry Lewis. But Sahl, I kept thinking, is truly the wave of the future. His comedy, fresh and original and alive, makes other clowns sound awfully dated and tired."

Academy president George Stevens invited Mort and Phyllis Kirk to the Governors Ball, but Phyllis wouldn't go because she had to work in the morning. Stag, Mort got up in front of the people at the Beverly Hilton and scored a personal triumph, tailoring an impromptu twenty-minute set to industry insiders. Still, if you didn't dig him, you weren't alone—Cecil Smith, covering the event for the *Times*, observed Laurence Olivier watching from the back of the room, never betraying a smile, much less a laugh, his face expressionless "as if he could not fathom what was going on."

Feeling better, the Oscars now firmly behind him, Sahl opened at the Crescendo on April 16, 1959, sharing the bill with trumpeter Dizzy Gillespie and his band. It wasn't a comfortable pairing, given Mort's antipathy for bebop and its general lack of structure. "I thought there was a lawless, anarchic tone to a lot of it," he says, "and some of it was pretty vulgar. I didn't go along with everything Dizzy did. He was a big anti-white guy, you know. Actively." Gillespie stayed until the end of the month, when baritone saxophonist Gerry Mulligan came in. *Look Forward in Anger* was taking off, and the cigarette girl at the Crescendo was selling copies of that album and *The Future Lies Ahead* to club patrons.

It was around this time that Lou Lotorto of the Sahl Cellar Shakers came down to Los Angeles for a visit. "I remember hanging out with Mort," he said, "and that was fascinating for me to observe. This is when I just fell in love with his brain and his person. We'd go hang out. I remember one day we were on the Strip somewhere, and Mort was making an appearance at a record store, signing albums. I remember Budd Schulberg coming in, and Mort was talking to Budd Schulberg. Then we went to see Norman Granz at a tennis club where Granz owned a membership. Wherever we went, it was

---

*Sahl had his revenge when he made Hopper a prime target of his twenty-minute set at the first annual Grammy Awards ceremony on May 4.

fascinating to see Mort doing his shtick. And by that evening, everything that had been distilled and discussed and molded and shaped after half a dozen tellings was there on stage and in final form."

The relationship with Norman Granz was troubled, Granz having appointed himself Mort's manager when the first record was cut. (Granz also managed Oscar Peterson and Ella Fitzgerald.) Says Mort,

Norman Granz was a very brilliant guy, but he was nuts. A real intellectual. He was my manager for most of a year, but he lived in Switzerland and there weren't any cell phones then. Somebody would say to me "We want you to go to New York" or "We want you to do a picture" and in as far as negotiating or anything, I couldn't ring him up and say, "What do we do?" He gave me a dozen cashmere sweaters he brought back from Paris and a Patek Philippe watch. He'd drive up to Ira Gershwin's and walk in with me and introduce me to Astaire and Judy Garland. He knew his way around, you know?

He absorbed me, but he was really crazy. He'd say, 'You've got a record contract with me. It says you'll make a minimum of so many records. It doesn't specify a maximum, so I can call you at any hour." I had nights when someone would come to my door every half hour till the sun came up and say, "You gotta record in half an hour." All night, every half hour. He detected a kind of independence in me that he thought was insubordinate. But he thought I was kind of a prestige item at the beginning, and then when he fought back he'd go all the way. He'd call Oscar Peterson in Montreal and say, "I found out that our friend is an ofay, a bigot." And he told that to John Lewis of the Modern Jazz Quartet. You would think that people would decide for themselves, but they didn't.

And he was very aggressive socially. He wanted to fire you before you could fire him. He anticipated that I was going to fire him, so he called me into his office, which was on Canon Drive, and he said, "I got news for you. I'm dumping you." *You won't have the drop on me.* He said, "I saw your television show. You're supposed to be a way-out thinker. You're *mild.* You're not even a liberal. You don't know how to make a commitment."

I said, "Well, who makes a commitment?"

He said, "Martha Glaser (who managed Erroll Garner) was a communist. *I* was a communist. You'd never do that. You're with this soft Roosevelt stuff."

I said, "This conversation has no future." I go to the door, and the knob comes off in my hand. So he gets on the intercom, and he says, "Mary Jane, call the Beverly Hills Fire Department." So she did.

He said, "I was a communist, and you're soft candy-ass liberal." Then they come through with the axes—through a wall—and he said, "If you repeat what I told you, I'll deny it under oath." Spoken like a true leftist.

In New York, Phyllis Kirk was being seen around town with NBC talent executive Dave Tebet and composer-arranger Bill Russo. *The Thin Man* was facing cancellation after two lackluster seasons, and despite an Emmy nomination for Best Actress, she wasn't exactly in mourning at the prospect of losing the series. "The glamour of acting on TV as a steady diet consists wholly of collapsing in a heap right after dinner and going asleep," she said at the time. The last week of filming had left her completely undone. "I was on Miltown, and drinking a cup of coffee became a federal case. Last year I had a rash and was swallowing bottles of some kind of green death."

Media profiles insistently connected her to Mort, who was seen as the steadiest feature in her unconventional life. To columnist Dorothy Manners she railed about conformity, saying that she was against people "dressing in the same way, thinking the same way, peering out from their little ruts to make sure they are just like other people in their little ruts." Yet, she began talking openly of marriage as if she really meant it. "Lately, I've been giving more thought to the idea of marriage, mainly because sharing life with someone I love is a fuller existence than doing things by myself. I've changed enormously in the course of just a few years. If I had married the boy I was engaged to at eighteen, both of us would probably be regretting it today. But now I think I'm ready for a good marriage to which I can contribute a lot."

She returned to Los Angeles after the Emmy Awards on May 6—she lost to Loretta Young—and by the time of Mort's opening at Mister Kelly's on July 6, *Tribune* columnist Herb Lyon was suggesting that Sahl might make his four-week stay at the club his honeymoon, describing the familiar couple as "an elopemental case." A few days later, Mort freely acknowledged as much. "Yup," he said, "I'm in love with Phyllis Kirk, but we have yet to set a date." Phyllis, meanwhile, remained on the Coast, certain she had landed a key part in the Richard Burton picture *Ice Palace*.

Hugh Hefner regarded the relationship with interest, not quite certain where Mort fell in his reading of the Playboy Philosophy. "He used to comb Vitalis through his hair, turn to me, and say, 'Are you still seeing Phyllis Kirk in California?' And I'd say yes. He'd say, 'While you sow the seeds of your own destruction, why do the girls you choose have to be so bright?' That time was the height of race-relations movies, and I was going to make a movie called *I Passed for Bright*. And Hef said, 'You got a choice. You can either be in love and be vulnerable, or make my decision to never know love and therefore be able to stand outside and solidly manipulate the relationship.' He said that with a straight face."

Phyllis never did show in Chicago, and when Lyon asked again toward the end of the engagement when he and Phyllis would wed, Mort responded with a recitation of his schedule for the remainder of 1959: "Currently in Chicago; still here as emcee of the Playboy Jazz Festival Aug. 7–8–9; star of a special Canadian network TV show Aug. 13; a splash into the big league of nightclubs, the Copa in N.Y.C. starting Aug. 20; into a new movie Sept. 9— *All the Young Men* with Sidney Poitier and Alan Ladd; and, finally, a Revlon TV spectacular Oct. 8 in the midst of shooting the flicker which goes into November. Any questions?"

Between his closing at Mister Kelly's and the start of the Playboy Jazz Festival, Mort did jet back to Los Angeles to see Phyllis and confer with producer-director Hall Bartlett on the new picture, for which he would once again be writing his own lines. "It's not too easy sometimes," he said of the task. "You've got to overcome a legacy of fifteen years of war pictures with such scenes as soldiers hiding dogs under their shirts as they board the troop transport heading overseas."

With *The Thin Man* winding down and Norman Granz now out of the picture, Phyllis arranged for Milt Ebbins to become Mort's personal manager, a role Ebbins had been playing in Peter Lawford's life for seven years. Superficially, it looked like a good fit: Ebbins started out at MCA, where he worked as road manager for Count Basie. Basie moved to William Morris, and Milt followed. By the end of the forties Ebbins was managing Basie, Buddy Rich, and Billy Eckstine, and had, for a while, handled Vaughn Monroe. By the time Phyllis put him together with Mort in August 1959, Ebbins had added Sarah Vaughan and Vic Damone to his client roster, and would eventually take on Elizabeth Montgomery and Patty Duke as well. He was also politically connected, as Lawford was married to Patricia Kennedy, daughter of

Ambassador Joseph P. Kennedy and sister to Massachusetts senator John F. Kennedy, a leading presidential contender.

Ebbins had an easy time of it at first. Mort was booked through the remainder of the year, but his career seemed stuck in overdrive—lots of work, but no real plans for the future. And the Morris office seemed content to keep it that way. Mort kept wanting to move into television, his best chance at permanence and maximum exposure, but all he ever got was the occasional guest shot. The splash he made on the Oscars prompted NBC to consider giving him his own special, but it was his subsequent success at New York's Copacabana that sealed the deal. The Copa was the nation's preeminent supper club, a Latin-themed oasis of dining and dancing on Manhattan's Upper East Side that was home base to such established names as Jimmy Durante, Sammy Davis Jr., Peggy Lee, and Perry Como. In 1956 the Copa hosted the final performances of Dean Martin and Jerry Lewis. Two years later, it became the scene of Johnny Mathis' New York debut. "I was trying to prove something," Mort says of the unlikely booking. "I was trying to gain full citizenship."

The Copacabana was a big room, a cavernous basement on East 60th Street that had originally housed a swank Prohibition-era nightspot. Outfitted with palm trees, silk coconuts, and, eventually, air conditioning, it seated, jam-packed, 650 customers and for years was the only New York club to put on three shows a night, seven nights a week. There was concern that Sahl, in his sweater and open collar, wouldn't mix well with Paul Shelley's tuxedo-clad orchestra or the razzle-dazzle of the world-famous Copa Girls. The booking, in fact, was the first of its kind for one of the so-called "new" comedians, who as a group were perceived as demanding and undisciplined. Proprietor Jules Podell decided to take a gamble on Sahl during the light summer months when he normally tried new talent. Says Mort, "Popsie Whittaker, the nightclub guy at *The New Yorker* was scandalized: 'You belong downtown.' You know, with the chanteuses—fictional New York. Jonathan Winters said, 'Why? Because [you think] he's too inside?' 'Yes, frankly, I do.' And Jonathan said, '*Inside* U.S.A.'"

On opening night, August 20, 1959, Sahl took the floor in a gray sweater, one of the town's morning newspapers under his arm, A-list celebrities like Kirk Douglas, Charlton Heston, Lee Remick, and Billy Rose ringside. In a solid rebuke to the naysayers, Mort Sahl gave the Copa, by Earl Wilson's reckoning, "its biggest premiere in months." With a presidential election year in the wings, he signaled a greater emphasis on national politics, skewering the likely contenders in a volley of short, electric bursts. Jack Kennedy, a youthful forty-two, was having one of those talks with his father when old Joe asked, "What do you really want to be, Son?" The junior senator from Massachusetts replied, "President, of course." To which Pop responded, "I *know* that. I mean what do you want to be when you grow up?" As far as Kennedy, who was seeking to become the first Catholic chief executive, was concerned, the hereafter was taken care of "but next year is driving him out of his mind." Some Democrats, meanwhile, felt that Adlai Stevenson could be elected "if only he could be nominated." He branded Vice President Nixon "a byproduct of our times" and wondered aloud if he was worth $100,000 a year. "I admit his chances look pretty good, but what about ours?" And then there was New York governor Nelson Rockefeller, who was promising children Little League polo.

The Copacabana was a model of efficiency in its own rough-hewn sort of way. Podell had well-known ties to organized crime, and for a while his partner in the club was mob boss Frank Costello. Mort marveled at the one time he had a heckler at the Copa: "The light went out over his table, and when it came back on, the table was gone." The three-week engagement was a surprise hit and summer record-breaker for the venerable club. ("SRO COPACABANA" boasted a full-page ad in *Variety*.) Veteran nightlife correspondent Tim Taylor, writing in *Cue*, said he amused himself by picking out those in the room who were clearly confused, the old diehards who were schooled to laugh at Durante and the Kean Sisters, but who could do no more with Sahl than stare. "It was quite an experience watching and listening to Sahl at the Copa," he wrote. "I doubt that he'll ever replace Joe E. Lewis in the hearts of the Copa habitués, but I, for one, will never forget his invasion of the celebrated cellar."

6

A PRETTY GOOD EXERCISE

The validation of a booking at the Copacabana opened a lot of doors for Mort Sahl. It was during his residency at the Copa that he made his first appearance as a panelist on *What's My Line?*, trading the open collar for a black tie, his panel mate to the left a frequent booster, *New York Journal-American* columnist Dorothy Kilgallen. At about the same time, Mike Nichols and Elaine May balked at fronting a previously announced special for NBC, and producer Joseph Cates offered the job to Sahl. "I'm the host—whatever that means," Mort told John Crosby. "Well, I made one picture—that means I can host a TV show. Look at TV—General Motors, Ford, and Revlon, right? Federal Theatre comes back to the people." Actually, the Pontiac job was the more problematic of the two, as he would be serving as ringmaster as well as satirist—jobs that did not necessarily go together. "I'll do something political—walking on ice, but for identity. All audiences are the same; it depends on what they've been weaned on. Most audiences have been weaned the wrong way."

All the Young Men was another war picture, this time set in Korea, exploring racial tensions within a small platoon of Marines. Writer-director Hall Bartlett (*Zero Hour!*) set the project up at Columbia with the understanding a major name would appear alongside Sidney Poitier, who had already been cast in the principal role of Sergeant Towler, a black man who assumes command when the white platoon leader is killed in action. By the time Mort joined the cast in early July, Alan Ladd had signed on as executive producer and Poitier's co-star, his production company now a full partner in the venture. A crew of seventy traveled to Montana's Glacier National Park for an October 5, 1959, start, the vagaries of weather stretching a twenty-eight-day schedule to a grueling fifty-four-day shoot. Nevertheless, Poitier would recall it as "a remarkably uneventful experience, except for some blister-ingly cold months in Montana and Oregon."

Mort wrote his own lines, air-expressing Dictaphone belts to Bartlett in Los Angeles. He also distinguished himself as the only member of the cast who was willing to grow a beard. Ladd, who he remembers as "a sweet guy, a good guy," had little of significance to do in the story, despite his first-position bill-ing over the title. "It's got a lot of subtlety in it," Mort says of the picture. "For instance, when one of the guys is wounded by Koreans the only one who has his blood type is Sidney Poitier. So it goes back and forth: *da-dum . . . da-dum . . . da-dum . . . I think they're trying to tell us something . . .* And Hall directed it, you know. You'd hear 'Rolling! Speed!' and he'd say, 'All right, tense up team!'" Even Mort's obligatory solo turn failed to come off, tarted up as it was with reaction shots of the men laughing mechanically. "It played," he says, "like someone came into the room while I was rehearsing. Awful."

While on location in Montana, he borrowed the sheriff's jeep and drove from Hungry Horse to Helena to wire material to John F. Kennedy at the Senate Office Building in Washington. The connection had been made through Milt Ebbins, and the initial phone call was not from the senator but rather his father, who caught up with him at Dick Carroll's haberdashery on Rodeo Drive. "This is Ambassador Joseph Kennedy. I understand that you're preeminent in the field of political humor. I want you to write some things for Johnny."

Jack Kennedy, of course, didn't have the nomination yet—he hadn't even formally announced—but he was the steady favorite among voters. The Gallup Poll, in a trial heat after the off-year election of 1958, put him at 59 percent over Richard Nixon's 41, and his star continued to rise into the early months of 1959. It was the vice president's July visit to Moscow, and news of his so-called kitchen debate with Soviet leader Nikita Khrushchev, that reversed the trend and narrowed the Senator's lead. Nixon, however, was hampered by a stiff, humorless appearance in public. Kennedy, by con-trast, had come to be regarded as a genuine wit, a quality his father thought could be sharpened as the campaign gained momentum. "I've heard you're the best at this," he told his quarry. "I don't want Nixon bludgeoned. I hear you can put the dagger in between the fifth and sixth rib." Sahl said he didn't make endorsements, but that didn't seem to matter to the old man, who, when he wanted something, was used to getting it. And so Mort Sahl, the quintessential outsider, began writing humorous jabs for an undeclared candidate, with explicit instructions and no promise of compensation.

"It seemed like a pretty good exercise," Mort says in retrospect. "I liked Jack Kennedy when I met him, but who would I be a supporter of? You know the kind of guys I like. [Former vice president and Progressive party candidate] Henry Wallace I liked. So I didn't enlist for the duration. I also let him know that I hoped one of the benefits of his election would be that I be allowed to do what I do, as he does what he does." Often the courier between the comedian and the senator was Pat Lawford; at other times it was legislative assistant Ted Sorenson or press deputy Pierre Salinger. Sometimes the lines were retooled from jokes in the act, but mostly they were new and of the political moment. "I did all this on the fly, at odd hours," Mort says.

Sahl's involvement advanced to another level when he was asked by Frank Sinatra and Peter Lawford to emcee the Democratic party's annual Jefferson-Jackson Day dinner at the Beverly Hilton. For Kennedy, the $100-a-plate fundraiser would be the culmination of a four-day swing through the state, during which his goal would be to see—and be seen by—as many Californians as possible. The event was set for Monday, November 2. On Sunday night, Sinatra found him dining with Dyan Cannon at La Scala and drew up a chair. "Mort," he said, "I need your help. I want you to write some material for me. I'm going to be working with Jack Kennedy and I'd really appreciate it."

The following night, Mort had to make sure he didn't use any of the lines he had supplied to either Kennedy or Sinatra. But for a few hours it didn't appear as if that would even be a problem. He was shooting interiors for *All the Young Men* at Columbia studios, six miles east of the hotel. Along around quitting time, he found himself mired in a scene with actor-singer James Darren and a frog trained to jump on cue. Hall Bartlett wasn't happy with what he was getting and kept at it as the dinner's 8:30 starting time approached. "Just to let you know, we're going to do this until we get it right," Bartlett said to him. "And, by the way, I'm with the other side."

Populating a reception before the big dinner that night were Milton Berle, Danny Thomas, Sinatra, Dean Martin, Lawford, and Shirley MacLaine. The senator with the piercing blue eyes took Mort's hand, shook it vigorously, and thanked him for what he was doing. Kennedy coveted California's eighty-one delegate votes, but Edmund G. "Pat" Brown, who was serving as honorary chairman, warned him that he could expect short shrift were he to attempt to enter the 1960 California primary—in which the popular governor intended to run as a favorite son. "Have you got any more one-liners?" the senator asked. "This looks like a rough crowd."

Kennedy held his remarks to twenty minutes. "It's a great pleasure to be here in California tonight," he began. "As I traveled around your state with its mild climate I was reminded of the fact that winter has come to the East. And it is a constant source of amazement to me that Governor Brown would want to leave all this for the chill of Washington, D.C." Later, on the way to Palm Springs in Kennedy's plane, a converted Convair, the candidate asked Mort why he admired Fidel Castro, whose forces had chased Cuban dictator Fulgencio Batista into exile. "I told him of my admiration for Castro, and that a revolutionary, I thought, appealed to all Americans—well, not quite all, for Americans view South American revolutionaries as a joke, the Russian revolutionaries as a horror, and the American revolutionaries as heroes."

Kennedy then grilled him about a joke Mort had told on television: The ambassador says to his son, "I'm putting you on an allowance. You're not allowed one more cent than you need to buy a landslide." What, he wanted to know, did that mean?

"It means your father is rich, for one thing."

"How much do you think he has?"

Mort didn't know. "Four hundred million," he guessed.

"He looked at me as if I were retarded and asked if I knew how much the Rockefeller brothers were worth. 'Liquid,' he said, 'about ten billion.' Then he looked at me and said, 'Now, that's money!'"

Mort Sahl's ambition had always been to play to an audience like himself—hip, musically sophisticated, attuned to the new realities of social and political engagement. He had slowly come to realize, however, that such an audience alone would never be enough to fundamentally change the way America laughed. Now there were two major television appearances in the offing that could significantly expand his reach in the marketplace: A guest shot on a new celebrity-laden variety series called *The Big Party* and then—finally—a network special of his own, *The Future Lies Ahead*, for Pontiac.

The Big Party was designed to alternate with the fading *Playhouse 90*, its premise being that a famous host decides to throw a party and invites an array of talented friends who, over the course of a long evening, do their stuff. It was live to the East Coast but not unrehearsed, and it did not rely on extemporaneous dialogue. Humorist Goodman Ace had created a similar program in the waning days of network radio called *The Big Show*, but where the latter was genuinely informal, *The Big Party* would merely seem to be.

"We want a spontaneous, ad lib quality," he said, "but make no mistake— every word, every cue will be written."

It was perhaps the illusion of spontaneity that prompted Goody Ace to settle on Mort Sahl for his first show, for which the host would be Rock Hudson and the guest mix would include Tallulah Bankhead, Sammy Davis Jr., Esther Williams, and Broadway showstopper Lisa Kirk. Mort's set, about halfway through the program, took its cue from Khrushchev's recent visit to Fox studios and led into his satire of airline disaster movies, only lightly touching on politics in deference to the show's deep-pocketed sponsor, Revlon. Otherwise, he occupied the periphery of the action, trading scripted small talk with Hudson, Kirk, Davis, and briefly breaking the fourth wall in acknowledging the capacity audience in CBS' Studio 50, the former Hammerstein's Theater on Broadway.

Both Jack O'Brian and the *World-Telegram*'s Harriet Van Horne headlined their reviews identically: THE BIG PARTY IS A BIG BORE. Generally mauled by the critics, *The Big Party* nevertheless scored a 19.6 Nielsen share, beating out *The Untouchables* and Tennessee Ernie Ford and serving as an excellent lead-in for the following month's scheduled telecast of *The Future Lies Ahead*. Unlike *The Big Party*, however, *The Future Lies Ahead* would be anything but live. The show, touted as a showcase for "young hopefuls" in a revue-style format, was videotaped over three days just prior to the Revlon broadcast, Sahl delivering two extended monologues, one labeled "cultural warfare" in the script, the other more lifestyle-oriented. His responsibilities were otherwise limited to a four-minute opening and introductions of new acts getting their first breaks on national television: French-born chanteuse Vicki Benêt, who was in the midst of a modest recording career with Decca; the screwball comedy team of Harvey Norman and Stanley Dean; a newly minted singing trio calling itself Joanie, Johnny and Hal; and comedian Lenny Maxwell. The rest of the hour was filled out with the production numbers considered necessary for all such programs, bringing size to an otherwise modest offering and justifying the "living color" in which it was produced.

The show was written by comedy veteran Jay Burton and twenty-three-year-old Woody Allen, though their contributions were mostly limited to connective material and the two commercials the sponsor required. "I remember being in my apartment with Jay Burton writing jokes for that," Allen said. "To me, the end of the rainbow was to write for Mort Sahl. And I contributed what I could, but it paled in comparison to what Mort would come on and do routinely of his own. I didn't know him at all. He was always very standoffish with me, and skeptical. He was skeptical of everybody."

With his CBS and NBC commitments behind him, Sahl briefly returned to Los Angeles, then left for Montana and location work on *All the Young Men*. He was completely out of touch, other than by wire, when Pontiac executives and agency MacManus, John and Adams gathered in New York for their first look at Joe Cates' $225,000 extravaganza. The show was set to go out on Saturday, November 21, but there was general agreement among those assembled that its best parts were the clever car commercials. "To hear them tell it," *Variety* reported on October 7, "if Pontiac can salvage 25% of the show it would consider itself lucky." *The Future Lies Ahead* was pulled from the NBC schedule, delayed until January to give Cates time to come up with a fix. The agency's TV head, Hank Fownes, told the trade press that tapes from the dress rehearsal and final run-through would be cut and edited into a new show, and that Sahl, still on location, would likely be called back for reshooting. But other than the new air date, their putative star was told nothing at all.

All the Young Men wrapped on December 12, 1959. By then, Mort was into his fifth record-breaking week at the Crescendo, paired on the bill with singer-songwriter Sam Cooke and looking forward to another holiday season with Stan Kenton. If he noticed items in the press indicating that sixty-seven-year-old Eddie Cantor and English pop singer Frankie Vaughan had been added to *The Future Lies Ahead*, he didn't let on. "I knew they were modifying it," he says, "because all of a sudden I'm doing an interview with *TV Guide* and they're telling me Eddie Cantor is in it. I got paid, but Milt Ebbins wouldn't put up a fight with anybody." To the *San Francisco Chronicle*'s Terrence O'Flaherty he said, "Only the title is the same. The content has been changed to protect the innocent."

The Future Lies Ahead finally got its nationwide airing on January 22, 1960. Three sections of the meandering talent show had been scrapped entirely: Sahl's cultural warfare monologue; Lenny Maxwell's spot in which he played all the characters in a prison vaudeville show; and a short musical finale in which Mort handed out fortune cookies to individual cast members, all of whom were inspired to conclude "The Future Lies Ahead!" To fill the extra time, Cates led with a solemn introduction by Cantor in which the veteran musical-comedy star, billed as the evening's narrator, underscored the purpose of the show. "This is the first time a company—rather than an individual—has made it their business, along with making new Pontiacs, to do something about new talent. So ring up the curtain for Mort Sahl in *The Future Lies Ahead*."

There followed a jumble of disparate elements: a frantic Snow White–inspired routine by Norman and Dean; a lengthy Pontiac commercial crowded with competing announcers; songs from Vicki Benêt (whom Sahl facetiously introduced as "an exchange student"); and a perfunctory set from the host himself on the challenges of dating girls from the Beat Generation. An eight-minute ballet contrasting Russian, Latin, and American rhythms ("The Dance Olympics") came next, followed by Joanie, Johnny and Hal and another Pontiac commercial, this one featuring actor Reginald Gardner as an English explorer discovering new car interiors. To round out the hour, Frankie Vaughan, hardly a new act but largely unknown in the States, contributed several songs in a separately produced finale that looked as if it had been shipped over from England. For the conclusion, Cates threw it back to Cantor, who brought the whole unfortunate experiment in committee-based programming to a close.

Although it seemed as if every TV critic in the country caught the show, eager to see how a full hour of network television could be allotted a man who had recently said, "The only honest thing on television now is wrestling," Sahl himself was not among them. At the appointed air time of 8:30 P.M., he was backstage at LA's Shrine Auditorium as the extra added attraction on a Stan Kenton concert date that included June Christy and the Four Freshmen. Thus distracted, he never saw the end result. The following Monday, Jack O'Brian predictably savaged the show from his perch at the *Journal-American*: "Mort Sahl, on TV at least, is consistent—he gets worse every time he goes on."

O'Brian aside, most reviewers expressed puzzlement over Mort's handling in what was ostensibly his breakout performance. "By and large this was a standard variety show with a commendable desire to show off young talent," Richard F. Shepard wrote in the *New York Times*. "Unfortunately, Mort Sahl, who was the host, had the spotlight for only one short segment. His monologue on the difficulties of dating the beatnik girl who is 'restructuring her environment' was a fresh, funny interval." The trade review in *Variety* noted a general lack of cohesion and suggested that "further rework and perhaps another postponement" was in order. "Could be that the Pontiac people were afraid that Sahl's sallies would be too far over the heads of the mass audience but they shouldn't have started with him in the first place instead of sitting on him as they did."

Although it didn't quite seem so at the time, Mort Sahl's one genuine chance at a broad national audience had come and gone in a haze of confusion. Never again would he have a showcase like *The Future Lies Ahead*; never again would he be anything other than a guest on network TV. "He was funny in his nervous brainy way," concluded the AP's Bob Thomas, "but he never got a chance to warm up. Perhaps, as many professionals claim, Sahl is too far out for the general TV audience. At least he should be given a chance at what he does best."

Mort Sahl's rupture with Norman Granz turned acrimonious with the filing of opposing lawsuits, Mort claiming $4,200 in back royalties and Verve responding with a $200,000 breach of contract complaint that he had refused to show for a June recording date. The actions effectively tied up two new releases just as he was coming off a Grammy nomination for his second album, *Look Forward in Anger*, and the release of his third, *A Way of Life*. Sahl, of course, was directly responsible for Shelley Berman's phenomenal success for the label. (Berman's second album, *Outside Shelley Berman*, notched advance sales of some 60,000 units based on the more than 200,000 copies of *Inside* sold to date.) And Jonathan Winters had joined Verve at Mort's insistence, recording *The Wonderful World of Jonathan Winters* during a stand at the Riviera Hotel in Las Vegas.

In the trade, *A Way of Life* was seen as more of the same, despite cover art by the prolific David Stone Martin that gave it the unmistakable look of a jazz album: Sahl depicted in Martin's signature style of bold lines and blotted shadings, his rolled newspaper at hand as would be the instrument of a celebrated musician. He took great pride in the cover, its look and resonance, just as he did in the acceptance and acclaim he enjoyed among the jazzmen with whom he appeared. Says Mort:

> It meant a lot to me. When I first got out there and I couldn't find my way—the audience was restless and all—it was always the musicians who would say, "Well, what did she say?" They'd urge me to get into a continuity. And "weird" did not disqualify you with them—being different. Of course, now it's a terrible conformity, but with them it was: *Go for it.* I liked their humor. And, of course, I loved their product because it spoke to you in a different language. They have a different way of expressing their contempt for the establishment, which I liked about all of them. And the way they talk is in a kind of

emphasis. I'd finish a monologue, and [trumpeter] Jack Sheldon or [trombonist] Milt Bernhart would say to me, *"Yeah Mort!"* So I was really—and still am—flattered.

One night, [drummer] Louie Bellson was in [the jazz club] Donte's, and with the L.A. traffic, the bass player, Ray Neapolitan, was late. Louie said, "Can you get up there and say something to the audience, Mort? Stall for about ten minutes?" So I did, and I got a few laughs. Then Louie sat down and he started in syncopation. He didn't just thank me. He got everybody's attention, and then he said, "I want to thank Mort Sahl for sitting in with our band." And that killed me.

Once while appearing in New York, Mort stopped in at Birdland, which had instituted a lunch matinee. Pianist and composer Lenny Tristano was on the stand, as was Tristano's frequent collaborator, alto saxophonist Lee Konitz. It was Konitz who turned to Tristano, who was blind, and said, "Hey, Mort's here."

Tristano called out to Sahl: "Do you want to sit in?"

"Well," he responded, playing along, "I didn't bring my axe."

And with that, Tristano reached under the piano and offered up a copy of the *New York Times*.

The question of marriage seemed to follow Mort Sahl wherever there was coverage in the press. Generally, he was portrayed as the most eligible of bachelors in a business populated by some the world's most desirable women. He saw little downside to his celebrity status, and reveled in being linked to the likes of Phyllis Kirk and Dyan Cannon in the national media. Even his occasional nights out on the town became the stuff of rampant speculation. In interviews, he readily acknowledged a preference for actresses and, as he often put it, "other female impersonators." Simply having lunch with someone like Susan Cabot was enough for some to presume a relationship.

Marilyn Monroe was another actress he saw on occasion, it being Jerry Wald's original plan to film *Let's Make Love* with Mort as Coffman (the part eventually played by Tony Randall) and Gregory Peck in the male lead. "I knew her because of Sinatra and being around the Morris office," he says. "I wasn't cruising her or anything. A couple of times I drove her down to Dolores Drive-In. She'd put on a scarf and dark glasses and we'd go down there and get hamburgers. . . . She was sensational, really a girl. When [husband

Arthur] Miller got into trouble [with HUAC], she took every dime she had in the bank and put it toward getting him out of that. She was *really* a chick. I was very impressed."

In October 1959, when Sahl sublet screenwriter Herbie Baker's Miller Drive house, Earl Wilson mistakenly reported it as a purchase and wondered: "The Phyllis Kirk marriage close?" By December, Dorothy Kilgallen was reporting that Mort and Phyllis had once again parted company, and that he was devoting all his attention to one Jane Langley, "beautiful west coast entry in this year's Miss Rheingold contest." In January 1960 he admitted to Wanda Hale of the *New York Sunday News* that, having settled on Hollywood as a home base, he would like to get married. "I thought of proposing, but there are so few eligible girls out there. Barbara [Rush] got married [to publicist Warren Cowan], Phyllis is too busy with all that television she does and taking French and flying lessons."

What, he was once asked, did women want from him? He thought a moment. "Hilarity. Alcohol. Adventure. Escape. Danger. Reflected prestige. They think I'm what I seem to be on stage. And I'm not. Girls say to me: 'You analyze too much. Why don't you follow your feelings?'" He laughed. "That's ridiculous. If I followed my feelings, I'd be an outlaw."

In early February 1960, Mort Sahl left Los Angeles on a four-month tour that would take him through Chicago, New York, and then back to San Francisco for another stand at the hungry i. But his first stop in Chicago wasn't Mister Kelly's nor the Blue Note, but rather the venerable Chez Paree, an elegant supper club in the city's Streeterville neighborhood that was on a par with the Copacabana in terms of size and prestige. As with the Copa, longtime observers thought the booking ill-advised, but the connection had been made through Jane Dick, whose husband, industrialist Edison Dick, was a partner in the club. Relishing the booking and refusing to be intimidated, Sahl made the transition with no adjustment in style or technique, lining up a choice selection of his favorite targets—Richard Nixon, *Life* magazine, the city's continuing police scandals ("the last outpost of collective bargaining"), network television, Dwight Eisenhower, juvenile delinquency, Cape Canaveral ("Disneyland of the East"), Jack Kennedy, Congress, the Soviets. "Sahl," reported *Variety*, "proved that 'individual perception' is just that—in a regulation nitery as well as any other."

It was on a Wednesday morning during this particular engagement that Mort, subdued and thoughtful, taped an extraordinary radio interview with WFMT's Studs Terkel. "You represent a new kind of humorist," Terkel began. "The misused phrase 'sick' is used here. It's as much a cliché now as the word 'beat.' What's your feeling when you're told you're a 'new kind' of humorist?"

Well, you know, Studs, first of all, if I represent a new kind, where are the others? Let's get back to that. If it's a new trend, I'm pretty lonely for a guy who's part of a movement. . . . One of the ironies of our time, and I say this at the risk of sounding pedantic, and I don't want to become too scholarly, but I go into this at this depth because I'm in a role of justifying myself perpetually. One of the ironies is that you can go on the stage and be generally cynical about the entire human condition, and not even entertain hope for our future as human beings, and you'll be considered a good, wholesome, all-around red-blooded comedian. If you are specifically cynical about institutions that aren't worthy, you're then called "sick" and negative. And it's always interesting: if you accuse anyone of cynicism, they always say, "I'm being realistic." It's a conditioned response.

I was just on the Coast, and gag writers who work in television, which they consider mass media—and [for which] they are turning out saccharine family comedy—had a stag dinner. When they went to the stag dinner, they all became profane—that was their degree of release. I mean, they didn't tell the truth, but their reaction against years of oppression is to degrade themselves rather than those who oppress them. So it means they went from a saccharine ignoring of the facts to the other extreme of obscenity, but they never once came in contact with the truth. It's sort of a magnetic polarity.

Digging in, Terkel asked about Sahl's approach as a humorist "without giving away trade secrets." Was there a way of developing material that he used every evening?

Oh, sure. I'll tell anything I know; I'm ignorant in a lot of these areas, too. It's just a synthesis. I read as many papers as I can get my hands on—because of a basic curiosity, not because I'm well disciplined in my work by any means. And then the jokes grow from night to night. It's liable to be anything, but it starts . . . like, I'll tell you the way an area will grow, just as an example.

It starts initially when, perhaps, one Republican candidate says, "Jack Kennedy is a Catholic." So the joke will grow. In other words, he comes out and says, "Why doesn't Kennedy take a stand on birth control?" So I said to the audience, "Kennedy has not taken a stand on birth control, but I think there are more important issues than birth control facing us." So that got, really, nothing. But then that grew from night to night to a point where in three weeks it had become this: "Well, I see that one candidate said that Jack Kennedy is a Catholic. And he read other bulletins through the evening. Then he said: Let's face the fact that being a Catholic will condition Kennedy's behavior." Then I put it out to the audience: "But that isn't necessarily true. Vice President Nixon is a Quaker and it hasn't conditioned his necessarily."

And then we go from that to the point that someone comes up to me and says, "What do you think about birth control?" And I say, "I don't think about that at all. I'm thinking about disarmament most of the time as a major issue." And then I point out that maybe ignoring the issue of birth control is a traditional role with men so we can't relate that politically. And then if *that* doesn't go anywhere, I take a further avenue—you see, it goes a million ways—that I'm thinking about disarmament, I'm thinking about the hydrogen bomb, and a girl comes up to me and says, "Do you think a Catholic can be president?" I say, "Oh, sure—if we're here." Then we're off with the hydrogen bomb, and I finally wind up with Kennedy saying, "Please accept me as a senator, not on a basis of my faith. In other words, as far as I'm concerned, the hereafter is taken care of—but November is driving me out of my mind."

Sahl filled the early months of 1960 with club dates and emcee duties at testimonial dinners and the like, but the Pontiac debacle rendered him radioactive when it came to television. Briefly there was talk of a series based on columnist Art Buchwald's exploits in Paris, but negotiations fell apart after *The Future Lies Ahead* was aired. Aside from an occasional guest shot as a panelist on *What's My Line?* the only man who seemed willing to put him on network television was Steve Allen. The former *Tonight!* host had gone prime time in the fall of 1956, battling Ed Sullivan and ABC's *Maverick* on Sunday nights. In 1959 he was moved to Monday nights, a "ratings graveyard" as Allen later described it, and NBC relocated the entire show to the network's color studio complex in Burbank, California. It was there, on the March 14, 1960, episode of the *Steve Allen Plymouth Show*, that Mort, in a rare shift from satire to parody, delivered one of his more unusual performances.

"Steve really wanted to know everything that was on the shelf," he says. "He wrote fifty-four books! And when I did a routine on his show, making fun of his intellectual curiosity, I played him. Producer Billy Harbach helped me rehearse it, and Herb Sargent and I wrote it while Steve was out of the studio—we called him out on a ruse." Harbach had a duplicate of Allen's suit tailored in sharkskin, and gave Mort an identical pair of glasses. A full opening, complete with the NBC peacock, fills the screen and then collapses into chaos—mangled names and a new 1960 Plymouth almost plowing into a dancer. Mort emerges from the wings with a book under his arm, taking aim at Allen's penchant for lofty reading recommendations. "Good evening and welcome to another show for Plymouth," he announces. "But first I'd like to recommend this book to you. It's great that you can be a better person while watching this show. I just read this on my way from the dressing room. Every American should read this book. It's called *Is Your Fallout Shelter Termite Proof?*

"Now I think we should get the show started," he says while seating himself at the piano, "with a little music by one of my favorite composers—me. I would like to play a number from my 958th record album, which is called *Steve Allen's 958th Record Album*. Although I may never sell a million records, I may *make* a million records." The scene switches to series regular Pat Harrington Jr. playing announcer Pete Hanson during an abortive Plymouth commercial. "Before going on," says Mort, returning to center stage, "I'd like to recommend a book I read during Pete's commercial. It should be on the shelf of every American regardless of his country: *Are We Lagging Behind China on the Crabgrass Problem?*"

Mort, as Steve, then introduces a bug-eyed Don Knotts playing Mort. "Tonight I want to tell you this story about a liberal traveling salesman and the reactionary farmer's daughter," Knotts, in an ill-fitting pullover sweater, begins nervously. "Right away you've got a basic conflict . . ." Cutting him off, Sahl reappears with yet another book. "It's a book you owe it to yourself and your country to read. It's called *Is Your Unborn Baby a Communist?*"

After dropping a number of plugs ("I have a brand new album out called *Music Steve Allen Didn't Write*") guest star Tony Martin is asked to name the song he would sing. "I don't sing anymore, Steve. I just come on and do my plugs." The audience interview segment is hijacked by Louis Nye posing as a tourist, and the billboard girl, an Allen prime time tradition, gets knocked to the ground when the cover of a gigantic photo album is thrown open. "Next week on the show is the lovely Jayne Meadows," Mort declares, displaying an oversized glamour shot of the current Mrs. Steve Allen, "in answer to your many requests—and also because we get her at a very good price." Two more book recommendations are wedged in before the show ends with an anarchic crush of guests reminiscent of the stateroom sequence from *A Night at the Opera*. In skewering Steve Allen's considerable ego, Sahl's parody pulled very few punches. "He loved it," Mort says of his response to the ambush. "When we went to air he laughed so hard he couldn't get his breath."

Steve Allen lasted just one season on Monday nights. His last show, on June 6, 1960, was heavily dependent on clips culled from previous broadcasts, so it fell to Mort to offer eight minutes of new content amid all the plaudits. ("We used to consider Mort a little more a member of the family than just a guest passing through the building," Allen remarked.) He started by bringing up reports of contaminated cranberries from the past holiday season, suggesting they'd be good for this year's Thanksgiving dinner with some spoiled turkeys he'd been reading about. Mention of November naturally got him onto the subject of the election, particularly a recent appearance by Vice President Nixon on David Susskind's *Open End*.

"Susskind would say, 'What about Red China?' 'or the UN?' Something like that. And Nixon would say—he'd sort of preface his answers by saying, 'Ah, yes, my wife and I were discussing that the other night at home, a quiet evening. She was over in the corner knitting a flag and I was reading the Constitution . . . prior to leading the children in the flag salute." He urged other presidential candidates go on television as well, maybe as summer replacements. He visualized Ike and Nixon slipping into the roles of Major Adams and Flint on *Wagon Train*, Nelson Rockefeller serving as the family patriarch in *Here Come the Nelsons* ("Try to be back before the recession, Ricky"), Adlai Stevenson starring in *Bachelor Father*, JFK in *Leave It to Beaver*.

Current events brought him around to the U-2 incident, the downing of an American spy plane over Russia:

As you know, there's been a lot of talk about the U-2 the last couple of weeks. That started on the first of May when the plane was shot down, and the president reserved comment until he could assemble all the facts, and weigh them, and discuss it with his advisors—and then deny it. So then Khrushchev turned around and said, "I'm sure the president didn't know about the flight." And the State Department said, "Of course he knew!" And the president said, "Yes, I've known about *all* the flights."

The president said, "Why are they so self-righteous? They've got a lot of spies in our country, too." Which they have. And if we're lucky they may steal some of our secrets and then *they'll* be two years behind.

While Mister Kelly's was Mort Sahl's regular venue in Chicago, like the Crescendo a place to which he could habitually return, he hadn't yet found a similar home for himself in New York City. The Blue Angel was too small, the Village Vanguard too musical, the Copacabana too fancy. The need, he said, was critical. "Today's forum is the nightclub," he told Danton Walker of the *New York Daily News.*

> If a man has something he considers serious and important to say, he can put his thoughts in a book—but you're not sure the book will be read. Or you can hire a hall and hope somebody shows up. In a club you don't have to wonder. The people come, and they listen. They laugh, too, and that's the way to bring them in. I've never laid claim to being a comedian. I had to create a place for myself in theaters and clubs. Then I forced myself into larger places. Now the clubs don't need big orchestras and dancing girls. They want a guy who can stand up there and talk. I think of myself more as a journalist—I've always worked that way.

It took the failure of a Latin-themed nightclub called Casa Cugat to create a lasting forum for Sahl on Manhattan's East Side. Partners Ralph Watkins and Leonard Green gave the Cugat six months to catch on, but even its namesake, bandleader Xavier Cugat, acknowledged it was "virtually impossible" for a modern nightclub to compete with television. By the spring of 1959, Watkins and Green were mulling a shift to jazz, a form of entertainment largely missing from home screens, and the change came about in June when the narrow performance space on 48th Street, just east of Lexington, was renamed Basin Street East. In the beginning, the booking policy tended to favor bebop, never a heavy draw, and it took time to find a proper balance. By the end of the year, with mainstream acts like Benny Goodman and the vocalese trio Lambert, Hendricks & Ross filling the room, Basin Street East was establishing itself as one of the city's key venues for jazz.

Watkins was an old hand at the club business, a saxophonist who had his own band for a while before opening his first place, Kelly's Stable, in the thirties. His first Basin Street was on Broadway, the second in Greenwich Village. And at various times he had Basement Street East, the Royal Roost, the Famous Door, and the Embers. It was Green, president of Mercury Artists, who had pitched the idea of a club built around the persona of his friend Cugat, envisioning a stable New York venue for his agency's Latin music division. "It was a plush room, and our customers were society types," said Green, "but it just didn't go. We were about to give up when Ralph Watkins suggested the jazz idea." Lennie Green booked most of the talent, while Watkins handled the day-to-day workings of the club. "There was a third partner, a guy named Moe Lewis. He was with Ralph originally, because Moe was connected with The People. In those days you had people; we used to call them 'The People.' Mob types, but nice people, very well behaved. Moe was the partner who made sure that no one bothered anyone and that everybody got taken care of, the police got taken care of, and that everything worked the way it was supposed to."

When, after jamming the place with Peggy Lee at $10,000 a week, Green suggested Mort Sahl, Watkins, who hadn't heard of him, nixed the booking of a comedian just as the new policy was catching on. "I said, 'Ralph, this is different. Mort Sahl isn't just a comic. He's a *jazz* comic. He appeals to people who like jazz.' I just made that up. Ralph said, 'Really? I didn't know there was such a thing.' I said, 'Sure. They'll love him here because he's a jazz comic.'"

Once again, Sahl was considered a risky bet when brought in to work Holy Week as the club's first nonmusical attraction. As insurance against the traditional Easter slump, he was presented in tandem with former Kenton vocalist Chris Connor, a Basin Street favorite backed by conductor-arranger Richard Wess' fifteen-piece orchestra. Late for his own opening ("probably busy taking his tie off," suggested Earl Wilson) Mort took aim at an easy target: "The Chicago Police Athletic League is an organization that encourages kids to go along with the cops on their burglaries." Basin Street East was on a roll. Up against big names like Lena Horne at the Waldorf-Astoria, Jimmy Durante at the Copacabana, and Les Paul and Mary Ford at the Latin Quarter, Mort Sahl held his own, pulling capacity business and surprising even the most hardened of café observers with what *Variety* called "ropes up" business. Halfway into the engagement, Watkins and Green signed him for a minimum of three weeks per year for three years, and on closing night, a Wednesday, there were turnaways at the door. "It was a great club," Mort remembers. "Even the audience was talented. They were awake."

Since it had been nearly seven years since Mort Sahl's debut at the hungry i, his April 25, 1960, opening at the "i" was attended by members of the press, local radio and TV figures—and Robert Rice, son of playwright Elmer Rice, who was researching a lengthy profile for *The New Yorker*. The span of time inspired reflections and—invariably—comparisons in the press, but it was generally agreed that Sahl was in fine fettle. Among the topics he touched upon: Charles Van Doren ("He hooked us into thinking, then sold us out"), Fidel Castro ("He's my age—32—and what bugs me is that he's got a whole country"), and holidays as observed in the South ("They close the banks and open the schools"). To *San Francisco Examiner* columnist Dick Nolan, Mort appeared withdrawn as he dutifully circulated among the guests, happily ceding the spotlight to his parents. "There's a lot of bickering between Mort and Enrico," a beaming Dorothy Sahl told Nolan, "but it's just like between two brothers. Mort feels his entire career began with Enrico and the hungry i, and he'd rather be in San Francisco than anywhere." Harry, more reserved than his ebullient wife, was reflective. "I'm glad Mort turned out to be the kind of comedian he did," he said. "In my day the comics got laughs by hitting each other with newspapers."

Variety's account noted the price of admission ($3.00), Sahl's weekly salary ("something in the neighborhood of $4,000"), and the general nature of the crowds ("squarer, older, better upholstered, and definitely tourists—no more Beats and college kids"). None of this seemed to affect the act much. "Sahl rolls along for 57 minutes, which is a pretty big dose. And the only shadow of doubt comes from those skeptics who knew Sahl five years ago— they point out that if Sahl hasn't changed, the crowds have: the laughs sometimes come in odd, i.e. wrong, places; Sahl seems to be working harder than he used to, etc., etc. But that is a minority, if hip, view. On the whole, Sahl remains the same, and is drawing business."

It was during Sahl's four-week stand at the "i" that *Time* estimated his earnings at more than $300,000 a year. Under questioning, he admitted to some personal idols: Mark Twain ("a prism through which the young country expressed itself"), Herman Melville ("he had scope and virility, didn't internalize"), Thomas Paine, Albert Einstein, Edmund Wilson, Theseus, and

George Bernard Shaw. Considering that he regarded Franklin Delano Roosevelt as a father figure, he allowed as how Dwight Eisenhower might qualify as a "stepfather figure."

In all, it was a good month, the first Mort had spent in the Bay area in more than two years. "Enrico, Mort, and some others—we all hung around together eating, telling lies, and getting laid," said Herb Caen. "Enrico had a door charge at the 'i,' and sometimes he would take over from the doorman, collect the cash, and we'd all be off to Reno. It was an unforgettable time."

As the national conventions approached—the Democrats meeting in Los Angeles, the Republicans in Chicago—there was a general assumption that Mort Sahl would be providing color commentary for a major television outlet. "Sahl," predicted the *Herald Tribune*'s Marie Torre, "will be one network's insurance (NBC's most likely) against viewer ennui during the convention coverage, his assignment being to unleash good humor when the proceedings grow dull—and dull they can grow, if you remember the last conventions on TV."

It seemed a natural fit, but there were no network offers forthcoming, despite occasional expressions of interest. It fell to a local station, KHJ, to put him on the air in the Los Angeles market in a nightly recap of convention happenings, predictably titled *The Future Lies Ahead*. (The call letters, Sahl explained, stood for "Kennedy Hates Johnson.") Stepping up, the Hearst newspapers then engaged him to cover the conventions as a columnist, giving him a national platform despite his widely known involvement with the Kennedy campaign. Sahl himself vehemently denied any undo influence. *Newsweek* helpfully reported that he had contributed to exactly one speech. ("Just a one-shot deal for both," the magazine assured its readers.) The truth was a bit more complex, the candidate genuinely wary of savaging a figure as beloved as the outgoing president. "Kennedy," says Mort,

> would look at the speech and say, "You know, you're getting to be pretty flippant. This guy's General Eisenhower." I'd say, "You're not going to beat him with that attitude." But inside I thought the argument had merit. I didn't tell him that. I said, "I had good luck with Eisenhower. I'd go to his fallibility." And we went round and round about that. I was with him in Palm Springs, and then back up at the Hilton, the Beverly Hills Hotel, the Biltmore. And then down at the convention. I wasn't always invited into those private things, but he

always had those over-the-shoulder remarks to me. He'd say, "A worthy cause even *you* might tolerate."

What truly inoculated Sahl against charges of conflict was his unwaver-
ing support for Adlai Stevenson. "I had taken Stevenson's word: 'You must
do missionary work among the heathen, because your audience is the most
oppressed majority in the world.' He told Democrats to believe in their
latent power—and, of course, they didn't." Kennedy, he remembers, had
a way of saying something funny and then watching for Mort's reaction.
"Well," he'd say, "I know I'm not up to the standard of your *real* hero."

In the runup to the conventions, the Crescendo was outfitted like a campaign headquarters. A banner extending out over Sunset Boulevard read:

OUR NEXT PRESIDENT
MORT SAHL

In the lobby stood a voting booth for "Mort Sahl's Galloping Poll" in which
the ballots were decorated with squares and ovals, and a note instructed the
respondent to "mark X in the square or in the egghead."

Sahl told Murray Schumach of the *New York Times* he wasn't worried of
being put out of work should a Democrat be elected president. "It is not my
ambition to become court jester to the Democratic candidates for president.
They think I agree with them. They are lucky if they agree with me." Even
with a Democratic landslide in the fall, he was confident enough Republicans would remain in office to supply him with material. "If you are a Republican and plan to vote, you have a choice of Richard Nixon."

In the days prior to the start of the Democratic National Convention,
the Crescendo was aswarm with delegates, party functionaries, some candidates, notable out-of-towners, and more than the usual complement of
local celebrities. Lionel Hampton, a Republican, brought his big band in,
providing a solid balance to the evening's satire. "I like fun," Mort would say,
"but we don't have time for jokes. We have to overthrow our government."
Chet Huntley, Douglas Edwards, and Walter Cronkite were observed one
evening sharing a table. "Feel free to laugh at the political jokes now," he
advised them from the stage. "It's not treason until November."

Central to the high-profile convention attendees were a core group
dubbed "the Clan" by UPI. A not-so-veiled reference to the group surrounding Peter Lawford and his wife, Senator Kennedy's sister, the Clan consisted

of Lawford, Frank Sinatra, Shirley MacLaine, Dean Martin, Sammy Davis Jr., Tony Curtis, and Janet Leigh, fervent Kennedy supporters all. Heading the lonelier "Draft Stevenson" contingent were Robert Ryan, Jan Sterling, and Jessica Tandy. "L.A. International Airport received [Senate Majority Leader Lyndon] Johnson, Kennedy, and Stevenson in the past two days," Sahl wrote in his first dispatch for the Hearst papers. "The confident Kennedy's comment was, 'I am here to accept the nomination.' Johnson said that he would accept the nomination, but running the nation's business, he barely got here. Stevenson's philosophy seems to be, 'I don't want the nomination, and I am not here.'"

That afternoon, Sahl and co-host David Susskind taped a ninety-minute preview for KHJ heralding their nightly "unconventional look at the convention." They promised to "seek truth from such common people as Zsa Zsa Gabor and other grass roots individuals" and planned to interview outgoing DNC chair Paul Butler, campaign managers for the four leading candidates, Milton Berle, Steve Allen, and others. The two men then separated, Susskind returning to Chicago, where he had a movie in production, and Sahl heading for the Beverly Hilton, where the hospitality had been flowing for hours. For delegates who didn't have $100 to buy their way in to one of the twin banquets, a parking lot adjacent to the hotel had been set aside, and more than three thousand attendees swarmed the host bars that covered the asphalt. Then a lavish buffet supper was laid out for a thousand or so visiting members of the news media—press, radio, television—replete with movie stars, Olympic athletes, poolside interviews, and tart observations from the likes of Hedda Hopper and Groucho Marx. "They once wanted me to run for governor of California," Groucho said. "I'm corrupt enough to be a politician, but if I'm going to be crooked, I want to get more money than they're paying me on television."

Mort arrived at the International Ballroom, the larger of the hotel's two halls, with Dyan Cannon, who was described in one wire dispatch as "a sultry young lady currently on television in something called *Full Circle*." He proceeded to seat her at the multi-tiered head table, which was otherwise reserved for the candidates, a selection of party leaders, Sammy Davis, Tony Martin, Judy Garland, and, at the opposite end, Eleanor Roosevelt. On the dais, Kennedy, being the front runner, bore the brunt of the abuse. Milton Berle, who assumed the podium first, wielded each line like a blunt instrument. "You'll have to excuse Senator Kennedy," he said as the candidate momentarily left the stage. "He's been drinking pabulum on the rocks. But don't worry about the senator—he's got a clean bill of health from his pediatrician." Sahl took a similar tack, telling the crowd that if Kennedy didn't make it "he can go back to school and write a term paper on what he did this summer."*

The sharpest material was directed at the opposing party. Of Nixon, Berle said, "The American public should give him their undivided suspicion." Of Eisenhower: "Come January, he will leave the White House—if he can find it." Turning to Adlai Stevenson, Berle said, "I'm going to keep voting for you until you win." When Sahl took the stage, he recounted Kennedy's bravery in the Pacific as a naval officer. "The senator went to Washington to be decorated with some other heroes, and President Truman made his usual speech about how he would rather be getting one of the medals than be president. All of the other heroes agreed with him—except that one tall lieutenant from Massachusetts." Introducing "Mom" Walker, chief telephone operator at convention headquarters, he said, "They have good exchanges for a convention—like RUthlessness, BLitz, AVarice, and MAchine." Then he told the audience that he wasn't as concerned with politics as with the Russians: "Khrushchev says he can bomb any American city. And I want to know if he's taking requests." In his Hearst column, Mort remarked on the success of the dual event. "The Democrats just held a $100-a-plate fund raising dinner which garnered $300,000," he wrote. "Now poor people can run for office."

The actual convention failed to generate much suspense, Kennedy gathering up delegates at a furious pace. Johnson and Missouri Senator Stuart Symington (who had Harry Truman's endorsement) were quickly left behind, making Stevenson, the subject of the biggest airport rally in city history, the only possible barrier to a Kennedy victory on the first ballot. As events got under way at L.A.'s Memorial Sports Arena, Stevenson arrived at the Biltmore Hotel's convention headquarters some four miles to the north. While those staffing the Draft Stevenson office across Pershing Square worked frantically to slow Kennedy's advance, he introduced Mrs. Roosevelt to an overflow press conference. Easily the most beloved figure in the Democratic party, she said that she doubted a ticket headed by Kennedy could win in November, citing fears of JFK's Catholicism and his seeming

---

* The nagging issue of Kennedy's youth was underscored by the men who made up his campaign team. Ted Sorensen, who was busy drafting JFK's acceptance speech, was thirty-one; Sorensen's assistant, Richard Goodwin, was twenty-nine; Robert Kennedy thirty-three; advance man Kenneth O'Donnell thirty-six; Pierre Salinger thirty-five. Mort wondered if the nation was searching for a "son-figure."

inability to deliver the Negro vote. "The strongest ticket we could put up would be Stevenson and Kennedy," she concluded.

The other candidates, each figuring he had a chance only if Kennedy were held short of the necessary 761 votes on the first two ballots, were hopeful that Mrs. Roosevelt's dramatic statement would be the thing to stop him. Meanwhile, Kennedy's own forces—and many independent strategists—felt her move had come too late to make much of a difference. Johnson, the candidate with the second-most delegates, was holding steady with the more than five-hundred votes he expected to receive on the first ballot. So Monday's emphasis on the former Illinois governor tended to dominate the TV recaps.

When Mort took to the air at 10:30 P.M., David Susskind was still in Chicago overseeing location filming of *A Raisin in the Sun*. To fill Susskind's chair, he turned to the most passionate political junkie he knew—Phyllis Kirk. Though he and Phyllis had largely gone their separate ways—at one point she had been linked in the columns with Gene Norman—there was still a powerful connection between them. When she returned to Chicago in June 1960 to appear in a production of *The Country Girl*, she assured Herb Lyon, who seemed unnaturally interested in the matter, that she and Mort would never wed. It was just a friendship, she insisted—all the while feeding Lyon piquant items about his favorite nightclub comic. Of late, Phyllis had been prominent in the movement to save Red Light Bandit Caryl Chessman from the California gas chamber, a battle that ended with Chessman's execution on May 2.* She was also one of thirty film and TV stars, along with Peter Lawford, Edward G. Robinson, Shelley Winters, and Frank Sinatra, to sing "The Star Spangled Banner" during the convention's opening ceremony.

Sponsoring the telecast was Lytton Savings and Loan, and watching from his home in Holmby Hills was the flamboyant Bart Lytton, finance chairman for the California Democratic party, whose support for Jack Kennedy had mysteriously given way to a strident and quixotic push to make former Connecticut governor and ambassador Chester Bowles the party's nominee. (Bowles, it should be pointed out, had already endorsed Kennedy.) A former screenwriter, Lytton quickly became incensed at what he was seeing on screen, and he climbed into his Cadillac for the short drive to the new Lytton Savings building at Sunset and Crescent Heights, where the broadcast was taking place.

---

* On the matter of capital punishment, Mort liked to say that he was for it. "You've got to execute people," he reasoned. "How else are they going to learn?"

The panel that first night consisted of Mort, Phyllis, Irv Kupcinet, and writer-comedian Bill "Jose Jimenez" Dana. The panelists had just finished interviewing New Jersey Governor Robert B. Meyner, who spoke warmly of Adlai Stevenson. (Meyner was married to the former Helen Day Stevenson, a distant cousin.) Lytton abruptly walked onto the set, his white dinner jacket flaring on screen. Knowing that both Sahl and Kupcinet favored Stevenson, he admonished, "Let's not make this a rally for one man."

There followed a few moments of stunned silence.

Kupcinet said: "This is a television first. I've never heard of a sponsor breaking into a show like this before." Phyllis tried to get the discussion back on track as Mort sat dumbfounded, one of the few public times he was ever at a loss for words. "This is the last in a series of these shows," Dana whispered into his mic. Kup made several references to Lytton's "highly irregular" behavior, but Lytton stood his ground through a commercial break. "I have been accused of being everything except partisan," Mort complained. "I have never been part of a group large enough to be called a minority." He implied that he would not participate in the remaining programs, but seemed to relent when Lytton reappeared and apologized for his outburst. In response, Mort suggested the name of the show be changed from *The Future Lies Ahead* to *Bart Lytton Prevents*.

Viewer interest in the opening session at the Sports Arena was low— NBC took an early Arbitron rating that showed only about 30 percent of the nation's TV sets were tuned to the convention—but what some saw as Lytton's attempts at censorship made news and ginned up viewer interest at the local level. The papers all covered the incident, as did the wire services, *The Huntley-Brinkley Report*, and *Time*. An outraged Steve Allen withdrew $10,000 from Lytton Savings, and in the *Los Angeles Times*, Cecil Smith, who expected the Sahl-Susskind matchup to be "an irreverent gasser," averred as how "the best shows at any convention are, of course, in the periphery—even as unofficial a periphery as the nightly Mort Sahl-Phyllis Kirk roundup." Adorning Smith's column was not a picture of Mort, but rather one of Phyllis, a wary three-quarter profile, her big eyes suggesting that the reader brace for the unexpected.

Sensing a ratings bonanza, Lytton phoned Mort and told him they should keep the feud going. "I've got to keep threatening you, and you've got to keep attacking me." Publicly, both Lytton and KHJ insisted the program would continue. "I'll be on the air again tonight," he announced, "and so will Mort. You might say I was an irate sponsor who didn't want the program to become a one-man rally. After all, I'm a Chester Bowles man." In the days to come, guests on *The Future Lies Ahead* would include Ted Kennedy, Governor LeRoy Collins of Florida, Kennedy campaign director Larry O'Brien, syndicated columnist Drew Pearson, and Pearson's associate and eventual successor, Jack Anderson.

The publicity didn't hurt business at the Crescendo, where Mort was playing to capacity audiences twice nightly before making the three-minute drive to the Lytton building. "Kennedy came down to see me," he remembers. "I walked out at the beginning. Before I get my bearings, I just kind of riff until I find something. He was in the back with Pierre Salinger and Larry O'Brien. I said, 'Well, Marilyn Monroe is at liberty.'* I have an idea for her. She was married to the world's greatest intellectual, Arthur Miller, and the world's greatest ballplayer, Joe DiMaggio. So I think she should be married to Adlai Stevenson, and then Kennedy can be jealous of him twice.' I heard his fist hit the table. And he said: 'Goddamnit, there he goes again!' I heard him. But that didn't stop him. The next day I was with him. By that time Ebbins had apologized to him."

In a break with tradition, Stevenson had visited the Sports Arena on Tuesday, sparking a wild fourteen-minute demonstration on the convention floor. His backers were predicting a fifth-ballot victory for the reluctant candidate, while Stevenson himself was quietly floating the idea of a cabinet position in the new administration. "I wonder if the Kennedy people have considered that a Secretary of State named Stevenson might run for the presidency in 1964?" Sahl mused in his column. "In fact, if he were late one morning, I am sure the Administration would get nervous and wonder where he is."

Stevenson basked in the adoration that rained down on him from the galleries of the 15,000-seat arena, another roaring crowd of 3,000 surrounding the building and awaiting his appearance outside. Yet, nothing had been left to chance by Kennedy's disciplined team, which had coolly and confidently amassed enough publicly committed delegates to put him over the top. The alphabetical roll call on Wednesday night ran all the way to the delegation from Wyoming, whose votes narrowly clinched the victory. In the runup to the vote, Mort witnessed a confrontation between Bill Blair and Ambassador Kennedy at Peter Lawford's beach house. "Joe Kennedy stopped Blair.

---

* Sahl had just had dinner with Monroe and knew that she had engaged in an affair with her *Let's Make Love* co-star Yves Montand.

'When is your man going to concede to Jack?' And he put his cane in front of him and wouldn't let him go through the door."

That night, David Susskind (who referred to his panel mate as "the Peck's Bad Boy of entertainment") was back on the set at Lytton Savings, where the talk centered on who Kennedy would pick as a running mate. Symington had shown enough strength to ensure his consideration, but Kennedy was thought to prefer Senator Henry M. "Scoop" Jackson of Washington state. Still, the smart money was increasingly on Johnson, who was the first of the four major candidates to have his name put in nomination, and a man who would serve to strengthen Kennedy's appeal in the South. "There is much talk here of new leadership in both parties," Sahl had written in his Wednesday column. "Young men are acceptable . . . if they have the same old ideas."

The plan for Friday, announced the previous week, was to have the eventual nominee make his acceptance speech in a gala event at the city's Memorial Coliseum, a brief walk from the Sports Arena. Some 90,000 seats were made available free to the public through schools, PTA groups, and labor unions, with reserved "ringside" seats to be had for a $10 donation to the Democratic Central Committee. Acting as bait would be two hours of entertainment featuring Mort, Phyllis, Sinatra, Sammy Davis, Steve Allen, Edward G. Robinson (reading from Walt Whitman), Mercedes McCambridge, Ralph Bellamy, Vincent Price, Barry Sullivan, and Jan Sterling—all gathered in the hope that all 105,000 seats in the huge amphitheater would be filled for network coverage of Kennedy's prime time address.

It was, however, a July afternoon in Southern California, and when the entertainment began at 4:00 P.M. the temperature in the direct sun was close to ninety degrees. The weather had a predictably adverse effect on attendance; the Coliseum's emergency hospital staff logged a record 100 patients, most the victims of heat prostration. Crowding the schedule was a pageant called "Forty Eight Plus Two," a salute to the new states of Hawaii and Alaska, and various youth bands, drum corps, and drill teams. When the final convention session was gaveled to order at seven o'clock, attendance stood at 41,000. Limited to just a few comments, Mort memorably announced that Vice President Nixon had wired his congratulations to Ambassador Kennedy: "You haven't lost a son; you've gained a country." He concluded his brief stint with the Hearst papers by ruminating on Lyndon Johnson's strength in the South, the striking similarity of the various candidates, and the role of machine politics in securing the nomination for Kennedy. "I object to wealthy people seeking public office," he wrote. "It's more traditional to attain public office and THEN become wealthy." He made fun of the convention slogan ("The Democrats Care"), TV newsmen with their electronic backpacks, and Bobby Kennedy's political ambitions. He concluded: "The Democratic Party leadership kept saying it was tough to come up with a ticket that would satisfy everybody—and then went on to prove it."

The convention had the entirely unintended effect of rekindling the relationship between Mort and Phyllis Kirk. Phyllis began frequenting the Crescendo again, even as Dyan Cannon was reported in one of the columns as "gazing fondly" at Mort. But Phyllis' ambitions, always on display, wore on him. "I went to La Scala with her every night," he remembers. "And one night I was in there and she'd go to every table—work the room. She was always in business." She asked him to re-introduce her to Jack Kennedy, which he did.* "The next day she showed up at his suite at the Beverly Hills Hotel without me. Of course, since Kennedy met so many people, he worked on a system of associations. As soon as she walked in he said, 'How's Mort?' She said, 'How would I know? I'm not his keeper. I'm a person, too.' So he threw his hands up and wouldn't talk to her."

While still at the Crescendo, Mort took her upstairs one night to see Lenny Bruce who, after a long absence, was back at the Interlude on a four-week booking with Mavis Rivers. "There were about four people in the room," Mort remembers. "You know how you get—you confide in them. He said, 'Did you go downstairs to see Mort?' Applause. 'He's great.' He didn't know I was there. And he said, 'He'll be all right if she doesn't emasculate him.' And he made a clipping gesture with his fingers. I walked out of there and went down to the Gaiety Delicatessen. I ran into Army Archerd, and I said to him, 'That guy—he's supposed to be my friend. He shouldn't be talking like that.' I think I said I was going to pop him. Then Lenny called me that night and said, 'You're upset about that, huh?' I said, 'Yeah.' 'Well you didn't say you were going to hit me, did you?' It really bothered him. Army Archerd had told him that already—in a matter of minutes."

In his *Daily Variety* column, Archerd's lede sent Lenny to the woodshed: "Gene Norman decides on the future of Lenny Bruce at his Interlude and Crescendo. L.B. is skedded for four weeks in the upstairs haven for limp-wristers, and three below at the Crescendo. . . . Bruce's opening night

---

* Kennedy had visited the *Thin Man* set in 1958, and had been photographed with Phyllis and Peter Lawford.

material made Don Rickles (also debuting, at the C. with Frances Faye) sound like a temperance leader." He reported Sahl as "mortified by some of the filth" in Lenny's act. "That's what it was—and particularly one remark aimed at him was grounds for a good punch in the nose. And we wouldn't have stopped this one."

Lenny Bruce was not yet using the words on stage that would lead to arrests in various cities, but he delighted in stretching the bounds of what was, in 1960, considered good taste. Mort was a genuine Puritan when it came to language, steadfastly refusing to work blue and disliking the inclination in others. Phyllis' tendencies were more calculated, and her occasional expletives were yet another source of tension between them. One night between shows at the Crescendo, he wandered over to Phyllis' house to give her an emerald ring and ask her to marry him. As she watched television, a box of chocolates at hand, he said, haltingly, "I've been married. I never thought I'd do it twice. But this thing had come up. I really thought we could help each other through the mortal storm." And while he was fumbling for words, she turned to him, free of makeup and pretense, and said, "What the fuck are you talking about?"

It was, he later said, like a lash across his back. "That was just like writing on the wall. I felt like belting her. I think she took too much for granted. She could have had some good times, because I was really crazy about her. But God didn't want that to happen." There was a point when Phyllis told Mort she had met a wonderful man and that she was in love. Mort knew the guy—he was gay. "But that was all right," he wrote in *Heartland*. "She was a great nurse, provided you had a great problem—like being a homosexual or losing your television series." When she eventually did marry, in 1967, it was to writer-producer Warren Bush, whom she knew to be an alcoholic.

"She had kind of a wall about being elegant, planning the future," Mort says reflectively. "She thought I was like a wild card, you know? 'When we're married I'm going to get into investments and you're not going to have to work.' She was always planning. Like the best-laid plans, of course, it never happened. She said great things about me right up to the end, but you can't build your life on that. The chicks don't know how important they are. They have a disproportionate view of how important they are, and they build castles of sand on that. She was a nice girl, but she wasn't the raw material of a love affair."

7

MY LIFE HAS NO DISSOLVES

Mort Sahl didn't travel to Chicago for the Republican National Convention, but instead followed network coverage from Los Angeles, airing his views on KHJ and again via the Hearst papers. The TV deal was closed only at the last minute, Mort wary of going on the air again for Bart Lytton. With two albums at the ready, Norman Granz stepped in, and Mort's fifteen minutes of nightly commentary were covered by Verve. In Minneapolis for an Ella Fitzgerald concert, Granz told the *Tribune* he spent $11,000 "bailing Mort Sahl out of the hassle inspired by the Democratic National Convention."

Mort found commenting from a distance of some two thousand miles oddly liberating, the big picture aspect of the job helping to keep the foregone conclusion of a Nixon nomination in perspective. "The Republicans are meeting in Chicago's International Amphitheater," he noted, "which is situated strategically near the stockyards. Where else can you nominate a presidential candidate and watch baloney being made at the same time?"

Mort Sahl at the hungry i, recorded in April 1960, reached back to the previous summer for its material, covering Sahl's engagement at the Copacabana, Nixon's trip to Russia, his kitchen debate with Nikita Khrushchev ("If he continued to run against the Russians instead of the Democrats there's no telling how far he could go"), Khrushchev's own September visit to the United States, and the general topic of communism as a world threat. Timed to hit stores in June, Mort's fourth album for Verve wouldn't have seemed very timely were it not for the downing of the U-2 on May 1. The decision was made to add nearly twenty minutes of new material, an entire side of *at the hungry i* that was actually taped at the Crescendo, yielding, in Mort's words, "true stereophonic sound with 409 miles between the left and right ear."

On May 5, Khrushchev addressed the Supreme Soviet for three-and-a-half hours, his news about "aggressive acts . . . by the United States of America" coming at the end of his remarks. Caught off guard, the U.S. administration confirmed that a weather observation plane had gone missing over Turkey after the pilot reported oxygen trouble. The following day, NASA identified the "weather" pilot as Francis Gary Powers, a statement that prompted Khrushchev to reveal that Powers had been captured "alive and kicking" and that he had made a full confession. On May 11, President Eisenhower assumed personal responsibility for the U-2 flights.

"So they got Powers," Mort said, summing up the situation for his audience at the Crescendo.

They're going to try him, you know. But they'll let him go because in France, Italy—all the European countries—it'll go over big that they don't have capital punishment. That's a good propaganda weapon, because they hate us over there for having capital punishment. And, as you know, there's a big scuffle going on in this state now about capital punishment. Largely, oddly enough, the religious groups want capital punishment, believing that you must pay for the error of your ways, even if a man is occasionally executed unjustly. And they believe in that, even though they made a Very Large Mistake once. . . . So, Powers is off, and he's got the bomb under his seat, the ejection seat, and he's got a poison needle. And he's to use those—those are the alternatives. And then the Russians caught him in the searchlights and started shooting at him, and he chose a *third* alternative, I gather . . .

What's happening to the national morality? We've had two spies in our history—Nathan Hale, who said, "I regret that I have but one life to give for my country." And Francis Powers, who's quoted as saying, "This shatters all my plans." It's depressing. So now we have surplus U-2s because the president has suspended the flights. So they were purchased by an entrepreneur, and you'll be hearing more about that later, probably in one form or another. Maybe you'll be walking around Los Angeles and these leaflets will drop down from the sky and they'll say: YOUR PICTURE HAS JUST BEEN TAKEN AND IS AVAILABLE FOR TWENTY-FIVE CENTS.

When word got out that *The New Yorker* was preparing a major profile of Mort Sahl, Henry Luce ordered a *Time* cover story rushed so that it would appear first. Says Mort, "There were always a lot of guys from *Time* talking to me, taking me to Mercurio, a place near the Time-Life building—iced grapes and stuff. It was very baronial with Luce. They really put their nose to the grindstone, that crowd."

Where *Time* correspondents all over the country were enlisted to gather material for a *Time* cover profile, a man like Robert Rice was essentially on his own. With no hope of beating *The New Yorker* to the newsstands, *Time* ran a kind of mini-profile in its July 25 convention recap, covering Sahl's nightclub and television work while the Democrats were in town. Gone was the "sick" label that had plagued his previous mentions in the magazine, replaced with more admiring coverage that presaged the full cover story to come: "First and still the best of the New Comedians whose specialty is topical humor, Mort Sahl, 33, is emerging as the most successful political satirist in the U.S., a sort of Will Rogers with fangs."

When Rice's seven-page article appeared in *The New Yorker* a few days later, it was titled "The Fury" in reference to the watch inscription Mort had given his friend Paul Desmond. Much text was given over to descriptions of Sahl's onstage manner, his way with a line, the basic hostility that, Rice contended, drove him from within. "Mort Sahl," it began, "a dark and savage wit who spends most of his working life fulminating through the haze, late at night, from the stage of one nightclub or another, is almost certainly the most widely acclaimed and best-paid nihilist ever produced by Western civilization."

Dispensing with any presumption of a moral compass, Rice spoke with an array of eyewitnesses: Dave Brubeck, Desmond, Mort's mother, Enrico Banducci, others who declined to be identified by name. Brubeck and Desmond talked of their joint gigs with him, Brubeck lamenting the basic problem of having him open for you. "Mort's impossible to follow," he said. "He demands so much of an audience that it hasn't the strength for anyone else." Desmond, recounting their time on the bill with him at the Crescendo, reflected on the evolution of his material over a period of weeks: "It's like watching a garden in time-lapse photography."

Mort's chronic depression was on display, although it's attributed to the notion that he's appalled by the world he lives in. "If this were a movie," he told Rice, "there would now be a dissolve, but unfortunately my life has no dissolves. I have to live every agonizing moment of it." His early days were recounted in considerable detail, while completely missing the obsession with American movies that shaped his view of the world and held it to impossible standards. "After all," he said, "if we couldn't laugh about these things, we might do something about them." At one point, as if to under-score Rice's contention of nihilism, he took aim at *Pogo*, the beloved comic strip written and drawn by Walt Kelly. "What kind of a civilization are we living in," he demanded, "when a possum says something and we all say, 'I wish I'd said that'?"

All the Young Men came to theaters nearly a year after its completion, an apparent stiff held by the studio for the less demanding audiences of sum-mer. Mort saw it as a catalog of war movie clichés, dreary and predictable and useful only as a target for ridicule. He told an audience at the hungry i:

> Before I forget, I want to mention I have a movie coming out. It's called *All the Young Men*. I hope you see it; it's out in August, I think. It's about the Korean War, and it's cast the way movies are cast today. It's amazing—there's hardly any women working in pictures. Remember? Stars? You know how they always thought America was a matriarchy? It isn't. These chicks try to be actresses until they're thirty. Then they quit and marry an actor and express themselves through charity. You know—The League for Retired Movie Horses and all that . . .
>
> But here's the way they cast a movie today. This picture stars Alan Ladd. See, you got a male star. That's how you get your money from the bank. Sidney Poitier is in it. He plays a platoon sergeant in the pic-ture. He's in the picture because you've got to have respectability—a Broadway actor. Then they have James Darren for teenagers and the title song. And then [world heavyweight champion] Ingemar Johans-son is in it for the audience which must be subpoenaed. And I'm in it. And my appeal is somewhat indeterminate at this point. It's those people who chase [deposed South Korean strongman] Singman Rhee with rocks. Right?

When producer-director Fletcher Markle and his wife, the actress Mercedes McCambridge, discovered Mort Sahl during a 1956 performance at the Fair-mont Hotel, Markle sensed the soul of an actor and vowed to one day cast him in a dramatic role. "He was sort of the basement Orson Welles, very man-nered," says Mort. They became friends, and it was through the couple that Sahl met Marlene Dietrich. Markle was working in episodic television at the time, but didn't have the right material at hand until he began producing a new anthology series for MCA's Revue Studios called *Thriller*. The NBC series hadn't yet premiered when he came up with a story titled "The Black-Eyed

Stranger" by the Edgar-winning mystery writer Charlotte Armstrong. It centered on a TV writer who overhears a plot to kidnap a girl and manages to avert the crime by abducting her himself. Retitled "Man in the Middle," it was well suited to a guy Markle regarded as "a Hamlet who always wanted to play a comedian." He thought, in fact, that it had the potential of opening up a whole new career for his friend the nightclub comic. "If Sahl chooses, he can become a great actor," he predicted at the conclusion of filming.

Markle, who also directed the episode, denied that using Mort Sahl in any way qualified as gimmick casting. "Mort carries the show," he assured Dwight Newton, who was showing interest on behalf of the *San Francisco Examiner*. "You'll be impressed." Newton, who knew an enthusiastic producer often oversells a product, was mildly skeptical, having seen Sahl's earlier dramatic outings, particularly *Playhouse 90*. "Oh, he's not the leading man type," Markle conceded. "He's no Rock Hudson, but he registers with tremendous strength. Like Yves Montand, and he reminds you of Yves. The seamy lines of his face burn out of the screen at you."

Mort was in Los Angeles shooting "Man in the Middle" when he was contacted by a man named Ernie Anderson, whom he knew as John Huston's press agent. At various times Enrico Banducci had investors in the hungry i, and one of them was Huston, the celebrated director of *The Maltese Falcon* and *The African Queen*. Huston was in Reno, filming one of the decade's most anticipated productions, *The Misfits*, with Clark Gable, Marilyn Monroe, and Montgomery Clift, and August 5, 1960, would be his fifty-fourth birthday. Anderson was assembling a surprise party and wanted Mort Sahl to take part in the evening's entertainment.

The *Misfits* company was headquartered at Reno's Mapes Hotel, and Anderson had enlisted manager Walter Ramage's help in pulling the event together. Ramage offered the hotel's Fable Room for the party and put Anderson in touch with a ninety-five-year-old Paiute chief who would make tribal members of the guests of honor. (August 7 would be Mrs. Gable's birthday.) The event got out of hand when friends and acquaintances of the Mapes family showed up and filled the room, leaving precious little space for the cast and crew of Huston's picture.

Huston entered at eight-thirty and was appropriately flabbergasted when the entire assemblage yelled, "Happy birthday!" He was, says Mort, "so drunk he didn't even know I was there." Both he and Kay Gable were inducted into the tribe, and Huston's Paiute handle became Long Shadow. Later, Long Shadow tried introducing Mort to Marilyn Monroe, unaware that Mort had known her for years, and, in a haze, Monroe didn't seem to recognize him. She took his hand and, in an apparent gesture of greeting, put it on her breast.

"Don't be afraid, Mr. Sahl," she said.

"I'm not afraid."

"How wrong you are. We're all afraid."

Despite the free-flowing liquor, it wasn't an easy crowd to engage. Mort did a variation of the routine he did for the Oscar telecast, but couldn't get a grin out of Monroe's husband, playwright Arthur Miller, the author of Huston's screenplay. Montgomery Clift, he observed, was in a haze too. Clark Gable, a notorious drinker, was on the wagon that night. "He went upstairs, came down in a suit, had an obligatory 'Good evening,' and went back upstairs with his wife. No hell-raising. Clift stayed there until he dropped."

The story in *Time* hit with the August 15 issue, Sahl rendered on the cover in muted colors with a long needle held aloft, surrounded by balloons bearing deft caricatures of his frequent targets—Ike, Johnson, Kennedy, Nixon, Stevenson. Inside, the coverage (titled "The Third Campaign") began on page 42, accompanied by a photo of the subject on stage at Mister Kelly's, hands in motion, a thought issuing forth, a standing room crowd paying rapt attention. There were numerous researchers on the job, Mort remembers. "It was like taking an exam for the CIA." The resulting profile, written by contributing editor John McPhee, didn't allege nihilism and specifically absolved him of the "sick comedian" label the magazine had so eagerly saddled him with in earlier days. Instead, he was portrayed as a sharp-witted rabble rouser in the best tradition of the topical satirist.

Historian Arthur Schlesinger was quoted as describing "a mounting restlessness and discontent, an impatience with clichés and platitudes, a resentment against the materialist notion that affluence is the answer to everything, a contempt for banality and corn—in short, a revolt against pomposity. Sahl's popularity is a sign of a yearning for youth, irreverence, trenchancy, satire, a clean break with the past." Then came testimonials from some of the walking wounded. "Wherever there is political bloat," said Hubert Humphrey, playing off the cover art, "Mort sticks a pin in it." Adlai Stevenson was portrayed as fiercely admiring: "I dote on him." Senator Kennedy, when similarly queried, spoke of his "relentless pursuit." Of whom? he was asked. "Of everybody!" he responded.

"He does not tell jokes one by one," McPhee wrote, "but carefully builds deceptively miscellaneous structures of jokes that are like verbal mobiles.

He begins with the spine of a subject, then hooks thought onto thought; joke onto dangling joke, many of them totally unrelated to the main theme, till the whole structure spins but somehow balances. All the time he is building toward a final statement, which is too much part of the whole to be called a punch line, but puts that particular theme away forever."

Mort's lifestyle was expressed in terms of quantities. His rented home on Miller Drive in Beverly Hills was stocked with fourteen radios, four television sets, two hi-fis, eleven electric razors. In the driveway and garage were three cars. On his wrist, on a single band, he wore two "monstrous, oyster-shaped gold watches worth $610 apiece." At one time, it was noted, he owned forty watches—which were sometimes strewn carelessly about the house.* "A friend, visiting him one day, picked up a magazine and out fell a $300 chronometer."

Gradually, a portrait of the artist as idealist emerged. "If I criticize somebody," he is quoted as saying toward the end of the piece, "it's only because I have higher hopes for the world, something good to replace the bad." High hopes in a bad world, McPhee suggested, are invariably good for a laugh. "Nobody here is proud of our times, although you hear a lot about our way of life," Sahl pointed out. "I'm not saying what the Beat Generation says: 'Go away because I'm not involved.' I'm here and I'm involved."

Sahl's four-week run at Mister Kelly's in August 1960 marked his return to Rush Street following a year's absence. In the interim, Hugh Hefner had abandoned the bedroom behind his *Playboy* office and purchased a brick and limestone residence on North State Parkway that he dubbed the Playboy Mansion. With the addition of the house next door, Hefner had seventy rooms at his disposal, eventually adding an underground pool, cabana bar, and a full-scale bowling alley complete with automatic pin spotter. As a showcase for the Playboy lifestyle, it became a stopover for celebrities visiting town or passing through on the way between coasts. "Hefner's house in Chicago was like a cocoon," Mort says. "I'd get off in the snow, and he had a chauffeur there and the Mercedes. He'd take me to the house, and I'd go up to my room. He had everything in there—a robe and toothpaste and razors. You could come down and eat in the dining room, or you could stay upstairs. They'd duplicate everything in the room. I wouldn't miss a beat, and I'd be off to Mister Kelly's."

In Chicago, the *Time* cover story was on newsstands citywide. Better balanced than the *New Yorker* profile, if not quite as probing, Mort nonetheless

---

* "I like to spend money on cars and watches because they don't have the imperfections of people," he once said.

took to referring to the venerable Luce publication as *Snide, the weekly news-magazine.* "I respect their function," he qualified, "which is, first, to elect Nixon and, second, to inform the public." Fresh from the conventions, he devoted fully thirty of his fifty minutes on stage to the newly minted Democratic and Republican nominees. "Some people claim Nixon is trying to sell the country, and Kennedy is trying to buy it. At the Los Angeles convention I had a hunch about how things were going right from the start when the minister delivered the invocation and said, 'A little child shall lead them.' You know, Kennedy had to have Lyndon Johnson on the ticket with him because he can't get into Washington without an adult. And Nixon picked [UN Ambassador Henry Cabot] Lodge [as his running mate] because conservative Republicans approve of anyone getting out of the United Nations. Right? Right!" He found time for Fidel Castro, Huntley-Brinkley, the Newport Jazz Festival, network television, drug manufacturers, and capital punishment. Still, it all came back around to politics, the three-month race for the White House now at full tilt. "It's all over but the doubting," he concluded. "My considered opinion of Nixon versus Kennedy is that neither can win."

Adlai Stevenson caught the act more than a dozen times while Mort was in residence at Mister Kelly's. He was the best of audiences, says Mort. "He understood everything in the margins." Mort also paid a visit to Stevenson's seventy-acre estate at Libertyville, admiring the Art Deco mansion Stevenson constructed on the property in 1938. "He doesn't stand on ceremony or have any protocol," he said of his host, "and yet the dignity is indigenous. Only trouble is he's so charming he usually steals your girl."

From the Letters page of *Time* magazine:

Sir:
Congratulations and all that jazz to TIME on a real gasser of a story on that chick-loving weirdo I dig, that bug Mort Sahl. "Wild, huh?"
ROBERTA THALER Reseda, Calif.

Sir:
Sahl is the embodiment of the cynicism, moral decay, and retreat from responsibility which currently infect this great land.
TIM TERRY San Marino, Calif.

Back in San Francisco, Sahl was set to tape an appearance at the hungry i for an Ed Sullivan special, the first of a once-monthly series called *See America with*

Ed Sullivan. At various locations, Sullivan and his crew were recording guests who had connections to the town—Johnny Mathis, Dave Brubeck, Dorothy Kirsten, the San Francisco Ballet. Putting Mort on stage at the "i" would give the show its quintessential North Beach moment, given that visitors had long since chased all the genuine color from the scene. "The Chamber of Commerce ought to put out a pamphlet on the beatniks," said Henri Lenoir, proprietor of the Columbus Avenue saloon Vesuvio. "They've brought more tourists to this city than Fisherman's Wharf or Chinatown." Lenoir was doing his part by displaying Hubert "Rube the Cube" Leslie in a window seat. "I give Hubert two hits to sit in the window so I'll have a beatnik to show tourists."

The night of the taping, Mort and Herb Caen were joined for dinner at Enrico Banducci's apartment by a delegation from the *Misfits* company, then they all drifted over to the "i" to watch Sullivan record a performance by a lively new folk act called the Limeliters. John Huston put on a waiter's jacket and walked on camera during the introductions to offer Sullivan a glassful of cocktail cherries. "The club seems to be a political science classroom where drinks are served," UPI's Fred Danzig wrote. "Sahl got off a couple of speedy, iron-clad lines of irreverence about our presidential candidates. While the entire routine seemed heavier, more forced and less incisive than usual, it was a treat seeing him operate in his so-called native habitat."

On the heels of his triumph in Chicago, Sahl uncharacteristically decided he needed a week's vacation. Rather than taking off for Palm Springs or Las Vegas, he chose instead a destination that guaranteed minimal relaxation and maximum aggravation. "It was just whimsical insanity," he admits. Returning briefly to Los Angeles, he made arrangements to visit Russia, his ancestral home, to see, as he put it, "how the other seven-eighths live." Accompanying him on the trip would be Patricia Manley, thirty-one, a strikingly beautiful blonde who worked as a designer in the wardrobe department at NBC.

The couple flew to Moscow on October 1, and immediately encountered trouble. "I landed at What-Do-You-Call-Him Airport, named after the guy who invented airports, and an hour later I was in the Hotel Berlin with nobody but a lot of Red Chinese technicians. Fantastic. If you tried to call out on the telephone, the guy from Intourist would come in and say, 'Who are you calling?'"

John Chancellor had just been posted to Moscow and was still getting used to the place. "He used to have to fly to Denmark to buy butter," Mort recalls. There was no phone book, and when he asked for Chancellor by name, they demanded, "Why do you want to talk to an American journalist?" Intourist always seemed to be absent whenever he wanted to change money, ask questions, or talk to someone. "He was very eager to show me Lenin's tomb, a collective farm, and the ballet."

The hotel was decidedly downmarket. "It was deadly. It looked like [San Francisco's seedy] Mission Street." The room itself was tiny and cell-like, with a bare light bulb dangling from a wire and a single chair standing in the corner. The mattress was stuffed with straw. "I went down to the coffee shop and said, 'Can I get some scrambled eggs?' They had an apparatchik traveling with me, and he said, 'Hasn't your great god Eisenhower developed something more advanced than a prosaic egg?' I said, 'Don't start with me—I've got more on him than you have.' Unbelievable!" When Mort and Pat went out to eat, they saw "a lot of people on the streets because the rooms in the apartment buildings are so small. The people I did meet looked like they were scared to talk to you or looked blank. No humor." He did find some minimal reminders of life in the U.S. "I mentioned *Time* magazine and they glowered at me—just like at home." And for kicks, he said, he tried tipping: "It worked."

One day of the place was enough, but it took another twenty-four hours for the couple to reclaim their passports and arrange a flight. "The KLM guy got me a ticket out of there," Mort says. "I went to Holland, and I went to Paris. Screwed around, and came back." In Copenhagen, he told a wire correspondent he had ended his visit to Russia "because I couldn't stand the leveling of a whole people." The Soviet state, he said, left them no privacy. "It reminded me of George Orwell's 1984 society, really frightening. I can use a lot of this in my show, but I'm afraid most of it will be on the same line as Bob Hope's recent crack about his TV set in Russia—it watched him." The man advised him that he'd probably never be allowed back into the USSR once his comments got out.

Mort's response: "Promise?"

In February 1960, a bulletin from the William Morris Agency announced that Mort Sahl, "the sweater-garbed satirical comedian," would embark on a concert tour that fall, his first ever. "Sahl will be available to local auspices in October and November in a two-hour program which will feature another well-known act in addition to his inspired monologues." Inquiries were directed to the agency's Concert and Special Attractions Division, where a string of twenty-seven one-nighters was eventually assembled. All the engagements, apart from the first, would be for a specified guarantee against a percentage of the house. Depending on the venue, the guarantee would range from

$2,500 to $3,500, the percentage from 55 to 60 percent. In the aggregate, Mort stood to clear slightly more than $100,000 for a month's work.

The tour got under way October 11 in a 4,800-seat auditorium on the campus of the University of Minnesota. (Many of the stops were in college towns—Lansing, Ann Arbor, Berkeley, Princeton.) To open the show, the Morris office enlisted the Limeliters, who delivered fifty minutes of standards and obscurities, with an assortment of French, Yiddish, and Russian tunes rounding out the set. Sahl took the second half of the evening, sticking principally to politics with the election now less than a month away. He ended the performance on an upbeat note: "Pretty soon we won't have to be holding these meetings in secret anymore."

At a top of $3.50, the gate amounted to $11,782 that first evening—a near sellout. Combined with the next four stops (Baltimore, Washington, Princeton, Philadelphia) the Sahl tour grossed more than $45,000 in its first five days alone. Hardly content with doing just one show a night, he took to jetting around the country in his off hours, emceeing fundraisers, generally with Adlai Stevenson. "One day I did a breakfast with the Democrats, with Stevenson, I flew to Chicago and did a show, and then I flew out to Seattle and did a show that night. Just unbelievable. I flew to Minneapolis on charter to do a rally for Kennedy with Myrna Loy. All the ladies liked Stevenson—Betty Bacall, Mercedes McCambridge."

At New York's Morosco Theater, he and Stevenson headed an all-star rally with host Melvyn Douglas just hours before Douglas would be back on stage in *The Best Man*. Their supporting players that afternoon included Bacall, Loy, Henry Fonda, Tom Bosley, Anne Bancroft, Jason Robards Jr., Tallulah Bankhead, James Thurber, and Orson Bean. Douglas began by introducing all the personalities seated on stage, then brought on "the man who calls himself the next president of the United States." Sahl said news of President Eisenhower out on the campaign trail had left him depressed: "After a clear record of eight years, I hate to see him involved in politics." He was a hit with the partisan crowd, but nothing compared to Stevenson, who got the day's biggest ovation and nearly as many laughs.

The tour rolled on: Cincinnati, Pittsburgh, Town Hall in New York City, where a second performance had to be added and folding chairs placed on stage to accommodate the overflow. The extraordinary demand led to a Thanksgiving weekend booking at Carnegie Hall, to which Mort promised to come with "new hostilities." In Washington, he held a news conference in which he touched briefly on his trip to Russia. "I traveled with a young lady," he said. "If you take a guy with you, they think you're defecting." In Detroit, he emphasized that it wasn't Kennedy who "made the real rebuttal to Norman Vincent Peale and those Protestant ministers [objecting to the Senator's Catholicism]. It was Adlai Stevenson when he was in St. Paul. Adlai said he found St. Paul appealing and Peale appalling." Then he added: "These can't be the original candidates—they must be the road company."

The stop at Seattle's Orpheum Theatre was sold out, as was Portland's Paramount and the Santa Monica Civic Auditorium, the new home of the Academy Awards. The first eleven concerts brought in $91,173, and with seventeen more yet to be tabulated it was estimated the entire tour would gross between $225,000 and $250,000. He laid off the night of the election, November 8, 1960, figuring it would be too difficult to garner an audience, and told Army Archerd he longed to star in an updated version of *Mr. Smith Goes to Washington*. "I want to do it so badly I can taste it," he said.

That night, Mort threw a party at his house on Miller Drive. The invitation list, he claimed, was carefully divided between Democrats and Republicans. Half the living room was decorated with Kennedy posters while the other half festooned with Nixon banners, and crying towels labeled KENNEDY and NIXON were on display and available for use. TV sets tuned to network coverage were placed in every room. Among the nearly two hundred "friends, Republicans, and Democrats" accepting his nonpartisan hospitality were Shirley MacLaine and husband Steve Parker, John Huston, Natalie Wood and Robert Wagner, Joan Collins and Warren Beatty. It was a long night; Kennedy's razor-thin victory wasn't assured until dawn, long after the last of the guests had struggled home.

Sahl's final tour dates gave him room to comment on the election results, telling a Berkeley audience that, in the end, he liked Kennedy's imitation of Roosevelt better than Nixon's imitation of Eisenhower. "I identify with Kennedy—I couldn't prove myself to my father either." The outcome was so close, he said, it was ridiculous. "It doesn't seem that we've made up our minds as a nation. Every time Kennedy walks down the street now and meets a couple, he knows that one of them doesn't like him."

The Berkeley appearance at the 3,500-seat Community Theater, coming one night before the official wrap-up at San Francisco's Masonic Auditorium, was a homecoming of sorts, Mort recalling his aimless days in the local coffee houses before auditioning at the hungry i. "I think we're approaching new frontiers when an audience as big as this will hold its attention span this long," he concluded at the end of his seventy-minute set. "I have a message for the Democrats. I hope you all get jobs. And for the Republicans, there'll be another meeting downstairs after the show."

The *Thriller* episode "Man in the Middle" aired on December 20, 1960, opposite *The Tom Ewell Show* and a new ABC series called *Stagecoach West*. As directed by Fletcher Markle, Sahl's measured performance, playing to his stage cadences if not his intensities, wasn't to all tastes. While fans generally liked what they saw, others sensed minimal range and a general lack of experience. Marlon Brando, with whom he took long walks in the Hollywood Hills, seemed only to notice the things he didn't like. Mort says, "When I tried to be naturalistic, scratch my hand or something, he'd say, 'Please don't do that. It's so unattractive.'"

The AP's Cynthia Lowry thought the episode miscast: "Mort Sahl has a prickly and rather remote personality even when he's being an actor instead of a comedian." Dwight Newton's verdict came in the December 22 issue of the *San Francisco Examiner*: "From his first dramatic role in this week's *The Thriller* [sic], Mort Sahl can go no place but up. Oh, he looked the part of the tormented writer caught in the web of a kidnapping plot, but he had great difficulty reading lines. His untrained voice couldn't shake loose the monotone of his nightclub routines. In some of the most desperately tense scenes he could have been reciting the alphabet backwards for all the emotion he conveyed. But don't sell Sahl short in the drama department. His manner is hypnotic, his appearance is electrifying, his serious seamy face compels attention. All he needs is acting mileage, and lots of it."

The election of John F. Kennedy came at a time of great uncertainty in the nightclub business. The talent shortage was acute, the *Los Angeles Times'* nightlife editor, John L. Scott, acknowledging a commercial scene that had always been driven by big names. "Unfortunately," he wrote, "as far as the larger local supper clubs, where the overhead is astronomical, are concerned, there are only about a dozen 'names' who can assure an owner a profit for an average engagement." In comparison to the Las Vegas model, where dinner and an hour of star talent served as loss leaders for the gaming tables and slot machines, big city clubs had to make their nut on $7 minimums and $1.25 highballs, and often depended on expense account business to keep the doors open.

Dave Brubeck still played the clubs, and was a potent draw when correctly handled, but he distinguished between good club owners and bad. A good owner, he said, always had a good piano in tune, controlled drunks, noisy air conditioning, and "tip-happy" waiters and waitresses. Still, Shelley Berman and the ascendant Bob Newhart were abandoning the clubs because of hecklers and the random noises of bar service that upset the precision of their acts. Mort twitted them for it, saying that he liked nightclubs and thought they were getting a bum rap. "Bob should remember that without Mike and Elaine, Shelley, Jonathan, Orson, and myself opening doors, entertainers like himself would never have had a chance to get into the business. It was difficult at first, but once we had the people putting their drink down and listening, we had an audience—an audience that is increasing every day." As for the "noisy drunks" Newhart specifically complained about, Mort took note of the watered-down drinks typically served in clubs. "I've played nightclubs for seven years, and with the price and size of drinks I don't know how anybody can get drunk unless they were loaded when they came in."

Yet, Mort, too, was sensing the urgency in moving on, and he admitted to the *New York Times* that he had taken the *Thriller* assignment expressly because he was "very anxious" to expand his career beyond the nightclub circuit. The November 27 issue of *American Weekly* devoted itself entirely to "The Changing Face of Show Business," and while Sahl was prominently pictured representing nightclubs, there was no supporting text for the category, movies and television and even classical music taking up the space instead. Back were the same familiar figures—Ethel Merman, Mary Martin, Bing Crosby, Dean Martin, Fred Astaire. In a Q&A at the outset, Jackie Gleason, then appearing in the hit Broadway musical *Take Me Along*, was invited to pontificate on matters of pay television, talk radio, and the evolving role of advertisers in the arts. Gleason was asked if he thought "the Mort Sahl-type comic" would take over the nightclub business. "No," he answered, "for the same reason I think so-called controversial and spectacular pictures will fade. These straight-talk-type comedians depend on shock value for their laughs. But people get used to absorbing shocks pretty fast. Personally, I think they aren't comedians at all. I also can't think of anything more unsatisfying than trying to be intelligent in a nightclub. What's the point of talking politics and sociology to a bunch of drunks?"

The November 1960 release of *The Next President*, Mort Sahl's final LP for Verve, neatly coincided with Norman Granz's sale of the company to M-G-M for $2.5 million. ("He sold his company for $1 million," Mort said, fudging the details, "and 35 cents good will.") His first four albums had cumulatively sold 125,000 units, making him one of the label's few profitable recording artists, but still something of a cult figure compared to Shelley Berman, whose populist angst had moved nearly 1,000,000 copies of his three releases. And where the category was Spoken Word when *The Future Lies Ahead* appeared in 1958, records from Sahl, Berman, Dave Gardner, Jonathan Winters, Bob Newhart, and Dayton Allen, among others, were now being grouped and binned under Comedy.

Berman would remain with Verve, but Sahl's availability made him a welcome addition to the talent roster at Frank Sinatra's new label, Reprise. Scrambling to get a topical album on the new Kennedy administration into stores as one of its initial releases, the company arranged for its engineers to record Mort's April 17, 1961, opening at the hungry i, where business had gone soft and where he would play a month at deep discount to help get Enrico Banducci back on his feet. By now, the "i" had reached its physical maturity, a descent down a steep flight of stairs landing customers in a narrow room dominated by Banducci's hand-tooled bar. On a wall opposite the bar was a sign: WE ARE ALL HUNGRY FOR LOVE, BREAD, KNOWLEDGE, PEACE, ETC. (which, said Banducci, pretty much "explains the joint"). Beneath the sign were framed photos of Mort, Shelley Berman, Bob Newhart, the Limeliters, the Gateway Singers, Stan Wilson, and the Kingston Trio. To the left of the bar was a space honoring the intent of the original hungry i, with tables suitable for sandwiches and coffee and lively discussions. To the right was the Other Room, a discreet upscale restaurant. Between the two was the low-ceilinged showroom with the $2.50 cover charge and the canvas chairs with the single wide arms on which to balance drinks—and a small hustling army of Japanese waiters ready to bring them.

Sahl's appearance was like the return of a favorite son, and Banducci arranged a news conference to welcome him back. Scheduled to arrive at noon, Mort swore he hadn't been told when he ambled into Enrico's Cafe, the hungry i's sister establishment, a couple of hours late, a dozen or so of the city's press corps having been serenaded in the interim by the proprietor's violin solos. Conservatively attired in a gray suit, he laid down an extemporaneous statement of principles regarding the new team in Washington. "Intellectuals are now socially acceptable," he announced. "I'm interested in the Administration, not in the cuisine at the White House or the social side of Jackie Kennedy. And I wouldn't pay any attention to Caroline even if an eagle absconded with her on the White House lawn." When asked about the challenge of the new versus the old, he replied: "You have to work with what you have. Nixon means nothing anymore and neither does Eisenhower. People identify with the winner, and I think half the country has already forgotten that they voted for Nixon. But things still need to be said, and guts are required on several levels. I'm no oracle, though. I'm feeling my way just like you."

He opened at the "i" a few days later, thanking the audience for coming out on Academy Awards night and commenting on some of the non-winners in the categories already announced. Having recently played Florida, he brought up Castro and the CIA-sponsored invasion of Cuba that was to become known as the Bay of Pigs. "Our ambassador to the United Nations, Adlai Stevenson, categorically denied our participation in this invasion. He made a speech in the UN. And he said that Castro can look to our government for help 'if he has been rejected by his own people.'" He allowed the laughs to start bubbling up and then added, "Stevenson should know," the explosion covering his final words on the subject.

"Now. Where are we? Oh, yes. Stevenson. The official line of the party is that Stevenson never had it, but Kennedy has magic . . ." Which, eight minutes in, brought him to the topic on everyone's mind. "As you know, a few remarks have gotten into the press about what I've said about the New Frontier. And a lot of people haven't known what to make of me. The Democrats, as a matter of fact, feel completely misled by me, because I used to criticize President Eisenhower and Richard Nixon, and now I'm saying a few words about President Kennedy and his administration. And the Democrats feel that they were misled. I misled them. I could say the same thing, but I won't tonight." He laughed his quick, nervous laugh as punctuation, the audience joining in.

> I'm being facetious. But Democrats didn't know what to make of me because, initially, I was kidding about President Eisenhower. And then I kind of kidded Nixon for seven-and-a-half years, which is approximately seven years and two months longer than Kennedy kidded him. But that doesn't matter. After the election, I immediately, you know, was going ahead with the material. And I'd be up on the stage at various clubs—whether it was Basin Street in New York or the Crescendo in Hollywood or the Fontainebleau in Miami—I'd get up and say the same thing.
>
> Actually, I thought Kennedy was going to lose. I had a lot of jokes ready about his father coming out the next day in disenchantment and

saying, "What's happened to our values? Does money mean nothing?" That's what I was working on. So I did all these jokes. Now the Democrats are coming backstage. They come back in committee because they're really the ruling party now. And they come backstage and they say to me, "You just criticized President Kennedy." And I'd say, "Yeah, that's right, that was me." And then they'd say, "We're appalled. We thought this was what you wanted." And I'd be forced to say, "You didn't have to do it for *me*."

He made note of Robert Kennedy's appointment as Attorney General ("Little Brother is watching you"), talked quite a bit about television and guesting on *Jackpot Bowling* (to where NBC had exiled Milton Berle), and got into a debate with Steve Allen on *The Nation's Future* over whether there were any taboos for comedians. ("Yes, there are taboos, but we're not allowed to discuss them.") Flying to Florida led to a lengthy discussion of stewardesses and how the relationship between passenger and server deteriorates over five hours "like a microcosm of a bad marriage." Then he was off on Timex watches, David Susskind, and network censorship under the new administration.

I had hoped all that nonsense had ended with Eisenhower. Now we're in this period of reverence again. And it's a question of where you can go with it, because the press is on a honeymoon with this administration. I even find Republicans saying, "I'm pretty happy with the way it worked out." That'll give you pause for thought if you're on the Democratic council. We have this pyramid now, and, as I say, you've had an influx of intellectuals here. And before you would kid the New Frontier you would have to scrutinize it, you'd have to examine who the president has appointed, and you'd find, for instance, Edward R. Murrow as a good example. He's head of the United States Information Agency. He recently said that he would like the president, as a propaganda weapon for the Russians, to drop copies of *Life* magazine on the Russians. Now you know they don't get *Life* or *Time*, see? This goes along with their claim that they are ahead of us in certain areas . . .

He doesn't want to take every edition, he wants to take the inauguration edition. Have you seen that edition? It's exciting. It was all gold, and it was fifty cents, and they happened to have some left over. They want to drop these on the Russians—not in stacks but separately, of course. That can all be worked out if Congress approves. So, of course, Fulbright and a lot of those guys started asking about it, what would happen with it. Now, first of all, can the Russians read the captions? Well, Murrow held that they wouldn't have to. They'd see an inauguration and they'd know what happens with democracy because it's obvious enough. And there are some great pictures in the issue, if you will recall. There's a picture of the president with his father, who he was recently reunited with, as you recall. Remember he was gone for a long time? And they're riding together in the car. That's where Miss [Louella] Parsons had said that the president looked like a movie star—Judge Hardy and Andy. . . . Did you read that? She said that Kennedy's handsome enough to be a movie star. He can retire at fifty-one and go into pictures. Of course, we could go on all night if we started speculating on what producers would handle him. Hitchcock! He could work for Hitchcock. *North by Northwest* with John Kennedy being pursued across Mount Rushmore, right? By the head of the House Rules Committee, right? With good shots of Kennedy climbing on his own face . . .

The queues at the "i" were up the stairs and out into the street for the first time in months, Sahl delivering a well-paced fifty-three minutes of topical satire that relied on neither Nixon nor Eisenhower as targets. "Something new and old was added to the hungry i recently," Herb Caen reported in his column. "The new: A turnaway crowd, with hopefuls lined up ten deep. The old: Mort Sahl, back in his red-bricked cave and licking his familiar wounds in public—a more incisive and sharper-edged commentator than ever." Mort was preceded on stage by a black gospel group called the Grandisons and Anita Shear, a flamenco singer, but the drawing power was all his, and it was clear by the end of his first week that he would leave Enrico Banducci and the hungry i on solid footing upon his exit in May.

It was a measure of Reprise's eagerness to get the new Mort Sahl album into stores that retail ads for it began appearing before it had even been recorded. The plan was to drop the first six Reprise albums as a group, Sinatra's *Ring-a-Ding Ding!* accompanying initial entries from Sammy Davis Jr., Mavis Rivers, Joe E. Lewis, and Ben Webster. But *The New Frontier* couldn't be cut and mastered quickly enough, and the other five went out ahead of *New Frontier*'s May 1 release date. The emergence of a major new label brought strong press attention, making *The New Frontier* the most widely

reviewed of all the Sahl LPs. But with an avalanche of new recordings hitting the stores, the market for comedy albums was softening, and those
expecting Mort Sahl to go easy on the charismatic Kennedys began looking
elsewhere for political commentary.

"Welcome to the monthly Mort Sahl opening," was the way he began his
first set at the Crescendo on May 22, 1961. It was a tacit acknowledgment of
the treadmill he was on, and for the first time in recent memory the room
wasn't filled to capacity. The material wasn't quite as fresh, Sahl working
the same Kennedy lines he had used at the hungry i and, subsequently, on
The New Frontier. Highlighting the jokes he would have used had Kennedy
lost the election only served to underscore the trouble he had skewering
an administration that was scarcely four months old. Suddenly, nobody
wanted to hear how young the new president was, or how much his father
may have spent to get him elected. It was a new world for a comedian who
had come to regard club patrons as the bedrock of his audience, and now,
suddenly, they seemed to be slipping away.

He was also facing new competition, new comedic figures who were starting to draw serious attention. The same night as his Crescendo opening,
Phyllis Diller made her Los Angeles debut at the neighboring Cloister, having established herself at San Francisco's Purple Onion and through some
thirty appearances with Jack Paar. The Onion also served as incubator for
the Smothers Brothers, who had made their first appearance with Paar in
January. Over at the hungry i, a chain-smoking black comic named Dick
Gregory was shaking up the topical humor category, playing on the absur-
dities of racial prejudice. "I sat in a restaurant for nine months," went one
of his choice lines. "When they finally integrated, they didn't have what I
wanted." Having worked a lot of third-rate places, Gregory had landed a last-
minute booking at Chicago's Playboy Club only four months earlier. "They
call me the Negro Mort Sahl," he liked to say. "In the Congo they call Sahl
the white Dick Gregory." Then the "i" had a guy named Harrison Baker, who
billed himself as "The Last of the Well Comedians." While Baker positioned
himself as the anti-Sahl, doing mildly topical stuff in the un-edgy spirit of
Bob Hope, he freely existed in Mort's shadow, another comic who walked
through the door Sahl so decisively kicked down.

"Mort was the forerunner of all these people," Enrico Banducci said.
"They all wanted to be another Mort Sahl."

8

I'M STILL IN BUSINESS

Mort Sahl's June 5, 1961, opening at Basin Street East brought fresh scrutiny from a public eager to see how he handled a Democratic president after seven years of savaging Republicans. "Of course I attack Kennedy," he said indignantly when Arthur Gelb raised the issue in a review for the *New York Times*. "I resent the idolatry. What's happened to the two-party system? Why are we suddenly so united? I feel evangelism is needed in all areas." To Gelb, however, Sahl didn't appear to enjoy Kennedy as a target the way he did Eisenhower. "He sometimes seems to have trouble eking out his Kennedy material with nonpolitical quips about Jacqueline Kennedy's interest in clothes and about the size of the Kennedy family: 'There was a rumor that the Cubans were going to assassinate the Kennedys—if they had enough ammunition.'"

A few days later, after appearances with Ed Sullivan and as a mystery guest on *What's My Line?* Mort used John Crosby's column in the *New York Herald Tribune* to announce his retirement from television. "I don't like doing TV," he said sourly. "It's killed the enthusiasm of the performers." *Newsweek* picked up on his comments and ran its own interview in the June 26 issue. "It isn't television to come on every six months and do the stuff you've been doing in clubs," he elaborated. "I feel the [Sullivan] show is going in one direction with the dog acts and stuff. Then Sahl comes on. It's like asking the audience to turn around and go in a completely different direction. You're rushed. You're reciting. The show doesn't grow naturally. We're not doing any more of that kind of television." Then, as if on cue, the phone rang and within two minutes he had agreed to do a one-hour special for the BBC in July. "But in the U.S.," the *Newsweek* item concluded, "the most articulate and satiric single voice in the land will be given a reasonable hearing only in saloons."

The BBC special was promoted by a young Canadian actress turned producer named Helen Winston, who was in England to set up a feature film based on Hugh Lofting's Doctor Dolittle books. Sahl agreed to a fee of $8,400 and expenses, installing himself at the Dorchester and taking a week to acquaint himself with London before recording the show at BBC Television Centre on July 16. His trip, which took on, in some respects, the appearance of a state visit, began with a press conference before thirty TV and drama critics, Kenneth Tynan positioning himself on the floor at his feet. In subsequent days he was reported shopping ($25 for a Mont Blanc pen, $5,000 for an E-type Jaguar), admiring the new American embassy in Grosvenor Square, and visiting the House of Commons as a guest of the British humor magazine *Punch*. "I'm very impressed," he commented. "It's just like Congress—not many people there and most of them asleep."

The studio held an invited audience that included Peter Sellers and the notorious Conservative peer Lord Boothby. Introduced as the next Secretary-General of the United Nations, Sahl, who had been warned not to make any cracks about the royal family, tried approaching American subjects from a British viewpoint. On Joseph P. Kennedy: "You may recall he was in the embassy here in charge of Edward R. Murrow." (The audience, remembering the ambassador's prediction that Hitler would win the war, booed his name.) On compact British automobiles: "Our cars are different. You know, clocks up front and in back—different time zones." On Soviet-American relations: "Our dogs are affectionate and can fetch newspapers. Russian dogs don't show affection, but they are all engineers." He claimed that he once taught college math, telling how he distinguished between the exact and inexact sciences: "I drew a woman on a couch, and I explained to the class that in mathematics you moved across the couch and got the girl. In philosophy you never reached her. And in psychology you discovered she wasn't the right girl for you anyway." Sometimes, the hand-picked audience could be heard laughing when they shouldn't have been. "The studio theatre claque, who must have palms like champion Rugby fives players, made such a row at the wrong moments that I missed some of the satirist's throwaway lines," complained the *Observer*'s Maurice Richardson.

Filled out with singing star Georgia Brown, the Leo Kharibian Dancers, and the Johnny Dankworth Orchestra, *The Mort Sahl Show*, despite the fact it was essentially American in tone and outlook, was, on the whole, a more successful showcase for its star than *The Future Lies Ahead*. It was transmitted on July 19, 1961, to a reaction that was decidedly mixed. *The Daily Mail* reported "a small number" of viewer calls to the BBC, most of them complaints. "He was effective enough on this first hearing to make us realize how timidly our own sacred white elephants are treated. . . . There could be room here for just one Mort Sahl." But, the tabloid admitted, he "turned out to be less funny and less biting than his build-up promised."

Sue Cardozo, Frank Sinatra's press agent, had been given the job of guiding Mort through his stint at the BBC. According to her, he and actress Joan Collins, in town to film *The Road to Hong Kong*, had an affair "in no time flat." ("That was me bouncing off the walls," he says today.) It was all over by the time he left for Paris, but not before he had arranged for Collins' face to grace the cover of his new LP for Reprise, which carried the working title *Mort Sahl on Relationships*. It was a striking concept, considering that he was about to be dragged through the pages of the nation's papers over one particular relationship he thought was over.

For a guy who was twenty-seven before he could afford to take a girl to dinner, Mort Sahl was a quick study, learning the way of things in a business where friendships were transitory and sex a commodity to be bartered or sold. "Sinatra used to show movies at the house," he recalls. "Nobody had prints then. He'd call anybody; he'd call [filmmakers William] Perlberg and [George] Seaton for stuff. I'd leave the Morris Office—I had an office there. I'd leave there about six-thirty and I'd go up to Ira Gershwin's. Judy [Garland] would be there, and Frank, and Fred Astaire. Oscar Levant when he was hanging around. George Axelrod. Jack Lemmon. Anyway, I went up to Sinatra's house one night, and I took Dyan Cannon. And he took one look at her, and he homed in on her. And then I saw someone call him into the hall. It was Hank Sanicola, who was, theoretically, his manager, but really what he was was the guy who collected the money at Caesar's Palace—he just wasn't his manager. And he said to him, 'Frank, it's not nice to hit on your friend's date.' And he never even got an argument."

Apart from Cannon and Joan Collins, Mort was briefly linked in the columns with actress Nancy Olson, who was divorced from lyricist Alan Jay Lerner and living in Brentwood for the summer. The date was arranged by Bill Harbach, but Olson could tell from the outset that Mort was used to running with a faster crowd. "I found him absolutely fascinating and smart as he could be," she remembered, "but quite odd. You know, I'm a doctor's daughter from Milwaukee, Wisconsin. Need I say more? After a couple of nights' dinners with me, it was like: Oh, my god . . . No!" She laughed. "My nickname in college was 'Wholesome Olson.' Does Mort Sahl want anything to do with Wholesome Olson? Probably not."

They weren't all actresses. There was a beautiful Indian girl named Chilendra Jones, who worked as a receptionist at *Time*, and Rosita Valencia, who taught the cha-cha in Miami. The one who stirred up the trouble was Pat Manley, the costume designer who was Mort's traveling companion on his abortive trip to Russia, and again during his fall concert tour. "We were on this trip, just Mort and I," she said. "We had discussed marriage, and were going to get married when I found out I was going to have a baby. We didn't get married because Mort felt these were not the right circumstances."

Manley, a photogenic widow with two young children, was working on the Steve Allen show when they met in 1960. Mort, she said, had given her money and had paid her hospital expenses. She was expecting support or a settlement of some kind when she decided to go public, retaining a lawyer and posing for pictures with the baby, who was born on July 5, 1961, and given the name Adam Matthew Sahl. "I filed this suit just to get everything cleared up and on the record," she told the press. According to the paperwork, she was seeking $1,035 in monthly support and legal fees of $25,000. Through a spokesman, Mort admitted affection for her ("She really moved me") but refused to concede the baby was actually his.

After articles appeared in the *Los Angeles Mirror* and the *Examiner*, the wire services picked up on the story, bringing it to the attention of *Time*, where it headed the magazine's "People" column on September 1. ("Asocial satirist Mort Sahl, a disciple of birth-control advocate Sir Julian Huxley . . . had a population problem of his own.") A hearing took place in Superior Court on October 4. "My own attitude is simply this, that there has been a child brought into this world, and I have reasonable doubts that this child is mine," he said in a prepared statement. He lamented the stigma "that unfortunately must flow from a proceeding of this kind" and stressed that if it was proved the baby was his, he would "like any father who is interested in the baby's welfare, do anything that will be compatible with his real interests."

But the suit was thrown out of court on the grounds that the mother had sued on her own behalf and not her son's. The judge gave her fifteen days to file again, insisting the boy's interests were more important than hers. She refiled two days later, generating more press and setting off a series of negotiations. When the case was quietly dropped from the court calendar in early November, terms of the settlement were not disclosed. It only came out much later that she had accepted a onetime payment of $35,000 in exchange for agreeing to relinquish the baby to the Children's Home Finding Society. Paternity was never firmly established, and Pat Manley dropped from sight, never to be heard from again.

Milt Ebbins had helped Mort find the Herbie Baker place on Miller Drive—Baker was a client—and when that lease ran out, Ebbins moved him to producer Arthur Loew Jr.'s house about a mile away, also on Miller. Mort liked living above Sunset, where he could peer down on the Crescendo and count the house. With the lease coming up on the Loew house, he began looking for yet another hilltop home to rent. Used to a 270-degree view of the world, he noticed a house under construction near the top of San Ysidro Drive, just steps from the western lip of Franklin Canyon. "You don't have to rent a house," his business manager told him. "You can buy it."

The three-bedroom, two-bathroom house, a rustic mid-century on a third of an acre, was completed in the spring of 1961. When Mort left town, he put a decorator named Phyllis Pinto in charge of furnishing it. "Bunkie Knudsen ran Pontiac," he remembers. "He made me a great convertible with a 421 V-8, and when I built my house, the decorator did the house and then I paid her by giving her that car. I'd never driven it, so it worked out pretty well. She did everything. I was in New York, and she did the whole house so that I could walk in and live in it. And it was wild—Japanese and very serene."

He had the place fitted with eleven speakers for his hi-fi system and had closed-circuit TV installed so that he could see who was at the front door. Actress Cloris Leachman saw the newly decorated house with her husband, director George Englund. "It looks like a set," she observed, "but there's no movie in it."

After a promising start, Mort Sahl's movie career was going nowhere. "It's a sick business," he said in 1959, seemingly bent on antagonizing the industry. "Actors can't produce pictures, but they're trying to. They're buying screen stories—largely western and war pictures—that they would take suspensions for if they were under contract. . . . The producers can't get a rage up at anything anymore. They came out here thirty years ago and insulated themselves in the San Fernando Valley. Everything they do is on film—little bits and pieces far removed from what life really is. They have no contact with real, live audiences. . . . Our government is worried about Fidel Castro's brother. I'm more worried about the relatives in the movie business."

Even before *All the Young Men* came along, he was thinking in terms of producing his own movies and selecting his own roles. "What would I do if I had $2 million to make a picture? I'd do a story about today—not in costume and not on the moon—about the problems of America, such as the relationship of men and women and how they are competing for domination. And I would make it with actors who can act, not some tired old movie star, a girl one-third his age and a bunch of TV actors in the background."

Late in 1959, when it was announced that Sahl had been added to the cast of *Ocean's Eleven,* he wired Frank Sinatra:

SCHWEITZER SAID BECAUSE OF NUCLEAR TESTS HE DIDN'T KNOW WHAT WAS GOING TO HAPPEN TO THE WORLD'S POPULATION. THAT'S EASY—THEY'RE ALL GONNA BE IN OCEAN'S ELEVEN.

Then director Lewis Milestone culled the script and Mort's part was eliminated.

Early in 1960, Jerry Wald announced that he would cast Sahl in *The Bohemians*, playing a French writer in love with an American girl studying in Paris. (Meade Roberts' screenplay, it was noted at the time, was suggested by Puccini's *La Boheme*.) Wald kept *The Bohemians* on his schedule for nearly two years, at one point adding Pat Boone to the cast, but eventually decided not to make the picture. Sensing a disconnect with established producers, Sahl formed Moraga, an independent production company, and began optioning properties. *Two Against Tomorrow* was the first, followed by an original backstage comedy called *We Sing, Tomorrow!* After declaring that he wanted to remake *Mr. Smith Goes to Washington*, there were exploratory talks with Columbia Pictures, which held the rights, but nothing came of them.* Eventually, Otto Preminger, whom he knew through Paul Newman, offered him a part in *Advise and Consent*, but it was only a cameo, one day's work playing himself. Preminger, it could be said, owed him one. Early in 1959, the producer-director wanted Duke Ellington to compose the score for *Anatomy of a Murder* but was too intimidated to ask him. Says Mort: "I made the call."

---

* Sahl's interest in the property may have inspired Columbia, through its Screen Gems subsidiary, to develop a *Mr. Smith* TV series for the 1962–63 season.

✧ ✧ ✧

As a harbinger of turbulence to come, Sahl dismissed the William Morris office, as well as his business manager, on the eve of his Crescendo opening on September 7, 1961. Unhappy they had set up another tour for him, virtually a carbon copy of the wildly successful one of the previous year, he was once again taking matters into his own hands, having now burned through the town's two biggest agencies, MCA and Morris. "I was the national hero," he complains, "and these guys didn't even want to represent me. And at that time they got fifteen percent of the concerts, Ebbins got ten, and the business manager got five. And I had to hire the press agents, Rogers and Cowan."

The club was SRO that night—Henry Fonda was turned away—but when Mort took the stage, he gazed out at the audience and saw Morris president Abe Lastfogel and his lieutenants seated ringside—a demonstration of just how difficult it would be to disentangle himself from the agency. With him on the bill was twenty-year-old Joanie Sommers, a powerful singer of pop standards and show tunes who had already recorded two albums for Warner Bros. and would be joining him on the new tour. ("No more folk singers on his tours," reported Army Archerd.) Subject matter ranged from the Kennedys to Castro, Adlai Stevenson, Senator Barry Goldwater ("Goldwater is Jewish and Episcopalian. That's what I like—somebody who's Jewish and does something about it"), science, satellites, integration, and sex. "Don't go into my personal life," he said, moving along. "I try to stay out of it."

Mort describes the tour that followed as "an invention of the Morris office, because they knew I had a big college audience." The touring company, comprised of Sahl, Sommers, the Lou Pagani Trio, and a road manager in the person of Milt Ebbins' brother Bernie, was set to cover thirty-six cities in forty-five frantic days. "It was a back-breaker," Mort says. "I was in a different town every night. Then the manager doesn't show up. He sends a hired hand to get the tickets and get the luggage. And it turns out to be kind of meaningless. It was an endless pot of money, but I thought they were going to work me to death."

Milt Ebbins was taking ads in college newspapers along the route, but the halls weren't filling as they had just a year earlier. There was also an unusual amount of attention focused on Joanie Sommers, whom Mort remembers as "a very family-oriented Catholic chick." A film crew from David L. Wolper's production company was following her around for a TV documentary called *Story of a Singer*, and her final performance on the tour, at Santa Monica Civic Auditorium on November 25, was to be recorded for a new Warner Bros. album called *The Two Sides of Joanie Sommers*. Mort, too, was being taped, by Reprise, after a September recording date at the Crescendo had fallen through. A malaise of fatigue settled in, and the mad rush between cities got to be a grind. He fell ill in Tucson after an appearance at the University of Arizona, and a stop in Phoenix was scrubbed on a day's notice.

The whole benighted enterprise limped into Southern California on November 24, and Sahl promptly found himself embroiled in a controversy with the musicians' union. He had always been proud of the fact that he worked entirely alone and traveled light. ("Mr. Sahl, why don't you use any Negroes in your act?" he said an activist once asked him.) So he made sure that Joanie Sommers, who opened the show with a set of six songs, was, along with manager Ted Wick, entirely responsible for her own backup musicians. And, for all previous stops on the tour, those musicians had been a trio assembled by pianist Lou Pagani. Now for the final two stops on the tour, Pagani was set to play a November 24 date at Pasadena Civic Auditorium. Following that, with Warner Bros. poised to record the show in Santa Monica, Wick was quietly planning to replace the Pagani trio with the fuller sound of a sextet assembled for the occasion by veteran studio arranger Bob Florence.

All this sounded innocent enough, but where AFM Local 47 was apparently willing to look the other way with a trio, a sextet came dangerously close to a double-cross, the arrangement flouting the union's longstanding requirement that a singer had be backed by at least twenty-one musicians in either hall. Word of the arrangement reached union ears just prior to showtime in Pasadena, and the performance was delayed as frantic negotiations took place backstage. Seeming slightly bewildered by the uproar, Mort went out and began reporting on the harangue to the sparse audience, unsure of what to say about it since he had played both venues with the Limeliters the previous year.* Pagani and his men were forbidden to work, and unable to hire another eighteen card-carriers on the spot, Sommers was forced to sit out the show, leaving Mort out on stage alone—overcompensating, he admitted—for a withering two hours and twenty minutes.

One marathon performance didn't diminish the prospect of another, and they went sailing into Saturday night's date in a stalemate—Sommers and her manager unable to afford the full band the AFM required, Mort

---

* While the Limeliters played their own instruments, Sommers wasn't a musician—just a chirp (in trade lingo) who fell subject to the rule.

maintaining hands off while justifiably angry that Wick had allowed the situation to get so completely out of hand. Saturday became a repeat of Friday's debacle, albeit before a larger audience, and with Sahl better prepared, laying into the union as he had more extemporaneously the previous night. Promoter John Moss, who was left out of the discussions, said he was aware of "some dispute" but acknowledged he wouldn't have covered the cost of the extra musicians in any event. The show, he estimated, grossed "around $2,500 at Pasadena and around $3,700 at Santa Monica. We lost money on each."

For his trouble in covering for Sommers on the nights she couldn't work, Sahl was threatened with blacklisting by AFM vice president Max Herman, who was angered by the anti-union cracks he made on stage in Pasadena, maintaining the barrage made the on-site musicians ill at ease. "He knocked hell out of us," Herman complained. Then Ted Wick, the instigator of all the trouble, asked MCA, which booked his client, to make a demand of Moraga Productions for the money owed her for the two performances she was forced to sit out, disingenuously maintaining that Sommers had a contract for the dates and venues and could not perform "through no fault of her own."

Spent, Mort gave a thoughtful interview to the *Los Angeles Examiner*'s Ted Thackrey in which he dismissed Wick and Local 47 and considered instead the lessons learned from earlier stops along the route—Bloomington, Salt Lake City, Kansas City, Peoria, Pittsburgh, Omaha—where topicality gave way to regionalism and a new set of political realities were taking form. "And it was kind of wild," he said.

> I mean, there we were doing our part to reverse the business slump for the airline companies—and all the time, I see by the papers, it was the auto industry that needed our help. Well, let me tell you, friend. That joke almost got me ridden out of Detroit on a rail.
>
> It's not just that people are touchy. I mean, that's not bad. So you kind of insult somebody in the audience and he begins to burn at you, but in a minute or so you've insulted somebody else he doesn't like, and it's okay, right? But sometimes you come up with something that gets no reaction at all. You begin to wonder if someone's called a practice air raid alert and they've forgotten to let you in on it, it's so quiet. You get a loud silence with a gag, say, about Khrushchev. And when you check real quick and find out the audience is still there, only just kind of silent, you wonder why. Well, there's an easy answer.
>
> In Denver, they know all about the corruption on their own police force, right? And in Detroit they know that *Time* magazine called their

town a depressed area, right? They're interested in that—but Khrush-chev? Well, maybe he used to play third base for the Tigers. . . . What I mean is, they're insular. They only know and care about what affects their own little part of the world—and it's that way in an awful lot of towns. And it worries me. I mean, now and then I catch myself *thinking!* That could be bad, right? Maybe it's part of the wave of conservatism that I heard about sweeping the country. I don't know about it myself, but I do know that on campuses where I appeared, the only organized student groups were in the conservative camp. It may be an indication. On the other hand, maybe it means nothing. I mean, it could be just the same old story—anything to be different from Dad, right?

You can understand how the kids feel, though. They have an idea the liberals let them down badly in the last election, right? I mean, the lib-erals elected a Harvard man with $450 million. And the conservatives were running a man who wanted nothing more than to be allowed to join the country club, right? Since the election, though, both parties have been acting strangely. The Democrats spent eight years under Eisenhower complaining about being an oppressed majority. Now, I think they're apprehensive about their victory. And the Republicans are acting even stranger. They're suspicious about Rockefeller. And they're quizzical about Goldwater. And they're very, very silent about Nixon, right? It's funny about that, too. I mean, he loses one election and right away he's dead as far as they're concerned. He's nowhere. Well, he spent eight years just a step from the presidency, and if he was as inept and incompetent as all that—I think I want a refund.

Mort Sahl on Relationships was an answer to Frank Sinatra's squeamishness over Sahl's continued attacks on the Kennedys, an album, in concept any-way, relatively free of political content. Sales had been disappointing for *The New Frontier* and it was thought a change in subject matter, if not neces-sarily in tone, might salvage the franchise in a category that was now seen as overcrowded. The tipping point came in 1960 when *The Button-Down Mind of Bob Newhart* seemingly appeared out of nowhere and shot straight to the top of the charts. "After that," observed Capitol Records president Alan Livingston, "everybody got into the act." Eager to get in on the comedy explosion, Capitol bought *2,000 Years with Carl Reiner and Mel Brooks* from World Pacific, convinced it had been mishandled, and reissued it as their own. "Maybe it never made the charts," said Livingston, "but that '2,000 Year Old Man' was big."

By the time *Relationships* appeared in December 1961, there was nowhere left to go in the comedy category, and even Newhart's sales had fallen off dramatically. "The newness," Newhart suggested, "wears off, I think. . . . You develop a certain cult—100 or 200,000 people who'll buy as a matter of course. That first album sold 875,000 last count . . . it was the highest seller in Warners' history. My second album sold 200,000. See what I mean?"

There would be no more breakout hits until parodist Allan Sherman's *My Son, the Folk Singer* appeared in October 1962. And no more albums for Mort Sahl, whose relationship with Reprise was quietly brought to an end.

Nineteen sixty-one had been a difficult year as old avenues of expression—records and concert tours—fell away and new opportunities were in lamentably short supply. In searching for another way to define himself, Sahl found the answer was surprisingly close at hand.

It came in the form of a feature motion picture directed by his friend Marlon Brando, a western inspired by the legend of William "Billy the Kid" Bonney and Lincoln County Sheriff Pat Garrett. Drawn from Charles Neider's 1956 novel *The Authentic Death of Hendry Jones*, the story portrayed the characters as a pair of bank robbers until Bonney, known as "Rio" in the film, is double-crossed by Dad Longworth and left for capture by the Mexican authorities. After five years in a Sonora prison, Rio, unrepentant and bent on vengeance, escapes and heads north to Monterey, where he finds that Longworth has gone straight and been elected sheriff. Their superficially friendly encounter, as portrayed by Brando and co-star Karl Malden, stakes out the boundaries of the conflict to follow:

LONGWORTH

You know what you're going to do?

RIO

No.

LONGWORTH

You're going to stay to supper.

RIO

Well . . . I'll tell you. I was just pokin' through and thought I'd stop in and say hello. But it wouldn't look too good, me hanging around your town . . .

LONGWORTH

You let me worry about that.

RIO

Well, now, you better think about it . . . 'cause I'm still in business.

The movie, titled *One-Eyed Jacks*, took two years to make and reportedly cost $6 million—twice its original estimate. Cast in the lead, Brando
took over direction after Stanley Kubrick withdrew and Karl Malden, who
had directed one film, declined to replace him. At Brando's request, Mort
worked the wrap party and received a Zenith shortwave radio for his trouble. "He drank about a gallon of tequila and was playing the bongos," Mort
remembers. "The cast gave him a belt with a gold buckle as a gift. He was
staggering around, and he said to me, 'You think I'm a damn fool.' I said,
'No, you're human. What you're doing is human.' He said, 'Am I human??'"

Sahl hadn't seen the film at that point; nobody had. And yet he's seen it
so many times since he can no longer recall the first time. ("I would go anywhere it was playing," he says.) When it opened in New York in March 1961
he was playing the Crescendo, and when it went citywide in Los Angeles
he was at Basin Street East. "When people reject you, often you have made
that your own choice," he wrote in *Heartland*. "When the door is closed, you
have bolted it from the other side. I can take this all the way to the level
of the president of the United States. I served notice on Kennedy that I
was going to attack him, and *he* didn't reject me. The core of neurosis is to
think people ostracize you after you've submitted your resignation. Talking
to Kennedy after he was elected and telling him you're not coming to dinner
and you're going to go your own way is Marlon Brando's confrontation with
Karl Malden in *One-Eyed Jacks*. They had been bank robbers together, but
now Malden is the sheriff. The bank robber looks at the sheriff and says, 'I'm
still in business.'"

The self-image had been evolving over a period of decades, from Mort's
movie-saturated childhood in Los Angeles to the notion that he was on the
job to save America, to save the ideal of America as put forth in the Hollywood films he absorbed so readily. The previous year, Murray Schumach of the
New York Times had asked him what he would do if the country miraculously
emerged a Utopia. "Then I see myself like some hero in a Western series," he
replied, "riding out to a saloon and someone saying to me, 'What will you do?
Where will you go?' And I say, 'I'll be heading for another country.'"

He began talking about a legacy-building shift in his career, proposing
to drive the national conversation with a nightly commentary on network
television. It was part of what he called "The Plan," and he described it in an

interview with the *Hollywood Citizen-News*, nervously twisting paper clips as he spoke. "I think I could do it," he said hopefully. "I think it would go over very well. I'd do it five times a week, and just comment on the day's happenings on the newsfront. I think once the audience got used to it, it would really go." The Plan also included a book he would write, as well as a syndicated newspaper column. "Everybody else does it. Why couldn't I?"

He talked up *One-Eyed Jacks*, his search for the perfect woman, his desire to one day conduct a jazz band.* And when his questioner raised the threat of overexposure, he dismissed it with a wave of the hand. "I think you'll find that most of the people who are 'overexposed,' as you say, are merely not turning out good shows. One bad show is overexposure, really." The key, he maintained, was in appealing to the best in people. "People will believe what they want. If you talk to the worst in people, the worst part of them likes you. Try for the best, and that part digs you."

Implementing The Plan required him to be more open to TV work, and in that regard the year 1962 began promisingly. On January 12 he starred with Henry Fonda and Lucille Ball in a nostalgic ninety-minute spectacular assembled by Leland Hayward titled *The Good Years*. Based on a bestselling book about the period working up to the start of World War I, it was a hodgepodge of music and narrative, with Mort's topical observations limited to headlines half a century old. Other segments required him to impersonate bodybuilder Eugene Sandow, experiment with a newfangled shower bath, illustrate man's tribulations in learning to fly, and demonstrate the first getaway car used by a forward-thinking gangster. "I was way out of my depth," he says of the experience. "I got a ton of money. Lucille Ball came into rehearsal. She had a later call and a lot of doubts about the script. She said, 'How's it going?' And to kid her in the terms of an M-G-M musical, I said: 'The show is off. The dean doesn't like swing.' You know what she said to me? 'The dean doesn't have to worry about this show.'"

Sahl gave a number of interviews while *The Good Years* was in production, always taking care to mention The Plan and the fact there had been discussions with two of the three commercial networks. Henry Fonda, a longtime fan, had a better time with the show than the critics who universally panned it. "The presence of Mort Sahl proved almost a complete loss," mourned the AP's Cynthia Lowry. "It was impossible for him to be sharp, topical, and

---

* Sahl eventually funded bands for Kenton trombonist Dee Barton and Bill Russo, among others, but never fronted one himself.

satiric on such lively, controversial issues as Teddy Roosevelt and J.P. Morgan, the elder." Cecil Smith, in the *Los Angeles Times*, deplored the greatest misuse of talent, material, and time he could recall. "I am not usually in favor of capital punishment," he wrote, "but last Friday night at ten I would have been happy to have seen three men hanged—namely producer Leland Hayward, writer A.J. Russell, and director Franklin Schaffner."

Infinitely more promising was the pilot for a proposed series called *Joe and Josie*. The producing company was Four Star, whose president, Tom McDermott, offered Sahl a spec script by director-playwright Garson Kanin. "It was *The Marrying Kind*," says Mort, recalling the 1952 comedy-drama written for Judy Holliday by Kanin and his wife, the actress Ruth Gordon. Mort's character was Joe Belfer, a driver for Luxor Cab who yearns to be out on his own but knows that the price of a hack is way beyond his means. He has set up his wife, Josie, in her own hair salon, and they live in Philipstown with their six-year-old son. If it went, the series would be a co-production between Four Star, the Kanins, and Moraga, the production company Sahl had formed with Milt Ebbins. With the deal set, the first order of business was to settle on an actress to play opposite him. "To show I wasn't above such things," says Mort, "I lobbied for them to cast Dyan Cannon in the part because I was dating her at the time."

Cooler heads prevailed, and the part of Josie went to Cloris Leachman, who proved a perfect match for Sahl's philosophical cabbie. In the pilot, Joe picks up a fare at the airport and tells him of his dreams of independence as they make their way into town. Listening with considerable interest is the millionaire banker Charles Eliot Burton, played by Edward Everett Horton. When they reach their destination in lower Manhattan, Burton gives him two one-dollar bills and expects twenty-five cents in change. Joe gives him every opportunity to let him keep the change as a tip, then is finally sent across the street to a newsstand to change one of the dollars. Feeling stiffed, he sullenly delivers the last nickel and is handed a folded piece of paper. "That's your tip," says Burton, who disappears into a building with his name on it. Joe unfolds the paper to finds it is a check for $3,240—the exact price of a new cab.

Paired with as fine an actress as Leachman, Mort did his best work as an actor in *Joe and Josie* and feels that she undoubtedly upped his game. "Her dedication and concentration were absolute," he says. "She was nuts all the remaining hours of the day, but at work she was the best." Their chemistry was on full display in a giddy scene in Joe's cab after he has cashed the check and is lovingly fondling the bank envelope crammed with bills. Behind the wheel as Joe clambers into the back seat, Josie dons his yellow cap and says, "Where to sir?"

"Twenty-one thirty-one Broadway—the Acme Cab Exchange."
"Yes sir!"
"And don't spare the horses!"
"No sir!"
"There's an extra fiver in it for you if you make it by midnight."
"Yes sir!" she responds, giggling uncontrollably. "How'd it go?"
"Like a dream," says Joe. "I dreamt I robbed a bank. You know all the trouble I have when I go to the bank?"
"Oh yeah."
"I walked in there and said, 'I'd like to cash this, please.' 'Yes, sir. May I see some identification please?' 'Certainly. Why not? My driver's license.' 'Yes sir.' 'I'd like it in tens and twenties,' and that's the way it came—wang, wang wang. One hundred, two hundred, five hundred, one thousand, two thousand . . .'"

Producer-director Marc Daniels gave *Joe and Josie* a smart look, shrewdly incorporating second-unit footage shot in New York with backlot and interior scenes made at Republic Studios. Everyone seemed pleased with the result, and the show looked like an easy sale to ABC. At Sahl's "regular monthly opening" at the Crescendo, McDermott and his wife could be seen ringside, but Mort's attitude toward the series appeared to sour as a deal proved elusive and talks for a nightly news commentary went nowhere. "As far as the comedy series is concerned, it's sort of scary to be tied to one thing for a period of years," he said to a correspondent for *Variety*. "But with my luck this series probably will sell and I'll be stuck." He was a bit more sanguine in June when it looked as if *Joe and Josie* wouldn't sell after all. The time for the network committing to a new series had passed, and there was only a slight chance it would be picked up as a mid-season replacement. Being tied to one thing for a period of years would not be a worry after all.

Immediately upon finishing *Joe and Josie*, Mort left for San Francisco and the hungry i, but the old magic wasn't there anymore. The audiences were older, more affluent, able to pay an admission charge that had climbed all the way to three dollars. And, having grown used to big rooms and concert tours, Mort's sets lacked the discipline of earlier years, when a lean thirty-five minutes served him to best advantage. Then, too, the first days of his four-week stand found him mired in controversy. The trouble began almost a year earlier when Herb Caen was between marriages and squiring around town a twenty-three-year-old fashion model named Lily Valentine. An exotic mix of Chinese, French, and Russian heritage who spoke six languages fluently, Valentine was a local fixture who, in her capacity as Miss Pacific Festival, served as Nikita Khrushchev's interpreter during the Soviet premier's 1959 visit to the city.

"She was a stunning girl," says Mort. "I met her, and wanted to see more of her. I talked to [TV writer] E. Jack Neuman. I said, 'What do you do if your friend's got a girl?' He said, 'Well, you ask him. Like a gentleman. You've got instincts. Use your instincts. You don't go over his head. You ask him if it's okay.' So I went to Herb. I said, 'How serious are you about this girl?' He said, 'Not at all. She's way too dumb.' So I said, 'Do you have any objection if I call her?' And he said, 'I don't know how long you'll be able to stay awake. She's really dumb.' So I called her and had dinner with her. We got along pretty good."

Enrico Banducci would stage big Italian buffets at his place in North Beach. One night, Mort was in line and John Huston was behind him. Caen, in a fury, pushed his way through the crowd. "You've stabbed me in the back," he sputtered, sticking a finger in Mort's face, "and I'll get you. As far as I'm concerned you're dead. The column made you, and it's going to break you. *You're dead in the Chronicle!*" People turned and stared.

> I said, "You said you didn't care." And he started yelling at me in front of everybody. I said, "I don't want to jeopardize our friendship. I know everything I owe to you and I love you." They finally pulled him away. Huston's standing there holding his plate. "Well," he said, "we've just seen a man in love." I said, "He told me he didn't love her." He said, "I didn't say with *her*."
>
> And from then on Herb would never take my calls. Or talk to me. She called him and tried to straighten it out. The power of a woman. Here's this young chick. She took the phone and said, "Now, now, Herbie, behave yourself . . ."

Caen wrote of the relationship between Lily and Mort, hopefully proclaiming its demise in a June 1961 column:

As the Big Colyumists would put it: The hot flame kindled here by Mort Sahl and Model Lily Valentine has flickered out. Gorsh, what fun to write purty like that . . .

A Big Colyumist, specifically Earl Wilson, picked up on the item when Sahl opened at Basin Street East and Lily Valentine was on display ringside. A month later, Louis Sobol reported that Mort had resumed with Chilendra Jones after Lily "flew off to Europe, miffed because Sahl was dodging marriage."

Caen resisted the temptation to comment on Pat Manley's well-publicized lawsuit, and in November ignored the local stops made on Sahl's tour with Joanie Sommers. He was, however, present when Mort opened at the "i" on January 31, 1962, this time casting a critical eye upon what he had previously only singled out for praise. Under the heading PRODIGAL'S RETURN, Caen bemoaned the length of the set—an hour and twenty minutes—and a "disquieting" penchant for kind words and name-dropping that seemed to leave the capacity crowd in a state of shock: "The metamorphosis is regrettable, but, I suppose, inevitable. Mort Sahl is now a member of The Establishment, and the old, fearless rapture has been replaced by wariness: you don't stay in the power elite by belting it, and it's difficult to remain an iconoclast once you've become an icon yourself. Although I'm one of the oldest Mort Sahl fans extant, I refuse to wear an 'I Like Icon' button. Come back, come back from wherever you went!"

"That's Lily," Mort says. "He's mad about Lily." The item ran on a Friday, and that night Sahl spent the first ten minutes of his opening set "answering" what Caen had said in his column. "I don't want to be penalized if he strikes out with a girl," he told the audience, which reportedly found the situation uncomfortable. "San Francisco is in terror Herb Caen won't mention it." The attack didn't go over well, and was universally condemned in the press. "I had the luxury of having my feelings hurt," Mort acknowledges. "I wouldn't do that now. I knew Herb had an unfair advantage. There's a certain irony in the fact that he forced me on people. As [humorist] Finley Peter Dunne said, 'After you have the victory parade through the arch, they take the bricks one by one and hurl them at you.'"

Variety's William Steif caught the show and seemed to line up with Caen in observing that Sahl, as a member of the "Coldwater Canyon Clan," had achieved a sort of conformity with his non-conforming peers that made some of his act "sound awfully close to simple name-dropping." Still, Steif acknowledged, a lot of the essential qualities of a Sahl performance came through. "For instance, when he's talking about Dr. Fred C. Schwartz' Christian Anti-Communist School, 'from which I got an incomplete last semester,' he's at his best. He's funny in his comments about the [John] Birch Society and [its founder] Robert Welch, about Richard Nixon and California Governor Pat Brown ('Brown attacked Nixon with a blunt instrument—his wit'), Eisenhower, the CIA, and last year's Geneva Peace Conference ('the Red Chinese could audit but they couldn't go for credit')."

The whole enterprise was an unhappy one, and Sahl was on edge throughout the engagement. At one point it was reported that he was being sued for $5,000 by a Mrs. Cathy Russell of Salinas, who alleged that when she waved at him while dining in the hungry i's Other Room, he grabbed her arm and tipped her flat onto her back. "However," said manager David Allen, attempting to put the best possible spin on the misunderstanding, "Mort *did* apologize . . . in his own way. He asked me to throw her out."

Sahl was still smarting from having placed a full-page ad in *Variety* touting his friend Brando for a Best Director nomination, a costly gesture that went completely unacknowledged by the actor, who seemed vaguely embarrassed by the idea. And while he was still in residence at the "i," Dorothy Kilgallen ran an item about his tensions with Milt Ebbins. "The problem is reported to have started when Sahl's 'concert tour' did poorly, grew when he called off a Broadway production, claiming his material wasn't ready, and was not helped a bit when he encountered troubles with the musicians' union in California. Mort blames Milt for his professional miseries, but Milt blames Mort, saying he's stubborn and difficult to reason with. Well, Norman Granz could have given Milt a fill-in on that scene."

On February 28, Sahl retreated to the Crescendo, where Gene Norman was doing his best to enliven L.A.'s moribund nightclub scene by offering a bill that incorporated two other established headliners: the George Shearing Quintet, which stayed on for nearly an hour, and singer Nancy Wilson.* Irritated by the overstuffed nature of the thing, Sahl balked at doing a second show as curtain time approached 2:00 A.M. "What is this?" he demanded of Norman. "A jazz concert?" Business justified the bold programming, tables jamming the aisles as county fire officials looked the other way. "I now have a 'commercial' act," he told the first-nighters, who included Paul Newman

---

* Shearing and Wilson had released the seminal jazz album *The Swingin's Mutual!* on Capitol the previous year.

and Joanne Woodward, Janet Leigh, Tony and Judy Franciosa, and fellow jazz hound Jack Webb. "It's half politics, half sex—to reach a common denominator. And I throw pies later." He went on to relay JFK's congratulations to astronaut John Glenn ("You did very well for someone who isn't in the family"), characterized Frank Sinatra as "the President West," and riffed on the impact of the Committee for a Sane Nuclear Policy ("There's fallout in my milk").

Upon finishing at the Crescendo, he left town for an extended period, seemingly intent on countering reports that he was having trouble pulling in trade. He sold out a week at Freddie's in Minneapolis, played four standout weeks at Mister Kelly's, his first Chicago appearance in two years, managed a guest shot on Ed Sullivan's April 8 broadcast, and returned to his native Canada for a short stay at Montreal's El Morocco, a booking that yielded a half-hour documentary that aired on the CBC. He landed in New York in June, not simply to play Basin Street East, but also to host and deconstruct *The Tonight Show* for a week. In terms of network television, it would be the most prominent and creatively successful thing he'd do all year.

9

THE MEANING OF THE WORD *LOYALTY*

"Jack Paar was not a phenomenon I had indulged in," says Mort Sahl. "I was out chasing girls all the time, so I wasn't home for *The Tonight Show*. And he, of course, had made it his own for five years." Paar, who was as far removed from Steve Allen as anyone could possibly be, had announced his retirement from late night, opting instead to do an hour of prime time a week for the 1962–63 season. Game-show host Johnny Carson was chosen as his replacement, but due to Carson's ABC contract, he was unable to assume the job until October 8, 1962, leaving *The Tonight Show* without a permanent host for seven months. NBC's solution was to switch stars weekly, turning the program and its support staff, including announcer Hugh Downs, over to a colorful grouping of unlikely candidates that included, for the first thirteen weeks, Art Linkletter, Zsa Zsa Gabor, Spike Jones, and Bob Cummings. Mort found himself among them, sandwiched between singers Pat Boone and Steve Lawrence and scheduled for the week of June 11.

"I never liked the *Tonight* show," he told the *New York Herald Tribune*'s Joe Hyams during a brief stopover in Los Angeles,

> but it was pure television. I felt Jack Paar was courageous, but his knowledge was limited. He attacked the press, which was marvelous. He thinks the worst thing the press did was attack him. He'd go out of his mind with the blowing up of the Maine. The trouble with the show since he left it and guest hosts have come on is it is too much like a Friars' meeting, with everyone kissing each other. I plan to put on new people, colorful people who aren't performers. There's no use talking to artists. they're hopeless. They haven't said anything since they all stood up and sang "Happy Birthday, Mister President."

The NBC people said they want me as I am. I'll do the news for fifteen minutes two times a week and have guests like Governor Brown, Richard Nixon, Governor Stevenson, Otto Preminger, and Gore Vidal. I'd like to invite the president, but he doesn't come on unless he's running. I do intend to do a good deal of talking about the man-woman situation. You know: Women are highly competitive but they don't have the guts to really compete. They just give you a lot of trouble at home and say they have fine minds too. I'll try and get some bright-os like Inger Stevens. I want a chick who fights like a chick, not like a man.

As the 11th approached, the political figures started to peel away. Senator Barry Goldwater, for example, wired regrets because of scheduling pressures. "I guess," said Mort, "he's afraid there'll be no one to watch the country if he comes." The one exception was Governor Pat Brown of California, who was never shy about seeking out the spotlight, but who was nixed by NBC because he was locked in a tight race for re-election with Richard Nixon and it was feared he would trigger the equal-time rule. "We're throwing out the desk," Mort declared. "Who wants to sit at a desk? The place will be rigged for coffee house conversation, not for interviews. The show has always been interview. I'll have some people sitting around talking about girls. If an Adlai Stevenson drops in, I won't say, 'What do you think of Algeria?' That's interview. I'll say, 'We're talking about girls, Governor. What do you think about girls?'"

Paar's writing staff remained behind, and it was up to them to supply jokes to the temporary hosts, an onerous task when Art Linkletter was in the chair and a world-class challenge when the guy out front was as famously self-sufficient as Mort Sahl. Twenty-five-year-old staff writer Dick Cavett recalled his first exposure to Sahl the previous year at Basin Street East. "It was stunning," he said of the performance he attended with his friend Woody Allen. "It was as if someone had come out and started a painting somewhere in the middle of the frame, and then worked on a corner of it, and then another part, and then back to the first part, and then on to another one, until he seemed to satisfyingly fill the whole thing. Woody once used an odd adjective, what he once referred to as 'that great canine intelligence.' That wonderful face with the great canine intelligence . . . He said, 'Whenever I see him I think everybody else should quit the business.' I was willing to go along with that. I had never seen anything like it."

As intimidating as the job seemed to be, Cavett was able to channel Sahl's sensibilities to the extent that he became one of the very few people to ever write credibly for him:

> It was hard to write for Mort because you felt so inadequate. There was one line he did that was about pigeons. The thrust of the joke had to do with the testing and re-testing of atomic bombs. One country made another country start testing again, and so on. And the news item was simply that the United States Army had re-recognized the value of carrier pigeons. (This sounds like a gag, but it was true.) Some genius re-raised the subject of carrier pigeons, and the punch line was something like ". . . which of course means that the Russians will now start re-testing their pigeons." It got a big laugh, and I thought: I was Mort Sahl for just a moment there.
>
> Another one: It was a time of scandalously rotten streets in New York, potholes everywhere, and Mayor Wagner's administration was being pummeled for not doing anything about this. Mort's punch line was, "Wagner needs criticism like this from me like he needs a hole in the street." That got a big laugh. And I remember a joke about the Cal-Neva Lodge, which was in the news because Sinatra had an interest in the place. Explaining to those who might not know that one end of it was in California and the other in Nevada, he said that you could meet a girl at the bar, take her to the lounge and violate the Mann Act.

The first show, taped at NBC's Radio City studios, drew mixed notices, Sahl not quite sure how to spark an exchange among guests like Hugh Hefner and Otto Preminger when their principal topics of conversation were themselves. (Mort's line on *Advise and Consent*: "It opens June 8 and closes June 9.") He brought on one of his personal heroes, the acerbic radio comedian Henry Morgan, who cleared the air by remarking on the sheer abundance of plugs, then later repaid the compliment by telling the Associated Press that Sahl was about through. ("He's turned into a lecturer on politics and no one wants that.") The presence of Swedish-born actress Inger Stevens lent piquancy to the occasion, as she and Mort were being linked in the gossip columns. ("I was trying to get something going there," he admits.)

Tuesday's show, with novelist Gore Vidal, came closest to a political discussion. Vidal, a resident of upstate New York, had recently run—and been defeated—for a seat in Congress. However, the presence of producer David Merrick (who, Mort said, "imports flops") repeatedly turned the subject back to the theatre, stifling whatever political observations that managed to bounce forth. Harriet Van Horne of the *New York World-Telegram* watched nearly an hour of the show and thought Sahl was doing well. "There were no screaming laughs. There were no particularly brilliant comments on the day's news. But as Sahl explained, 'I'm here [at NBC] all day and I am at a club called Basin Street all night'—a circumstance that would dull the sharpest of wits. Whatever Sahl's failings, let it be noted that he avoids clichés (save for the clichés of his own private mythology), he is almost never vulgar, and he does not throw pies."

Even the dissenters in the press gave him credit for his nervy bookings. Without any politicos to fill the time, he opted for jazz acts that rarely got seen on network TV—Dave Brubeck, Carmen MacRae, Jackie and Roy, Nancy Wilson, the Oscar Peterson Trio. He booked Woody Allen, who had previously been on with Jack Paar, and gave comedian George Carlin his first *Tonight Show* exposure. "NBC," Mort recalls, "was under the reign of Dave Tebet. He gave me a very hard time, but I didn't realize he was seeing Inger Stevens—and I was quite taken with her. Nobody would tell him no. He was the Vice President of Talent—that meant he went back and forth [between coasts] once a week. They didn't want Woody, and they didn't want Carlin. And they really raised it from a non-issue to a major issue. I thought they were both talented; I didn't expect them to change the world but I thought they ought to be heard. Herb Sargent was sort of my sidekick through all that. I remember coming in the first night and looking at that board with the names of the guests, and a lot of people on the board weren't definite. I said, 'How're we doing?' Herb looked at the board and said, 'So far you have Adlai Stevenson and Joe Williams.' That was the state of the show. A guy came in from the Morris office. 'I'm Joe Wolfson. What can I do to help you?' And Herb said, 'Go away.'"

Sahl's most audacious guest list came on Thursday night, when he assembled an all-female panel for a discussion of the "Man-Woman Equation." (This from a guy who had recently said, "A woman's place is in the stove.") For the occasion he ditched the pullover sweater and donned a jacket and tie. Tellingly, all his guests were actresses: Suzy Parker, Felicia Farr, Susan Strasberg, Geraldine Brooks, and Inger Stevens. The result, depending upon who was doing the judging, was either explosive or banal, insightful or sophomoric. Nobody came down in the middle.

"You wouldn't believe how tough it was to get a panel of sharp chicks together," Mort told Copley TV correspondent Don Freeman.

We had seventy-five percent fallouts. Cancellations. Chicks must think I'm Mr. Abrasive. Anyway, that show brought the biggest mail response I've ever had. Talk about women and you get mail, which shows what's on people's minds. Chicks wrote in to tell me off, but— get this—they did so in my terms, using the four-syllable words, playing the intellectual. What can I say to them except, "You've proved yourself as an intellectual. How do you intend to prove yourself as a woman?" Right?

I never had any trouble with chicks when I was a gas station attendant. Then I made it and all the chicks I began to meet were actresses. Actresses always competing. All an actress really wants to be is an actor. I used to look up at these beautiful chicks in Hollywood. Goddesses, I thought. Listen, I found they're the most inadequate people in the world. They run scared. You love me today, actresses say, but you'll turn me down in two months. Unbelievable. And "career girls." The ambition of most women is to settle down and make a broken home. And girl writers—the worst. Did you read Rona Jaffe's latest book? I'm in it—she calls me Mort Baker, and I'm the soul of morality, which I consider highly insulting. Sometimes I think my life is like a bad TV show that keeps getting renewed every year—and all the chicks are reruns too.

Sahl was back in Los Angeles when Lenny Bruce played what would be his last stand at the Crescendo, a two-week engagement as part of a grab bag of a bill that included vocalist Ann Richards, vibraphonist Terry Gibbs, and the Chad Mitchell Trio. There was, by this point, ample evidence that he had influenced the direction of Lenny's act, but where he pushed boundaries with politics and lifestyle, Bruce was doing it with irreverent topics and, increasingly, language that left him open to arrest. "I didn't want to play him anymore because he got too rough on the stage," said Gene Norman. "Sally, his mother, said, 'Gene, Lenny loves you, you've gotta give him a chance.' So, sure enough, I brought him in and he was terrible. He was disconnected, wandering all over the place. One night, a couple sat in front of the stage and at one point the man got up and said, 'You're disgusting.' They actually confronted him. He said to them, 'You can't laugh 'cause you can't cum.' Jesus, I wanted to crawl under the table. Everyone heard it. Only by the grace of God the sheriff didn't bust me."

One night in July 1962, Mort got a call from Gene Norman asking him to cover for Lenny, who had been arrested in the Crescendo parking lot. "They'd send plainclothes policemen to attend his performances and take notes," he says. "They'd arrest him if he used any blue material. Then Gene would have to go over to the sheriff's station on San Vicente and bail him out. Gene said, 'I didn't know they were cops.' I said, 'Couldn't you tell that they resented getting a check?'"

With plans to go to Monte Carlo as soloist for the Marquis de Cuevas ballet company, Yvonne Craig arrived in June 1958 to spend the summer studying in Los Angeles. Quickly, she found herself, at age twenty-one, working in feature films and TV. Lithe and photogenic, Yvonne had a natural affinity for the camera and little interest in a conventional show business career. She played precocious teenagers and the occasional lead, working steadily but lacking the ambition that might otherwise have given her a shot at stardom. By 1961 she was separated from her first husband, actor-singer Jimmy Boyd, and going around town as part of a threesome with her younger sister Meridel and Milt Ebbins' brother Bernie. One night Bernie took them to see Mort Sahl at the Crescendo. "I saw his show and thought he was brilliant!" she wrote in her autobiography. "Bernie took me backstage to meet him and we all went up to Mort's house afterward. He was bright and funny and I was smitten."

Craig took to hanging around the William Morris office, just happening to be on hand whenever Mort was in the building. "We kept running into one another by accident," she said, "and finally he asked me out." The relationship got off to a slow start, primarily because the tour with Joanie Sommers was looming and Mort would be on the road for the balance of the year. Then there was the matter of Pat Manley and the paternity suit, which compelled him to keep a low profile. It was almost a year before they were spied having lunch in the commissary at Universal-International, where Yvonne was working in an episode of *The Wide Country* for Revue. "She reminded me some of Joan Collins, who saw Mort quite often when he was in London last year," remarked columnist Sheilah Graham.

There were other women, of course. Mort was widely reported to be pining for Inger Stevens, who was linked to a number of prominent men. (After her death in 1970 it came out that she had been secretly married the entire time to a black producer named Ike Jones.) Actress Tippi Hedren was considered Mort's steady girlfriend at the time she was making *The Birds* for Alfred Hitchcock. He was also seeing actress Julie Newmar, who at five-eleven towered over him. "I don't think I'm his type," Newmar told Hedda Hopper, refusing to take him seriously. "I think he likes me because I provoke him." It was only after steadily seeing him for a period of months that Yvonne learned about Stevens. "I'm watching him on the *Today* show, and he says, 'Will you marry me?' to Inger Stevens! I didn't know anything about her. I was stunned."

And while Yvonne's career was heating up, Mort's was cooling down. Movie roles were periodically floated, but nothing ever came of them. Stanley Kramer talked of wanting him for *It's a Mad, Mad, Mad, Mad World* but a firm offer never materialized. In October, he shot a one-day cameo in a picture called *Johnny Cool*, which was populated by second-tier Rat Pack personalities and nominally produced by Peter Lawford. Later that same month he traveled to El Cajon, east of San Diego, for a humiliating ten days at an impossibly plush nightclub called Art's Roaring 20s, where he reportedly set the record for the sparsest attendance in the club's brief history. By December 1962 he was hanging out with his pal Paul Newman and reduced to accepting a pep talk from an old nemesis.

Sahl's favorite restaurant had always been Jean Leon's La Scala, an Italian place that appealed to the somewhat younger set in Hollywood, Leon having been all of twenty-eight when he first opened his doors on Little Santa Monica Boulevard in 1956. It was one of those affairs with tufted leather booths and hanging wine bottles and dishes named after the regulars—*grenadine of beef a la Paul Newman*, *veal steak Barbara Rush*, *veal scaloppini Mort Sahl*. Jack Kennedy was known to like the food at La Scala, his favorite meal being fettuccini with clam chowder (which Leon once admitted was actually an Italian soup). One night there was a commotion when Peter Lawford sent for thirty orders of lasagna to be delivered to him in Palm Springs, where the president was known to be visiting. And seated at a back table were the couple who, for want of a few votes in Cook County, might otherwise have been on the receiving end of such an order—Mr. and Mrs. Richard M. Nixon.

"I was with Newman," Mort remembers. "He was drunk that night. Joanne would let him out with me because, among the wives, I had the reputation of a boy scout: I wasn't going to let him wander with anybody, and I wasn't going to let him get too drunk. Newman's at the bar, and he says to me, 'Jesus Christ, you wouldn't be alive if it weren't for him. Why don't you have the courtesy to send him a drink?' So I sent over a note and said: I'D LIKE TO BUY YOU A DRINK. A note came back, and it said: I'LL HAVE SOME

WINE IF YOU'LL JOIN US. So I then put it into the act: 'I verified it was Nixon because he tried to make a deal.'"

Nixon had just lost California's gubernatorial election to Pat Brown, and had famously told a group of reporters they wouldn't have him to "kick around any more" because it was his last news conference. "I went over to the table and I introduced myself and sat down. The wine steward came over and asked what Nixon had ordered to eat. Nixon said cottage cheese and meatloaf. The wine steward asked what wine he would like to go with that. Nixon said, 'What would you recommend?' I thought it was a toss-up between Ripple and Thunderbird, but the guy said, 'Well, Mr. Nixon, how about the Rothschild?' Nixon said, 'No, we're going to have an American wine.' He was very adamant. The wine steward blanched because he saw his money going out the window. He said, 'What year?' Nixon said, 'This year.'"

After dinner, Nixon said: "Don't forget to keep a candle under my ass, and under Kennedy's too. It's good for America. You're the Will Rogers of our time." When the check came, Sahl grabbed it, seemingly grateful for both the company and the advice. Paying with his Diners Club, he noted on the receipt that the meal was a deductible business expense and his guests were Mr. and Mrs. Nixon. "Did you discuss specific business?" the slip asked. "Yes," he scribbled, "we discussed excessive taxation and the possible overthrow of the United States Government."

Mort Sahl's nervous energy, which served him well when he was working constantly, began to turn on him when bookings grew scarce. Like a powerful engine forced to idle interminably, he seemed bent on any chance for engagement. "It was very unpredictable behavior a lot of the time," said Yvonne Craig, who was perfectly happy devoting her downtime to reading and relaxing.

> I don't know what triggered it. I do know that we used to go to dinner together, and I was always on tenterhooks because you never knew when somebody was going to come up to the table and interrupt your dinner. I understand perfectly that nobody likes that to happen, but you never knew whether he was going to say, "Hey, sit down and have a drink with me," or whether he was going to grab them by the throat. I fended off people by saying, "Oh, could you excuse us because this is the last night we're going to see one another. . . ." But it was scary to watch because he was wiry and volatile, and you just never knew how he was going to treat strangers.

December brought no prospects for work, and Mort ended up losing an announced part in a *Dick Powell* episode called "Charlie's Duet" to Tony Franciosa. He sank into a deep depression, and Newman, who counted Mort, Gore Vidal, and Arthur Loew Jr. among his small circle of friends, grew worried. "Paul Newman just adored him," said Yvonne. "Mort hit a spell where he was catatonic. He would sit in his living room and stare into space and rock back and forth. They saw it and said, 'We really have to do something about this.' I said, 'I know it. I don't know what to do.' Paul or Joanne—one of them—said, 'We know a psychiatrist, and he needs to see that person.' And that's how he got to Dr. Rogowski." Dr. Alex Rogowski was a Beverly Hills psychoanalyst on the staff of the USC School of Medicine. "It lasted a long time," she continued.

> I think it did some good. He went to see Dr. Rogowski a lot—I mean like four days a week—and he seemed to be getting rid of a lot of stuff. But because he was charming, Rogowski, I think, fell under his spell. Mort would go in and tell fun tales and things like that, and that's not helping him. You need to say, "We can't do this. Why are you trying to mesmerize me if you are truly interested in getting your act together? You need to talk about that." And I think toward the end he just didn't.
>
> I met with him once because Mort said, "You need to talk to Yvonne." Rogowski said to me, "He says he doesn't sleep." I said, "He sleeps." He said, "Why do you think he said he doesn't?" I said, "I don't know. I heard a conversation the other day. He said to somebody, 'Do you know why they want my opinion? Because I'm God.' Maybe he thinks God doesn't sleep, so he can't."

The few dates Sahl landed in early 1963 were emcee duties, fundraisers for Pat Brown, who was paying off campaign debts after a bruising campaign against Nixon. ABC's Howard K. Smith came out from New York to tape an interview at the house on San Ysidro, and having been on the cover of *Time*, Mort was invited to the magazine's fortieth anniversary party. In March he was tapped to speak at a Democratic dinner in place of UN Ambassador Adlai Stevenson, who was unable to make it. Instinctively, he took the needle to what had once been his core audience. "I know it's peculiar that I should be replacing Mr. Stevenson at this dinner," he began, "but the Democratic Party has a history of accepting less than Stevenson." The response, by his own account, was tepid laughter and some hissing.

"I had eight years with Ike and Nixon," he told UPI's Vernon Scott. "I got rich on the Republican administration. The Democrats laughed at my jokes about the presidency and the vice presidency, and the Republicans enjoyed a laugh on themselves. But things are different now. The Republicans are still laughing, but the Democrats aren't. It is said the president is willing to laugh at himself. That's fine. But when is he going to extend the privilege to us?"

The first real work of the new year didn't come until May, when Sahl made a guest appearance with Johnny Carson on *The Tonight Show*. He reportedly signed a contract with Capitol Records that same month, but nothing ever came of it. When he opened at the Crescendo at the end of May, it constituted his first club date in seven months—and the booking was for a paltry ten days. When he tried to engage Gene Norman in a serious talk about the business, he was politely rebuffed with vague comments about the new tax laws and little else. Gene had Ella Fitzgerald coming in behind him at $10,000 a week, but nothing seemed right about the club he had come to regard as his home base, and audiences weren't packing the room as they had only a year earlier when George Shearing and Nancy Wilson sweetened the bill.

He took to using his Monday nights off trying out new material in Santa Monica, something he would have never done—or had time for—in previous years. (One of these days, he liked to say, he was going to lead a freedom march down Ocean Avenue—if he could find a place to park.) David Sheehan, a columnist for the *Independent*, found him at one of his favorite bistros, Chez Jay, munching on peanuts and refining his swipes at the administration. Mort would talk of watching Kennedy's inaugural address and wondering when he was actually going to be told what he could do for his country. And that he'd been waiting ever since that day, afraid to take a steady job so as to be completely ready when the president finally told him what he wanted him to do. "It was just a tremendous overture with no first act," he said. "I'm still waiting."

Ironically, Kennedy did seem to know what he wanted of nightclubs and high-end restaurants, and had said as much as early as 1961. In April of that year he proposed $1,700,000,000 in tax savings for companies investing in new machinery and production facilities, while tightening deductions on expense accounts, dividends and interest, and overseas income. Of the president's proposals, it was his assault on what he called "expense account living"—lavish entertainment, country club memberships, business gifts, and the like—that would hit clubs and restaurants the hardest. "Too many firms and individuals have devised means of deducting too many personal

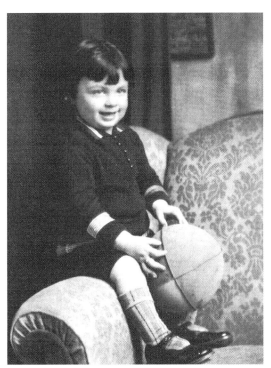

Morton Lyon Sahl, Montreal, circa 1930.
(Mort Sahl)

Wearing the Prop and Wings
of the U.S. Army Air Corps,
1946. (Mort Sahl)

Enrico Banducci. (San Francisco Public Library)

Outside the new hungry i, which was situated in the cellar of San Francisco's International Hotel. (© Bob Willoughby/mptvimages.com)

Newlyweds Sue and Mort Sahl, July 1955. (© Bob Willoughby/mptvimages.com)

Caught in performance at Mister Kelly's, February 1957. (Grey Villet/Life Picture Collection/Getty Images)

The Crescendo and the Interlude on the Sunset Strip, July 1957. (Bruce Torrence)

Recording a commentary segment for NBC's *Nightline*, 1958. (Mort Sahl)

With parents Harry and Dorothy Sahl and actress Joanne Woodward on the set of *The Sound and the Fury*, 1958. (Mort Sahl)

Phyllis Kirk. (Author's collection)

With Hugh Hefner and Playmate Joyce Nizzari during the first annual Playboy Jazz Festival, Chicago, August 1959. (Mort Sahl)

Backstage at the Playboy Jazz Festival with idol Stan Kenton. (Mort Sahl)

Chatting with Sammy Davis Jr. during rehearsals for *The Big Party*, October 1959. (CBS Photo Archive/ Getty Images)

For his role in *All the Young Men*, Mort was the only cast member willing to grow a beard. (Author's collection)

Talking with Senator John F. Kennedy at a New York banquet honoring Eleanor Roosevelt, December 7, 1959. (© George S. Zimbel/Harry S. Truman Library and Museum)

With his political hero Adlai Stevenson, circa 1960. (Mort Sahl)

Wielding a sharp needle on the cover of *Time*, August 15, 1960. (Author's collection)

As TV writer Sam Lynch in the 1960 *Thriller* episode "Man in the Middle." At left is actor Ashley Cowan. (Author's collection)

With impresario Leonard Green in his dressing room at Basin Street East, 1961. (Debra Green)

Out on the town with actress Yvonne Craig, 1962. (Author's collection)

The "new" Mort Sahl on stage at the Sands Hotel, Las Vegas, August 1965. (Mort Sahl)

China Lee. (Mort Sahl)

On the set of his KTTV show, April 1966. (Mort Sahl)

On the Sunset Strip with KLAC station manager Jack Thayer, November 1966. (Mort Sahl)

With Steve Allen on the set of Allen's syndicated talk show, 1969. (Mort Sahl)

The wedding of Mort Sahl and China Lee, October 30, 1970. (Mort Sahl)

Fatherhood, 1976. (Mort Sahl)

With Paul Newman,
circa 1978. (Mort Sahl)

With General Alexander Haig during the latter's quixotic presidential run, 1987. (Mort Sahl)

In *Mort Sahl's America*, 1996. (Mort Sahl)

At the 80th birthday *All-Star Sahl-ute*, June 28, 2007. Back row: Richard Lewis, Jay Leno, Norm Crosby, Kevin Nealon, Hugh Hefner, Ross Shafer, Drew Carey, Albert Brooks. Front row: Shelley Berman, Jonathan Winters, George Carlin, Mort Sahl, Harry Shearer. (John M. Heller/Getty Images)

The black Mort Sahl and the white Dick Gregory together on stage in Mill Valley, 2010. (Lucy Mercer)

Mort shares a laugh with his pal Robin Williams. "I wasn't the destructive influence his managers said I was," Mort comments, "and he wasn't a wild man, either. I really treasured the guy. He was a very pure soul." (Dan Dion)

living expenses," he said in his message, "thereby charging a large part of their cost to the Federal government."

Curiously, Sahl missed the full significance of Kennedy's proposal, both initially and later, in July 1961, when it was raised again as part of a prime time address to the nation. Trade groups began maneuvering behind the scenes, and brought their efforts out into the open in January 1962 when nearly a thousand restaurateurs descended on Capitol Hill, many taking Congressional leaders to lunch, others conferring with legislators in their offices. The National Restaurant Association declared its opposition to Kennedy's "ban on goodwill entertaining," estimating the annual cost in lost sales at $1 billion. A joint memo from five unions and eight employer groups followed, addressing Chairman Wilbur Mills on the eve of his House Ways and Means Committee's renewed consideration of the controversial proposal. It voiced fears that 200,000 jobs would be lost, representing more than $500,000,000 in annual wages.

Kennedy refused to back down, successfully steering the rule though Congress, but in July 1962 the Senate Finance Committee sharply restricted the plan, handing him a major legislative setback. Still, what most people seemed to retain from the skirmish was a coming reduction in deductible entertainment expenses. Business in clubs and bistros declined precipitously, and by December a lot places that had formerly booked name acts had switched to dining and dancing policies. On December 16, comedian Ben Blue closed his popular club on Wilshire Boulevard in Santa Monica, blaming a slump in business on widespread confusion over the new expense rules. Then came Mike Romanoff's announcement that he would close his world famous Beverly Hills eatery on January 1, 1963, saying businesses like his "have had it" with the government shift on tax policy. It was the high-profile closing of Romanoff's that sent shockwaves through the industry.

While the actual changes to the tax code were minor, given the draconian nature of Kennedy's original proposal, there was no convincing those eager to avoid potential trouble with the IRS. (It was also widely suggested that companies were using the threat of a crackdown as an excuse to cut back on employee expenses.) By March 1963, Gene Norman was reporting that combined business at the Interlude and Crescendo had dropped "at least twenty-five percent" and that he was electing not to book any talent for six weeks, at which point he said he would "reappraise the situation." Furthermore, in his capacity as president of the American Night Club Association, Norman described similar drops in business around the country. However, he remained optimistic that the situation would work itself out by summer.

"By that time people will have gotten used to the fact that they just can't write as much of their entertainment spending off to business."

Shelley Berman, while acknowledging the IRS role in the downturn, saw the problem in longer and more generalized terms, blaming indifferent managements who had steadfastly refused to modernize their operations. Many, he charged, were "still proud possessors of inadequate lighting (if they have any at all), inadequate sound systems, gaudy and undignified decor, inadequate sightline facilities, bad food, weak drinks, and maitre d's who would sooner leave a front table open than to give it away for nothing." Costs, he added, were keeping young audiences away when they were sorely needed to counter the natural attrition of older patrons. "I will give you a dollar for every person under forty-five you find at New York's Waldorf Astoria on any given night. It must cost a young couple at least $50 to have dinner and see a show there." Suggesting adjusted minimums keyed to age, he added, "I never drew a laugh from an empty table, and management never made any money from one. I can count the big, big nightclub draws on the fingers of one hand, and new ones aren't being developed. New talent needs a young following to launch it."

The steady drumbeat continued. In Minneapolis, Freddie's discontinued its name entertainment policy, as did its chief competitor, the Flame Room. In June 1963, Dorothy Kilgallen reported Enrico Banducci as admitting he'd like to sell the hungry i, having grown weary of the downturn in business. The other shoe dropped in July when Gene Norman abruptly sold his two clubs to a pair of corporations headed by publicist Sheldon "Shelly" Davis and attorney Theodore Flier. Nobody saw that coming, and Norman himself gave off no hints, having booked both rooms through October. In a statement, he vowed to serve as "entertainment consultant" to the new owners while devoting more time to his record label, GNP Crescendo. Mort, who was working a three-week engagement at Mister Kelly's, was shocked when he heard the news.

The trouble on the club circuit was mitigated by some uncommonly welcome news in network television. One of the guest hosts of *The Tonight Show* over the summer of 1962 was Jerry Lewis. And he, along with Merv Griffin, used the stint as a springboard to a talk show of his own. But where Griffin was doing time as a game-show host, Lewis was at the peak of his career as a movie star and a towering box office draw—number five in the nation. He drove a hard bargain in condescending to host a weekly show for ABC. Among his demands: two hours of prime time, live, with absolute creative control and a lavish budget befitting a star of his stature. While he and ABC declined to publicly discuss money, both parties acknowledged the forty-week contract was valued at more than $10 million.

"I'll be in complete control," Lewis boasted at a news conference. "It'll be something I've never done before. It'll be what people want—strictly entertainment. No song and dance stuff. No working under pressure with people who are frightened. This is going to be what this infantile medium should be—live. I'm going to play it loose. I'll be what I am with. I suppose I'll have guests. If they're hostile, I'll be hostile. If they're warm, I'll be warm. If they're zany, I'll be zany."

Mort Sahl had never abandoned his dream of doing a regular TV news commentary, even after he was rebuffed by all three networks. It fell to Jerry Lewis, at the behest of producer Perry Cross, to finally make it a reality. In August 1963 it was announced that Sahl had been signed for twenty appearances on the new Lewis show, making him a semi-regular. "The Morris office went in to have a meeting with him about the money," Mort remembers. "They said, 'We're thinking about Mort getting about $6,000 a week.' He says, 'You were, huh? You think he's worth that? Well, let me tell you something: He's not going to get six, he's going to get ten. Now get out of here! I've got work to do!' He's got to play it out, you know. The bad movie. 'And in addition, in the summers when we're on hiatus, I want to make a feature with him, for which he'll get $250,000 and 10 percent of the gross. And the first one will be a remake of *The Man Who Could Work Miracles*.' So that was all typed up."

As plans for the new series went forth, Hollywood's El Capitan, where Lewis and Dean Martin had hosted the *Colgate Comedy Hour*, and where Sahl himself made his prime time debut, was gutted and re-christened the Jerry Lewis Theatre. The danger of inflicting an unscripted Lewis on home viewers for 120 unrelenting minutes a week apparently occurred to no one.

Ahead of his first show, Lewis mused grandly about the people he would have as guests—Elizabeth Taylor, Brigitte Bardot, Sir Winston Churchill, maybe even Teamsters president Jimmy Hoffa. But when the show finally hit the air on Saturday, September 21, 1963, the billboard was a lot more conventional—Sahl, trumpeter Harry James, singers Jack Jones and Kay Stevens, essayist and critic Clifton Fadiman. What followed was a loosely rehearsed catalogue of Lewis' excesses that had households across the country tuning out in time to catch the start of *Gunsmoke* on CBS. Only those who stuck it out past the ten-thirty station break got to see Mort, in black tie, chat awkwardly with his new benefactor before being sent center stage to do his stuff like a contestant on Ted Mack's *Original Amateur Hour*.

"They were very uncomfortable with everything he did," Mort says of Lewis.

> Like when they didn't laugh in the studio he'd say, "What are you? A bunch of Arabs?" Then he built into his desk a control room—a duplicate—so if he didn't like the show on the monitor, he could override the director. And to make it competitive, he hired two directors. So one week it was Jack Shea, and the other week it was John Dorsey. He had all these elaborate plans. My section was the news. We called it "Mort Reports." And the set was made up of a lot of different sized globes. Balloons. And after talking to Herb Sargent, at the end of the monologue, instead of saying, "Back to you, Jerry," I throw this globe at him and I said, "Here. You wanted the world." Which he wasn't even insulted by 'cause he never listens to anybody.

The ten-minute segment was a mixture of old and new material, topical in format if not quite in content, and a solid hit with an audience desperate for something intelligent to laugh at. "It was nearly an hour and a half before the messiah of the nightclubs came on—but he was worth waiting for," Cecil Smith reported in his notice for the *Los Angeles Times*. "It was the first time, to my knowledge, that the true Sahl has been exhibited on television, his acid political wit unhampered. He snarled gleefully at both sides of the political fence. 'We're celebrating the centennial of the Civil War by having another one,' he said. And: 'Ole Miss is either a university or the president's legislative program.'" The *New York Times* described the show as "graceless" and "vapid," and even UPI's Rick Du Brow, normally one of Lewis' defenders, thought it embarrassing. A twenty-six city spot rating showed *The Jerry Lewis Show* drew nowhere near the numbers the star predicted on air (". . . some fifty to sixty million people—more than viewed the Academy Awards—are watching") and even NBC's broadcast of *The Seven Year Itch*, an eight-year-old movie, beat him handily.

The second show was appreciably better, with more big-name guests and fewer technical gaffes. Liberace, Peggy Lee, and thirties dancing star Ruby Keeler were the headliners, gamely cutting into the airtime Lewis had previously reserved for himself. "We go in to rehearse the show," says Mort, and Dorothy Brown, who was the continuity acceptance censor for ABC comes into the theater and sits in the back when I come on. And I start the monologue. She's making notes. Lewis walks out, he goes ballistic. He said, "My deal with ABC is that things go on the air live." He says to me, "Stop the monologue," so I do. She's protesting. The director said, "I have to block, so just say anything." Lewis said, "Say anything, but don't say what you're going to say tonight." So I pick up a paper, and it says in there that Governor Grant Sawyer of Nevada is thinking of not giving a license to Sinatra for the North Shore because he said, "I don't like the kind of person he hangs out with." I said, "So conceivably one of these anti-social types is Jack Kennedy."

Again slotted toward the end of the evening, Sahl had more topical material at hand, particularly with reference to Sinatra, whose picture kept popping up in a discussion of the nation's leaders on the first broadcast. Now he made specific reference to Sinatra's share in the ownership of the Cal-Neva Lodge and a report that he had hosted mobster Sam Giancana at the property, which aroused the interest of Nevada's Gaming Control Board. His seemingly innocent comment: "The Governor of Nevada is objecting to Sinatra's friends—who are Sam Giancana and the President of the United States."

The statement was allowed to go out live in the East and Midwest, but when the show aired via tape delay in the West, the audio was faded after the word "friends," leaving it to lip readers to complete the thought. Lewis, who pointedly mentioned on the first show that the network had four attorneys monitoring the telecast, predictably flew into a rage when he discovered the six-second deletion. In a blistering wire to American Broadcasting-Paramount Theaters president Leonard Goldenson, he contended the network had no right to do such a thing, and that if it ever happened again he would consider it a breach of his contract. Lewis, however, assured Goldenson he was not blaming him personally, but rather "some of the incompetent idiots" on the lower rungs of the organization.

The incident generated some press for the struggling series which, it was hoped, would inspire a badly needed spike in the ratings. Yet the network seemed to blame Mort Sahl for all the commotion and there was talk of eliminating him from the show. It didn't help that after Lewis' volley in the press, Mort chimed in and suggested that ABC owed both of them an apology. "We won't read the telegram to Eastern viewers," he said helpfully.

"They heard the line before it was cut. We'll only read the telegram to the West Coast viewers who didn't hear the remark."

Lewis remained steadfastly in Sahl's corner. Not only would Mort continue to appear on the show, he insisted, but there would be no attempts to censor what he said. "I've had some pretty aggressive agents," Mort said admiringly, "but nobody like Jerry standing up there. He's like Lancelot ahead of me with a spear." As for his spot on the third show of the series, "Jerry just tells me to go ahead. You know how these network guys are. They say, 'We don't understand Sahl.' Jerry says, 'I don't either, but I want to find out.'" Now firmly consigned to the last half hour of the show, Sahl appeared in a coat and tie and, possibly unnerved by the events of the week, delivered a weak set notable mostly for Lewis' elaborate introduction: "Our next guest has been called incisive, witty, and brilliant. He has been called too controversial, not too controversial. Well, he's been called too rough, too mild, too harsh, too gentle. Also constructive, destructive, and instructive. I feel that any comedian—and I believe this—who can inspire that wide a reaction deserves to be heard. I'd like to add to that list funny, unpredictable . . . and my friend. Here are the world . . . and Mort Sahl."

Behind the scenes, Lewis was plainly shaken by the bad ratings and terrible reviews. Soon all parties were sizing up Sahl as the sacrificial lamb, the one glaring thing obviously wrong with *The Jerry Lewis Show*. "Tom Moore and Ted Fetter from ABC came in and said to Lewis, 'The show stinks. We want to pull you off.' He says to them, 'Well, *he* caused all this trouble. If I cancel him, will you guarantee me thirteen weeks?' So I come down to the studio to rehearse and it's locked. He never paid me. I wound up showing up for work three weeks, and he never gave me the $18,000." Moore, the network head, told Hedda Hopper they were behind Lewis for the long haul. "No matter what the rumors are, Jerry is going to be fine," he said. "Mort Sahl is definitely off the show. Things are picking up and you can quote me: We have a winner."

With no income from the Lewis show, Sahl looked into playing the Crescendo again. With the exception of Dick Gregory, Gene Norman had leaned away from comedians, booking reliable music acts like the Mary Kaye Trio and Nancy Wilson in his final days as owner of the club. Now Mort approached Shelly Davis, who had added Jackie Mason and presidential impressionist Vaughan Meader to the year-end calendar. "Shelly Davis was a friend of mine," Mort says, "because he'd been a press agent." Davis said: "I've been told that the White House would be offended if I hired you and I'd be audited on my income tax. I heard you offended the president." Dumbfounded, Mort suspected Milt Ebbins was somehow behind it. "Ebbins used to return from Washington or Palm Springs or visit Lawford's home in Malibu and he'd say to me, 'They squeezed me at dinner: The Old Man said, 'Doesn't Sahl know the meaning of the word loyalty?' He would tell them he could get me to stop doing it. And every time he brought that up, I would react by doing three times as much material."

After one such paternalistic talk, Dorothy Kilgallen was moved to comment, "Goodness, Mort Sahl is being mighty harsh on the Kennedy family in his routine at Basin Street. His diatribes at JFK are rougher than they were at President Eisenhower." And a month later: "Insiders suspect that JFK and the New Frontier's pet gag man, Mort Sahl, have cooled it. In palmier days, Mort used to supply the president with smart lines—or so the legend went." Joseph P. Kennedy had suffered a debilitating stroke in December 1961, and hounding a lowly nightclub comedian into submission became the very least of his concerns. "I don't think it was Jack," Mort says of the president. "I think it was them trying to play up the power. Elmo Roper, the guy who did the surveys, came into my dressing room one night. He said, 'Don't believe the criticism. He loves you.' He gave me a big hug and whispered that in my ear. Ebbins, I think, betrayed me in a hurry."

"I heard about that kind of pressure on Mort at the time," said Steve Allen,

> growing, of course, as it would have, out of concern of the pro-Kennedy camp. I don't remember that it ever affected any of my programs or any of Mort's appearances on my shows. On my show he had complete freedom to do what he wanted to, because I always relied on his good taste and his good judgment. He never let us down. But this is really par for the course. Whoever is in the White House, and whatever comedian is doing jokes critical of the occupant, there is somebody—there at the White House or somebody's brother-in-law—who is talking to the comedian's agent saying, "Hey, a joke or two is funny enough." So I would think it almost certain that there was that kind of objection, that kind of criticism. It's inevitable.

Sahl ended his professional relationship with Milt Ebbins in August 1963, just as Jerry Lewis had seemingly delivered on something Ebbins had not—a regular commentary slot on network television. "He did whatever the Morris office told him. 'Keep him in the clubs. Don't go into television. Tell him to throttle back—they don't want to hear that.' And he covered his conscience by saying, 'Mort could have been a king, but he's just got a rebellious nature. And he rubbed everybody the wrong way.' But what he was really trying to do was to keep me in the corral. I was disappointed. He was kind of an elder figure for me. I pulled away because I thought he was trying to neutralize me."

Stung, Mort spent a good deal of time with Dick Cavett, who had come west to join the writing staff of the Lewis show. "He would call me a lot," said Cavett. "He initiated a lot of wonderful evenings." There were hearty meals at the house on San Ysidro, sometimes with Yvonne Craig, but often not since she was working frequently. Cavett wondered about the absence of other people, the apparent isolation in which Mort seemed to live. "I think there were people who felt self-conscious, even uneducated around him. They felt: I'll just make a fool of myself trying to keep up with him. And they couldn't keep up with him. He suffered from that, I think. That's one of the most complimentary things in my life—that Mort liked me."

The Jerry Lewis Show limped along until November 19, when an agreement was reached with ABC that would pay Lewis $4 million to settle his contract. The show was, he later acknowledged, a disaster. Referencing the million he spent upgrading the El Capitan, he added, "I was so busy getting the proper facilities and fixing and making it the kind of perfection I think our business warrants, I forgot the show. I forgot a minor thing called Get Funny. Some of the pressures that were brought to bear? They were my fault that I allowed them to be brought to bear. I cannot blame anybody but me." The final show, it was announced, would air on December 14.

"I left Mort's house so late one night that the sun had risen," Cavett recalled. "And I had to drive back to my little apartment in Bel Air. Now, how can you stay up and be so bright and so funny for so long? It started with dinner and it lasted 'til 4 or 5 A.M. or whenever the sun comes up in California. And just before I left, he was leaning on the car, passenger's side window, talking through it. He said, 'Twenty-eight years in California, and it's hard to think of anybody I can call up as a friend.'"

A few days later, Mort was seated at his dining table enjoying his usual breakfast of coffee and orange juice. He had the radio on, and was reading the *Los Angeles Times*. It was 10:30 on a sunny Friday morning, almost exactly ten years to the day since his debut performance at the hungry i.

The date was November 22, 1963.

PART TWO

ANYWAY, ONWARD

10

THE NATION'S CONSCIENCE

"I was shocked," Mort says, "but I knew it was going to be twenty-four hours of communal crying and I was waiting for some facts—where, how many, who. And I remember Adlai [Stevenson] had told me, 'He mustn't go down where there are ads up that's he's wanted for treason.' He advised him against going, and Bobby didn't want to listen to anything Adlai said. Really humiliated him."

The president's assassination brought all normal life to a stop. Stores closed, theaters emptied, schools let out, and network programming became one continuous news report that included the live shooting of a suspect while in the custody of the Dallas police. Since he wasn't working, still smarting from the Jerry Lewis debacle, Mort remained sequestered in the house on San Ysidro, riveted to the TV and devouring even more than his usual diet of newspapers and magazines. Yvonne Craig was filming an Elvis Presley picture called *Kissin' Cousins* at M-G-M, so there was little to distract him from the onslaught of media.

Sahl had once again jumped agencies, moving to the newly formed General Artist Corporation, where chairman Larry Barnett, a thirty-seven-year veteran of MCA, was dutifully pitching three different series ideas to the networks. But suggesting a political satirist in the days following a president's murder bordered on bad taste, and there were no takers. In fact, the two solid offers of work that did come only peripherally involved GAC.

In New York, a play by Lorraine Hansberry, her first since *Raisin in the Sun*, struck its director, a friend of Phyllis Kirk's named Carmen Capalbo, as being perfectly suited to Mort Sahl. The title character in *The Sign in Sidney Brustein's Window* was an irritable Jewish intellectual, an artist and writer. Capalbo, whose off-Broadway revival of *The Threepenny Opera* had notched more than twenty-six hundred performances, described it as "a mammoth part," a challenge for a seasoned actor, much less a complete novice. "I've never seen a more difficult role," he said. "Except for three pages in the third act, he's on stage the entire time." Incredibly, Capalbo was able to convince the playwright and her two producers that the role would be a manageable stretch for Mort Sahl, as well as newsworthy casting. The resulting announcement in the *New York Times* came on February 24, 1964, the cast consisting of Mort as Sidney Brustein, Rita Moreno as his wife, Iris, and Peggy Cass as his sister-in-law. Indeed, the part so closely resembled him that Hansberry felt it necessary to emphasize that in no way would the play be tailored to suit him—lest the impression spread that it was written with him in mind.

While plans for *Sidney Brustein* went forth, Sahl accepted a two-week booking at the Copacabana, his first club date in eight months. Business for New York's biggest and best-known nightclubs had dropped to levels not seen since the Depression, and the Copa had actually posted a loss for the year 1963—the first in its history. Management responded by overloading the bills, and so Mort found himself part of an unlikely grouping with actor Eddie Albert and singer Barbara McNair. On opening night, he seemed to acknowledge being off his game by ambling onto the floor in a tie and jacket, explaining to the audience that he had been delayed in traffic and "didn't have time to undress." A Steve Allen appearance the previous day had been equally off-key. Again, the coat and tie, and, again, a somewhat haltingly delivered routine that failed to gain traction with the studio audience. Drawn from notes and a single section of the Sunday *Times*, it was an oddly dispiriting performance that caused Senator Hubert Humphrey, another guest on the program, to observe that Mort was "getting a little soft on Republicans." In the main, the Copacabana engagement was notable for being the first time any aspect of the assassination found its way into the act. "Melvin Belli must be really confused now," he remarked in briefly discussing the trial of Jack Ruby, the killer of Lee Harvey Oswald. "He insulted everybody in Dallas except Jack Ruby—and then RUBY fired him."

As Mort Sahl was struggling to re-establish himself in a segment of the business he had single-handedly revitalized, a second wave of comics influenced and inspired by his example were gaining in prominence, none more so than twenty-eight-year-old Woody Allen. "I never, ever was going to be a performer," he said. "Never had a thought in my mind of doing it until I saw

Mort Sahl. And I thought to myself two things. I thought: Well, you may as well quit because everything great in comedy has now been done by this guy and there's nowhere to go with it. Everything is just over. The other thought I had was: Gee, I would like to do that. What he's doing is so inspiring. Why am I just writing in a room for other comedians? Why don't I get up and do that? Look at him—he's just *amazing*. It would be so much fun to do that."

Happy in his role as a journeyman writer, it took five years for Allen to work up the courage to audition at the Blue Angel. By 1961 he was a regular presence at the club, having perfected a character Arthur Gelb described as "a Chaplinesque victim with an S. J. Perelman sense of the bizarre and a Mort Sahl delivery." In Allen's surrealistic world, a girl he fancied listened to Marcel Marceau records, a struggling artist he knew attempted to cut off his ear with an electric razor, and an "authentic, ethnic folk singer" he admired still sported a leg shackle. He described what he did as "creating verbal cartoons" such as when he was thrown out of NYU for cheating on his metaphysics final. "I looked within the soul of the boy sitting next to me," he admitted.

In November 1963, Allen was the subject of a profile for the *New York Times Magazine* in which Mort's name was invoked more than once. "Somewhere in the back of my head I suppose I'd always thought about telling the jokes as well as writing them," he said in the article, "but I'd never had the nerve to talk about it. Then Mort Sahl came along with a whole new style of humor, opening up vistas for people like me." By then, he had advanced to the Bitter End and regular appearances on shows as varied as *Candid Camera*, *Jack Paar*, and *Hootenanny*. "It was just like when you hear a great, great jazz player," he said fifty-two years later, "and you think: God, I'm going to go out and buy a trumpet or a clarinet and take lessons because this guy looks like he's having the greatest time. And so Mort was 100% responsible for my becoming a comedian."

When Shelly Davis, the new owner of the Crescendo, finally got over his reluctance to book Mort Sahl, it was for the Interlude, the little upstairs space Sahl hadn't played since 1958. Brought in on a four-week guarantee, he wasn't paired with anyone else at first, and Davis' ads laid it on thick:

THE NATION'S CONSCIENCE
MORT SAHL
RETURNING TO THE SITE OF HIS SPRINGBOARD TO FAME!

Opening night, Sahl's first on the Strip in nearly a year, was consistent with his other performances of late—little political content, and what was there was so soft as to be deemed out of character. Part of it had to do with the assassination—still an open wound for audiences after just six months. Then there was a general disengagement that took place when the charismatic young president was followed into office by a polar opposite in the person of Lyndon Johnson. "He made so many things about government popular," Mort said of Kennedy, "that it made my job easier. Still, there are limitations. You can't get a laugh with Hubert Humphrey; they don't know who he is. Even Adlai Stevenson doesn't evoke any response. And there's no reaction to Bobby Kennedy, which is something President Johnson made note of. I've been laying off Goldwater because he's too easy a target. His position is defined; all you have to do is trigger the mechanism and it explodes—witness all the 19th century jokes the other fellows are using."

"A less toxic, less furious and somewhat less stimulating Mort Sahl has launched a month-long stand at this spot," began the notice in *Daily Variety*. "Even off form, he's still about the sharpest comic-commentator extant, but his devoted followers may be disappointed at the slightly mellowed, seemingly more inner-directed version of Sahl they are apt to encounter, if the opening night performance is accurately representative of the current phase of his disposition as a humorist. 'The Nation's Conscience' seemed poorly prepared for his stint. His material seemed dated and blunt."

Whatever had thrown him off—the assassination, prolonged periods of inactivity, a precipitous dip in income, depression—it wasn't enough to keep the people—*his* people—away. Attendance built steadily, fueled by word of mouth, and by the end of the run he was doing four shows a night to handle the throngs. Davis, the new impresario, was delighted, but with Sahl's revitalized schedule—he was booked to go into New York's Café Au Go Go in June, Basin Street East in July, and rehearsals for the Hansberry play in August—he wouldn't be available again until sometime in 1965. And by then the Crescendo and Interlude would be no more, the victims of unpaid taxes, changing tastes, and a business model that was no longer sustainable. The building would briefly house a rock music venue known as The Trip and then fall to the wreckers, the site made into a parking lot for the adjacent Playboy building.

Just prior to Mort's opening at the Interlude, Mike Connelly of the *Hollywood Reporter* ran a one-line item in his column: "Mort Sahl and Yvonne

Craig have called it a day." The split may have come because Yvonne had been linked in the gossip columns to Elvis Presley, a relationship she described as platonic. Or tensions may have resulted from the simple fact that she was working constantly while Mort was not, or that she was getting movies when Mort hadn't been offered one in years. "He used to say to Milt Ebbins, 'James Garner became a movie star. I don't know why you can't do that for me.' And the reason Milt couldn't do it for him was because Mort did every-thing off the top of his head—so that three nights running he did not do the same show. If you got him on the first take you probably got it, but if you asked him to do it again, and it was somebody else's lines, it wouldn't happen. He was not an actor."

Syndicated columnist Harrison Carroll phoned Mort for a statement. "She's a wonderful girl," he responded. "We had no fight. We just adjourned, but it's permanent." Two weeks later, Carroll reported raised eyebrows at La Scala when the two made an appearance and had dinner together. "Mort and I will always be friends," Yvonne said. "I'm not sure what's going to hap-pen. We are trying to figure things out."

As the 1964 convention season approached, Mort Sahl expected to land another commentary gig, as he had with KHJ in 1960. He told *Variety*'s Jack Pitman he was available to repeat for RKO-General, the station's owner, but expressed an unabashed preference for network exposure. "GAC has been trying to stoke interest in him at the webs," Pitman reported, "but so far no takers. Implying a status quo on the net's reaction, Sahl says 'it's all up for grabs.' At CBS, he jabs, political punditry 'is not a funny issue,' and 'NBC is like out to lunch.' With ABC, 'it's not a matter of morality—they're worried about libel.' (More likely the 'equal time' clamor.) Re: his ardor for the jour-nalistic role, the elder statesman of the nightclub 'new wave' explains, 'I just think the conventions would be too much fun to miss.'"

Finally, in May it was announced that Sahl would indeed repeat for KHJ, and he appeared at a cocktail party thrown by the station's manager to make it official. Instead of again pairing him with David Susskind, this time there would be a trio of observers for the Republican National Convention in San Francisco: Sahl, former California governor Goodwin Knight, and KHJ news commentator Clete Roberts. At the party, all three men took their turns at the mic, but attention was focused primarily on Mort, who was perceived as the senior member of the team as well as the most quotable. "General Eisen-hower is finally taking an interest in politics," he said, repurposing a line he had originally used in 1956. And: "Lyndon B. Johnson is the only president who ever put the country in his wife's name." It was stressed that KHJ's coverage would go on the air after the networks had finished for the night, and that it would have a "human, lighter touch." Emboldened, Mort again pressed for a nightly news slot on one of the networks. "I had an offer to do 45 seconds of news at 11:14 but I turned it down," he revealed. "Can you see people asking me what I'm doing all day? 'I'm waiting for those 45 seconds at 11:14.'"

It was Mort's stretch at Café Au Go Go that broke the curse, the miasma that seemed to envelope him in the months following the president's murder. The scene, a basement coffeehouse in Greenwich Village, placed him comfortably within feet of such familiar establishments as the Bitter End, the Dugout, Pizza Plaza, the Village Corner, and Snooky's Luncheonette. Owned and run by a Wall Street account executive, it needed a restorative shot of class after a late-model Lenny Bruce had gotten himself (and the proprietor) arrested on an obscene language charge in a room otherwise known for its burgers and sundaes. Present for the opening night embrace were Paul Newman and Joanne Woodward, actor Robert Preston and his wife, Henry Fonda, and Warren Beatty. It was a far cry from his difficult run at the Copa where, as he said, "I emceed dinner." Now thoroughly back in his element, he drew the generous press attention a return to form so richly merited.

"There is something persistently juvenile in Mort Sahl's appearance and bearing, supported by his working costume of slacks and pullover, that reduces any signs of increasing age (the guy is now 37) to nothing more serious than the symptoms of an undergraduate hangover," wrote John Canaday in the *New York Times*. "When he grasps the microphone at the Café Au Go Go, 152 Bleecker Street, for an hour's monologue, he has the air, at once cocky and nervous, of the dean's worst problem child. With the highest I.Q. and the most erratic scholastic record on the campus, he had come to another exam unprepared. In an excess of empathy, you are immediately rooting for him in his necessity to bluff through once again. You needn't worry. The laughter at the Café Au Go Go is continuous."

It was to the Café Au Go Go one night that Newman, with whom Mort was staying in Westport, brought Richard Burton and Elizabeth Taylor. Burton, to whom Yvonne Craig took an immediate dislike, was appearing in John Gielgud's modern-dress production of *Hamlet* at the Lunt-Fontanne.

According to Yvonne, the party tried slipping in after the lights dimmed, but Taylor was spotted anyway and a commotion ensued. "Everyone wanted to see Elizabeth Taylor and Paul Newman," said Mort. "And they all swamped over the stage and finally into my dressing room. A guy from the *New York Post* said to Burton, 'What are you doing here?' Burton said, 'Well, I always come to see Mort.' The guy said, 'Why?' Burton said, 'Mort is rare. He's not burdened like the rest of us actors with the words of an author—the words are his own.' I would have liked it better if the author hadn't been Shakespeare."

On site for the Republican National Convention, Mort found himself battling an utter lack of suspense in Barry Goldwater's eventual nomination, a certainty that contributed to making the GOP's quadrennial event one of the dullest in memory. KHJ's coverage, distributed to a network of stations up and down the state, was laden with commercials, but there were still occasional observations that trumped the gaffe-prone proceedings on CBS, NBC, and ABC. Considering Oregon governor Mark Hatfield's address, in which he grouped the John Birch Society with the Communist Party and the Ku Klux Klan to the obvious displeasure of many of the attendees, Sahl said the charismatic young leader seemed to him "the Dr. Kildare of politics." Later, once the nomination had been cinched, he revealed that Hedda Hopper was happier about the Goldwater victory than anything since she had heard a rumor that Hitler had turned up alive in South America.

It was generally thought that Senator Goldwater was more vulnerable to the sting of satire than LBJ, who undeniably took office under the most horrendous of circumstances. But it would not be an exaggeration to say that political comedy came creeping back into fashion with Mort Sahl's June appearances at Café Au Go Go. And now, in August, he returned to New York to effectively seal the deal with a month-long stand at Basin Street East, partners Watkins and Green apparently unconcerned that he had just recently spent three high-profile weeks appearing in the Village. Taking the stage on opening night in a bright orange sweater, he immediately zeroed in on Goldwater, explaining that he had just played the Sombrero Playhouse in the senator's hometown of Phoenix. Driving around the city, he told of passing a Goldwater's—one of a chain of department stores founded by the senator's family—and seeing a banner that read: GIANT SALE—EVERYTHING MUST GO—SHOES . . . DRESSES . . . TVA . . .

While at Basin Street, Mort cooperated with a profile for the *Saturday Evening Post*. "Isn't that a great comment on our society?" he said of his supposed earning power. "What do you do when you're antiauthoritarian? For me, you get up on a nightclub floor and attack authority. I mount my neuroses every night, and I'm a big hero." The Kennedy people, he pointed out, never understood him. "They don't think you have a philosophy. They think if you're not for them, you're against them. It's like, 'Who do you think you are?' And you say, 'I think I'm me.'" It was better, he decided, to remain on the outside looking in at his targets. "It's a mistake to meet them," he added, "because they're all good guys when they can relax and be themselves. I had a great time talking to Nixon, and I wasn't coming on with the ax like I used to." Asked about his own politics, he allowed as how he was against the Republicans for what they were, and against the Democrats for what they weren't. "I run a very elusive course, leaning a bit to the left to correct for drift in the country."

Rehearsals for *The Sign in Sidney Brustein's Window* began the week of August 17, 1964. Mort acknowledges it as "a big mistake all the way around," but at the time he thought he could pull it off because, he said, the role reminded him so much of himself. "Except he has the courage to whisper. He doesn't have to *geshrei* all the time. He doesn't have to be hostile." The production, capitalized at $125,000, was set to open on October 5, but the play itself was a rough draft desperately in need of sharpening. It needed all of Lorraine Hansberry's time and attention, but having fallen ill with pancreatic cancer, she wasn't up to the job. "If there had been time," wrote Rita Moreno in her autobiography, "Lorraine may well have streamlined and refined the play, but with so little time to prepare the production, and little input from her, we could only hurtle from one emergency to the next." After a few wan appearances, the playwright vanished to her sickbed, and co-producer Robert Nemiroff, her ex-husband, tried making all the fixes himself.

At first, everyone was on book, and the casting of Mort Sahl appeared to be a gamble that was destined to pay off. "The play went so well for the first week," said Carmen Capalbo, "I was almost sure that nothing would go wrong." They got it on its feet, but the material was daunting for everyone, not just Mort. "Every speech in the play starts with, 'Sidney . . . ,'" he remembers. "Everybody talks to me; I'm the king of the neighborhood. 'Sidney, I wonder where my life is going.' 'Sidney, I love you.' 'Sidney . . .' So when people used to get hung up rehearsing, they'd say to the director, 'Line, please.' I'd say, 'Sidney! I'm sure it's Sidney!'"

The very qualities that made Sahl an extemporaneous comedian, unburdened, as Richard Burton so aptly put it, with the words of an author, conspired against him when essaying the role of Sidney Brustein. "He had seemed like such a brilliant choice," said Rita Moreno, "but he never did learn his lines, and then he vanished too." It was a slow fade that took nearly four weeks. "The director, Capalbo, wanted me to learn to play the guitar," he says. "Cliff Robertson came over. He said, 'You don't have to do that. I did *Orpheus Descending*. Just have him turn away from the audience and play. I did it all season.' Well, that's not good enough for them. I got awful tired with guitar lessons and rehearsals. One morning, I leaned over to rinse my mouth while brushing my teeth and I couldn't straighten up. I lost my balance. I hit my head on the sink." Robert Nemiroff's co-producer was Burt D'Lugoff, brother of Village Gate impresario Art D'Lugoff and a doctor of internal medicine. "He says, 'You need some sleep. Here's a prescription.'"

Yvonne Craig, in New York to read for a part in Susan Slade's comedy *Ready When You Are, C. B.!* was there for the worst of it. "What did they give him? Something . . . chloral hydrate, I think. And that's a kind of chloroform. [D'Lugoff] was writing prescription drugs for everybody in that company. 'If you can't sleep, I'll give you something that will allow you to sleep, but then, if you can't get up for the rehearsal, then I'll give you this.' And he was allowed to do that because he was a physician." Famously abstinent, Mort had no resistance to such powerful drugs, and his inability to memorize lines only worsened. "I think it's the same thing that happened to him in movies. He doesn't do other people's lines. If they had said, 'Let's improvise *The Sign in Sidney Brustein's Window*,' he'd have been home free. But they didn't handle it well. I mean, if you're the producer or the director, you go and you say, 'Look, this is not working out. You're still holding a script. We are going to open in three weeks, and I need you to either dump it and know those lines, or fess up and give it up.' And nobody ever did that. He went to the theatre and it was locked!"

Sahl contended that he reported sick on September 10, a Thursday, while Nemiroff insisted that he hadn't. On Friday, he flew to Los Angeles to see his doctor, and rehearsals continued with the stage manager reading Sidney's lines. The following Monday, he was barred from returning to work, and Capalbo was instructed to start auditioning replacements. Nemiroff told the press that no illness claim had been made until Tuesday, and that Sahl's employment had therefore been terminated. A meeting on Wednesday failed to resolve the matter, and Actors' Equity was formally notified.

"At this point, no charges have been filed against Mr. Sahl with Equity," D'Lugoff told the *Times*, but he added that he had a month in which to file and that he would be guided by the advice of his attorney.

Mort remained in New York long enough to see the part of Sidney Brustein recast with Gabriel Dell, a former Dead End Kid, and the withdrawal of Carmen Capalbo, who walked the plank for his inspired casting of a comedian with no acting chops. As Yvonne was preparing to take Mort to the airport, she threw out the pills D'Lugoff had prescribed. "He hadn't had them for about three days while they sorted this out: Is he going to stay in the city? And is he going to do the play?" On the way to the airport,

> he had what looked like a grand mal seizure, and I thought he was joking because we were talking about Peter [Lawford]. Peter had always believed that there were ghosts in houses where he lived, so I said, "Oh God, Peter . . . he's so full of it. He's so worried about ghosts." And Mort's hands started to shake. You know how people do: "*I'm a monnnsterrrr.*" I thought that's what he was doing, and then I thought: Well, that isn't his sense of humor, but okay. Then I realized that he was having a seizure, so the driver pulled over. There was this horrible person who was with us. He called himself Bombay, and he was a thief. (God, Mort knew some people.) Bombay threw him down in the seat. I didn't think he should be lying down, and so I picked him up again and started rubbing his back. God, I am so lucky I didn't paralyze him because he did not need his back rubbed—he had broken the thoracic vertebrae.
>
> We took him to Roosevelt Hospital, and the guy said to me: "Is he a drug addict?" Immediately. I said, "No!" Then I said, "Well, he was taking sleeping pills, but I took them away from him the other day." And he said: "Lady, you put him into drug withdrawal."

Mort was transferred to Columbia Presbyterian Medical Center, where it was reported that he had injured four vertebrae and was suffering from extreme fatigue. ("You've broken your own back," the doctor told him.) His condition was listed as good, but he would be in the hospital for several weeks. When he was released in mid-October, he was in a brace and forbidden to work until January. But that wouldn't be the end of *The Sign in Sidney Brustein's Window*.

✧ ✧ ✧

When offered an hour of live election wrap-up on KCET, the NET affiliate
in Los Angeles, Sahl took the gig, even though the UHF station wasn't
widely received in the area and he was still in a back brace for at least half
of each day. Titled *I'd Rather Berate Than President*, it was set to air the
night after the election, but on election night he learned the station had
decided to pre-tape his remarks for review. Incredulous, he balked, and
station manager Jim Robertson said that he didn't blame him. "All I want
to do is get to the people," Mort told *Times* columnist Hal Humphrey, "and
to do that you have to be on TV. This country needs a social critic. There
are worse things than communism, segregation, Jimmy Hoffa, and Republicans, but you wouldn't know it from watching TV." Once again, he found
himself venting to the media rather than being an integral part of it. "I've
seen *That Was the Week That Was* go far beyond what I would do, but it's on
NBC every week. I asked the William Morris Agency to go to ABC and get
me a late-night thing to compete with *The Tonight Show*. They kept telling
me ABC wasn't interested, then the network hires Les Crane and bills him
as 'controversial.' Now I'm with General Artists Corporation, and when
Steve Allen quit his syndicated show with Westinghouse, I didn't get the
job. But General Artists signs this Regis Philbin after he takes over for
Allen. Is that wild?"

As a consolation, GAC got him on *That Regis Philbin Show* for two guest
appearances and a week as co-host. Against his doctor's advice, Mort took
the bookings, which paid union scale, and was defiantly seen around town
again with Yvonne, notably at Phyllis Diller's November opening at the Crescendo. "I was very down," he comments. "I was worried I was never going
to work again. I was just going to float down the River Styx. So I didn't know
how to handle anything, including love. Yvonne lived way the hell over at
Sunset and Western. She'd drive over to the house every day. Long drive.
She had a Corvair. And her sister didn't like me much. Half of the rap was
that I was unorthodox. Nobody knew what to do with that."

The producers of *The Sign in Sidney Brustein's Window* weren't finished with
him. Still to be sorted out in arbitration were charges that Sahl had failed to
appear for rehearsals. The production, they contended, never recovered from
the expense of having to replace him, their reserves dissipated to the point
that a loan of $8,500 had to be secured from "someone close" in order to keep

the show open. And now, as Lorraine Hansberry lay near death and the play staggered toward its closing, they were seeking relief through arbitration.

Granted a hearing by Actors' Equity, each side was to select a representative. "I asked Paul Newman to represent me," says Mort. "I was out of my bailiwick." Newman, however, balked. "If I tell them the truth," he said, "you're not an actor at all. You don't have the commitment. All you think about is broads." Mort was incredulous: "I said, 'You mean I should be grateful because you won't help me?' And he said to me, 'Does anybody that tells you the truth run the risk that you'll never talk to them again?' I said, 'Yeah.' And I walked out." After several hearings, an internal Equity committee ruled that Sahl had indeed breached his agreement. Fined $1,000, to be donated to the union's welfare fund, his sole consolation was that "they were forced to call me an actor for jurisdictional purposes."

The decision cleared the way for the producers to seek $25,000 in damages, the money to cover costs associated with the cancellation of ten previews and the postponement of the opening from October 5 to October 15. Apart from the money, the time lost, the bad publicity, and the broken back, the ultimate cost was the loss of Paul Newman's friendship. "That was the way it ended," says Mort. "I'm sorry that's the way it ended, but he wouldn't throw me a rope. He said all I thought about was Yvonne, that I wasn't a disciplined actor. And I thought he was ducking the fact that I was getting crucified. I thought a lot about that in Hollywood—nobody wanted any part of any conflict. I thought the guy loved me. I loved him."

Work picked up in 1965, but there were still long stretches of inactivity. Producer Bill Harbach offered him a guest shot on ABC's version of the Sullivan show, *The Hollywood Palace*. ("When vaudeville died," Bob Hope once quipped, "the box they put it in was television.") With a Q Score that was scarcely a blip, Mort was an obvious choice to sub for host David Frost on *That Was the Week That Was* and little else. In Washington to play a club called the Shadows, he attended a Nixon press conference and took the opportunity to visit the White House, where he encountered Lady Bird Johnson and lunched with Ted Kennedy. Asked at a National Press Club luncheon, at which he was both guest of honor and principal speaker, what he thought the difference was between JFK's New Frontier and LBJ's Great Society, he replied, "A short memory."

Faced with an anemic nightclub scene, Sahl arranged to spend the greater part of the year at the hungry i, commencing April 26. ("Comedian Mort

Sahl, having more downs than ups recently, opens a four week run next week at the hungry i, scene of his glory years," Herb Caen noted sourly.) Another four weeks would come in October, and then an indefinite run beginning November 29. It all started out well enough. Opening were the comedy team of Jack Burns and Avery Schreiber and Broadway vocalist Lainie Kazan (making her club debut). The first night was a sellout, Sahl mining considerable material from his stint in Washington. ("At the CIA they have a sign: Keep to the Right.") A review in the *Oakland Tribune* carried the headline, MORT SAHL GREAT AS EVER.

Then, a couple of weeks into the engagement, his voice weakened, a matter he laid to laryngitis. (It had been giving him trouble for several months.) A visit to the doctor determined the problem was something worse—polyps. Ordered to keep quiet between sets, he took to communicating with bits of paper. An interview with Dick Nolan of the *San Francisco Examiner* became a clash of wills, Mort employing scribbled notes and hand signals to maintain control. On stage, the voice was hoarse, the throat raw, but the content had new vitality since he found he had to up his game with a target like Lyndon Baines Johnson. "You start by using an invented exaggeration about life on the LBJ ranch," he explained to UPI's Merriman Smith, "and then you discover he really *does* herd cattle in a white Continental." He closed as scheduled on May 22 and returned to Los Angeles, where he underwent surgery to remove a benign polypoidal tumor from his larynx at Cedars of Lebanon. "It's evolution," he explained on a scrap of paper. "If we don't protest enough, we lose our voices."

The surgery forced him to cancel a booking at Mister Kelly's, but in July he was back on his crusade to save America, first in Atlantic City, then, significantly, at the Sands Hotel in Las Vegas, where he shared the bill with singer Patti Page. It was Jerry Lewis who suggested the booking to Sands entertainment director Jack Entratter. "The reason you're not working," Lewis told Mort over dinner one evening, "is because you do the news. We've got Chet Huntley, so we don't need you." When he asked if Mort had ever worked in Vegas, Mort, of course, replied that he had. "Well," said Lewis, "you ought to work there again." And, impulsively, he phoned Entratter to close the sale. "Jack," began Lewis grandly, "how would you like to be the first guy to present the *new* Mort Sahl?" Entratter, formerly Jules Podell's general manager at the Copacabana, paused to let the question sink in. "I didn't like the *old* Mort Sahl," he said. Undaunted, Lewis pressed his case: "He's gonna wear a tuxedo. And he's gonna do as much time as you want . . ." Snowed under, Entratter agreed to the booking and gratefully ended the call. "And I want equal billing," Lewis shouted as the line went dead. "Remember now," he cautioned Mort, "you gotta change your act."

"There's more appreciation of satire now," Sahl told the *Los Angeles Times*, "so I decided to take the great leap and confront the lost faces along the Strip." The performance became a high-profile repeat of his turn on *Hollywood Palace*, Mort once again eschewing the sweater for the tuxedo Lewis had promised. Introduced as the "new" Mort Sahl, he emerged from the wings to hang his orange sweater on a coat rack that constituted his only scenery. "This is our flag now, right?" he said. "It's at half-mast now, symbolically."

He faced the same skepticism in the trades that had dogged his first Vegas booking in 1959, when Gisele MacKenzie imperiously limited him to twelve minutes. Entertainment columnist Charles Champlin covered the opening for the *Los Angeles Times*, and deplored how the nightclubs that had collectively been Sahl's forum had mostly gone dark or topless. "The club thing is over," Mort agreed. "But I think TV can be the second stage of the booster." With a friend, he said he had worked up a storyboard for a kind of illustrated commentary on the news. "People keep asking: Can I reach the audiences? And do they want to be reached? They want to be reached, and of course I can reach them—if I have the platform."

The platform finally arrived in the form of a Susskind-style talk show, an open-ended slot on Saturday nights on WNEW, the Metromedia station in New York City. The offer sprang from Sahl's appearance at the Sands, as did a November 21, 1965, booking with Ed Sullivan—his first in three years. Originally titled *Mort Sahl's People*, the show would be taped at WNEW's studios on East 67th Street, a short walk from Hugh Hefner's unused apartment, where Mort would be living over the course of his twenty-six-week contract. The format, blandly described by the *New York Times* as "various guests talking on various subjects," called for a lot of interaction with a studio audience, Mort providing cohesion and controversy as he sought to mold the show into the sort of news commentary he had been proposing for years.

The station's general manager, Lawrence Fraiberg, had been in charge of sales at San Francisco's KPIX during the years Mort was making his name at the hungry i. Newly arrived in New York after a long stint at Metromedia's

Washington outlet, Fraiberg had the idea of placing the show with the company's entire group of five stations, eventually syndicating it to other markets as well. To boost media attention, the colorful Fraiberg bought out Sybil Burton's trendy new discotheque Arthur and threw a launch party. Then he delayed the show's premiere a week to allow the Sullivan appearance to sink in with viewers.

The experience over at CBS, however, became a harbinger of trouble to come. "I walked in," Mort recalled,

> and Sullivan said, "Do what you did in Vegas." I did it. I opened by starting with, "Lyndon Johnson . . ." and Sullivan said, "Hey, hold on, what's this?" I said, "It's the story about my meeting Johnson." Sullivan said, "You never met Johnson." I said, "As a matter of fact, I did." "That's *not* what you did in Vegas." "Yes, it is." "Well, I don't think people want to hear about your meeting a president. It's not believable." Oh, well. I went a little further and he said, "Why can't you talk about things that are funny . . . like that great comedian . . . his name doesn't come to mind . . . the little red-headed guy." I said, "Woody Allen." "Yeah. Why can't you do what he does?" So I said, "Why don't you hire him?" "Well, I told you I'd use you, and I keep my word. Now, do what you did in Vegas." "This *is* what I did in Vegas!"

Sullivan, Mort figured, had obviously had a change of heart and was trying to provoke him into quitting. "How about doing something on Ronald Reagan and George Murphy?" Ed suggested, trying to steer the subject away from Vietnam. Civil rights was out, too, he added, saying that he had gone through all that with Harry Belafonte. The torture continued until Sullivan finally said, "Why don't you come and see me in my office tomorrow at ten o'clock?" When he went back, Mort ran into comedian Jack E. Leonard in the hallway. "What are you here for?" he asked.

"I'm replacing somebody," Fat Jack replied.

With press attention at a peak, *The Mort Sahl Show* opened for business on Saturday, November 27, 1965, at 10 P.M. The *Times'* Jack Gould thought the host off his game, his skills as an interviewer lacking. Sahl did, however, make news with his very first guest, Judge Joe B. Brown, who presided at the Texas murder trial of Jack Ruby. It was Brown's opinion there was no connection between Ruby and Lee Harvey Oswald prior to the killing, and that the alleged assassin of John F. Kennedy wasn't even shooting at him. "I really think that Oswald was shooting for [Governor John] Connally and the president got in the line of fire," he told Mort. "He had cause to hate Connally. When Connally was Secretary of the Navy, he refused to change his discharge." John Chancellor, now director of the Voice of America, discussed the government's propaganda arm under Mort's softball questioning, and Walter and Miriam Schneer, authors of *Invitation to an Inquest*, sharply criticized the FBI's role in the Julius and Ethel Rosenberg espionage case. "Mr. Sahl could have a workable format going for him," Gould concluded, "but he will need to dig beneath the generalities advanced by his guests. Oddly, the humorist's monologues on matters in the news were the show's weakest link. Some of the quips were dismally tactless. But with experimentation *The Mort Sahl Show* may make it; a late-evening period of outspokenness could be a welcome complement to the existing innocuous chit-chat."

Ratings for the first show, which went up against network offerings like *Gunsmoke* and the *NBC Saturday Night Movie*, were described as "fairish." In line with Gould's comments, station executives began to prod their unmanageable host toward a sharper, more adversarial line of questioning, on a par with the confrontational Joe Pyne, who was driving Saturday night ratings at KTTV, the Metromedia outlet in Los Angeles. "The station started to tell me what guests to book," said Mort. "We argued all week."

The tension was evident as he began the warmup for his second show, for which the guests were to be activist James Farmer, Betty Shabazz, the widow of Malcolm X, former studio head and playwright Dore Schary, and animal activist Cleveland Amory. As Bennett Korn, president of Metromedia's TV division, watched from the audience with a group of friends, Mort announced that the crowd had been salted with plants. "James Farmer is going to be attacked. He doesn't know it. It's a setup and it's supposed to pass for controversy . . . but it isn't." He then proceeded to lay into management. "Mort," said Yvonne Craig, who was in the studio, "warmed up the audience by saying, 'Hitler didn't kill enough Jews and the ones he killed were not on *my* list.' And Korn was sitting there with twelve of his friends, all of whom had to have lost relatives in the Holocaust."

The show went on as scheduled, but in the general malaise that followed, there could be no doubt about the damage that had been done. Korn, who, like Fraiberg, had worked his way up from account executive, was a proponent of highbrow programming, having once been married to concert

pianist Moura Lympany. The previous year he had fired David Susskind for
devoting an episode of *Open End* to "The Sexual Revolution in America"
without prior clearance. Now he prepared to sack Mort Sahl for a remark
he hadn't even made on air. Three days after the show went out, WNEW
announced that Sahl had "breached his agreement with us and we have terminated his contract." While a chastened Larry Fraiberg declined to explain
the exact nature of the breach, Abby Greshler, Sahl's agent of the moment,
suggested his client had merely taken off on the station and its executives
"in a kidding way." After having achieved the thing for which he had spent
three years striving, Mort Sahl had managed to destroy it all in the space of
two weeks.

"Mort was livid," Yvonne remembered. "He said to me, 'Why would they
fire me?' I said, 'Because of what you said. They all have to have lost relatives, Mort.' He said, 'They know I'm iconoclastic. I would never say that on
the air, but they hired me because I'm iconoclastic.' And I said, 'Yeah, but
now they don't trust you because they're afraid you'll say it on the air.' He
truly was surprised."

For his producer Sahl had selected Bob Bach, a fellow jazz enthusiast
who was the creator and associate producer of *What's My Line?* ("He tried
to shut me up all the time," Mort remembers. "There were no conservative
censors—only liberals.") Bach would eventually return to Goodson-Todman
after years as an independent producer. Suddenly out of work, as was the
rest of the staff, Bach attempted to move on. Three weeks later, still at liberty, he finally received his business cards as the erstwhile producer of *The
Mort Sahl Show*.

11

A VAST SPIRIT OF PESSIMISM

By the time of the WNEW fiasco, Mort Sahl and Yvonne Craig had been an item in the columns for three years, splitting frequently but somehow always drifting back together again. To Yvonne, Mort was bright and funny and "just neurotic enough" to be attractive to her. "People use to say, 'How can you go out with him? He's so cynical.' And I thought: The truth of the matter is *I'm* cynical. He is not." Yet Mort's volatility and his obsessive nature were bound to wear on anyone close to him. "It was hard knowing me," he admitted, recalling a story that Enrico Banducci liked to tell. "Once, when he went to pick up [Paul] Newman at the airport, he said, 'I love Mort.' Newman said, 'I love him too.' And Enrico said, 'But can you stand him twenty-four hours a day?' Newman said, 'Hell, no.'"

"He was very intense," Yvonne conceded. "And I don't think people can live at that kind of intensity." He was also impossible to please, something she observed in his relationship with his parents. "One of them called one day, and I overheard the conversation. He said, 'Yeah, I'm doing such-and-such in blah, blah, and then I'm going on to Jules Podell's and I'm doing da-da-da.' He's saying all of these things, and then he said, 'Yeah, uh huh, okay . . . well, goodbye.' And then he said: 'They never ask how I am.' I said, 'They can't win with you because the other day your mother called you and said, 'How are you?' and you said, 'Have you no interest in my career?' They could never win."

Sometimes, their breaks were lengthy. Yvonne entered into a months-long relationship with actor Vince Edwards—TV's Ben Casey—that ended when Edwards impulsively married another actress. And Mort was briefly linked to actress Bara Byrnes while Yvonne was spending time with Elvis Presley. When the subject of marriage came up, it was Yvonne, not Mort, who was wary: "By that time we'd been through so much, I knew I couldn't ever say that I would take him 'for better or worse.' We'd already used up all the 'worse.'" They parted in New York, Mort down on his luck and impossible to be around. "I was having a big intermission," he says. "I wasn't working a lot. They were really toying with the idea of just rubbing me out. Like an eraser. I was running around trying to get work."

Playboy's Playmate of the Month for August 1964 made pop culture history. Margaret "China" Lee became the magazine's first Asian centerfold, a beautiful New Orleans native who had been a Playboy Bunny since the age of nineteen. Reared as one of eight siblings in a strict Chinese household, China (pronounced Chee-na) was working as a hairdresser when she bet one of her brothers she could get a job at the new Playboy Club. Used to waiting tables at her family's Chinese restaurant, House of Lee, China was a natural for the job, strong and buxom with a take-charge attitude. She was brought to Chicago to work the original club on Walton Street, then helped open the St. Louis and New York locations as a Training Bunny.

"She was the Door Bunny and I was a waitress," recalled Elaine "Teddy" Howard, who met her in New York in 1962. "The Door Bunny is the girl who is privileged to wear the black satin bunny costume, and she greets everyone who comes to the door and asks to see the member's key. She's really in the spotlight, and in New York it was all glass in front with the winding staircase. China could be seen all night long by passersby, at the door and through the glass, so it was very dramatic and very sexy."

The other girls considered China a tough number, competitive and no-nonsense. "She was known to the rest of us as a barracuda: Club slang for a Bunny you didn't want to cross," wrote actress and author Katherine Leigh Scott, "Bunny Kay" at the New York Club. China was a champion bowler, an expert swimmer, and a prize-winning equestrienne and jumper. She pitched for the Bunny softball team, winning the title in the girls' division of the Broadway Show League. ("My windmill pitch is unhittable," she boasted.) She played a hooker in the movie *The Troublemaker*, gracing the cover of the soundtrack album and singing its love theme, a Cy Coleman tune called "Here I Go Again." She was in San Francisco for the 1965 opening of the Playboy Club at Portsmouth Square when she encountered Mort Sahl, who was working a two-night benefit for Muscular Dystrophy in one of the club's intimate showrooms.

They had met before, just once, in Chicago. "I was working at Mister Kelly's," Mort says. "Chicago went all night—it wasn't like New York. New

York *used* to be like that. Everybody went up to Muskett and Hendrickson, a twenty-four-hour drug store that had a restaurant in back. Whenever I finished at Kelly's I'd go over there, and they served a little filet with cheese on it. She was coming in with Tony Bennett and somebody introduced me to them. I just met her to say hello, and I never saw her again." In San Francisco, Hugh Hefner had given him the use of a limousine. "She was closing the club and I gave her a ride home. I played it with my old technique, which is to stay on the *other* side of the car. Never even shook her hand or anything. I said, 'We'll see each other again in L.A.' I wasn't exactly the stereotype of all the guys she met at Playboy."

He phoned a couple of weeks later, having briefly escaped to Los Angeles after the humiliation of the Sullivan cancellation and the tepid response that greeted the first *Mort Sahl Show*. "When he called to ask me out," China remembered, "I said to him that I had a date and that I couldn't go out. He sounded like he was holding back tears, and I knew something was wrong. Then he said to me, 'What about your roommate? Can she go out?' And to myself I said: Oh, my God. He doesn't even *know* my roommate. So I said, 'Well, wait a minute. Let me try to find the guy I'm going out with tonight and see if I can make it for another night.' He picked me up in his Cobra and we went up and sat at Mulholland to talk. He was sobbing in his car, so that's how I got hooked. He was so alone; he just thought that everyone was against him. He didn't know where he was going. Even though he had a television show in New York, he was a mess."

He flew back to New York for the second *Mort Sahl Show*, reconnecting with Yvonne Craig—who was passing through town—in the process. Earl Wilson reported seeing the two of them at the Playboy Club in early December, then Mort was spotted again, this time stag, with Henry Silva, Don Adams, and Vince Edwards. When Harrison Carroll saw him in Hollywood the following month, it was amid reports that he was carrying a heavy torch for Yvonne. With him at Ruebens, Carroll reported, was China Lee.

"I got him back to work," said China, who only had to work Saturdays at the Los Angeles club to cover her living expenses. She pushed him to take gigs wherever he could find them—The Golden Bear, a funky folk music hall in Huntington Beach, a place called Caesar's Palace Room in Inglewood, Doug Weston's Troubadour, which was, up to then, strictly a music venue. Then the opportunities began flowing again—a movie role at M-G-M, a couple of club dates, the lead in a production of *A Thousand Clowns*, a play he loathed. Shelly Davis proposed naming his new Westwood nightclub Mort Sahl's Uprising. ("It's really unique," Mort said. "It's not even owned by the Mafia.") But the best thing to come along was also the most unlikely. As if to bestow one of life's rare second chances, Metromedia came calling again, this time with a show for the Los Angeles market.

The new West Coast incarnation of *The Mort Sahl Show* was made possible by Bennet Korn's exit from the conglomerate in January 1966. Mort had always enjoyed the friendly approval of Metromedia's founder and chief executive, an unconventional businessman and onetime communist named John Kluge. ("Keep it up!" Kluge would call out to him. "Great! Go to it!") The program director at KTTV was a longtime staff director named Jim Gates. It was Gates who had just presided over the shaky renewal of KTTV's license, the FCC having acted despite complaints that the station, with its freewheeling weekend talk shows, was creating a platform for "kooks, perverts, and fanatics." With the renewal now safely in hand, Gates was acting to replicate the hugely successful *Joe Pyne* show and its black counterpart, *Louis Lomax*, by expanding the station's talk franchise to seven nights a week. "The audience has more intelligence than given credit for," Gates said. "We're trying to give them conflict, we're trying to make them think."

The initial lineup gave Tuesdays and Thursdays to Pyne and Lomax, respectively, the latter being a Yale-educated journalist and author. Mondays and Fridays went to Tom Duggan, an abrasive newspaperman, formerly of Chicago, while Wednesdays belonged to attorney Melvin Belli. Duggan, a heavy drinker, proved unable to handle two nights a week, and in April Gates announced that Duggan's Friday night slot would be turned over to Mort Sahl. For writing and performing ninety minutes of fresh commentary, Sahl would be paid $650 a week.

"One day I got a call from Jim Gates," remembered Bob Lally, one of the station's seven full-time directors, "and he said, 'I think we have a new one coming in, and it's right up your alley.' It was Mort Sahl. I was delighted because I had been a big fan of Mort's. I had seen him at the Crescendo years before, had all of his albums. It turned out that we really clicked—personally as well as professionally."

With a set resembling the host's den and a studio audience of about ninety, the new show, titled simply *Mort Sahl*, made its debut on April 15, 1966. Positioning himself as "a sort of cleansing agent of the entertainment business," Sahl opened the show with a soliloquy, "Where Have I Been?" but gave over most of the broadcast to his continuing fascination with

Hollywood. That first night he welcomed playwright George Axelrod, director Ralph Nelson, and actress-comedienne Ann Elder. The following week
his guests were George Englund and Shelly Davis. The show was catching
on, but Gates, who was dating actress Ursula Andress at the time, pushed
him to land some bigger names, like some of his friends.

Reflecting the pressure he was under, Mort said he was shocked that
Paul Newman, Frank Sinatra, and Steve Allen were giving him the brush.
"They've all moved in with the Establishment," he complained in an inter-
view. "'We don't like Vietnam either,' they say to me, 'but what can we do?'
These are the same guys who thought Goldwater was a murderer. I called
Bill Cosby to come on my KTTV show a couple of weeks ago and he said he
didn't do local TV now, but if he did he'd go on the Lomax show. I thought
that was pretty funny."

The show moved through its early days with an eclectic mix of guests,
marquee names remaining hard to come by. Satirist Stan Freberg came on
for the third episode, ACLU attorney Stanley Fleischmann for the fourth.
They settled into a comfortable routine, taping Monday nights so that Mort
could take club dates during the week. Bob Lally's search for a proper tone
for the show was evident in the ever-changing telops—MORT AGAINST
THE MADNESS, MORT VS. INSANITY—that led in and out of the commercial
breaks. *Mort Sahl* quickly developed a cult following, and the waiting list
for tickets to the Monday night tapings stretched from weeks to several
months out.*

One of the show's most fervent admirers was a Harvard-educated actor
and comedian named Marc London. Known primarily for a *First Family*–
style comedy album called *The "President" Strikes Back*, London was striving
for visibility in Hollywood, where he would eventually land a prime writing
berth on *Rowan and Martin's Laugh-In*. But in the spring of 1966, London
wasn't working, and after watching the Sahl show one night on KTTV, he
decided it could use a resident stock company doing topical skits and he
conspired to pitch the idea himself. A small, impoverished group took shape,
with London recruiting his former comedy partner, writer Pat McCormick,
and McCormick bringing in actor-comedian Jack Riley. Ann Elder, who
already knew Mort and considered Riley her best friend, rounded out the
foursome, her inclusion being, as she put it, an "easy sale" as far as Mort was

---

* Actor James Mason could sometimes be seen in the studio audience, seated alongside his seventeen-
year-old daughter Portland, who was a fan of the show.

concerned. Jim Gates embraced the idea, and on June 17, eight weeks into the show's run, its Friday night time slot expanded from ninety minutes to two hours to accommodate the change.

The set was modified, a world map and three clocks suggesting the stern surroundings of a small newsroom. Sahl was introduced from off-camera (although he preferred a cold opening) and stepped into view in a powder-blue sweater to announce the new format. "I know my audience the way Dr. Frankenstein knows that monster," he declared, confident in the belief that he was now delivering the strongest show possible. "My name is Mort Sahl. This and other problems in a moment."

Not all of the new features worked. A straight segment on happenings around town—the Bolshoi at the Shine Auditorium, *Funny Girl* at the Music Center, Grad Night at Disneyland—fell flat, and a rant about the previous week's guests, Carl Reiner, Norman Jewison, and Eva Marie Saint, who had appeared to promote their picture *The Russians Are Coming! The Russians Are Coming!*, came off as vicious rather than funny. It wasn't until the fifth segment of the evening that the show found its balance, with Ann Elder taking the stage as NBC News correspondent Nancy Dickerson to report on the upcoming wedding of Lucy Baines Johnson. The sets were spare even by *Our Town* standards, but the comic energy collectively generated by Elder, Riley, and London—the six-foot-seven McCormick sat very noticeably in the audience—gave the show a terrific bounce. They sat in on the discussion segment with guest Buck Henry, Mort introducing each of them individually and giving a nice plug to Henry's new series, *Get Smart*, which hadn't yet premiered. As if to illustrate the new strain of satiric thinking on the show, Elder suggested getting a tape of *Supermarket Sweep*, a frantic new game show produced by David Susskind and Daniel Melnick, and running over it the audio of Susskind accepting an Emmy for *Ages of Man*.* The show signed off at 1 A.M. having run out of gas, but Lally and station management knew they had something new and exciting on their hands, and *Mort Sahl* soon became the creative standard for all local programming produced in Los Angeles.

Concurrent with the new TV series, Sahl's movie career began to take off again. In April, just as the KTTV show was being launched, he played a

---

* ABC declined to provide the video.

cynical nightclub owner in a labored comedy called *Three for a Wedding* at M-G-M. The film's nominal stars were George Hamilton (whom Mort labeled "the Peter Lawford of our time") and Sandra Dee. It was then allowed a year to ripen on the shelf. By the time of its release as *Doctor, You've Got to Be Kidding!* Hamilton's brief vogue as a movie star had passed.

In July, Sahl appeared in a considerably better picture titled *Don't Make Waves*, playing Lingonberry, an eccentric Malibu homeowner bent on selling his cliffside house to Tony Curtis. Afforded a better director in Alexander Mackendrick (*The Ladykillers*, *Sweet Smell of Success*) and permitted again to write his own dialogue, Mort turned in a spirited performance, explaining at one point that an unfinished construction project on the property wasn't a pool but rather a bomb shelter. "I started digging it during the Eisenhower administration. Then I stopped digging it during the Kennedy administration. Now I'm wondering if it's big enough . . ." Made during the peak of the KTTV series' popularity, parts were found in the film for Ann Elder and Marc London, and even China could be glimpsed in a couple of shots.

Sahl also contributed a brief cameo to *The People Trap*, a dystopian look at the population explosion that was made for ABC's *Stage 67*. The hour-long drama aired in November to widespread critical acclaim, and was repeated in January 1967 by popular demand. As a group, the three films helped re-establish him as a viable supporting player, but little came from the exposure apart from fresh material for the nightclub act. As Mort once indisputably observed: "Anybody can act, but the only one who can do what I do is *me*."

With everything going so well that summer, the grievances Sahl had nursed over the lean years following the Kennedy assassination came bubbling to the surface. Reflexively, he was conditioned to lash out, and he talked of a "conspiracy" to keep him unemployed. "Even my agent and my publicity man were on me to quit making what they called the wrong kind of joke," he said to Hal Humphrey in a piece for the *Los Angeles Times*. "'You're getting bitter,' was their line to me. I had to get rid of both of them." He said that he realized he was running the risk of being seen as paranoid, but he couldn't stop himself. Humphrey, the most ardent of admirers, buried such sentiments in the body of the article, preferring instead to lead with the happy news of the new contract with Channel 11. Anger, he reasoned, was what Mort Sahl trafficked in, the product he so expertly bottled and served up in performance. The column's headline reinforced that notion: "Angry Mort Sahl Joins KTTV Fold."

Then came the forum of a profile in *Newsday*'s weekend magazine, a long interview with Mike McGrady, who normally covered the civil rights movement and the war in Vietnam. Sahl was in town to play a one-night stand at the Canoe Place Inn in Hampton Bays, another gig China had pushed him into taking, and stopped off at a motor inn long enough to meet McGrady and spill his guts over a cup of coffee. All those he saw as having betrayed him were called to account, and the strident delivery that served him so well on stage had a curdling effect in such an intimate conversation.

First in the dock was Milt Ebbins. Mort went over the business of Ambassador Kennedy recruiting him to write jokes for the campaign, and how the national sense of humor didn't suddenly change when Kennedy was elected in 1960. "Well, Ebbins and Lawford started living at the White House and at Hyannisport. They became star-struck. And they came to me and said the president didn't like what I was saying and I was to stop it. And they said to me: If you listen to reason, you can be a king. But if you don't, you're not going to work."

Hearing this, the tone and substance of it, McGrady knew he wasn't going to be able to run it without first giving the accused a chance to respond. Reached in Los Angeles, Ebbins denied the conversation ever took place. "That's an absolute untruth," he said. "At no time was he told not to say anything. There was not, not ever, a conspiracy to hurt this man. Kennedy may have asked, 'Gosh, what happened to Mort? He was such a good friend of ours.' It may have been that he wasn't invited to Washington social functions. But I was never told to keep him quiet. Look, I like this man very much. Mort Sahl is a great, great talent. It's so sad. No one did anything to this man."

Next came the Morris office. "The heat started in July of '62," Mort said, correctly pinpointing when proposed changes in the tax laws regarding deductible expenses began to have a dampening effect on business in clubs and bistros nationwide. "And you know what kind of heat? Well, this is a capitalistic country. And the William Morris office, which made as much as $65,000 a year in commissions from me, didn't want to work for me. Some of the strangest reasons—they'd tell people: His work habits are very bad, he doesn't show up. Well, you know, they can be very forgiving when a dollar's involved. But not in this case."

Sam Weisbord, a senior executive at the agency, was the man who worked closest with Mort. "That isn't true at all," he responded. "In the first place, he would have had to earn $650,000 to pay that commission. He never did. We didn't drop him; he dropped us. What happened was that some of his business turned bad. While he was with us we had moved his salary way up—to keep making that kind of money you've got to play before a packed house. Every career waxes and wanes. Mort was no exception." Then Weisbord added: "I've always felt that those who live by the sword must be prepared to perish by it. Sahl's kind of entertaining, his approach, made him a lot of enemies."

Then Sahl's indictment turned to his press agent, Warren Cowan of Rogers & Cowan. "My press agent made $1,000 a month with me. And then he said, 'I don't like what you're saying about *our* president.' And then the liberal community in Hollywood—my employers in television and pictures, the bookers—they're almost all registered Democrats, they're all Jewish and they all think they're liberals. They started practicing a blacklist on me. The word got out that I would not listen to reason and be a king, I gather. And so it stopped." Cowan recalled it differently: "I can't remember anything like that. I might have said that Jack Kennedy was so popular that it was a mistake to go on attacking him. Once I told him I didn't think he should wear sweaters anymore. But not in a million years would I tell a client what he could or could not say. I really think that's kind of psychotic."

Mort pressed on. "Not only the work stopped," he said, "but the phone stopped socially. Paul Newman was about my best friend out there. Nothing." (He conveniently forgot about the friendship-damaging exchange he had with Newman over Actors' Equity and *The Sign in Sidney Brustein's Window*.) "These are all Democrats," he continued. "Franciosa. Sidney Poitier, he looks at me kind of strangely. And if you talk to people—say you're a third party—and you say, 'How's Mort Sahl? How's he doing?' the color goes out of their faces. God knows what these people heard." McGrady asked whether this just might have been a natural reaction to his attacks on the late president? A cooling of affections?

"No," he insisted, "they were told. I mean, things didn't just peter out. My phone stopped. Nobody knew me. Now the rationale starts in. Steve Allen and several other people say, 'Well, the reason you don't see Mort anymore is because people don't want to hear that anymore. They like President Kennedy.' Well, my reaction is: I know this is Utopia . . . It's simply not true. If it were true, people wouldn't laugh. I can give you any number of examples of this. *The Dean Martin Show*—never. *The Hollywood Palace*—no." (Yet he had actually played *The Hollywood Palace* the previous year—and would do so again in the spring.) "*The Jerry Lewis Show*—fired, not told why; nobody says anything. And the audiences are laughing. That's just the reason you are fired. That's my point. The concept of conspiracy is not against me, it's against the American people, to keep them in abysmal ignorance. Now the people don't have to support me, they merely have to hear me—that's what it's all about. The whole *function*."

He told of getting thrown off the Sullivan show, about how he wouldn't go along with the host's mandate to lay off Johnson and Humphrey. "Now I know that fascism can come via the Democratic Party too. And I know that it can come in a blue suit, not on a white horse. I've seen it. Yes, sir. And my job is to play it up. And all of it shadowboxing—no one will own up to it and everyone's looking the other way and saying people don't want to hear it." He related Joe Kennedy's line: "Doesn't Sahl know the meaning of the word loyalty?"

Sahl went on to attack the press, especially the guys, he said, "who start off writing for jazz magazines and wind up writing for the *New Republic*." The irony wasn't lost on McGrady that while Sahl was on the attack, things were breaking right for him again, a phenomenon his subject credited to "certain people who still want to make money." McGrady checked with Frank Liberman, a press agent who worked with Mort for a period of nine months. "I don't know what he tells his analyst," Liberman said, "but Mort Sahl's conspiracy is against himself. He's hostile, he's . . . no, don't use that word. Let us just say mercurial. That covers so much."

That night, McGrady took in the show at the Canoe Place Inn, seated among "a tanned audience of weekenders" that laughed steadily and gen-erously while not quite delivering the guffaws sought by most comedians. "The particular beauty of Mort Sahl," he concluded, "is that he does not go for a laugh lodged in the belly so much as a reaction centered in the cere-brum. The demands on the audience are great, but this audience was more than willing to meet the demands. Rambling, digressive, discursive, and yet always trenchant and to a point. What Mort Sahl does—what he has always done—is put a mind on display, a mind at once marvelous and strange."

When McGrady's article ran on July 16, 1966, the fourteenth episode of *Mort Sahl* had just aired, the series by then having doubled the numbers logged by Tom Duggan in the same time slot. ("Dear Messiah," began a fan letter from an admiring viewer. "Continue to deliver us from evil.") At a point when ratings for KTTV's other talk shows had either stalled or declined, presumably the result of overexposure, the Sahl show was gaining momentum with its expanded format and its quartet of earnest young satirists. Tuning in a couple of weeks earlier, viewers could delight in Ann Elder and Jack Riley as a husband and wife interviewed in the lobby after the premiere of *Who's Afraid of Virginia Woolf?* "It was a wonderful movie," Elder enthused, "about how two people can have a meaningful relationship by hurting each other equally." On the same broadcast, Pat McCormick gave a compellingly loony performance as a Timothy Leary–like prophet of LSD forced to hire a "reality sitter" for his infrequent periods of lucidity.

Balefully staring such good fortune in the face, Sahl doggedly focused on the bleak side of his life. The blacklist was still on, he reminded the *Times'* Charles Champlin, noting that he remained an untouchable to the networks. "I've made a vocation of not fitting in," he added unnecessarily. When Shelly Davis tried opening Mort Sahl's Uprising at a Parisian-style shopping complex called Le Drogue Store, he was refused an entertainment license by the Police Commission, further proof, Sahl charged, of a conspiracy. Indeed, Davis got a sixty-day license only after the two men parted company, but then Mort discovered that Chief of Police William H. Parker had merely confused him with Lenny Bruce.

Lenny, by that time, was considered an undesirable by the British government as well as Chief Parker, who knew all too well of his drug and obscenity arrests. Mort stopped being branded a "sick" comic as soon as *Time* lifted the label, but his vague association in the public mind with Lenny Bruce had never ceased to grate on him. "His area of interest was the urban hipster," Mort says. "Jazz. Chicks. Dope. He thought I was naive. He was very warm; I liked him a lot. But I never thought he was going to be legendary. . . . I can remember back to when he embarrassed people in the audience. But Gene Norman didn't endorse that. He was playing the urban hipster; this is all a joke and we should all be in on it. You know—packaging and advertising, and he was right to that degree."

At the age of forty, Lenny Bruce was broke. He hadn't had a TV appearance since 1964, when Steve Allen put him on and then had to shelve the tape. He spent his days working on appeals. ("It's chic to arrest me," he once said.) On stage he rambled from one subject to the next as in a catatonic state. "When he was working the Crescendo—and Ann's 440 Club in San Francisco—he was really writing," said Maynard Sloate, "and he was creating all of the funny stuff that he did, the routines that were brilliant in my opinion. . . . And then, unfortunately it didn't last because he became an addict. That'll get your sense of humor every time."

Lenny's last live performances were under the aegis of record producer Phil Spector, who underwrote two sparsely attended weeks at Hollywood's Music Box Theater in February, 1966. "He became completely obsessed with the law," said his mother, Sally Marr. "He got so that when he went on stage, he never did anything anymore—the glue bit, the airplane bit. 'Hey, do the airplane bit!' 'What about the Palladium bit?' And he'd bring out the papers and he would just talk about the law."

On the evening of August 3, 1966, Lenny Bruce was found dead of a her-oin overdose, the inevitable end to a steep decline, an act of self-destruction the fiercely abstemious Mort Sahl couldn't possibly fathom. "I saw Lenny last about four months ago," he told Chuck Champlin in an interview for the *Times*. "He looked very, very sick." He recalled Lenny's early promise, his originality and frankness. "Then the dirty words thing became a crusade with him. Friends of his—FRIENDS!—were pushing him to test the laws, they said. It was suicidal for him. Then the pressure was on the owners and he couldn't get hired. We used to have a private thing. He used to say he was being crucified, and I went along with it. I'd say, 'Hey, man, but don't forget the resurrection.'"

In the years following the Kennedy assassination, Mort Sahl paid scant attention to the federal investigation into the president's murder. The occa-sional comments he made in his act tended to center on attorney Melvin Belli's unsuccessful defense of Jack Ruby, there being no real comedy to be mined from other aspects of the tragedy. When the President's Commission on the Assassination of President John F. Kennedy, a panel led by Chief Justice Earl Warren, presented an 888-page report on its findings to Lyndon Johnson on September 24, 1964, there was little surprise in the fact that the so-called Warren Report fingered Lee Harvey Oswald as the sole gunman. At the time of its publication, Sahl took note of the report—and the news coverage surrounding it—but never bothered to actually read it. Following Johnson's election in November, Mort tended to focus on the president's steady escalation of the war in Vietnam, something he rightly felt was tear-ing at the very fabric of American society. "They'll have to kill me if they want to shut me up," he declared in a TV interview. "America is sick. She suffers from an anarchy of the spirit. She desperately needs self-criticism, and there's almost nobody willing to give it."

Early speculative writings on the assassination, in both books and articles, were largely dependent on press accounts and eyewitnesses who naturally varied in what they saw and heard. It was only when the Warren Commission Report and its twenty-six volumes of testimony and supporting documentation were published that analysts finally had a common source of inquiry and evidence on which to base their studies. Authors and academics flew into action, and after a gestation period of some eighteen months, books critical of the commission, its methodologies and conclusions, began appearing in the summer of 1966. The first, which began life as a master's thesis, was *Inquest: The Warren Commission and the Establishment of Truth* by Edward J. Epstein. In his book, Epstein detailed the inner workings of the commission and the divisions within it, particularly those regarding whether or not Kennedy and Texas Governor John B. Connally were struck by the same bullet—a crucial point in establishing whether Oswald could have done the deed alone. It was, wrote Eliot Fremont-Smith in the *New York Times*, "the first book to throw open to serious question, in the minds of thinking people, the findings of the Warren Commission."

Epstein's work inspired public reactions on both sides of the debate. Former Kennedy aide Richard N. Goodwin suggested that an independent group look into Epstein's charges that the commission's investigation of the assassination was inadequate. Senator Edward M. Kennedy said that although he hadn't read the Warren report—and had no intention of doing so—he was satisfied that it represented "at least conclusively" the results, which he believed to be accurate. Two additional books covering the same ground appeared in August 1966. *The Oswald Affair: An Examination of Contradictions and Omissions of the Warren Report*, written by Leo Sauvage, the American correspondent of *Le Figaro*, was as dispassionate as the Epstein book and equally critical of the Warren Commission. And, as did Epstein, Sauvage alleged a conspiracy to kill the president.

Neither book, however, inspired the controversy that attended Holt, Reinhart & Winston's publication of *Rush to Judgment*. Its author, a New York attorney named Mark Lane, had been invited by Marguerite Oswald to represent her son's interests before the commission, a job he was ultimately prevented from doing by Earl Warren, who was convinced that Oswald was the lone assassin and directed the investigation accordingly. Frustrated in his efforts to serve as an adversary counsel, *Rush to Judgment* became Lane's brief for the defense, the case he would have made before the commission had he been permitted to do so. A vigorous self-promoter who projected a calm professorial image on camera, Lane did a lot of television in support of his book, contending the Warren Commission Report was a fraudulent document designed to hide the fact that there were two gunmen firing at the presidential motorcade in Dallas, thus providing the basis for a charge of conspiracy.

KTTV, meanwhile, was announcing its fall schedule, the most ambitious in its seventeen-year history. Along with sixty hours of color programming a week and the strongest lineups of sports and children's shows in the Los Angeles market, the station upped its game by adding David Susskind to its eleven o'clock rotation, joining stalwarts Joe Pyne and Louis Lomax, newcomer Regis Philbin, and Mort Sahl, whose slot on Friday nights continued to draw strong numbers. Jim Gates was always pushing for controversy— the kind the bombastic Pyne was so skilled at exploiting—so Sahl decided, with Bob Lally's concurrence, to devote the whole program on September 9, effectively the season kickoff, to Mark Lane and *Rush to Judgment*. The show, treated as a one-off, went well, drawing an extraordinary volume of viewer mail. ("I got a huge student audience from UCLA," Mort remembers.) The series returned to its regular format the following week.

Mort, recalled Ann Elder, was a pleasure to work with.

> We would go up to his house three or four days before the show, and we would read these sketches off of those shirt boards that Marc wrote on because we were all poor. (We were struggling so we used Marc London's shirt boards [from the laundry].) We would read these sketches off to Mort, and he would sit there behind his desk in his house and he would look at us with that beautiful grin and that little glimmer in his eye, and then something that we would say would trigger an idea in him—and he liked that very much. And then he would add something. . . . Mort was never critical of our work, but he would add to it. He'd say, "Oh! You've just brought up something. That reminds me . . ." And we would go off on that track. Rather than saying, "That's not funny." He never did that.

For a brief time Elder was seeing Mort on the side, but she saw there was no future to it.

> We went out two or three times, and I could tell that it wasn't going to click. He was too intensely brilliant for me, and he was obviously

enchanted at this point. He was just coming off Yvonne Craig, and then he was kind of enchanted with China—and who wouldn't be? So I was that middle girl for a while, maybe two or three weeks, and we really became such good friends. It wasn't a romantic situation; it was infatuation on my part. I remember having dinner with him, during which he spent most of the evening telling me how much he adored Yvonne. I thought he was so sweet, so kind, and so charming about the fact that he missed her so. I thought: Wow! What's wrong with her? Why isn't she still with him?

Mark Lane's appearance on *Mort Sahl* was a watershed event for both the show and its host. Fascinated by Lane's book and mesmerized by the author himself, Sahl began reading the Warren Commission Report. Earl Warren, it turned out, was his commission's own worst enemy. Having already come to the conclusion that Oswald acted alone, Warren blocked staff lawyers from investigating leads that may have led to other conspirators, particularly in Mexico where a supporter of Fidel Castro named Silvia Duran was rumored to have had an affair with Oswald in the weeks just prior to the assassination. ("You just can't believe a communist," Warren reasoned. "We don't talk to communists.") In deference to the Kennedy family, he denied commission members access to the president's autopsy photos and x-rays, permitting them only the hand-drawn diagrams contained in the autopsy report. He only reluctantly agreed to interview Mrs. Kennedy, giving in to pressure from commission lawyers while permitting none of them to be present for her testimony. And he honored Attorney General Robert F. Kennedy's request not to testify at all, although Kennedy knew of secret attempts to assassinate Castro that could have provided a motive for a reciprocal attempt on the life of the American president. Any one of these decisions, taken on its own, would have been enough to excite conspiracy theorists. Then there was the report itself. "Judging the report as a literary work," wrote Dwight Macdonald, dissecting it for *Esquire*, "I find the style and the form are not well calculated to produce the desired effect on the reader, i.e., that he is getting at last the definitive account, complete and objective, of what happened in Dallas. . . . It obscured the strong points of its case, and many are very strong, under a midden-heap of inessential facts."

Having decided that his own inability to land work was due to an industry-wide conspiracy, Mort found it easy to embrace Mark Lane's contention that the president's death was also the result of a conspiracy. And he wasn't alone: The results of a Harris survey released in October 1966 showed that only one in three Americans thought that Oswald was the lone assassin. Among those who either felt, or came to feel, that a conspiracy had brought down the president were Robert Kennedy and Lyndon Baines Johnson.

"I was skeptical about the conspiracy thing in the beginning," said Bob Lally. "And when Mark Lane came on the show, I perceived Mark Lane as a very self-aggrandizing guy—he was in it for money, he was in it for a lot of things. Not that he didn't believe in what he was writing, but I just thought: Well, this is all crap. When he was on the show—I don't remember if he gave it to me or I just inherited it—I got a copy of the book, *Rush to Judgment*. About three or four months later, I went on vacation for a few weeks and I went to Hawaii. And I tossed the book in my suitcase. I got over there, and I read it over a period of about two days. There was a lot of wild-eyed stuff in there. If only five percent of it was true, then there was a conspiracy. That made me a believer in the conspiracy."

On October 14, just a month after Lane's initial appearance on the show, Mort had him on again, this time with Ann Elder, Marc London, and Jack Riley dramatizing portions of the Warren Report. Lane appeared a third time in November, this time with actor Robert Vaughn and Victoria Adams, a witness to the assassination. There was concern at the station that his growing obsession with the killing, while energizing a core audience, was alienating more casual viewers. Then, as if to counter this, Mort was added to the weeknight lineup at KLAC, Metromedia's pioneering talk radio outlet, where Joe Pyne held down the morning drive time slot. "I needed a new platform, people with ears," he explained. "I wasn't doing anything for four years and I've got to get the ears back."

The "Two-Way Radio" phenomenon was growing, and station manager Jack Thayer brought in Mort Sahl, whom he perceived as left wing, as a balance to more conservative voices like Pyne and all-night moderator Ray Briem. Mort, however, denied that he was a liberal at all, telling *Times* radio columnist Don Page he thought "direction" more important than "position," and that his liberal followers weren't getting the message. "I'm not a friend of the Democrats. They haven't been for anything since 1948. I'm an independent, which has become an alien force in America." Then he added: "My function is to let people know they have not been rendered impotent, and mobilize them to unite in force—tell them 'you can do better.' Then, of course, when they attack, you push them back and bring them on again." He acknowledged that talk radio was still an experiment, a movement, as he characterized it, to replace talent entirely. "Yesterday a guy tried to bring a record into the building," he said, "but the guard caught him."

Mort was working his nightly three-hour shift on KLAC when he opened at the hungry i on November 21, 1966. Enrico Banducci set aside a broadcast area for him in a corner of the Other Room, allowing diners to observe him taking calls from Los Angeles while perched only steps away from the show-room. North Beach had changed dramatically from just a couple of years earlier when the first topless club, the Condor, emerged from what had once been a sidewalk café. Practically empty on weeknights, the "i" struggled to remain relevant with occasional bookings of high-profile acts like Mel Tormé, Dick Gregory, and Godfrey Cambridge. In terms of name talent, the only other venues left in the city were Bimbo's, an outfit called Basin Street West (no relation to Basin Street East), and the venerable Venetian Room, where singer Vikki Carr was winding up a three-week engagement.

At a press conference, with China and Banducci looking on from a nearby table, Mort identified the "two great issues" of the day as the assassina-tion of John F. Kennedy and the war in Vietnam. "I'd vote for anyone in 1968—even Ronald Reagan—who gets us out." Somebody asked, "Even Dick Nixon?" And he replied, "Even Dick Nixon." On the radio, he said he was sensing "a vast spirit of pessimism" in his listeners. It was caused by a false American foreign policy "where we send our young men off to die fighting for dictators all over the world." And he characterized the drive to bring economic equality to blacks as a sell-out. "They've bought into our insane middle-class dream instead of trying to reform us. They're now say-ing, 'Baby move over; I want a place at the trough.'" The nation, he went on, "was not founded on consumer values. If Thomas Jefferson could see us now . . ." Warming to the idea, he said the only incorruptible men he'd met that year were Senator J. William Fulbright, auto safety advocate Ralph Nader, and Mark Lane. At the mention of Lane's name, he volunteered with absolute certainty that Kennedy had been killed by at least two gunmen fir-ing a minimum of five bullets.

The media blitz paid off in packed houses at the hungry i, where the week-end top had now risen to $4. Sahl moved on to Las Vegas, where a leased line to KLAC was run from the lobby of Caesar's Palace. Fighting a bad case of laryngitis, he struggled to fill the hotel's lounge, Nero's Nook, where his jibes at LBJ drew, according to *Las Vegas Sun* columnist Ralph Pearl, nothing more than "knowing nods and a rare chuckle now and then from the café goers catching Sahl, whose cerebral comedy is a wee bit too grown up for the bettors, boozers, and lovers." Mort and China shared a gloomy Christmas in Sin City, and were there on December 28 when KTTV publicly announced that he had been fired.

Mort and China had been preparing to leave for Las Vegas, having loaded their bags into Mort's Cobra for the five-hour drive, when they saw Jim Gates coming up the driveway. Gates had in hand the new Nielsen numbers, which showed that *Mort Sahl* had gone from a 3.0 share to a 1.0 "virtually overnight." The show, Gates told him, "has taken a drastic drop in the ratings, I think because you talked too much about the Kennedy death." Gates emphasized, however, that it was low ratings that forced the cancellation of the program, and not any of the topics it tackled. "I have to believe him on the face of the statement," Mort later told Don Page. "After all, I presume they're honest men." Stunned, he said he asked Gates who he thought they would get to replace him. "To my shock, I was told there were rumors I may be replaced by either John Rousselot [of the John Birch Society] or Stan Freberg." Through other sources he heard that his radio show was also in jeopardy.

On the way to Nevada, Mort reflected on the thirty-nine weeks of episodes he had done for the station, and decided the Kennedy assassination *had* to be the underlying factor in the pressure on Metromedia to cancel the show. "Outside sources," in other words, were banding together to stop him from talking. With the KLAC microphone still at his disposal, he went on the air to voice his suspicions to listeners and stir up a storm of protest. It worked: Signs appeared on telephone poles along Sunset Boulevard calling for demonstrations in front of KTTV. The station's phone lines lit up, and an estimated 35,000 letters flooded the mail room. On December 29, Sahl flew back to Los Angeles to give the press his side of the story, which amounted to the station's "business consideration" being wholly and directly related to his criticism of the Warren Commission Report and his inquiry into the conspiracy to kill the president. The station, he said, had sent him a memo in early December ordering him to "lay off" the Kennedy probe because it was causing viewers to tune out. "I cannot believe I'm that dangerous, and I don't think they're turning me off because of that."

Just prior to the press conference, he had officially received his most recent Nielsens from KTTV management. They confirmed a drop from his peak rating of 3.0 to 1.0 for the eleven o'clock hour, and a bounce to 2.0 for the midnight hour. In the aggregate, these numbers represented an audience ranging from 51,000 to 80,000 viewers. Then, the seemingly impossible happened. At the conclusion of the press conference, he was called back to the station, where an advance copy of the competing American Research Bureau ratings for November had just been received. The ARB showed a consistent 4.0 rating, sometimes peaking to a 5.0 or higher, representing as many as 250,000 viewers per quarter hour. Mort was promptly awarded another thirteen-week renewal and a bump in salary. "Chuck Young, the station manager, said, 'I'm man enough to say I made a mistake, if you're man enough to come back.'" Sahl returned to Las Vegas, where he humbly announced to his KLAC listeners, "The people have spoken—you really can move mountains."

The first episode of *Mort Sahl* to be taped after the series' calamitous renewal was aired on January 6, 1967. With thousands of letters having poured into the station, a triumphant opening shot was easy to arrive at. "It's the movies," Mort says of the influence that had come to govern his life. "The day Chuck Young rehired me, we staged *Mr. Smith Goes to Washington*. I went in there with all the letters. You know: 'People want the boys' camp!'" He laughs. "Although Mort Sahl, the performer, says, 'Are they kidding? A boys' camp? Threatening Edward Arnold??'" The applause in the studio was deafening, and it went on for several minutes. Typically, however, Mort doubled down on the troublesome topic that had nearly wiped him off the air, reasoning that Jefferson Smith, Capra's idealistic hero, would never have backed down nor allowed himself to be silenced. "The Kennedy assassination information grew on the KTTV program until it became a department," he wrote.

On January 13, KLAC newsmen Dave Crane and Al Weiman appeared to question the circumstances surrounding a supposed tape of the late Jack Ruby's voice. On the 20th, authors Penn Jones (*Forgive My Grief*) and Sylvia Meagher attacked the Warren Report, as did *Minority of One* editor M. S. Arnone. And on the 27th, Mark Lane made his fourth appearance on the show, lashing out at Capitol Records and an "audio study" of the assassination released just days after Ruby's death. (Lane's book *Rush to Judgment* was alluded to on the album as one of the best-selling recent works of fiction.) "We had probably every major 'expert,' author, whoever, on the assassination," said Bob Lally. "Mark Lane was on repeatedly, and all the other guys were there at one time or another. And that, basically, was the downfall of the show."

In late January, Warren Cowan advised Sahl to drop the subject, and for a while he did. "Cowan said, 'There isn't any blacklist, and if there *is* in this town, maybe you ought to go to another town.' This is a guy I'm paying. So I went on camera and I tore up my SAG card, because nobody was going to hire me anyway. They would all hide behind: 'He wasn't right for this.' Well, what if you *were* right for it? So now you can have a dead marriage and a house in Mandeville Canyon?" But he still insists he wasn't acting on the basis of a latent death wish. "I just wanted to convince people that we weren't crazy." The next few shows featured guests like Stan Kenton, Francis Ford Coppola, and screenwriter Bob Kaufman, a close friend. Yet the Kennedy assassination was always a topic of discussion, even when it wasn't reflected in the makeup of the guest list. The whole nature of the show changed. Where once the focus had been on topical comedy and, where appropriate, controversy, the comedy had almost entirely given way to outrage.

After a considerable period of underemployment, Mort Sahl was now overworked and exhausted. Just the TV and radio shows alone accounted for seventeen hours of air time a week, not including preparation. And a club date, such as for the hungry i or Nero's Nook, added another fourteen to twenty hours a week in front of audiences. "It's zombie-ville," he admitted to Charles Denton of the *San Francisco Examiner*. "For some reason I seem to be either unemployable or indispensable. I never seem to be in the middle."

In February, he tore off his microphone and stalked out of an interview being taped for the Chicago-based *Phil Lind Show* when the interviewer asked him why he was changing his style "to become a lecturer on political issues." On TV, he asked two UCLA students opposing the imposition of tuition under the Reagan Administration if they were going to "sell out" to the Establishment, and the resulting argument, including several rambling, sleep-deprived monologues on the part of the host, dominated the rest of the show. "For a long time," he said wearily toward the end of the taping, "I've been warned by people in the 'in' group that you'd better be careful, because your meetings will be broken up, there'll be planted hecklers. That supposedly is supposed to come from the Right. That's not where it comes from. You know, I know where the enemy is, and I'm not surprised by them, but on the other hand, that doesn't mean I want to put up with them."

Where the anger and the irascibility really came out was on the radio, where all forms of life had equal access to him and the process of call screening, as dictated by station policy, was minimal at best. Cranks got under his skin, and unlike the station's other personalities, he couldn't let go. A caller one night wondered why people, according to Sahl, were afraid. To get appropriations through Congress, Sahl explained. To keep the FBI huge. "The leading countries of the world have atomic weapons—that's made people afraid. And as we've watched the world go closer and closer to the brink to serve privileged interests economically, that's made people afraid." The caller told him that he talked like "those philosophy people" with awfully big sounds.

"You're old enough to know some big words," Sahl responded.

"I'm wondering," continued the caller. "What the hell is everybody so afraid about?"

"They're afraid of being blown up."

"Excuse me, excuse me—"

"One-hundred and thirty-seven men were killed in *Vietnam* last week. They're afraid of being *killed*. Aren't you afraid of being killed?"

"No, I'm not."

"You're *not*, oh?"

The exchange grew more heated until Sahl told the caller that five hundred-thousand men were going to be murdered in Vietnam. "Doesn't that *scare* you?"

"No."

"You're not afraid of going to war with China?"

"No."

"Buddy, why don't you buy a paper and *grow up*? Or else go *die* somewhere?" Mort terminated the call. Three minutes later:

> I want to remind you of something. Last July I was in Washington five days and I spent three of them with the president. Do you know any radio announcers who do that? Everybody's got to stop playing games with these old ladies. *I don't want to hear about that. The country's coming apart.* Now all of you have to get off your fannies and *do* something about it. Forget the radio station. That doesn't *mean* anything. Like that—like this punk who just came on before you and said he doesn't know what everybody's afraid of. And when I answer him he says, "I don't know any big words." The anti-intellectualism. The defeat of the spirit. The lack of optimism. The separation of love and sex. The exploitation of the American woman. The lack of hope in the American child. The betrayal of the intellectual movement in the State of California through the university. It shows we're *dying*. That's what it's really all about, man . . .

Sahl's defense mechanism, if it could be called that, was to take fewer call-ers and lecture the ones he did take for longer and longer stretches of time. "When somebody was unusual," he says, "I let them go on. And I wouldn't do the station I.D.: '*And don't forget to get your carpets cleaned . . .*'" Listener-ship for the show that had once had the second-highest Hooper ratings in the market began to slide, and in April Jack Thayer announced the dismissal of his latest experiment in balance. "The decision to release Mort was in no way a disparagement to his ability as a comedian or commentator," he said in a statement. "It's strictly a matter of incompatibility over policy." There were howls of protest and charges of censorship, all misplaced according to the *Times'* Don Page. "Mort Sahl was fired because he did not follow the pre-cepts of two-way radio," Page wrote in a postmortem. "Management, more than fair and tolerant, finally excused him after the program became one-way radio, Sahl's way, without the give-and-take format."

Over at KTTV, Mort was admonished not to mention KLAC or attack Thayer on the air. The warning, however, played more as a dare to him, and he did exactly what he was told not to do, using, in effect, one Metromedia outlet to bludgeon another. And then there was the steady drip of assassina-tion conspiracy, which was still a part of every show. "They told me to stop talking about the same thing," Mort recalls. "I said, 'What if I charge you with censorship in the press?' They said, 'If there's any *new* evidence, but you can't keep repeating yourself.'" All the obsessive and vitriolic content pushed out the sketch players, who no longer fit into a format that had once been modi-fied just to accommodate them. "There was a drop in what we were doing on a regular basis," said Ann Elder. "Once he did his tirade and it became Mort's deal, he wanted to figure out who really killed Kennedy—and he believed it wasn't just one person. And that became his *raison d'etre.* Therefore, we were no longer useful on his TV show. There were no sketches to be done anymore."

In May, while Mort was in Washington for a date at the Cellar Door, he and China were invited to a dinner at David Brinkley's Georgetown home. Also on the guest list, he was told, were Secretary of Defense Robert McNa-mara, columnist Rowland Evans, and Ethel and Robert Kennedy. Set to address the National Press Club, Mort also found himself invited to the White House where, subbing for his friend John Chancellor, he escorted Chancellor's wife, Barbara. "We get over there," remembers Mort, "and Johnson switches partners." The dinner for six couples included the wife of Senator Edward Kennedy. "So I sat with Joan Kennedy. And then things came out. For instance, she says, 'What are you going to do while you're here?' I said, 'I'm going to see Bobby tomorrow.' She says, 'Then he's not mad anymore.' I said, 'What would he be mad about? That I'm destroying my career? For the illusion of the family?' I pushed it as far as I could."

That next evening was an awkward affair, with China seated between Evans and a visibly agitated Attorney General, while Mort was paired with McNamara. "And the conversation was so innocuous that it had to be an effort," Mort said. Kennedy, he observed, made little pyramids of paper napkins and looked like a man really eaten around the edges. "I still did the shows in the club, so I ate the first course and I left for the club. Bobby turns to China and says, 'Did Mort ever write for my brother? Why does he say he wrote for him? Why wouldn't I know about it?' And China, who was never a wallflower, said, 'He was sitting there for an hour and a half. Why didn't you ask him?' But he just maintained that brooding silence."

Mort, said Bob Lally, was a "true believer" in the best sense of the word. "The general manager of the station was Chuck Young, who took a lot of heat from the Warren Report, Mort's attacking it. He called up and said, 'Look, this has to stop. You can't just keep doing this forever. We've got to get back to entertainment.' So we came back after this big confrontation to do a show, and I recall that either Chuck or Jim Gates was actually in the booth with me, and we faded in on the show and did the opening title, and out walked Mort carrying like ten volumes of the Warren Report and plunked it down on the stool. Whoever it was who was in the booth said, 'Oh, shit. That takes care of that.' And that show never aired. He just couldn't let it go."

The cancellation of *Mort Sahl* was announced the following day, the stated reason being Mort's seeming inability to follow station directives. "Despite our protests, he would talk on his show about personal matters with management," said Jim Gates. "He had been criticized about his material being repetitious and lacking in entertainment. There was no issue of free speech involved, although he claimed that we wouldn't let him talk about the Kennedy assassination." The last new show to be aired featured Jimmy Lyons, singer Phil Ochs, and *Realist* editor-publisher Paul Krassner. Ironically, the following week, the time slot was filled by a re-examination of the findings of the Warren Commission with attorney Louis Nizer and panelists replying to an earlier broadcast featuring five critics of the report. The week after that, a whimsical comedy team, Bob Arbogast and Jack Margolis, took ownership of the Friday night time slot, but their ratings never approached those of *Mort Sahl*, which had remained steadily in the 4.0 to 5.0 range to the very end of its run. Their show, *The Arbogast and Margolis*, lasted just sixteen weeks.

Losing the KTTV show was a terrific blow to Mort, who saw it as his job to push boundaries and inflict a certain measure of discomfort on station management. "Sahl may have become more intensely embittered over the state of the Establishment and the paths it was leading us down," wrote Hal Humphrey, "but part of the change is in his former fans, who naively expected him to join them when they became the party in power and joined the Establishment." Sahl himself recalled being confronted one day in a store by *Twilight Zone* creator Rod Serling, who told him that he didn't appreciate being attacked on the air. After a heated exchange, Serling withdrew, only to reappear moments later. Half apologizing, he took Mort's hand and told him to "keep up the good work."

12

UNCONTAMINATED BY REASON

On February 18, 1967, a news conference took place in New Orleans. The man who called it, District Attorney Jim Garrison, said that an investigation by his office had shown that the assassination of President John F. Kennedy was the result of a plot hatched locally, and that he claimed jurisdiction in the case because of a Louisiana law "which forbids conspiracy of any kind." In response to a question from the *New York Times*, Garrison explained why he had opened the investigation: "Last November, I began looking into the question because Oswald had spent six months in New Orleans shortly before the assassination. I went through the twenty-six volumes of the Warren Report and there were some questions raised. As a result, I began the investigation. The investigation led to new leads, which we followed out, and other leads were uncovered." His hand had been forced, Garrison said, by disclosure of the investigation in the *New Orleans States-Item*. "We were making good progress until the publicity."

Ten days later, Garrison arrested a man called Clay Shaw, accusing him of having taken part "in a conspiracy to assassinate John F. Kennedy." A Louisiana native, Shaw was a decorated war veteran and one of the founders of the New Orleans International Trade Mart, a nonprofit formed to promote trade through the Port of New Orleans. Oswald had been seen passing out pro-Castro leaflets outside the Trade Mart a few months before the assassination. Shaw, in an interview, said that he had once seen Oswald distributing the leaflets but had never met him.

Word of Garrison's allegations and his arrest of Shaw reached Mort Sahl by way of a news report. "Is he corrupt?" Mort asked China, whose eldest brother would eventually become sheriff of Jefferson Parish. "No," she said. "I've known him ten years. He's incorruptible."

Mark Lane went down to New Orleans to meet Garrison, and Mort followed, intent on landing an interview for his TV show. "When I got in the cab I said, 'Take me to 6400 Owens Boulevard.' The cab driver said, 'That's Jim Garrison's house. I'll drop you at the corner; I don't want to get shot.' So we're driving along and we pass a movie theater where Lane's movie is playing, *Rush to Judgment*. I said, 'Have you seen that movie?' He said, 'You mean *Russian Judgment*?' I said, 'Do you think any of it is true?' He said, 'God, yes. Those bastards in Washington will do anything.' I said, 'Do you think Johnson was involved?' He said, 'God, yes. I hope so.' So I ring the bell at Garrison's house and I'm confronted by this monster in a bath robe. I said, 'I've come to shake your hand.' He said, 'I hope you're going to do more than that.'"

The weeks following the cancellation of the KTTV show were particularly tough for Mort Sahl. Consumed by the assassination, he found himself blocked creatively and unable to leave the subject alone. In June, he was booked into Redd Foxx's new club on La Cienega, the site of the former Slate Brothers. *Daily Variety* covered the opening:

> A capacity house was on hand to greet Mort Sahl with solid, sustained applause as he began his two-week stand Friday (16). Sixty-seven minutes later, the applause wasn't quite so enthusiastic. In between, there were a handful of instances of general laughter, some spontaneous applause at some of Sahl's remarks, and, occasionally, an isolated ripple of chuckles at Sahl's monolog of the way things are in the U.S. political establishment. But the most persistent sound was Sahl's voice, droning on interminably as he trudged back and forth between the comedian's and polemicist's platforms, being neither particularly funny at the former, nor particularly convincing at the latter.

After a brief intermission, Sahl returned to the stage with content he would normally have reserved for television. He introduced Mark Lane, and the two men launched into a general discussion of the case Jim Garrison was building in New Orleans. After about ten minutes of this, an audience member began asking Lane who killed Kennedy and if he believed Garrison. Angered by the repeated interruptions, Sahl demanded that the heckler be ejected, something management declined to do. Eighteen minutes in, he remarked that he had tried to bring civilization to the crowd, but that they obviously weren't ready for him. And then he stalked off, leaving a cha-grinned Lane to hold the platform by himself.

It was a bizarre, polarizing performance from a man who had never been shy about going his own way, and business for the engagement, fueled by negative word of mouth, fell off dramatically. Sahl adjourned to Chicago, where he followed Dick Cavett into Mister Kelly's. To columnist Mike Royko he renewed his contention that the Kennedys had blackballed him, and then held a news conference to commend Royko and the *Daily News* for printing the story. The *Tribune*'s Will Leonard, an unabashed admirer since Sahl's 1954 debut at the Black Orchid, found the strident aspects of the act dismaying, particularly the assassination material and the attacks on Earl Warren. "Back at Mister Kelly's for his tenth engagement at Rush Street's top landmark," Leonard wrote, "he shows practically none of the old improvisational dexter-ity that made him unique. Now he spends most of his time with a tale, witty but possessed of the sound of an oft-repeated lecture, of his quick visit to the office of President Johnson in the White House. He professes to be so magnificently unimpressed that he must have been quite impressed."

Friends urged him to lay off the assassination, or to at least couch the material in the satiric tradition of the act. "He called me one time from the road," remembered Yvonne Craig, "and said, 'I really got the zingers in about Kennedy and de-de-de . . .' And I said, 'As long as it's funny.' It's supposed to be funny; that's why you go and see a comic." Irv Kupcinet had a particu-larly virulent reaction to the performance, fueled in part by Penn Jones' assertion that the unsolved murder of Kupcinet's daughter, Karyn, was con-nected to the conspiracy to kill Kennedy. "Kup said, 'What you're suggesting is indecent,'" recalls Mort, "'and it doesn't belong in a comedy club. I knew Jack Ruby here, and he's a patriot.' So, being the negative guy I am, when anybody said, 'Don't do it,' I did four times as much. Because I thought I must answer the voice of integrity."

In time, the conspiracy Sahl blamed for keeping him unemployed got conflated with the one he saw as being responsible for the death of the president. "One afternoon," remembered Ann Elder, "Jack and I, and maybe Marc London, were all in Mort's car. We were going somewhere—God knows where—and I remember very vividly that Mort pulled the car over, curbside, and he went to a pay telephone. He said, 'Sorry, I have to make a phone call. Hang in there with me, pals.' He was on the phone for, I don't know, two minutes. Then he came back and said, 'Yeah, they're still after us.' And I said, 'They're after who?' He said, 'All I can tell you is, they *know* I'm onto them.'"

✧ ✧ ✧

Work came sporadically over the summer of 1967, and Mort Sahl became a hard sell to the relatively few venues outside of Las Vegas that were still booking comedians. There were a couple of weeks at a small supper club in Columbus, and a week's stand at the hungry i. "I am," he told a reporter for the *San Francisco Chronicle*, "the permanent opposition to the Establishment, since there is no opposition politically anymore. I have become everyone's conscience through some weird set of circumstances. I have become, ironically enough, a positive force. It isn't that I've changed, it's that America is so hell-bent on suicide that I'm in the unlikely position of standing at the edge of the cliff and saying, 'Wait a minute. Have you thought this over?'" The paper's Charles McCabe considered such talk the sign of a swollen ego, and suggested that anyone who viewed himself that way needed help. "He has lost his touch as a witty commentator," rued Philip Elwood in the *Examiner*, "because much of his material has become self-centered. Thus even the Kennedy murder mystery has become, rather than a collection of curiously ironic samples of inconsistent recent history, merely a situation which Sahl can use to lecture his audience and display his own prejudiced conclusions."

Still, while many were writing him off, opportunities, however infrequent, were coming his way. Putting Mort Sahl back on stage in a New York theater was the idea of Michael Brandman, the general manager of the New Theatre on East 54th Street. Brandman had a solid hit on his hands with the comedy *Scuba Duba* and wanted to extend his management to a second house, specifically the vacant East 74th Street Theater. Again borrowing Hugh Hefner's East 71st Street pad, Mort settled in for rehearsals and two weeks of subbing for WNBC's Brad Crandall on Crandall's nightly radio program. Brazenly continuing his focus on the Warren Commission, he urged the listening public to embrace his campaign to save the country. "America is the only line between civilization and Hell," he told them, "and even if you don't care, give your kids a chance." He went on to charge that the president was killed by neo-Nazis because "he charted a plan for the end of the Cold War via Cuba, and he fought the right wing, which controls the spy apparatus and much of the military apparatus in this country. He died for the finest thing he ever did."

On his last night as Crandall's substitute host, more than 13,000 calls jammed the studio lines. But while he was busy proving that he could still engage an audience and deliver ratings, the new stage show, which had acquired the title *An Evening with Mort Sahl*, was stubbornly refusing to take shape. The opening date got pushed back to Friday, December 1, then

Mort announced that Jim Garrison would be one of his late-night guests during the show's limited run. Elaine May, who was fascinated by him and serving as co-author of the scripted portions of the show, was puzzling over the structure of the thing but couldn't get much further than dividing it down the middle. "The first act was to be an Elaine May show," remembered Ann Elder, who, along with Jack Riley and a Second City colleague named John Brent, was to be in the show, "and the second act was to be a Mort Sahl show. And Elaine was to direct both acts." Mort naturally assumed that his part of the show would be a variation on his nightclub act, and that whatever involvement he would have in the first half would be scripted and worked out in advance.

"Elaine," said Elder,

couldn't have been nicer. She said to me, Jack, Brent, "Why don't you all come up to our apartment tomorrow night with Mort? Let's try a get-together and have dinner." She was doing everything she could, although this was not necessarily Elaine's strong suit. We all said, "Okay. Fine." So we trooped up to her apartment at, I don't know, East Fifty-Fourth. Big, huge apartment. I'm still young, in my twenties, and I think: Wow!! I didn't even know apartments looked like this in New York. Jack Riley goes, "Wow!" Elaine, at this time, was married to a psychiatrist—that's her husband, David Rubinfine. Anyway, we're in this rather huge and kind of darkly-interesting apartment. I think that Jeannie Berlin, her daughter, was around. Elaine said to me, and to Jack Riley, and to John Brent (who was trying to figure out a way to have his cocaine over in a corner), "What is it you do?" I said, "Exactly what do you mean?" "Well, I've got to put together a show with all of you, and Mort, so I'd like to know: What is it that your characters do?" A very legitimate question.

Jack Riley and I looked at each other, because we didn't do characters in those days, we just did impressions. I said, "Well, we do a satire of the news." Now, remember, this was 1967, and Elaine looked at us and said, "Wadda ya mean a satire of the news?" She really didn't know what we meant. "Well, I play one character, sort of a news hound, Jack plays something else . . ." She said, "Can you give me an example of what you do?" So Jack Riley and I attempted to show her what we did, and what we attempted to do was a bad newscast. And she was just totally off—she didn't get it. And I don't blame her. She said, "Wait a minute. What are you basing this on?" I believe Jack Riley said, "Well, we do this based on the nightly news." And she said, "Okay. Where is that?" We said, "Television—every night at six o'clock." She said to her husband, "Honey, get the television set out." They dragged the TV set out of the closet—I'm telling you the truth—and they plugged it in. And I'm sitting there with Elaine May, her husband the psychiatrist, Jack Riley, and Mort Sahl, who was about to leave the room as fast as he could, watching Walter Cronkite do the six o'clock news—because that's just what she watched us do a satire of. And she looked at Walter Cronkite, and then she looked back at us. And she actually said, after the show was over, "He's wonderful! Does he do that every night?"

Mort disappeared. "The script wasn't ready," he says, "and Elaine May's contribution made me very nervous. She never saw the message part of me. She said, 'Why don't you do a sketch about how the world is falling apart and Walter Cronkite is reading weather reports?' And I said, 'Do you ever watch the CBS News? He doesn't do weather reports.' So I lost confidence in it, and there was nothing to open with, so I didn't go." According to Michael Brandman, Sahl didn't show for the technical rehearsal, nor the dress rehearsal. "I was there for four weeks," said Ann Elder, "and I talked to Elaine almost every night. I understood her frustration, but I respected Mort and I could never have proceeded with a project that I didn't believe in. I felt terrible for him."

Brandman cancelled *An Evening with Mort Sahl* on less than a day's notice. In the press, he estimated his losses at $20,000, including $6,000 in advance ticket sales. ("We have been hung up good by Sahl," he fumed.) Back home in Beverly Hills, Mort ducked the inevitable phone calls. Acting as his spokesman, Enrico Banducci put out word that Sahl was en route to San Francisco, where he would give his side of the story during a press conference at the hungry i.

"Here I am, big as life," Mort said from the familiar stage. "You can see I'm not hiding from anyone." Perched on a stool, he read from a prepared statement:

I did not walk out. I told Brandman of the progressive difficulties we were encountering and warned him in a registered letter three days before the technical rehearsal that this show was not ready for the public . . . There were union disputes which the producer refused to negotiate. No settings were constructed. Not one rehearsal was held.

I was never paid. I finally informed Brandman that since no actors were hired, no material was prepared, and nothing was in shape, it would be impossible to open. He then insisted that I go on alone and do my monologues. I refused, since the advance sale was predicated on a revue with other performers, not on my club act. . . . I'm hoping this can all be ironed out because I hate to see another year go by in America without political commentary just because I couldn't get along with some people.

The demise of *An Evening with Mort Sahl* left its star with a clear schedule and no immediate prospects for work. At odds with China, he boarded a plane for New Orleans and headed for Jim Garrison's office. "I didn't just come socially," he said to Garrison. "I want to know what I can do to help."

At six-foot-six, Garrison was an imposing character, the sort of man who thrived in a city where flamboyant public figures were an honored tradition. As the fiercely independent district attorney of Orleans Parish, he took on machine politics, judges and mayors, and began a cleanup of Bourbon Street that was popular with practically no one. Witty and well read, he was known to bury his adversaries under literary and historical allusions. It was Louisiana senator Russell Long who first suggested to him that the Warren Commission Report was not exactly a flawless job. Garrison looked into the matter, and his thinking on the assassination, the war in Vietnam, and the federal government in general changed completely. Financed by a group of local businessmen, he jumped into the work that was to define his public image and dominate his obituaries.

Garrison had first seen Mort Sahl in New York, likely at the Blue Angel. He said, "I thought he was tremendous, coming out with his rolled-up newspaper, and, obviously, from the top of his head was this great mind. So I stayed to watch the second show, and there was not a line repeated." The D.A. was dubious when Sahl told him that he was there to help. "Everybody who saw him said, 'What is a big star like Mort Sahl doing in New Orleans talking to Garrison? What is he looking for?'" recalled Andrew "Moo Moo" Sciambra, who was handling field investigations for the Garrison unit. "People thought he was trying to get something. I mean, what did he expect to gain from getting involved with the assassination? So I guess you could say at first glance everybody had questions, but I think it's fair to say that very soon people found out that the only real reason for Mort being down there was that he actually wanted to help with the investigation."

They made him an unpaid investigator, issuing him an official-looking identification card in a smart leather holder. OFFICE OF THE DISTRICT ATTORNEY OF NEW ORLEANS, it said on one side. The other displayed his unsmiling photo, the unremarkable details of his height and weight, and Jim Garrison's neatly rendered signature. He took an apartment and began coming into the office every day, covering his own expenses and asking for things to do. "We would have been glad to give him expenses," said Garrison, "not only because of his value [in] going out and talking to some witnesses when we were short-handed, but particularly his value with regard to morale when he was brainstorming with me. . . . He was a real asset for his great sense of humor at a meeting of the staff, because his sense of humor comes like lightning out of the blue." Garrison, it turned out, kept vampire's hours and enjoyed the easy access he had to his new volunteer investigator. "There were no computers then," Mort says. "He's sitting with the Warren Report, five in the morning [the phone rings]. 'Mort, it's Jim. Are you sleeping?' 'What is it?' 'This guy in volume seven—how'd he go from Montreal to Miami? Who travels like that? This guy works for the FBI.' And then I was calling him, and I began to see the grand design."

To buy groceries and pay the rent, Mort did college concerts and TV talk shows. His virulent antiwar stance made him popular on campuses. ("The kids know my passion is totally uncontaminated by reason.") But talk shows were easier to line up and more plentiful. Johnny Carson, in particular, made sure he had an income when work was light, booking him once, sometimes twice a month. The downside to shows like Carson's was that they paid the same union minimum. "You take all the risk on those shows and you get $265," Mort comments. "You had to lay your heart out there. It was tough." On January 24, 1968, he arrived at NBC's Rockefeller Center studios to make a routine appearance on the Carson show. "I met with Rudy Tellez, the producer, and said to him, 'Rudy, I don't want to throw you any curves. What's verboten on this show?' I've always done that, although the networks like to characterize me as an outlaw because it justifies capital punishment. Rudy said, 'Don't mention [RCA Chairman David] Sarnoff. It's the only No.'"

The show wasn't as tightly prepped as it later became. Says Mort:

The first thing Carson says to me is, "Haven't seen much of you." I thought: Oh my God, help bury me. I said, "Well, I've been living in New Orleans." He said, "You're kidding." You know—that crazy guy and all that. I said, "No, he's right. They don't wish you success because they're scared of the results." He said, "If that guy's legitimate, he's welcome to come on here." I said, "Give me a date." And he did. Then we go off the air. Stan Irwin [Carson's road manager] said, "You know, Johnny, you may have been precipitous. You don't want the show to become a circus." And David Merrick [another guest on the show] is there. Merrick says, "Yeah, you don't want some guy coming out here and distorting." They all started building on that. And then *I* became corrupt. I said [to Carson], "You're too much of a professional to let that happen to this show." Bite your tongue! It's easy to compromise; I wish I had more chances. I flattered him into it.

A wire was dispatched to Garrison, who immediately accepted Carson's invitation to come on the show the following Wednesday. The entire program—the full ninety minutes—would be set aside for Garrison and Garrison alone. The network pushed to have legal counsel on the panel, but Carson said that he didn't want it to look as if they were ganging up on him "like it was going to become another showdown or something." For the same reason, he also decided against having someone on the show with an opposing viewpoint, such as his own personal attorney, Louis Nizer, who was a defender of the lone assassin conclusion. "I went back to New Orleans," Mort says, "and I started to prep Jim just like you would for a presidential debate. I'd play Carson, and I guessed everything he'd ask with the exception of about one question. Jim said to me, 'There'll be a lot riding on this, and I'll have to be ready.' And then I said, 'Remember what Marshall McLuhan said: If he punches you and your nose bleeds, the American people will watch that, too. You don't have to be right . . . but you *are* right.'"

The broadcast, which aired on January 31 in New York, and the following night on the West Coast, came across as a huge disappointment for both sides of the debate. "I hope," said Carson, by way of introduction, "not to add more confusion. I hope in some way to illuminate what's been going on." Predictably, he was skeptical of Garrison's claims, reading off a chronology of Garrison's public statements that varied over time and seemed to conflict with one another. In May 1967 Garrison had said that the killing had been carried out by "a mixture of individuals . . . all anti-Castro oriented," while in July he said the assassins "were men who sought to attain a radical change in our foreign policy . . . individuals who were once associated with the CIA." Looking up from the paper, Carson said, "Isn't that terribly confusing? And don't you seem to be riding off in all directions?"

Garrison's response: "It seems like it, doesn't it?" He went on to say that each of the factors was "a characteristic of one being" and that they were not necessarily in conflict. "We have found that the Central Intelligence Agency, without any question, had individuals who were connected with it involved."

"You have absolute facts and proof of that?" asked Carson incredulously.

"Without any question. I wouldn't say so otherwise."

Carson repeatedly challenged Garrison's habit of characterizing allegations as facts. "What makes it a fact?" he would ask. "Because you say so?" Garrison spoke as if making his case to a grand jury, while Carson was sober, earnest, and well prepared on points of eyewitness evidence. "Aren't you taking inconsistencies in testimony during the emotion of the time, even self-contradictory testimony from even sometimes the most truthful of witnesses, and using that as tainting everything else that is very well explained?" Garrison's response: "I can't change the fact that it was an unusual moment and there were many people who were emotionally affected by what happened. However, we have located, with no trouble, many, many people who heard shots coming from the area of the grassy knoll. Practically none of these people were called by the Warren Commission."

At times, Garrison, who characterized the report's conclusions as "a fairy tale," was able to get the studio audience on his side, drawing laughs and occasional bursts of applause at Carson's expense. The host's conclusion: "I have to say, as a layman, I am still quite confused. . . . You are asking us and the American public to believe that a team of seven gunmen carried this out with precision, firing from various points that day in Dallas, which is a remarkable feat in itself, and disappeared into thin air, with no witnesses who ever saw any other gunmen or getaway vehicles, and a gigantic conspiracy in which nobody seems to have yet proved anything. You ask us to believe that. I find that a much larger fairy tale than to accept the findings of the Warren Report."

The takeaway for the press the next day was Garrison's assertion that the late Jack Ruby had been placed at Dealey Plaza by a witness just an hour before the assassination. A Dallas resident, identified as one Julia Ann Mercer, said that she saw Ruby driving a truck from which a man emerged with a rifle. "I looked right in his face and he looked at me twice," she was quoted as saying. "This is why I was able to recognize him when I later saw him shoot Oswald on television." It was later pointed out, however, that Ruby had his back to the cameras when he fired a single shot into Oswald's stomach and facial recognition from the screen would have been impossible.

Hearst columnist Bob Considine led his dispatch, datelined New Orleans, with the headline "Garrison's Guff." Considine dug into the inconsistencies in Garrison's claims, suggesting, as did Carson, that the district attorney had pursued a confused and reckless path on the way to Clay Shaw's indictment. "Friends of Garrison—and he has many in the state—still assume 'he must have something,'" Considine wrote. "They cannot conceive of his going so far out on a limb as to have it break and plunge him into scornful political limbo. They say he's much too ambitious a man to goof on any fool's chase." Jack Gould of the *New York Times* labeled the show "a journalistic dud," reminding everyone that the intermediary who arranged "Mr. Carson's mishap" was none other than Mort Sahl. And *Variety* characterized the confrontation as a "nightmare session" for Johnny Carson.

"Carson, of course, became furious," says Mort.

And then we started to get money in our office. People would send money and say: "I never believed you guys, but the way he tried to shut you up makes me think." And that was the end of me and *The Tonight Show*, and the end of Carson—we were friends. He cut me off, and they told me the show was unavailable. And Garrison wasn't saying much; I'd made a major sacrifice there. Then Carson had regrets, and the night of a Jerry Weintraub party [he] came up to me at the parking valet and said to me, "You were always great, and you were never any better than you were tonight. It was great to see you." But, of course, I had given up all those years. That was '88, and he cut me off the program [in '68]. So I was off the show for twenty years—and I never got back on.

"All the things he got involved in, I thought, were distracting from his art, his being a comedian," said Woody Allen. "But my feeling was that, as with any genius, these things are necessary. These eccentric excursions are part of what makes Mort what he is." Fortunately, there were other talk shows answering the demand for cheap, celebrity-laden programming, including two to compete directly with Johnny Carson in his own time slot. *The Joey Bishop Show*, originating live from Hollywood, debuted in April 1967 on ABC, and CBS would add Merv Griffin to its late-night schedule in August 1969. Most significant for Mort, however, would be Dick Cavett's new ABC show, *This Morning*, which would offer an uncommonly clever talk format to daytime viewers otherwise stuck with game shows, soap operas, and old movies. Originating from New York, Cavett hit the air on March 4, 1968, with Buckminster Fuller and actress Patricia Neal as guests, and welcomed Mort Sahl to the series for his first appearance on April 31.

Even with three or four bookings a month, income from the talk circuit rarely exceeded $1,000, and Sahl was constantly scrambling for other forms of work. "When the self-pity would come in, I'd say, 'Jesus Christ, Jim. I'm going to have to sell my house, and when we get to court they're going to crucify us.' He'd say, 'Yes. Aren't you glad you were born a man and not one of them?'" Mort remained in New Orleans through February 1968, then left for an open-ended engagement at the hungry i, where he would remain in residence for most of the year. "Mark Lane and I are helping [Garrison] collect some evidence," he explained to the press. "We talk to witnesses or stuff while we're out of town giving speeches or performing. Garrison has a small budget and can't afford to send one of his regular staff."

The "i" and its onetime cousin the Purple Onion had been in rough shape since rock had come to dominate the entertainment landscape, taking with it any hope of a younger audience. "The action and the future has shifted elsewhere," reported *Variety*'s Rick Setlowe, citing such venues as the Fillmore and the Avalon Ballroom. "That's where the kids are now," agreed Enrico Banducci. "They simply aren't interested in the traditional nightclubs." Seasonal business, the *Examiner* reported, was off 30 to 40 percent. Convinced that a more upscale clientele was his only salvation, Banducci was building a new hungry i, a fancy supper club near Fisherman's Wharf that would compete head-on with the Fairmont's classy Venetian Room. Money was so tight, however, that the Internal Revenue Service padlocked the doors for several hours on Mort's opening night, alleging the club was in arrears nearly $5,000 in employee withholding. "I've encountered pressure tactics before because we're getting closer," Mort said, charging a government conspiracy. "Even some of my oldest friends won't have anything to do with me now. They say I'm too dangerous to know. . . . Banducci is practically the only guy in America that will hire me now, and now they're getting into him."

Covering Sahl at the hungry i had come to be regarded as routine for the hometown press, and it wasn't until he played a place near Boston called Lenny's on the Turnpike that he got to talk at length about his work with Garrison. "I've worked with this man who works with hard evidence and works all night with it," he said in a profile for the *Globe*. "Nobody assumes anything. I don't believe in speculation and neither does Garrison. I believe in him very much."

On stage, he kept the act fresh, backing off on the assassination, saying only that "the only president ever opposed to the military was Kennedy, and we know where he is." He was otherwise classic Mort Sahl, with the pullover sweater and a rolled newspaper jammed into his back pocket. "I just flew across country from California," he began, "and I thought you'd want to know that in between there are fifty-six cities on fire." In the wake of the Garrison interview, Johnny Carson became a regular target, Sahl detailing his questioning of his guests "with his usual degree of stimulation." Carson, he said, "reads by the Evelyn Wood method [of speed reading] only following someone else's finger." Taking a page from the campus version of the act, he advised students in the audience to reject their parents. "The White House is like a furniture store in front with gambling in the back."

On censorship: "The Supreme Court has finally cleared Lenny Bruce. I think there's an argument there for speeding up the judicial process." On Hollywood: "In show business, Steve Allen is considered an intellectual—which gives you an idea of the standards." On U.S.-Soviet relations: "Johnson said he'll meet the Russians halfway, and then he went eighty-eight miles to Glassboro, New Jersey." The president, he observed, became popular overnight by declaring that he wouldn't run for re-election. It followed, therefore, that he would have been even more popular had he not run in 1964. And, paradoxically, had the country never heard of him at all, he would surely be the most popular person in the world. Sahl typically did about an hour. ("I used to do about fifteen minutes, but there wasn't that much wrong with the country then.") After inviting questions from the audience, he thanked them for coming. "I really dug your attention span," he told them.

He was back at the hungry i when Robert Kennedy was shot and killed on June 5, 1968, in Los Angeles. "Enrico wanted to close," he recalls, "but I said no." Kennedy's assassination came almost exactly two months after the murder of Martin Luther King in Memphis. "Mark Lane said that J. Edgar Hoover was the full-time enemy of King. Everyone was crying, but nobody was asking the right questions. I didn't believe the James Earl Ray story, and I didn't believe it with Bobby." His focus on the Warren Commission never wavered, but he saw the King and Robert Kennedy assassinations as a tipping point in American society.

"Mort," suggested broadcaster Elliot Mintz,

> was always preoccupied with the romance, the innocence of the country, and I believe he associated the assassination of [John] Kennedy

with the death of romance, the end of America's sense of innocence—
with the possible coup d'etat factor that was waved in the face of a man
who was clearly a maverick all of his life. I think the Warren Commission Report was so flagrant a misrepresentation of justice to him that
he took it personally. So, as in the case of all things with Mort, he began
with a global observation and then brought it down to a very personal
passion. He was touched passionately by the experience, and then
when given the opportunity to do something about it, the figure that
appeared most likely to do something about it was Jim Garrison. And
once he was introduced to Garrison, and got along with him socially,
personally so much, he was in. It pushed all of the Mort Sahl buttons.

In his most optimistic moments, the ones that underscored his basic faith
in America and the values that made it great, Mort Sahl reflected the ideals baked into him by his constant and repetitious exposure to American
movies governed under the Production Code. He saw everything he could,
as he had since about the age of eight, and was dismayed when a film ran
counter to the high-minded classics of his youth, works by master film-
makers like John Ford, Howard Hawks, and George Stevens in which cultural roles were firmly delineated and moral ambiguity was minimized.
The new cynicism that came with a spate of political assassinations and
the escalation of the Vietnam war had a withering effect on him and what
he saw as the country's spiritual health. He mourned the loss of traditional
Hollywood, even as he ridiculed the efforts of what he saw as the Liberal
Establishment. "In *In the Heat of the Night*, Rod Steiger played a bigot," he
said of the big mainstream success of 1967, "and Sidney Poitier played a
Negro—to the best of his ability." He loathed the breakout hit *The Graduate* and gave it a one-line dismissal: "*The Graduate*, a picture about a Jewish
kid with gentile parents."

The selling off of the Fox backlot, where he made his movie debut in 1958,
inspired the kind of tirade formerly reserved for the Eisenhower administration. "Movies are finished," he declared flatly:

The irony is calling [the new thoroughfare through Century City]
Avenue of the Stars. That's the end of stars. It's very nice of you to
say that. You know, it's very generous, but the fact is—goodbye stars.
Movies are finished for several reasons. The obvious reason is television, but there are less obvious reasons. After the witch hunts of '47
there wasn't anybody left in movies who said anything. They were all

driven out, and the irony was they didn't move to the right, which was the fashion. They just became eunuchs. They are not left or right. They don't write about anything. American movies aren't about America. They aren't about any of the things that bother us. Riding a horse or a space-ship to the moon . . . But they never make a good movie about American divorce or what's seriously hurting America. The country is becoming a kind of militarist armed camp. And that's reflected in our art. Our art is without direction. The only thing they are interested in in movies is that Negroes be allowed to be in bad movies. Let them be part of the mad-ness. Marlon Brando! What are the movies about? Overall, bestiality, voyeurism, fetishism, masochism, and homosexuality. Something for the whole family. They've had it. And I'm a great movie fan. I go.

In July he caused a stir on his first *Joey Bishop* appearance by predicting that Eugene McCarthy, should he gain the Democratic nomination, wouldn't survive a term in office. "If Senator McCarthy is elected president, he'll be assassinated within one year by the CIA." The line wasn't bleeped on the East Coast, where the show went out live, but it also wasn't bleeped on the West Coast, where, like the *Jerry Lewis Show*, it was seen on a three-hour delay. Hank Grant, daily columnist for *The Hollywood Reporter*, deplored the lapse, calling it irresponsible, but Bishop, struggling in the ratings, seemed to ben-efit from all the outrage—which included heated statements from both the Secret Service and the Federal Communications Commission—and invited him back four times that year. "ABC thought that if they got him," Mort says of the show's dour host, "Dean and Frank would come in every night on an informal basis. That didn't turn out to be the case."

After the RFK assassination, Sahl took to having the Warren Commis-sion Report and all twenty-six volumes of testimony on stage with him. "I felt the country had to confront it and settle it," he says, "and I was crazy enough to think we could do that. We never got to that; I tried. I did try to observe one thing, and that was to try to make it funny. I had a lot of jokes out of the report; I carried the report with me. And I took the book down and I'd read from it. And, of course, I'd fudge it to get the laugh." He con-vulsed an audience at the Village Gate by reading with relish from Volume XIII of the hearings, the questioning of a man who worked at Jack Ruby's strip club named Curtis LaVerne Crafard. At one point, Crafard was asked by assistant counsel to describe a dance called "The Dirty Dog." It involved, Crafard responded, two girls and a guy "and it can be made so filthy that it will almost turn a person's stomach *if they do it right*."

He touched on the New Testament, Chicago Mayor Richard Daley, LBJ, Hubert Humphrey, Marlon Brando, and the new Liberal Establishment that had pretty much replaced the old Conservative Establishment. "You know why the liberals say we should get out of Vietnam? Why it's a 'senseless' war? Because we're losing." His take on race riots: "I don't condemn those who steal color TV sets, nor to I condone them. I'm a liberal that way." As Vincent Canby concluded in the *New York Times*, "Mr. Sahl is giving a performance of nervous, fitful brilliance. If the point of view occasionally seems vitriolic to the point of paranoia, it's probably because the times may seem even more hopeless to the middle-aged than to the young."

Clubs were still the best outlet for him, and he managed to keep working with the notoriety he occasionally achieved on television, Cavett to Griffin, Griffin to Bishop, Bishop to Steve Allen and occasionally Mike Douglas. And then there was the new syndicated *Playboy After Dark*, which burnished his somewhat tarnished reputation as the hip guy *Playboy* readers aspired to be. It didn't hurt that he was the steady boyfriend of a groundbreaking center-fold, nor that Richard Nixon was elected president in November 1968. There was a widely circulated news photo of Dwight Eisenhower on his birthday holding a sign out his hospital room window that read: MAKE IT A HAPPY 78TH FOR ME—VOTE FOR DICK. "Frankly," Sahl confided, "I'd planned on getting Ike something smaller."

"It's really funny," he mused. "People say I've changed, that I'm not bitter anymore. Well, it's not me that's changed. It's them, the liberals who want to see me give it to Nixon. They'll hold my coat for me now." To *Playboy*, he described the evolution of his style as poetry. "It's a succinct stating of the case by distilling the issues—often to a single line. For example, how better could you have characterized the candidates than this: 'Humphrey says it's an ugly little war, but someone's got to do it. Nixon says it's an ugly little war, but fortunately we got to do it. And Governor Wallace says it's an ugly little war, but it's the only one we've got and we should be thankful for it.'"

More TV came his way. Merv Griffin invited him to guest host his syndicated talk show for a week, he was one of the nine harmless celebrities occupying *The Hollywood Squares*, and the Smothers Brothers taped an appearance in the round that gave him his first prime time exposure since *The Hollywood Palace*. Dick Cavett went prime time with a thrice-weekly hour on ABC, Steve Allen had him on at least once a month, Bishop and Griffin nearly as often. Then there were *Allan Ludden's Gallery*, *Kup's Show*, *Philbin's People*, a daytime game show called *It Takes Two* (with China), and guest shots on *Love American Style* and the Raymond Burr potboiler *Ironside*.

After Clay Shaw's March 1, 1969, acquittal, which took the jury just fifty minutes to decide, Sahl was undeterred. "We were going to arrest him and charge him with perjury—that's how he got off. Jim made a wonderful speech to the jury, which I had something to do with writing, where he said, 'If you don't do something about this, all I can promise you is that you'll never have the opportunity again.' And it was true." In the opinion of many, Garrison's case was sabotaged by a string of unreliable witnesses, including an insurance salesman whose memory had to be jogged three times by hypnosis and a man who once had his own daughter fingerprinted, claiming his enemies had often impersonated his relatives in their efforts to destroy him. Federal courts prevented Garrison from charging Shaw with perjury, and Shaw, who had to sell his house in the French Quarter to pay for his defense, sued Garrison and several of his backers for $5 million. Hearings in the suit were set to begin when Clay Shaw died of lung cancer in August 1974.

Once the five-week trial had ended, there was little investigative activity to occupy the staff, and the conspiracy movement began to splinter. In April, Edward Jay Epstein, whose *Inquest: The Warren Commission and the Establishment of Truth* was the first major book calling the integrity of the Warren Report into question, wrote a damning assessment of Garrison's investigation for the *New York Times*, and by extension questioned the work of Mark Lane, Penn Jones, and Sahl himself. "In view of the discredit he brought them," wrote Epstein, "it is not surprising that now some disgruntled critics have advanced the theory that Garrison himself was a CIA agent provocateur."

Mort, who had come to regard Garrison, like Stan Kenton, as a father figure, refused to pile on, maintaining his loyalty even as the press made a circus of Garrison's failures. (*Newsweek* charged that Garrison was guilty of "incompetence and irresponsibility as a public official," while the *New Orleans States-Item* called for his resignation.) "I may have believed in the case more than Garrison," Mort admits. "Because I was looking for a place to hang my hat, and it happened to be a time historically when the industry I aspired to, I think, lost its way. It isn't just that I was a Democrat or that Republicans got elected. The government made a date with me and didn't show up." However unsuccessful the prosecution of Clay Shaw had been, Sahl wore his role in the quixotic campaign as a badge of honor, the act of doing a noble thing regardless of cost or outlook. "You don't have to prevail," he said at the time. "You can live in a cell, as I have, and keep getting stays of execution and continue to cultivate your mind. Your job is to pose the questions and let the establishment answer them."

"Mort was never all that interested in getting to the bottom of *why*," said Elliot Mintz. "He was more interested in the curves. Friends of his would be somewhat frustrated about not being able to get a direct, simple, sound-bite answer [to the question] 'Who killed Kennedy?' Mort never answered that directly. . . . What he would do is put a bunch of pieces of the chess game in front of you. He'd move some of the pieces around and tell *you* to examine the board. Mort never told anybody what to do. Mort never told anybody how to think."

Back in Los Angeles, he endured the abuse that naturally flowed from Garrison's blunders. "An agent, Don Gregory, says to me: 'I don't know if you're right or wrong about this Kennedy thing, and I don't care. But the way you did it—you really wrecked your chances. I wouldn't have done it that way.' And I said, 'You wouldn't have done it at all.' Of course, I didn't know I thought that until I said it. I know a lot of people thought I came up short. 'Who does he think he is?' Well, just an American. That's what I thought *they* were." In May, as the dust was beginning to settle, Garrison and his staff presented him with a plaque:

To

MORT SAHL

The Best Friend

John Kennedy

Ever Had

From

Jim Garrison   Jim Alcock

Andrew Sciambra   Louis Ivon

New Orleans

May 29, 1969

"I came up with all that material about the assassination," Mort says, "and there wasn't any place to do it. I did that whole thing where I read the Warren Report on stage, and it was pretty funny, but I couldn't carry those books from city to city. I worked up at Marvelous Marv's in Denver, and I left the books there. I couldn't take them to New York. And I worked a couple of those comedy clubs—I knew that wasn't going to work. All the guys working around me were cursing.* And by that time I'd been around so long I was sort of a legend but they didn't know what kind."

Just as the Clay Shaw decision was being reported in the press, Enrico Banducci gave an extended interview to the *San Francisco Chronicle* in which he bemoaned the fact that at the age of forty-five he had "lost the touch" for picking the stars of tomorrow. "I can no longer use the old measuring stick," he said thoughtfully. Of the acts that had made the hungry i what it was, the Mort Sahls and the Shelley Bermans, he said, "They're through. They're yesterday's soup. Kids are not digging the comics. They go mmm-huh. They don't laugh." Two weeks later, the plush new "i" at Ghirardelli Square, with its 450-seat concert hall and its adjoining restaurant and bar, was padlocked once again by the IRS for back taxes. "I'm going to try to raise the $23,000 and open again," Banducci said. "I'm not sure I believe San Francisco wants a hungry i now. The nightclub business started going downhill about five years ago. Ten years ago there was only the Fairmont, Bimbo's, and the 'i' showing major talent here. So all those other guys said to themselves, 'The i's making a fortune. Why shouldn't I?' So now we have ten nightclubs, and the talent is playing one off the other. They're killing the business. Someone like Phyllis Diller wanted $25,000 a week, and an entertainer of, say, Frank Sinatra's caliber wouldn't even open his door at home for that." Bookings cancelled in the wake of the closure included Big Mama Thornton, Jonathan Winters, Roslyn Kind, Shelley Berman, and, of course, Mort Sahl.

Enrico managed to get square with the IRS only through the indulgence of his landlord, Ghirardelli Square owner and developer William Matson Roth. When he reopened in June 1969, the room was not packed with "super-stars" as he had promised, but rather reconfigured as a 400-seat theater housing the nostalgic stage musical *Dames at Sea*. "I was unable to change my ideas about what was going on in entertainment," he explained. "For one thing, I couldn't go for the loud noise of rock." With the closing of *Dames* after a six-month run, the hungry i folded for good. "Comedy today is on a very thin thread," he said. "Nobody has come up since Woody Allen, and that was almost ten years ago. You go out to even the second and third-rate clubs and all you see are folk singers." The corporation filed for bankruptcy in February 1970, Banducci listing liabilities of $363,733 and assets of just $9,056. In November 1970, he sold the rights to the name for $10,000, and it

---

* Mort used to see writer-director Billy Wilder at Dick Carroll's. Wilder would say, "I'm going to tell a joke. It's off color. You can have Mort leave the room."

has adorned the former Pierre's, a "wiggle-and-shake" place at the nexus of Broadway and Columbus, ever since.

By 1970 Mort's club work had dwindled to the point where he was playing split weeks at places like Basin Street West and Donte's, a jazz club in North Hollywood where he generally packed the house on Friday and Saturday nights. He filled his calendar with campus appearances—as many as three or four a month—where the Kennedy assassination was his primary topic. "I'm not one of those people who say Kennedy was a saint," he told a crowd of nearly five thousand at Cal State Long Beach, "but I miss him, and I miss the optimism that was around him. Since he was killed, the American people have been losing hope."

The assassination was more in the background when he did guest shots with Steve Allen and Dick Cavett, who had moved into Joey Bishop's late-night slot on ABC. Still, controversy followed him, such as when he threatened to punch John Simon, the acerbic theatre critic for *New York* magazine, on the Cavett show. Or when he played a week at the San Francisco Playboy Club and was picketed by a combined group of about thirty black militant and women's liberation activists. They called him a "pseudo revolutionary who is not interested in the freedom and liberation of black people or anyone" and denounced the club's "crass exploitation" of women and their bodies. "Probably Hefner hired them because there was no business," Mort says, dismissing the fracas.

It was in 1969 that Sahl first met journalist Lawrence Christon, who, as America's first comedy columnist for a major newspaper, would chronicle the burgeoning standup scene by employing the etiquette and criteria of a drama critic. "It wasn't just Garrison and a dwindling club presence that torpedoed Mort," Christon wrote.

It was the 60s themselves. The gaudy counterculture surge, Vietnam, the protests, the sit-ins, the Yippies, the racial tensions, the spilling out of the young Boomer id into tie-dye costumes, drugs and rock 'n' roll—this really was a revolution of sorts, with the decade bracketed by assassination. By the time it started rolling to a close and the Manson family committed those horrible murders, Joan Didion wrote that somehow those lurid acts were unsurprising, a fitting coda to an insane period. Mort himself phrased it best when he said that rebellion in the 50s was couched in literary terms (the Beats, etc.), but in the 60s it was the music. The strong current of anti-intellectualism that runs through American history once again flooded over into the general culture and society.

Mort Sahl was looking tired and older, the years of struggle having, at age forty-three, worn him down. He abandoned his trademark sweater for a buckskin vest, and his nightclub sets stretched to ninety minutes. It was time, he decided, to get married. "Women think sex is everything," he liked to say. "I think it's about twelve percent. The rest is rubbing the guy's neck and going out for tacos in the middle of the night and being a good listener. Remember how Gary Cooper turns to Jean Arthur in those Frank Capra movies and says, 'You know, tomorrow is my big test in court and I don't know if I can do it.' She says, 'I *know* you can do it.' He says okay and goes asleep on her shoulder. That's a woman—one in whom you can confide, even your doubts."

It took a while for him to decide that China Lee could be that kind of woman. When he first met her, he noticed her thick Southern accent and how she would lose her English when she got excited and revert to Chinese. "I'm a sharp-looking chick and I was a Playmate," she informed him, "and when a guy asked me to dinner in this town, I put him through Hell. I'd push him to the wall."

"Everybody?" he asked.

"Well, there was one guy I liked, and I was with him a long time."

"Whatever happened to him?"

"He went through the wall."

Mort told Paul Desmond: "I've met a girl—China Lee." Desmond said, "Don't you find her kind of aggressive?" Hugh Hefner was so devoted to her that he began to tear up when Mort told him that he was going to marry her. And he brought her to the Music Center when Stan Kenton was conducting the Los Angeles Neophonic. "I said, 'This is China Lee.' And he said, 'Young lady, I hope you like loud music.'"

Mort taped all of Jim Garrison's commercials when the District Attorney was running for re-election. "Twelve-thousand dollars—the whole campaign," he chuckles. "We're walking out of the stage at [New Orleans TV station] WWL. China went first, and then Jim, and then me. Jim said, 'Marry that girl.' He stood right by her. And I was embarrassed; I'm very Victorian. I said, 'Listen. I don't mind you arresting J. Edgar Hoover and impeaching Johnson, but stay out of my private life, will you?' He never laughed. He said to me, 'Do you believe in what we're doing?' I said, 'I do.' He said, 'Well, I'm here to tell you it's worth nothing if there's no love in our lives.' Big moment for me. He said, 'You better marry that girl.'"

China was volatile, but she was real. She pushed him and prodded him and bucked him up, and after an extended period of peace and contentment, he proposed. "I was never on one foot about that," he says in retrospect. "I recognized family was missing, and I was my father's son to a degree—that I'd propose before anybody gives me an elbow in the ribs. I'm very much for legitimacy." They set the date for October 30, 1970. ("I'm not getting married on Halloween," China vowed.) There were no engraved invitations, just phone calls to sixty friends.

> I said, "We're having a party Friday. Hope you can make it . . . and, by the way, we're getting married." Stan said, "If you can get her out of here to shop or something, I'll put the band around the house and I'll play the 'Wedding March' when she comes in." There were speakers all over the floor and Japanese plants everywhere. I said, "How can you get voicing out of the trombones if you have to spread them out?" He said, "You let me worry about that."
>
> China disappeared into the front of the house to dress with Elaine and Fran, her friends. I decided to be low key, so I drove down to Dick Carroll's store and bought a blazer, drove back, had a hot dog in the kitchen. Then people started coming in. We served dinner and everything. Kenton's band didn't play, but a lot of the guys did.

China, he remembers, was uncharacteristically nervous. "It was the first time I had ever seen her nervous. She was usually at the head of her class. Her mother was there; I think her sister, too. My dad was there. My mother had had a stroke. She would have loved it. She said, 'You've got to have a home. You've got to have something.' My dad wasn't so sure; I'm not even sure he wasn't prejudiced toward the Oriental thing. China's mother kept saying to her in Chinese, 'Why do they laugh whenever he talks?' She didn't know what I did." Said China: "My mother was just glad that I was getting married. She didn't care to who."

They got a defrocked rabbi, Herschel Lyman, to conduct the ceremony. "It wasn't the usual religious ceremony," said Mort. "He used a lot of quotes from Indian philosophers." Lyman, he says, got thrown out by the rabbinical council "for being like a hippie. He listened to Pacifica Radio and Alan Watts—that kind of stuff. So they weren't sure about him. He got up and said, 'Mort, tonight you're going to listen to me. Do you take this woman?'

"I looked at her and said, '*I sure do!*'

"And she blushed."

13

I HAVE MET MY DREAM GIRL

The war in Vietnam made the politicization of American comedy inevitable. While Mort Sahl managed to keep his iconoclastic bearings, the new trend in political comedy was decidedly partisan and inevitably divisive. On the right, Bob Hope was an unabashed hawk, his closest buddy Richard Nixon's vice president, Spiro T. Agnew. Hope's former co-star, comedienne Martha Raye, was seen in frequent TV appearances in a loose-fitting army uniform—she was an honorary Green Beret—and George Jessel, older than both of them, assumed the air of a senior officer, frequently photographed in a military-style uniform adorned with medals and ribbons, although he, like Hope and actor John Wayne, another outspoken conservative, was never in the armed forces himself.

On the left were the Smothers Brothers, who lost their prime time variety hour over issues of political censorship; Dick Gregory, who had evolved into more of an activist than a comedian; and clean-cut George Carlin, who, along with Woody Allen and Bill Cosby, embodied the new generation of comedians who wrote their own material and saw Sahl and Lenny Bruce as their natural forebears. "They'd have a general idea and let their thoughts flow," said Carlin, who included a deft impression of Sahl in his nightclub act. "There was more intimacy and less formality. They gave you their picture of life."

Mort was proudly antiwar before it was fashionable, yet gave prominent liberals as much grief as any conservative on the national stage. And while Bob Hope was embracing Agnew as "a wonderful guy," Mort was busy defining him as "the Richard Nixon of this administration." Hope, who was riding a wave of renewed popularity even as he transitioned from the role of comedian to American institution, cringed at such lines, saying that Sahl and his ilk were doomed to failure for going "a little too deep" and making people resent it. "I think Mort had a big chance to become a great comic," he said, "but people won't buy it if they think your tone, your outlook, is nasty. People just have to be sure of you." Sahl, however, didn't care about the love most comedians sought from an audience. "I'm still here!" he would say. "Trust me. Bob Hope represents the government, but I lead the revolution."

Mort took China to London for their honeymoon. "I have met my dream girl," he proclaimed. "The first woman I can talk with about the separate branches of government long into the night." Ensconced in Hugh Hefner's penthouse flat atop the Playboy Club in Mayfair, he invited the press in and let fly on a variety of subjects, including President Nixon ("If you were drowning twenty feet offshore, he would throw you an eleven-foot rope and point out he was meeting you more than halfway"); leading men Dustin Hoffman, Elliott Gould, and Richard Benjamin ("If any of those guys had been my roommate in college I couldn't have gotten him a date"); and their host, who was now widely known simply as "Hef" ("He says, 'Be a playboy, have a ball,' but the guy has had only three girls in all the fifteen years I've known him"). It was China's first visit to England, but their travels in Europe would become an annual ritual.

Mort's first job upon their return was a campus date at Niagara Falls Community College. He was doing some promotional work for Saab, and was given a new Sonnet to drive as part of the deal. Someone at the college served him a cup of coffee spiked with LSD, but he didn't know about flashbacks until he decided to drive home, virtually nonstop and fueled by coffee and a box of No-Doz. Along Interstate 40 near Winslow, Arizona, he started seeing things and went off the road, breaking his back again as he had in 1964. He didn't know how seriously injured he was when an Arizona Highway Patrolman found him wandering a grassy median complaining about rocks being thrown from a passing train. (The tracks, the patrolman noted in his report, were four hundred feet south of the road.) "He asked me if I didn't see all the people standing around," the officer recounted. Obviously hallucinating, Mort told him and a deputy sheriff who had stopped that he hadn't slept in six days and was taking Valium under prescription. He also insisted that there were five thousand Marines covered by landing nets all around them.

Taken to Winslow Memorial Hospital, he refused admittance for a drug reaction and hired a cab to take him to Phoenix. Saab collected the car and he flew home, where the true extent of his injury was diagnosed. A sport coat, several pairs of slacks, and personal effects went missing in the commotion, and Sahl went on Dick Cavett's show to accuse the Arizona Highway Patrol of theft. "The colonel commanding them called the Cavett show and said, 'We didn't treat him any different than we treat anybody else,'" he laughs. "I never did get them back." Ordered by his doctor to lay off performing, he sat out a five-day booking at Hollywood's Bitter End West and was promptly sued for $10,000. Two weeks later, strapped into a back brace, he played a weekend at Basin Street West, his first San Francisco appearance since the demise of the hungry i.

China was with him at Basin Street, and accompanied him to Chicago for an engagement at Mister Kelly's. The Marienthal brothers, whose chain of niteries had grown to include London House, the Happy Medium cabaret theatre, and London House North, had sold their holdings to the Chicago-based Arts and Leisure Corporation the previous year. Opening for Mort on a return booking was twenty-five-year-old Bette Midler, a campy graduate of the Continental Baths whose flouncy appeal and solid pipes would soon carry her to stardom.

"Sahl does the political thing during his current stand in Chicago," wrote Roger Ebert of the *Sun-Times*, "but it is part of a juggling act that includes every other subject in the contemporary zoo. Every time Sahl opens here, the columnists report that he covered everything under the sun, and then they list everything under the sun to prove it: Agnew, Ralph Nader, Vietnam, General Motors, Lockheed, etc., and you get the point. But what you can't understand, unless you watch him work, is the way he keeps seven or eight subjects in the air at once, and gets a lot of his laughs by transpositions and the integrating of non-sequiturs that, once you've thought about them, aren't."

The two-week stand at Mister Kelly's drew well, press attention focusing on Midler as much as Sahl, who some considered old news on his thirteenth visit to the struggling Rush Street institution. Now acting as Mort's manager, China was fiercely defensive of her husband and resented any sharing of the spotlight. It is also a measure of the trouble the marriage was in that she quickly sized up Midler as a threat and issued an ultimatum. According to the vocalist, whose act was as much comedy as song, China said she "would put my head through the wall if I ever spoke to her husband again." A few days later, on August 9, 1971, China filed for divorce.

"She wanted to get married," remembers Mort. "She's quite unusual, but she has one thing in common with all women: Although they pretend to be of successor generations, and they'll deprecate [those who came before], the dream and the wedding and proving to their parents that they're really good people—it always wins. We had a lot of glass in the house—you could look out over the mountains—and we had five dogs. It looked like it was going to be all right.

"Some guy asked me, 'What's it like to marry a Playboy bunny?' I said, 'You mean as opposed to a woman?' You're buying into the fantasy Hefner was trying to retail." It was, perhaps, too good to last. "She'd always say to me, at the most quiet moments, 'Do you know how lucky you are? That you have somebody who loves you? A great-looking girl who stays by you?' She'd say it to me all the time—and it got to be pretty charming. And then my luck ran out—right out the front door." According to the petition filed in Superior Court, the couple separated on August 4, 1971, after just nine months of marriage. The news, datelined Santa Monica, made the wire services.

"When she left me she went back to New Orleans. She used to go into the House of Lee, a huge place, and she'd sit in the back and drink tea. Her mother would come over to her and she'd flick her with the chopsticks in the head—which they do to the kids when they don't pay attention. And she said, 'Go home.' In Chinese. 'Why you here?' She said, 'I just came back for a little vacation, Mom. What's wrong with that?' She said, 'Don't give me that. You're married now. Take your problems there.'" Mort laughs. "They were really smart, but they aren't like Jewish people. They don't talk about it a lot; they lay it out there once."

One source of conflict in the marriage was Mort's allegiance to Stan Kenton and the Kenton band. "I loved Stan Kenton," said China. "I thought he was a great guy. I just didn't like his music." There were two exceptions: "Here's That Rainy Day" and, later, "Send in the Clowns," both slightly less bombastic than most Kenton readings. "I didn't like big band music, and Mort wanted to go out every night and listen to music. If I stayed home one night, he wouldn't talk for two weeks."

The new year brought Mort Sahl back to New York for his first appearance there in three years. A two-week stretch at the Upstairs part of Upstairs at the Downstairs drew healthy crowds for the first show but meager numbers for the second, a reflection, one observer noted, of a get-home-early pattern that was increasingly bedeviling Manhattan nightlife. Still, Sahl complimented his early audience on their collective resilience after an hourlong set: "I'm glad you all think more of relevance than of having a good time."

In between college dates, he took club work wherever he could find it. In a suburb of Detroit, at a place called the Top Hat, he was claiming many of the same victims he had ten or fifteen years earlier, thanks, chiefly, to their persistence on the national scene. On J. Edgar Hoover: "There's a great deal of comfort in knowing that the man who's chasing your son today chased your father in the Palmer raids." On Nixon's devaluation of the dollar: "The new sign on the president's desk should say: 'The half a buck stops here.'" On the president's historic trip to China: "All these years I thought he was an anticommunist. Even that's not genuine." And: "At least Marco Polo brought back spaghetti."

In what was to become a semi-annual event, China filed for divorce again in August 1972, and yet again in May 1973. "She was terrible," says Mort. "You'd have a fight with her in the house, then the phone would ring and it'd be some guy who was taking her out that night. She wanted to verify that she was still marketable, so she'd go to one of those Hollywood joints, an Italian restaurant, with some actor she knew." Although the wire services invariably got hold of the news, Mort declined to comment publicly, merely noting that he and Richard Nixon were both trying to learn to live with the Chinese. In between, he struggled to keep busy, with club dates hard to come by and even some of the Playboy showrooms cutting back to weekends-only bookings. He took to wearing denim in his campus appearances, Levis with matching jacket and a red bandana for color. "Move over, Will Rogers," he'd say in a blow for sartorial relevancy.

In the fall of 1972, he became a part of a late-night project for ABC called *Comedy News*, a parody of the real news that surrounded anchors Andrew Duncan and Kenneth Mars with the likes of Stan Freberg, Richard Pryor, Fannie Flagg, and the veteran radio team of Bob Elliott and Ray Goulding. Billed as Chief Washington Analyst, Mort appeared uncomfortable in a suit and tie, obviously pained to have a laugh track subbing for the essential feedback of a live audience. Soon he was back in a sweater and open collar, but the series, at ninety minutes, failed to gel, and it would take another three years for NBC's *Saturday Night* to perfect the fake newscast at a more manageable length of ten minutes. "We seem to be losing our sense of humor," comedian Alan King commented. "The press is intimidated. Public TV is intimidated. It's imperative that we hold things up to ridicule—make fun of things—and we just don't have social satirists anymore. There should be a place for Mort Sahl in TV, but he's working in a little club in Georgetown."

The new year brought a cameo on *Laugh-In*, a hosting stint on a locally produced series called *Performance*, and yet another divorce filing from China. They were back together again within a month, China still functioning as her husband's hard-nosed manager. "My job was to take care of everything so that he had no distractions," she said. "I handled all the money and paid all the bills. They used to call me the Dragon Lady."

A new comedy album, *Sing a Song of Watergate*, was released by Gene Norman's label, GNP Crescendo, in June 1973, a compendium of choice assaults dating back to Richard Nixon's days as vice president. "Gene saw a bargain," says Mort, "and thought he could make an album for $5,000. So we went down to Capitol Records and put some food and drinks out, got a bunch of people to come by, and I made the album."

It was Mort Sahl's first album since the 1967 release *Anyway . . . Onward*, which was the result of a short-lived deal with Mercury. Comedy albums had started paying off again with the emergence of a new generation of comedians, most prominently Bill Cosby, Flip Wilson, David Steinberg, and political impressionist David Frye. All, however, were relatively new discoveries compared to Sahl, who had been on the national scene for nearly twenty years. Paul Desmond suggested appending the album's title with the words "Apocryphal of Lie," but there were other similarly themed records—*The Watergate Comedy Hour*, Don Imus' *Son of Checkers*, "Tricky Dickie Rides Again"—crowding the marketplace. Despite glowing reviews and generous press attention, *Sing a Song of Watergate* didn't sell well, which meant there would be no further comedy albums from the man who had pretty much invented them.

Harry Sahl died on September 14, 1973, at the age of eighty-two. He had been living in a tiny apartment on South Hoover Street—the area of town he knew best—since the death of his wife in 1971. Incapacitated by a stroke, Dorothy Sahl had spent the last year of her life in a convalescent home on Beverly Boulevard. China would boost her spirits by bringing ice cream and talking cosmetics with her. Of her tradition-bound husband, who often demanded her full attention, Dorothy would say, "He retired—but *I* didn't."

Yvonne Craig kept up with the family through Mort's attorney, Richard Mark. "Mort," she suggested,

did a thing to his dad that he didn't realize he was doing. When his dad got older, Mort told him that he could support him, that he made enough money and that his dad should retire and do what he always wanted to do, which was write. Which meant: Now you have to write, Tootsie Pie. And his dad had no talent for it, although that was a dream of his. It's very difficult to be living knowing that your son is supporting you, that you said that you wanted to write, and that *you haven't done it*. So that puts a lot of pressure on you. I don't know whether Mort ever realized that, because he thought he was fulfilling his dad's dream, but in point of fact he was painting him into a corner.

China could never make friends with Harry, who remained distant and formal with her, but Yvonne had grown very fond of the old man. "He always called me *Yvonne*. I don't know why, but he always did. He was charming, he was kind of flirty, but I have to say that he was more in touch with his emotions than Mort was. It was interesting. Then, of course, Mort's mother died, and his dad was left alone and kind of at odds."

Burial took place on September 17 at the Valhalla cemetery in North Hollywood. "The Fire Chief of South Gate spoke at the funeral," Mort remembers. "He said, 'Harry was like a father to me. I never knew any Jewish people before.' Apparently it was easier to be his father than to be *my* father."

Mister Kelly's remained a reliable gig, the last of the original network of rooms Mort Sahl opened up to comedy. But Kelly's was soon to follow the hungry i, Crescendo, Interlude, and Basin Street East into extinction, another victim of changing tastes, aging audiences, and impresarios who either retired, fell ill, or simply gave up. New clubs occasionally opened, but they didn't last long, and by 1973 the dates Mort was landing were either weekends or split weeks. Still he kept at it, sustaining a level of exposure that kept him in the game until another breakout opportunity presented itself.

"Among my acquaintances," says Mort,

was Harvey Orkin. He was David Begelman's assistant, and when he went out of the agency business they made him the booker at the Las Vegas Hilton. This guy had been Richard Burton's agent. So he called me up and said, "I'd like to bring you up here, but of course they don't think anybody will understand you. Well, let me tell you what's happened: Louie Prima's had a stroke, and I have to find a replacement." I said, "Who're you going to get?" He said, "I'm not. I'm going to have to turn to you at the eleventh hour." I said, "I see." So he did, and they believed him. And I came in, although I had the flu. He said to me, "You'll be fine." So I went upstairs and went asleep. Then I got a phone call that said: "You're on in five minutes—and Barron Hilton is sitting down there." So I ran downstairs, and Harvey said, "Are you all right?" I said, "Well, I fell asleep." He said, "It's all going to be fine." I said, "Then you're going to be a hero." He said, "No. When it's fine, they will have thought of it." So I got on, and I said, "Good evening. I was upstairs sleeping. Now it's your turn." I did an hour, and when I finished, Hilton said to the manager, "Take that ground across the lobby and build him a room. Get him out of this one. Build him a lounge." And he did. I signed up for a year, and I stayed three years. The steady money was coming in again.

With the new room under construction in Las Vegas, Mort Sahl played a well-timed fortnight at the Shoreham Americana Hotel in Washington, D.C. Two days before he was to open at the Shoreham, Spiro Agnew resigned in disgrace. Then on the day of his opening, October 12, 1973, President Nixon nominated House minority leader Gerald Ford to be his new vice president. "That news came out at three or four in the afternoon," remembered Mark Russell, the self-described "verbal cartoonist" working the Shoreham's lounge,

and Mort's got a dinner show at eight o'clock. So I snuck down to the Blue Room and ducked inside the door to catch him. Dinner shows are always dreadful; they're sitting there carving into their steaks and the silver is rattling . . . awful. The band leader says, "And now ladies and gentlemen, Mister Mort Sahl!" The band plays, and he walks out. And they're barely paying attention. He didn't say, "Good evening." He didn't say, "Nice to be here." His very first words were: "Jerry Ford, huh? A member of the Warren Commission I might remind you. He said that the bullet came from the—" And we're on the grassy knoll during the dinner show.

The Casino Theatre dated from when the Hilton was known as the International, the newest hotel in Las Vegas and, reputedly, the largest in the world. The main showroom was big enough to support the likes of Barbra Streisand and Elvis Presley, while the smaller casino space was built for contemporary music acts like B.B. King, Damita Jo, and Ike and Tina Turner. It was generally considered too large for monologuists, and until Mort Sahl's arrival, the only comedian to work the place was Redd Foxx. The Vestal Virgin, the room Hilton had built for Mort, was more intimate, all chrome and mirrors with seating for 200. The initial deal guaranteed twenty-four weeks, to be played out in a series of four-week increments.

Sahl opened on December 21, 1973, alternating sets with singer-actress Becky Ilagan. "That's where the heavy dough was—and the chance to work every night," he says. "At the Hilton I did two forty-five minute shows. A very easy job. Always full. But they knew how to run a club. They made it just big enough, and they put in glass so that you could see it but you couldn't hear it. It was really manufactured chaos." Playing to regulars as well as tourists, he'd work in material of local significance—Evel Knievel jumping the fountains at Caesar's Palace, or the incessant presence of slot machines at grocery stores and gas stations. Always prone to movie references, he even spun a joke from childhood memories of *Lost Horizon*: "I get very lonely in Vegas, and I marry a chorus girl. We decide to move to Los Angeles to get stability—that usually got a laugh—and as we're driving to L.A. she grows older."

He got so that he could tell who was in the main showroom by the nature of the crowds they drew. "When Liberace's here, there's a lot of antique people in the lobby. They look like they'd be Justice Douglas' wife if he were sensible. When Johnny Cash is here, you don't have to look at the marquee to verify that fact. You just know it, because there're a lot of pickup trucks in valet parking." Over time, he came to adjust his delivery to the relatively short attention span of a Vegas audience. "What I did mainly was that I got rid of the excess. It was like I was Hope—I went from joke to joke for forty-five minutes. It was easy. Then I'd go right upstairs—I had a suite upstairs—and had my car in the back. But it was sort of maddening after a while. China would crack. She'd be there a few weeks and then she'd leave. She couldn't handle it; she didn't like the sameness of it. We'd drive up to Mt. Charleston once in a while. Or she'd take the Ferrari and drive back to L.A. Or she'd go to New Orleans."

China's father, Lee Bing, died of cancer on December 24, just three days into the new engagement. China was in New Orleans for the wake and funeral when she became convinced that Mort was cheating on her, and she seized the opportunity. "I thought: Now I have an out. I'm getting a divorce." In the past, they had always drifted back together—once when they made separate but simultaneous visits to a race horse they owned called Fighting Indian. But China was determined to make this one stick, and ultimately she would.

"She was never a Dragon Lady," said her friend Teddy Howard, "but there were a lot of people who were very jealous of her. I think she was proud of being tough, that she didn't feel that anyone could put anything over on her. She was a very, very good negotiator, and she felt, rightly so I think, that she did a lot for Mort's career. But it became too heavy on her, Mort being quite a bit older than China and a romantic at heart. Whereas, I think China was very much a realist in her own mind, of what was real to her, and she clung to those things. And I don't think Mort was tuned in enough to know when she'd had enough. I think that was probably their biggest problem."

Sahl continued to work the Hilton, did a little television (a Dean Martin roast, an episode of the unfortunate *Snoop Sisters* series), and played a fortnight at a New York club called Jimmy's, his first Manhattan booking in two years. Paired with Teddi King, he drew a healthy opening night turnout that included satirist S. J. Perelman. "What can you get Nixon that he hasn't already taken?" he asked rhetorically, turning his focus to the waning days of a calamitous presidency. "You really have to blame everything on McGovern because he ran against Nixon. If he let him run unopposed, he would have lost." Leafing through a copy of the *New York Post*, he paused. "Anybody know what Lyndon Johnson told Hubert Humphrey about Vice President Ford? 'He can't walk and chew gum at the same time' is what LBJ said. He said Ford played too much football without his helmet. But Nixon. I mean, what can you say about him except maybe he left his fingerprints on history? Seventeen of his staff are in jail, and fourteen are awaiting trial. I mean, is there life after Nixon?"

Although Mort was having a good year professionally, his new manager, George "Bullets" Durgom, wasn't happy. "Because of the continual Vegas thing," says Mort, "nobody knew where I went." Durgom, a former band boy for Glenn Miller who had managed everyone from Jackie Gleason and Frank Sinatra to Merv Griffin and the late Allan Sherman, wanted to stage a high-profile concert in Los Angeles, something attention-grabbing, but none of the existing clubs or theaters had the right kind of cachet. Then he was reminded of a one-man show starring eighty-two-year-old Groucho Marx that had been staged the previous year at L.A.'s Music Center, the most prestigious performance venue in all of Southern California. Durgom arranged to rent the Center's 745-seat Mark Taper Forum and managed to fill it on a Monday night in June 1974. It was a gambit that paid off brilliantly.

"Jokes about the SLA bring a political humorist into dangerous territory," wrote Dan Sullivan, theater critic for the *Los Angeles Times*.

Jokes about a coroner's jury following the events in Dallas are definitely off limits. But Sahl can do them, first because as a comic he always knows what kind of audience he's got out there (Monday night's, he correctly observed, was the liberal-guilty crowd from Beverly Hills); and second because as a man he is clearly laughing to keep from crying. He's there, he says, to remind us that we're not crazy. His mind, too, is boggled by the immense cloud of nonsense that passes in our society for truth; by the decline in American public morality from "Resistance to tyrants is obedience to the will of God" to "I am not a crook." All he's trying to do is sort it out for himself, and incidentally us.

June was also the month in which China's divorce was final. Three weeks later, Mort nixed a year-round offer from the Hilton to essentially double his time in the Vestal Virgin Room, citing the pending development of a weekly talk-variety show for Viacom. He signed with KTTV to do a nightly commentary during the House Judiciary Committee's impeachment hearings, and made a second Music Center appearance, this time on a Sunday night in the 2,000-seat Ahmanson Theater, the scene of the Groucho Marx concert. Ten days after that, he and China were remarried in Las Vegas.

"She took her time down there in New Orleans," he says, "and then she decided that we ought to be back together. And even though she didn't say it, I knew there was something ritualistic that convinced her. So I got the judge in Vegas to marry us in the tower of the Hilton. And she liked that." The date was October 30, 1974—exactly four years to the day from the first time they were married.

Nineteen seventy-four ended with the announcement that Mort Sahl would be teamed with conservative Los Angeles newscaster George Putnam for a nightly talk show on KCOP-TV, the station at the lowest economic end of the VHF spectrum. At first the show, which was Putnam's idea, was to be called *Talk Back*, which was the name of a nightly segment of Putnam's old newscast. Three weeks later, with the concept worked out more thoroughly, the show was *Both Sides Now*, playing off the Joni Mitchell song of the same title.

Putnam, who was thirteen years older than Sahl and dated back to the Fox Movietone newsreels he used to narrate with Lowell Thomas, had been off the air for a year. His strident political bent and mannered delivery had become a subject of parody, most prominently in the Ted Baxter character on the Mary Tyler Moore show. At a press conference, KCOP general manager Richard Frank framed the pair as "as far apart in political and social views as any two personalities in America today. Atmosphere they create will generate a sense of excitement and participation on the part of the viewer." In other words, *Both Sides Now* would hearken back to the manufactured controversy of the Jim Gates years at KTTV, spotlighting two venerated figures of the period. Sahl, said Putnam, was "so far left he makes Karl Marx look like a Goldwater Republican." Mort, in turn, said that he would be tolerant of Putnam's political views. "I don't think we can rescue him from his position, but he will be great to watch."

The first episode of *Both Sides Now* aired on January 6, 1975, and it appeared at first as if the show might actually work. Neither man cared much for Gerald Ford, who had assumed office with the resignation of Richard Nixon. "There is a kind of absentee or caretaker presidency in the country today," Putnam solemnly intoned, pointing out that neither Ford nor his vice president, Nelson Rockefeller, was elected. Sahl observed that former California governor Ronald Reagan was the only member of a new presidential commission probing the CIA who hadn't actually worked for the agency, and he quipped that the left-wing campus movement, famously infiltrated by the FBI, fell apart "when the government withdrew its financial support." They differed on CIA activities in Chile, Putnam considering it "money well spent," while Sahl decried Secretary of State Kissinger's stewardship of the agency's intervention there. The interview guest was Francis Ford Coppola, who had appeared on Mort's old KTTV show, and who was now the Academy Award–winning writer-director of *The Godfather* and *The Godfather Part II*. The inaugural episode ended with Putnam announcing something the audience would never see on television again. He then took Mort's head in his hands and kissed him full on the lips. "You kissed me," said Mort, a little astonished, "but do you respect me?" Responded Putnam: "I love you."

The notice in *Daily Variety* heralded "a stimulating and amusing program which should do well" for what it termed "television's newest odd couple." Dick Adler, a staff writer for the *Los Angeles Times*, was more reserved, longing for more flashpoints between the show's stars. "The real trouble appears to be that Sahl on his own has been mining both sides of the political street (as well as all four lanes of traffic in between for comedy) since he began, and doesn't need any needling from the right to make fun of liberals. Thus forced out of his natural territory, Putnam seems reduced to playing an Ed McMahon-like line feeder."

Concurrent with the start of *Both Sides Now*, which was taped just an hour before it aired weeknights at eight o'clock, Mort began another four-week stand at the Las Vegas Hilton, requiring him to go straight from the modest KCOP studio complex in Hollywood to LAX for the one-hour flight to McCarran International Airport. "I kept synthesizing my experience into the act," he remembers. "I'm talking about my own employability, and I'm standing out in front of La Scala waiting for the valet to bring my car. Carson walks out with thirty people he's taken to dinner. He says, 'Oh, Mort. What are you doing these days?' I say, 'I'm on Channel Eleven.' I don't have the guts to tell him I'm on Channel Thirteen. So then they drive away and they're all laughing. 'Ha ha ha! He's on Channel Eleven!' I made it into a whole routine."

Director Dave Dawson, son of former CBS president Thomas H. Dawson, had grown up in Miami Beach as a Mort Sahl fan. "Meeting him was special," Dawson recalled, "and the first meetings were cordial, and even very funny. But the more China got involved in the mix, the worse things became." There were "sooo many problems, from music to the set . . . especially the set. And once we got on the air, every day we thought would be the last." The volatile stew that was *Both Sides Now* began to curdle. Hecklers in the studio audience became a problem, and the tension between Putnam and Sahl quickly moved from the political to the personal. "In eight days the two guys began to kill each other on the air," said Rudy Tellez, whose Telco was the producing company. "It took eight days for them to hit venom and strike back."

The influential *Times* review echoed what those inside the station had already been saying. "Exactly what day it did start to fall apart, I can't recall," said Dave Dawson. "But most involved with the show were saying that the show that first week was 'too white bread.' And China was leading much of that. Or maybe I just heard her the most. . . . George, Mort, and I did get together a few times off the lot for dinner. Not many. And I had been 'encouraged' to tell them that they needed to get 'into it' more." Sahl found it easy to take Putnam's theatricality as condescending and dismissive, while Putnam sensed that his co-star wasn't as committed to the show's success as he. "I remember when he'd lose his temper," says Mort, "and I'd be looking at my watch because I had to get to the plane. And he'd say, 'Go back to your Mafia masters.'"

Rudy Tellez walked out on the show. "He wanted mock controversy," Mort says of Tellez. "In other words, Cleveland Amory would come out of the audience to talk about cruelty to animals. Then the next show was going to be gun control. And then the next show would be about how there aren't enough women cab drivers. All of that mock Jerry Springer stuff. He wasn't a real producer, he was a politician. He worked for Carson; he kept trying to use that. And then George, in order to oppose me, brought on Jack Ruby's sister. 'Jack loved this country enough to spare Jackie the trial.' And, of course, I knew better than that. He didn't know anything except for George to oppose it."

Putnam exited the show after eight rancorous weeks on the skewer, characterizing the self-made match with Mort Sahl as "a bad marriage." Mort remembers Putnam fighting a good deal with Rick Frank, who ran the station. "It was a combination of things," he says. "A lot of stuff was happening that was spontaneous, and he felt I had an edge in improvising answers. He liked to have the material in front of him, and he didn't want to appear ancient."* For Putnam, it was supposed to be an audience participation show. "When personalities became more important than the message, the rest of it fell apart . . . I do not have one word against Mort. I am talking about a beautiful idea which went awry. You've got to put down your own personal feelings for the sake of a show which is the thing; you've got to be a team player. The best thing I can say is that I lasted eight weeks with Sahl. It was a horrible nightmare that's over with."

Producer John Frook said the show would continue with Sahl and a series of guest hosts until one proved suitable as a permanent replacement. "If we had our druthers," he said, "we would have an attractive, eloquent woman whose philosophy and politics are to the right of center." A week later, the first guest host took the stage in the person of Hugh Downs, a man Mort had known since his days as Jack Paar's genial announcer. Politically, Downs had a libertarian streak but leaned Democratic. No fireworks erupted from his weeklong stint on the show, and after his departure the search for a permanent co-host was quietly dropped. *Both Sides Now* limped along for another eight weeks, Sahl commuting nightly between Los Angeles and Las Vegas, and came to an end on May 2, 1975.

Around the end of the year, it became known that Mort and China were expecting. "We went to Rome," he recalls, "and she had just been impossible. It was separate tables. Then we went up to the apartment in the hotel, Parco

---

* Putnam was sixty, Sahl forty-seven.

dei Principi, and it was *really* separate tables. Then I put my arm around her, and she got up in the morning—I was virtually a stranger by then—and she said to me, 'I'm pregnant and it's a boy.' She had a lot of that metaphysical stuff going. She had told me she could never have children, so, of course, she gets pregnant. She was thirty-four. Dr. Rogowski said to me: 'So much for the precision of my colleagues.'"

The storm clearing was brief; the two flew home on separate planes. Mort, however, was elated. "I thought it was great," he says of the prospect of having a child at the age of forty-nine. "I thought it was terrific. And I had an idea that maybe I had successfully made a commitment because I wasn't panicked by it and I thought it was wonderful." China, meanwhile, celebrated impending motherhood by once again filing for divorce. "I don't know what I'm doing with this guy," she complained to their friend Bob Kaufman. "He doesn't love anything; he doesn't love me." Kaufman did his best to reassure her. "He *does* love you," he insisted, "but he has a mission. He has to save America first."

In its bicentennial year, America seemingly had little need for saving. Mort worked only sporadically, taking campus dates and occasional week-ends at Donte's. In June, two concerts he gave at UCLA's Schoenberg Hall were taped by Home Box Office. The following month, he was part of NBC's coverage of the Democratic National Convention, commenting, along with John Kenneth Galbraith and William F. Buckley, for *Today*. "I'm looking for-ward to the political conventions on TV," he said. "You turn the channels and at first you think TV news is all the same. But take a closer look. Those TV newscasters all use different hairspray."

China, meanwhile, took her pregnancy in stride. "She only gained five pounds," Mort says, "so she didn't make a big deal of it." One evening, she and Mort rode down to Disneyland on the bus with Stan Kenton and his band. The Kenton organization was playing its annual week at the park's Carnation Gardens, a Gay Nineties–style dance pavilion where ghost bands and swing era veterans appeared throughout the summer. Contrary to all appearances, China was very pregnant, and Kenton asked her: "How do you think motherhood is going to affect you?"

"I'm looking forward to it," she said.

As they got off the bus in Anaheim, Kenton, in an aside to Mort, said, "She's scared to death."

In New York, the convention was serving as a "coronation" (as Buck-ley put it) of Jimmy Carter. Senator John Glenn, who was one of the two keynote speakers, indirectly furnished Sahl with one of the few genuinely funny lines he heard at the convention. Talking with an earnest young delegate, he mentioned that Glenn was the first man in space. "You mean that's Timothy Leary?" asked the delegate. Later, Sahl referred to Carter's press aide, Jody Powell, as the candidate's "director of revelations" and reported that California's frugal young governor, Edmund G. Brown Jr., was rooming at the YMCA.

He made more of an impression at a club on East 55th Street called Michael's Pub, where he was holding forth every night after the convention gaveled to a close. Michael's actually had two performance spaces. The Music Room was where pianist and former *Tonight Show* bandleader Skitch Henderson and his aggregation were appearing, while the smaller Bird Cage was given over to soloists and comedians. Primed with the latest political news, Sahl observed that back in 1776, when the country was much smaller, its best minds included Thomas Jefferson, Samuel Adams, and Thomas Paine. "Now we have Jerry Ford . . . Ronald Reagan . . . Jimmy Carter . . ." each name becoming a laugh line all its own. "Darwin," he concluded after a pause, "was wrong." He grinned wolfishly and said that he had been hired to provide "color" for *Today*. "NBC thinks I'm a liberal. That's one of the most insulting things I ever heard." Taking aim again at Jerry Brown, who was inexplicably waging a losing battle for the presidential nomination, he noted that when Brown was studying to be a Jesuit, he took a vow of silence—"on the major issues." Were Brown to actually win the nomination, he continued, his running mate would be "his inner self."

On the third day of the convention, China was at Hollywood Park, playing the horses with her sister Virginia, when her water broke. She was rushed to Cedars-Sinai, where the baby was born with a full head of hair. It was Bastille Day, July 14, 1976, and the boy was given the name Morton Lyon Sahl Jr.

Mort was on the convention floor at Madison Square Garden when he got the news. Partway through his ten-day engagement at Michael's Pub, he wouldn't be able to fly home for another week. Gene McCarthy was with him and offered his congratulations, adding ruefully, "They never forgive you if you're not there." Tom Snyder, who had come into Michael's one night to see the show, announced Little Mort's arrival on *Tomorrow*. Later, Mort met the nurse who attended the birth. She told him that whenever she passed the maternity ward, all the babies were laughing . . . and one was talking.

14

WHY AM I THE ONLY ONE?

During the period 1973–75, when work was infrequent, Mort Sahl had a project few people knew about—a book.

[William] Jovanovich [of Harcourt Brace Jovanovich] said to me, "I keep picking up these bios of Artur Rubinstein, Thomas Edison, who said, 'I always had a dream of making a light.' They go backwards about how they became great men. I want a guy who's in the midst of it, who is inflexible and who is convinced he is right—and we don't *know* if he's right yet. And you're that guy; you're in the middle of it." Pretty good. So I started writing it, and I'd go into New York and sit with him—he was the editor. Fascinating guy, Jovanovich. He was a Regent of the State of New York. Limo. Briarcliff. Lunch at Lutèce. Dinner at Périgord—a routine that was never broken. China comes into town. He says, "Mort's been telling me . . ." She says, "He hasn't told you everything. I *know* everything. I *see* everything." He says, "What are you talking about?" She says, "If Mort were disappointed enough, he wouldn't go on. But I would go on. I wouldn't die if he died, because *I* am a survivor. What do you think of that, Bill?" He says, "I think you're the most chilling young woman I've ever met."

Jovanovich was eager for a book that would not be dominated by the author's criticisms of the Warren Report or attract lawsuits for libel.

He said, "You've got to get a press agent. A lot of people are resistant to you." So he calls in John Springer. Springer says, "I don't think I can handle this." I said [to Jovanovich], "Do you know what the weight of the Garrison investigation is now? These guys are throwing the money back on your desk." He said, "You can't say these things in this book because [Clay] Shaw will sue." I said, "Shaw is dead. How's he going to sue?" He said, "Let me see your credentials." And he locked them in his desk—my credential from Garrison (which he never gave back to me). And then he wanted me to keep out of that area.

He didn't like the insubordination, and in the meantime I had a job. I was on a cruise ship. So I get on the cruise ship in Florida, and we're going to the Caribbean. I had a delivery in which I could indict someone by mentioning him. They say, "Here's Mort Sahl!" and I walk out and say, "Richard Nixon." And they applaud. It went downhill from there. They loved him.

The captain was Portuguese: "Can I have dinner with you?" He said, "I don't think you gauged this audience correctly." Anyway, I jumped ship. I got off in Puerto Rico, claiming illness, and went back to the Park Lane Hotel where Jovanovich had me, and we finished the book. He said, "That certitude is what this book is about. Don't ever be afraid of the page." He got out all these Flair pens and black pencils and said, "Let's go." Originally I had about 1,500 pages. He brought it down. I remember saying to him, "What kind of world are you building where I can't say this about an actor, but I can indict the president?"

Jovanovich didn't care for the title *Heartland*, which was Mort's inspiration. "He said, 'I don't know about this title.' We're at Lutèce, and he turned to a guy at another table. 'Would you buy a book called *Heartland*?' The guy said, 'No, not particularly.' He turned back to me and said, 'That's what's wrong with motivational research.'" The edited book was a snug 158 pages—no chapter headings or photo sections to impede the flow. What emerged was part autobiography, part statement of principles, part voice in the wilderness. "My experience is meaningless unless seen as a microcosm of America for ten years," Sahl wrote. "Here is the pain and ecstasy of a conscience out of control. It's not written in retrospect or triumph. It's a statement from the eye of the hurricane. It's a suspense story. Those who think of me as an outlaw will realize that I think of myself as the sheriff. Whatever else you find, you'll know what side I'm on."

Although buoyed by an early trade review in *Publishers Weekly* that pronounced it "a disconcerting but engrossing personal testament," Jovanovich was troubled by his own health problems and the author's insistence that he be allowed to "restore the integrity of the manuscript" by correcting "at least 49 substantive inaccuracies." The wrangling between author and publisher continued over the summer of 1976, delaying the publication of *Heartland* until September 30. The book was widely reviewed, the verdicts invariably divided. "Sahl has written a distinct social document, half-scream, half-whimper," wrote the humorist Jean Shepherd in the *New York Times Book Review*, "but who is to judge? One man's madness is another man's vision of truth. He ends with two questions: 'Is anybody listening? Does anybody care?' All working martyrs have been haunted by the same questions. However, as another great American humorist, George Ade, once put it: 'Don't pity the poor martyrs. They like the job.'"

Sahl used the book to settle a number of scores, a quality that prompted Paul Desruisseaux, in a profile for UC's *California Monthly*, to describe him as "a very likable guy who makes ex-friends easily." *San Francisco* magazine stirred the pot by licensing an excerpt from *Heartland* for its November issue and then commissioning Enrico Banducci, who was furious at the way he was portrayed, to write a rebuttal. In the book Mort credits Enrico with "a certain flamboyance which created a business" and then charged that he couldn't run it. "He had never discovered anybody at the hungry i except me. . . . Later on, the club was identified with people I had sent there, like Shelley Berman, Jonathan Winters, Barbra Streisand, and Bill Cosby, but they had all been booked by theatrical agents."

Returning fire, Banducci portrayed Larry Tucker as Mort's "crutch," the guy who actually thought up the funny things that Sahl uttered and then took credit for, pointing to Tucker's later success as a writer in TV and movies as proof. "He makes me out as though I didn't know music, and had no talent or foresight, and should have been a bootlegger," Banducci complained. "It's like I don't have the brains to spot talent and that I was in the same category as all the other nightclub owners, which I wasn't, or the hungry i wouldn't have been as distinctive and different as it was. . . . The thing was that Mort never suggested anybody who was any good. In fact, he would say that everybody was bad. He hated the Limeliters, for example. He loved Dave Brubeck, but Brubeck never played at the hungry i. If he had, Mort would have hated him, too."

Both men bent the truth in service of their own personal mythologies, with Enrico, courtesy of the magazine, getting in the final word: "Now with this book he's burned all his bridges behind him. He must hate all his friends, but then he really doesn't have any friends. . . . And now I get a call from *San Francisco* magazine asking for a photograph of me with Mort. Well,

I wouldn't be caught dead with him now that I've read his book." His parting line: "Mort Sahl is a phony."

Jovanovich's artwork and jacket copy did the book no commercial favors. The silhouetted image of a lone sheriff on the cover honored the author's own heroic view of himself, but it was confusing and off-putting to potential readers who knew Mort Sahl as a nightclub comedian and not a solitary figure on horseback. "Jovanovich was very fearless in the beginning," says Mort reflectively, "then he started backing away from all of it. I was going to clear the deck. I thought the candor was going to straighten out Hollywood." With the title and the physical look of the book suggesting a Louis L'Amour novel, retail sales were disappointing, particularly in an election year. There was no book club edition, no serialization other than in *San Francisco*, and no national TV exposure. The book had a small second printing and then disappeared entirely.

The presidential campaign of 1976 provided little in the way of material for an observer as acute as Mort Sahl. Gerald Ford, whom he was fond of referring to as Daddy Warbucks, had a sartorial style he described as "department store dapper." At a loss to say much positive about him, Sahl noted approvingly that Ford "had the best attendance record of anyone on the Warren Commission." Choosing between him and challenger Jimmy Carter, Sahl concluded, was like "choosing between Seconal and Nembutal."

In November, he was back in San Francisco to do election night commentary at a new rock venue called the Old Waldorf. Nearly six hundred people jammed the warehouse-like room at the Embarcadero to watch a giant video screen and hear Sahl's caustic commentary as he changed the channels. "Ford," he said, "looks like the guy at Safeway who okays your check, and Carter looks like a Peninsula lawyer who comes to the city to have 'a girl' cut his hair." Landing on cutaway shots of Democrats gathered at a party in Washington: "Five hundred people at the Hilton, and everybody gets an end cut." On black newscasters: "They look like they were made in the lab by white newscasters." On ABC: "Yesterday's cornflakes." On NBC: "What's on CBS?" And finally: "If we keep going we'll hit Channel 44 and the Dinah Shore show, and Nixon will be there with Robert Goulet to talk about his book."

"Any time Mort ever decides to write a screen story," Jerry Wald once said, "all I want is first grabs at it." In December 1976, Sahl made his first sale as a screenwriter, placing an original called *I Can't Talk to You Now* with Clint Eastwood's company, Malpaso. It was, he said, a comedy about "meaningful relationships, alternate lifestyles, the saving of the environment, confused sexuality. In other words, the promise of America." He had known Eastwood since 1957, when a close friend of Clint's was a cousin of Mort's wife, Sue. "She wanted me to get them in at the Crescendo without paying a cover, which I did. Clint, at the time, was building swimming pools in Van Nuys."

Eastwood was looking to expand beyond action parts, and liked the idea of doing a romantic comedy. "*I Can't Talk to You Now*," says Mort,

> is the story of a guy who is married to kind of an embittered dame. She drinks a lot, and he's a track coach at Pacific Palisades High. He sees this going nowhere, so he moves down to the Marina, gets an apartment and runs with a Doberman in the morning. He meets stewardesses down there. He meets Tony Curtis, who's an English teacher who has left Suzanne Pleshette, and who's down there trying to be half his age, using acid and getting sick. Clint rolls him up in a rug and brings him back to Suzanne Pleshette. She says, "What's this?" He says, "You made him this way—*you* take care of him."
>
> It's like that—it's a guy settling all the books. While he's down there, he's got a track meet coming up, and the head of the team is a Mexican kid, and his rivals on the team inform that he's illegal. Clint meets a stewardess, and when he falls in love with her she says, "You don't know how to have fun." So he picks her up—they're over by the sheriff's station where they've been running together—and throws her into the water. He says to the radio operator, "Are you on duty?" The guy says, "Yeah." He says, "Well, somebody's drowning out there." (Clint said, "What does that mean?" And I said, "It means America's drowning. He's gonna save America.") At the end of it, she comes back to the track meet, and she walks in and says, "Can I talk to you?" He says, "Yeah, but I have to do what they pay me for first. I can't talk to you now." And he goes out and runs the race with the kid.
>
> Clint loved it, and he bought it right away. I went out there, and I said to him, "I can get the money for this, so I'm going to do it. Will you direct it?" He said, "I want to do it, and we'll both direct it. You do the scenes inside, and I'll do the exteriors." So my first sale was a home run. I moved into the bungalow with him there on the Warner lot and I wrote it. When they made the deal, Warner Bros.' head of Business Affairs said to me, "What kind of money are you thinking of?" They

offered me $20,000. "You know," he said, "friendship will only get you so far." So I wrote it, and it was on the schedule with Bob Daly producing. He had it all set up. Then I was asked to do a rewrite, but there was no money involved—and at the time I resented that.

Mort refused to do the rewrite, a decision, in retrospect, he now says he regrets. *I Can't Talk to You Now* fell off the schedule, and Eastwood instead made another comedy for Warner Bros., *Every Which Way But Loose*.

The same month Mort Sahl turned fifty, Paul Desmond died in New York at the age of fifty-two. The two men had reconciled after Desmond's relationship with Susan Jaye Sahl had run its course, but never again were they as close as they once had been. Mort sadly recalls that he and Desmond were on the outs the last time they saw each other, when Desmond came into Michael's Pub during the Democratic National Convention. He had an attractive girl on his arm and passed through the Bird Cage on his way to the main showroom. "He used to go to Elaine's every night, get *very* drunk," says Mort. "His idea was: Go hear music, play if they want you to. He was smoking Kents or Carltons because he was that sick."* And drinking a lot of martinis. He gave me a real brush; he was pretty cold." By then, Mort knew it was lung cancer; the story was going around. "I didn't know the degree because I didn't see anybody. He dated a lot of those chicks that dated famous people—Barbara Howar, well-connected, and Jean Stein when she was around."

Desmond died by his own hand on Memorial Day—May 30, 1977. He knew he was terminal and, in the words of Jenna Whidden, his live-in companion, "He had no quality of life left." An obituary made the late edition of the *Los Angeles Times* on Tuesday, May 31, with a fuller version, under the byline of *Times* jazz critic Leonard Feather, following the next morning.

"When Paul died, I was working in real estate in Studio City," remembered Yvonne Craig. "Somebody said to me, 'Didn't you go with Mort Sahl?' I said, 'Yes.' They said, 'He's sitting out at the curb in his car.' I said, 'Are you serious?' They said, 'Yeah.' And he just, I think, wanted to talk about it. But he didn't come in, and so I didn't know whether he was really out there wanting to talk or what . . . and so I didn't follow through because I was busy."

At Desmond's request, there were no services, but there were three memorial parties, the first of which was hosted by Dave and Iola Brubeck at the Los

---

* For thirty-five years, Desmond had smoked unfiltered Pall Malls. Kent and Carlton were filtered, low-tar and nicotine brands.

Angeles home of actress Barbara Baxley. "I went to the wake for him," says
Mort, "and I told all these stories about him even though I hadn't seen him."
Bill Cosby, he adds, ended up with the watch Mort gave Desmond—*To the
Sound from the Fury*—which still grinds on him after all these years. "Never
gave it back, never answered me," he says of Cosby. "He's a bad cat."

After the slow collective demise of the first generation of clubs to welcome
comedy as well as music—the venues Mort Sahl opened to standup in the
mid-fifties—there was a fallow period in which a few new operations sprang
up, only to quickly fold under the brutal economic realities of the late sixties
and seventies. Rock was the dominant product, with only a scattering of
jazz venues seeking an aging and ever-diminishing audience. Then a handful
of clubs sprang up that were not for music at all, but rather for comedy—
full time, all the time. A harbinger of sorts was the Improv, which opened
as a single location in Hell's Kitchen in 1963, and hosted its first comedian,
the raunchy, politically tinged Dave Astor, the following year. Then there
was Jimmy's, a Manhattan club run by two former aides of New York Mayor
John Lindsey on the site of Toots Shor's old restaurant. By 1974 the downstairs room at Jimmy's had been given over to a rotating menu of names
that included political impressionist David Frye, David Steinberg, and the
ubiquitous Rich Little.

Out on the West Coast, the earliest of the all-comedy clubs was the Comedy Store, founded in 1972 by comedian Sammy Shore and actor-writer
Rudy De Luca. Housed in the old Ciro's building on the Sunset Strip, the
Comedy Store showcased young, emerging performers who took the stage
for exposure rather than income. Among the first name comedians to work
the room, for which a one-dollar cover was instituted, were Stanley Myron
Handelman, Martin Mull, Gabe Kaplan, and Richard Pryor. Ownership
shifted to Shore's wife, Mitzi, after their 1974 divorce, but it wasn't until
the club was ready to open its new 600-seat Main Room in 1977 that Mort
Sahl made his first Strip appearance since the demise of the Crescendo.
Says Mort:

When I went to the Comedy Store she said to me, "You can bridge this
for me. Nobody who lives here wants to do it." Milton Berle had said to
me, "If you bomb in Minneapolis, you get the check and you fly home.
But if you bomb here, they'll talk about it all month." Which is true.
So nobody would come, and she had no one but those kids. She said,

"You're kind of a bridge. You're not one of the great men of comedy, and you're not a kid. If you do it, then Shelley will come, and Joey Bishop will come." So I did, and I cut her a very thin deal on the money if it lasted a while. And then, of course, she told everybody, "That's my ceiling." She's a very strange dame. And I went over for her to Comedy Haven in Honolulu and then down to her La Jolla branch.

Sahl opened at the Comedy Store on August 10, 1977, and the advance press went heavy on the nostalgia. ("I was the hero to a generation and its shame," he acknowledged.) *Variety* called his reappearance on the local scene—it had been thirteen years since he had last played the Interlude—both "timely and welcome." A profile in the *Los Angeles Times* ahead of the opening portrayed him in a reflective and solitary mood. "Kenton said there should be a hundred bands," he said, "just as I've said there should be fifty or sixty people doing what I'm doing. Why am I the only one? I guess they need only one rabbi. I have people come up here for me to tell them it's okay to make bad movies. It's a split thing around here. People think they can make bad movies and then use the money to throw a pool party to help the Seminole Indians and everything is okay."

The stand at the Comedy Store was wildly successful, and Sahl was held over an additional two weeks. Soupy Sales followed him into the room, as did Dick Gregory and Shelley Berman—just as Mitzi Shore had hoped. In September, Shore signed him to play fifteen weeks over eighteen months, again giving him a regular forum just ten minutes from his house. When he played Shore's La Jolla location in October, he was feeling scrappy enough to dismiss the generation of comedians that normally populated such places. "Young comedians. Interesting," he said. "I hear a lot about David Steinberg. First of all, he's almost forty. And I don't see anything new there. He tells jokes about old people to a young audience. That's safe. And Bobby Klein. He satirizes Marlon Perkins and that show—what is it? *Animal Kingdom*? *Wild Kingdom*? And Carlin. He's doing Lenny, but he isn't really doing Lenny. And David Brenner: 'How about that airline service? But I love this town, I really do.' Right? The fact is there's nobody in this generation as good as Red Skelton. There's no one as good as Hope. It's a generation immersed in drugs and profanity. Very benign."

Mort began the year 1978 with an undisciplined set at Rodney Dangerfield's New York club that lasted nearly two hours. ("My father had it easy," quipped the owner, who was watching from the sidelines. "All he did in vaudeville was eight minutes.") With his drawing power on the wane, he was forced to cancel the midnight show when nobody showed up. It was the same story in Los Angeles, where a subsequent appearance at the Comedy Store drew a sparse opening night crowd, causing the man from *Daily Variety* to wonder if Sahl's brand of comedy had lost its audience.

As if to put club work behind him, Sahl accepted an offer to host a drive-time radio show in Washington, D.C., filling three prime hours a day on a station that was otherwise an all-news outlet. "I was in L.A.," he remembers, "and I got a call from [General Manager] Frank Scott at NBC. 'We know you did a talk show for Metromedia, and we'd like to build WRC as the call-in station.' So they offered me a pretty good figure, and then the station could promote everything. They gave me a Porsche, and they gave me a big condominium in a skyscraper in Bethesda, and cards to sign to eat at anyplace in town—the ad department was very efficient. So I went back and did it, and I made it pretty provocative."

The new show, called *The American Experience*, debuted in WRC's 4–7 P.M. time slot on October 16, 1978. "One thing I want to talk to the audience about is the American liberal," he told the *Washington Post*. "Now that he's running the country, I'd like to know how he explains the condition of it. I was on a television show in Chicago with Eric Sevareid and he kept saying to me—through his interpreter—America is well off because they caught Nixon. I was wondering why it's so wonderful now; it's almost comatose." To the *Christian Science Monitor* he added: "What we hope to do is shake people up, not convert anybody, and remind people of how strongly they felt before they became apathetic."

The Mort Sahl the nation's capital got on WRC was not much different from the one Los Angeles got on KLAC a decade earlier. "Okay, out there," he'd announce at the bottom of the hour, "it's time for the news. The big news for the day is that tomorrow you still have your jobs." Taking a call, he'd be solicitous one moment, cutting the next. "Hey, Mort, about this Guyana thing, I've been thinking about it and, uh . . ."

"Yeah, man, go on."

"I think this Guyana thing was some kind of experimental colony in mind control. It's a symptom of our society that people are willing to give up their free will. Don't you think so, Mort?"

"Yeah, it's like the next step after Civil Service."

Conversely, a critic of Israeli foreign policy was given short shrift. "My assumption is that you want me to join you in rampant anti-Semitism," he said, terminating the call.

Another caller: "I'm wondering if we really know the truth about this Guyana thing. I'm wondering if maybe the CIA or something went on down there and . . ."

"I'm wondering about that, too. Do we know how Jim Jones died and will we ever know? Guyana's an old stop for the American intelligence community, and they've lied to us once too often."

Baiting government agencies became a favorite pastime on *The American Experience*. "I talked about the CIA," remembers Mort, "and they'd call me from the CIA—they thought I was kind of amusing. 'You don't know the way the government works. We're listening out here and laughing.' But they *did* listen, and that switchboard blew out several times, it was so overloaded." Sahl's ratings were huge for AM radio at the time. "The station was ranked 18th out of 33, and they wanted controversy. Within ten weeks they went to No. 2," he said.

"I was working for NBC News in the same building," recalled anchor John Hart, who had made Mort's acquaintance while covering the '76 Democratic Convention in New York. "I'd go down and catch him every now and then, sit in the studio. I loved him from the moment I heard him say to a caller: 'We have only one purpose in life, and that's to be a human being. And it's a full-time job." Mort, he perceived, believed in the America that might have been. "It's that heart of his, it's a whole committed heart. He believed the movies and the songs like we all did. And he believed in the America that we seemed to be right after World War II—and what the great papers of the nation claimed that we should be. And his heart was broken."

Mort took occasional weekend jobs at clubs like Dangerfield's and the Old Waldorf, but he was essentially stuck in Washington for months on end. Eventually, the politics of the station got to be too much, and China hated all the snow. "Coming from New Orleans, as soon as it was dark, perpetually, she *really* got depressed," says Mort. "I used to take Mort [Jr.] out and drive around in the Porsche, show him all the monuments. He loved that. I'd drive him all around the Pentagon and the Jefferson Memorial and all. But China didn't like the town much. We made the social scene immediately because [John] Hart was there with his wife and all the journalists. Carole Simpson of ABC. Mark Russell was back there then. And [Ted] Koppel—very cynical.

It's the only place I've been, by the way, where somebody's got a party every night. And the only place I've ever been where people go back to the store because they've run out of liquor. I've never seen that—these half-gallon jugs and they're out in a couple of hours." There were bright spots, such as lunch with Gene McCarthy every Tuesday at Hamburger Hamlet. "We'd have a lunch and kids would crowd around and we'd talk about all the radical stuff. A guy came over from the *Washington Post* and said, 'Senator McCarthy, why are you and he friends?' And Gene said, 'Because we bring out the worst in each other.'"

After a few months on WRC, Mort was looking for a way out, homesick for California and eager for another shot at screenwriting. "It's an interesting thing," he says.

> When a deal comes, I look at it with stars in my eyes, and I never consider the reality of what it would be like. The town was toxic. I said, "They won't let me out of the contract." China said, "If you want to go, they'll be begging you to go. I know how to do that." And she did. She didn't agree to anything they wanted to do. They said, "You need more guests." So I had her on as a guest; she was great on the air. I'd do feminists—they'd be yelling at me. China came on the air to rebut them. She said, "This guy lets me stay at home. Or if I want to take pictures he buys me cameras. He rents me a studio. And he loves me, and you're going to replace that? It's phony. I'm a woman. I don't believe you." And the station said: "What about all the names you know? Why don't you have them on?"

Sahl obtained permission from NBC to leave his Washington show after just five months on the air, walking away from a base salary of $100,000 per annum. The station's publicity chief, Andrew Bergstein, said that Sahl had recently contracted to write pilots out on the coast for "two possible situation comedies." *The American Experience* aired for the final time on March 9, 1979.

Whether or not Mort Sahl had actually contracted to write TV pilots is now lost to memory, but he remained contemptuous of television and consistently kept his sights set on movie work. TV writers, he said, were "all fifty-five percent Jewish and have Scandinavian stewardesses as their second wives." Still, he insisted, there was a big market for political satire of some sort. "You don't see it on the air, that's for sure. Everything looks pre-taped. Most all the TV comics are about half a notch behind the Borscht Belt guys. Where does that leave me? Fighting for my life, as usual. They'll never let me work on TV because I clash with the programs. I either had my own, or I wasn't on. The same goes for pictures. In a sense, and I can say this immodestly, the two most successful pictures in the last couple of years were about me. *Annie Hall* (and Woody even says it) was very derivative. So was Chayefsky's *Network*. The only difference is that I didn't die on Channel Eleven. But the mad messiah with the army behind him was me."

Despite the collapse of *I Can't Talk to You Now*, he stayed friends with Clint Eastwood and was informally consulted on other scripts.

When Clint worked on *The Gauntlet*, Sandra Locke's character murders the guy who raped her sister. And I said, "You have to arrest her." He said, "I can't arrest her. She's like a sparrow." I said, "You have to." He said, "Why?" I said, "She goes over." All of Huston's dialogue [from *The Maltese Falcon*] came to me. "She killed your partner, she goes over!" And he thought I was crazy. It was almost a breach in our friendship. He didn't get the reference; all he was thinking about was the picture. I said, "No, this is the Code of the West. Bogie didn't cave in for the chick, and you can't cave in. They took your gun, they took your badge, they beat you up, they threw you in the water—she goes over."

Mort found screenwriting a rich source of material for his act, often blurring the lines between what was real and what wasn't. Emceeing a dinner for the National Association of Theater Owners, he said that he had just been asked to write a script by disgraced Columbia Pictures executive David Begelman. "He was allowed one call at the time." Half the act, he liked to say, was now about "failing upward" in the movies. "I sold the same script to Paul Newman, Robert Redford, Steve McQueen, and Clint Eastwood, and I'm finally going to make it myself. One hearing about the last one buying it would then decide not to make it, and the other one would say, 'Well, you worked for him. You must have great credentials.' When I was in the business two years I'd written three scripts, none of them produced, and a book which no one had read, and my price had quadrupled." Newman, he added, had engaged him to adapt a wildly comedic racing novel, *Stand On It*, for the screen. "What I'm really trying to write is Preston Sturges comedy. It's the only type of comedy I understand. Not nonsense comedy like *FM*, but comedies where things take on a life of their own."

Stan Kenton died on August 25, 1979. He was just sixty-seven years old but, worn down by years of incessant touring, seemed at least ten years older, stooped and heavy in his final appearances. "Every musician wants to go to Heaven," he once told Mort solemnly, "but he doesn't want to go through the kitchen."

"Stan," Mort recalls,

> had been back on the road in Reading, Pennsylvania, and we heard he had a fractured skull. We don't know if he fell or had a stroke or some guys beat him up, and Audree [Coke, Kenton's fourth wife and manager] became very secretive. "He's fine. He's fine." Bobby Troup even flew there to see him in the hospital. "He's fine." Then Stan came back, and he was having memory problems. I'd go down to see the band, and somebody would come over and say, "Great set, Stan." And he'd say, "Mort, who is that guy?" He had no memory, and he forgot a lot of the tunes. It went in and out; sometimes he was straight. And he slowed down a little bit. Then he went into UCLA, and I went up to see him—they had that request level on the top of the hospital. He said to the nurse, "Miss, do you think I could have some chocolate ice cream?" She said, "If I don't have chocolate, you'll take vanilla." And he said to her, "Are you Jewish?"
>
> Anyway, I was very worried about him in a most paternal way. We all were. Then Audree put up the cloak. "He's okay, he's okay." She wouldn't tell us anything. Then he said, "We're going to do a gig in Costa Mesa. I'm going to take a little time off. Pretty rank out there on the road." So I went down to the Black Angus with him. From Disneyland. They didn't have a table, and he said, "I just want to go home. I don't want to wait." Very uncommunicative. And then I would call the house, and she would say, "He's okay. He's just tired; he's resting." And then one day she said: "He had a stroke and fell in the shower." It was all very mysterious, and then the services were closed, so I couldn't go out there. I was fifty-two, and I thought the world folded. I couldn't believe it. He had a lot of meaning to Gene [Norman], too. Stan was like a way of life, I think.
>
> Stan intimidated China—and that's saying everything. Even Clint, six-foot-four, movie star, was intimidated by Stanley. I took Clint out to see him at King Arthur's Inn on Fallbrook in Canoga Park. Stan was

up on the stage there. Clint said, "Hi, Stan." Stan said, "How are you doin' with Maggie?" Clint says, "Oh, all right, I guess." Stan said, "How are you doing with China?" I said, "I hope I'm doin' all right." And then he said, "How are Bobby [Troup] and Julie?" I was so uncomfortable that I said, "What the hell is this? Family night?" And he said to me: "We're a small family, Mort. We have to take care of each other."

China Lee Sahl filed for divorce no fewer than five times during her first marriage to Mort, 1970–74. When they remarried, it took her just three months to file again. "When I got pregnant—and it was amazing I got pregnant—and Mort Jr. was born, I told him then and there that I would leave him when Mort Jr. left the house. I told him he could start seeing other women if he wanted, but to leave me alone. I would take care of the business, I would make sure things [got done], but I wouldn't be a wife." Mort followed with two filings of his own, once in 1977, again in 1978.

Neighbors on San Ysidro would report screaming matches, China clawing at Mort's shirt as they fought outside on the driveway. "She was very explosive," he says. "There was no derailing it once it got going. She broke a lot of crystal once. And she wouldn't be dissuaded when she thought she had been wronged." China, on the other hand, seemed proud of the fact that she could cow a man as naturally combative as her famous husband. "Mort was afraid of me," she said matter-of-factly. "I have a very bad temper." Frequently, she'd raise the specter of divorce, a threat so commonplace Mort would take it in stride. "Once she started yelling at me, and she said, 'I'm going to get THE divorce.' Like it exists all by itself. And the noise was so much that Mort got up—he was like three—and he came out of his room in his bathrobe and he said, 'What?' She said, 'I'm going to get THE divorce.' And he said, 'You can't divorce us!'"

Admittedly, marriage to Mort Sahl could be exhausting. "I think China felt she had to do everything for him," said Teddy Howard.

She had to take care of him. She was his filter with other people. And I can see why, in a way, she felt like Grace Kelly in *The Country Girl*, because China took any criticism—or anything negative—and it was immediately a fight. She was so protective of Mort—*genuinely* protective. Their fights were big when they did fight, but when I was married to Alex Trebek, and then when I was married to Peter Kares, we were all very good friends and there wasn't a conflict between them. I mean, she traveled with him, they did things together, she set up all of his performances, she negotiated when he would re-write film scripts, punch them up . . . Theirs was a complicated relationship.

Mort, China would charge, didn't want a father-son relationship, he wanted a pal—so it fell to her to be the disciplinarian. "That was a constant refrain of hers—you're not a father, you're a pal," says Mort. "I improvised a lot, because I didn't have a model. I didn't come from a large family, and we were always tight for money. My dad was always at work, so I really didn't know what to do. Teddy called China and said, 'You've got to think about this, because you're married to a supreme egotist. He won't allow a family; it's got to be about him.' So then I double-crossed them and I *liked* my son—in an effort to frustrate them. I'll go to any lengths not to be predictable."

In Mort's view, motherhood domesticated China. "We were a couple of vagabonds. We were all over the place, we were going out to dinner every night. But when she became a mother, there were three squares on the table and we ate on time—nine in the morning, twelve-thirty, and at six o'clock. She was making roasts and pork chops and mashed potatoes—great cook. She made lemon-pepper shrimp from the South. She had a fish fry up there for Kenton once—the whole band. We had it on his birthday—February nineteenth."

In time, China became known for the parties she gave, affairs that reflected an almost obsessive attention to detail. "She would do a Christmas every year that was fantastic," said Teddy Howard.

She would have an individual gift for each person—and there were maybe fifty people at the party. There would be Julie London and Bobby Troup. Clint Eastwood and a couple of his kids. (I never saw him bring a woman to one of China's parties.) Joanne Woodward and Paul Newman would be there, and then there would be people like Mort's dog walker. They weren't show business snobs. Kris Kristofferson, Eydie and Steve, Sam Peckinpah. It was like everyone let their guard down; there was nobody trying to impress anybody else. And I think that Mort and China together, as a couple, fostered that kind of atmosphere.

There were money worries, but they never seemed to affect Mort as they did China. "Money didn't mean anything to him," said Teddy. "The only thing it meant to him [was that he could] buy China beautiful jewelry. He always thought that she was beautiful, the way she dressed—everything. He spoiled her in that way. What he loved were cashmere sweaters, watches, and fancy cars—sports cars. Those were the three things. He and Jim Coburn would have their Ferraris and all that. They were very cute. They were little boys with toys." Mort worked sporadically in 1980—Yuk Yuk's in Montreal, Donte's in North Hollywood, the Entertainers in San Francisco. The rest of the time he brooded and worked on spec material for the film industry. "China would say to me, 'I can't stand you saying: See what they did to me.' I said, 'I never said that.' She said, 'Yeah, but you act like it.'"

China spent her days at the track. "I was a great gambler," she said. "And when I went to the races, it was because we needed money when he wasn't working. That's how we paid the bills. But I only did it as a business. I'm not a person who *has* to gamble. Like now, I don't even pick up a racing form. There's no reason for me to gamble." Mort recalls a time in Las Vegas when China's elder sister, Virginia, lost all her savings at the tables:

China said, "I'll get it back for you. I'll play blackjack and get it back for you." Which she did. Barron Hilton walked downstairs. He said, "China, is that you?" He went over to her at the table. "You're too smart for that. What are you doing?" She said, "I have a system, Barron." So he took her by the elbow, and he walked her outside. He pointed to the top of the hotel where the sign is. He said, "Why isn't your name up there?"

Every night, I would go down to the newsstand. She'd say, "Will you bring me back a form, Honey?" I'd bring her a *Daily Racing Form*, and she'd go into her office and sit there until the wee hours of the morning figuring it all out, then she'd call the bookie the next day. She *loved* all that.

China's gambling was a point of contention with Mort, but she could never understand why. "When I left him, he told everybody I spent all his money gambling. Well, let's put it this way: When he wasn't working, I went to the races, and I won maybe one day about $9,000. I gave him $3,000 in cash and I said, 'Here, go get yourself a watch. Buy something to make you feel better.' So he put the cash in his wallet, went out to eat, left the window [in the car] open, the door unlocked, and when he got back his wallet was gone—with the $3,000. And that's when we didn't have the money—I was going to the races to make the bills."

The press began to portray Mort Sahl as a has-been, a sort of ghost figure who aroused feelings of nostalgia rather than laughter. "He has survived on the lounge circuit," *People* magazine reported in a 1982 profile, "while writing screenplays that have not been produced, TV proposals that were inked but never aired, and a book (*Heartland*) that underwhelmed the market." The hook of the *People* article was a mild resurgence of interest in him as an actor. He played a brief cameo in *Nothing Lasts Forever*, a comedy-fantasy with *Oz*-like overtones that was produced by *Saturday Night Live* creator Lorne Michaels. Happy to have a part in any picture, Mort typically bit the hand that fed him, disparaging the late-night comedy franchise Michaels had built at NBC. "I was offended by the show the first time it came on the air," he said of *SNL*. "They've got the conventional liberal bias of Jewish kids in New York and L.A. They write a kind of hate letter to America. They're merciless to the working class. I'm tired of these smart kids. Their material trivializes the American experience. They've never fought anything seriously beyond acne. They're elitists, and it just won't wash."

More to his liking was the role of German *Kabarett* comedian Werner Finck in a five-hour dramatization of *Inside the Third Reich*, Albert Speer's best-selling memoir. The film was written and produced for ABC by his pal E. Jack Neuman, who saw him as obvious and necessary casting for the legendary co-founder of *Die Katakombe*, a club in Berlin where satirical jabs at the Nazis were tolerated into 1935. Pleased with the assignment, Mort saw it as a way of reminding people that he was still around and ready to work, as did the Music Center concerts of eight years earlier. "My whole life has been like that," he told *People*. "I get a hit in the bottom of the ninth."

However much he enjoyed being in front of audiences, his income was increasingly from screenwriting rather than performing. *Stand On It*, the property he adapted for Paul Newman, was acquired by Burt Reynolds, who would make it as *Stroker Ace* from a script by Hugh Wilson and Hal Needham. Through his friendship with director Sydney Pollack, he worked on the Dustin Hoffman comedy *Tootsie*. "We all wrote that one," Mort says. "Everyone contributed dialogue to that. It was a sign of an impoverished mind. A man dressing up as a woman? That's the oldest thing in writing—it always works. It went three times as long as it should because of Hoffman. Sydney, in comedy, wouldn't think that it would work, but [agent] Mike Ovitz did. I contributed some of the dialogue, but the original idea was from Don McGuire." Sahl's office at the time was at the Burbank Studios, the former Warner lot at which Columbia Pictures was now a tenant. "Al Sargent was in my office one day when Sydney stopped by. 'I love Mort,' Sydney said, 'but I don't know what he wants.' Al said, 'Why don't you make one of his pictures?' Sydney said, 'What if it's lousy?' Al said, 'Then it'll be behind you and you won't have to make any more.'"

The following year, Mort placed an original called *The Senator's Wife* with a short-lived production entity called Comworld. "That was written for [producer] Dick Berg," he says.

> They moved it over to a TV movie at Metro. Those were all sweetheart deals. When they'd fire someone at NBC, they give him a company and buy a script for him. So DeAnne Barkley was over there, and her husband was at CAA. Berg got a hold of it and they started rewriting it. Jud Kinberg, who had worked for John Houseman, came aboard. And Malcolm Stuart. They met at Dick Berg's to rewrite it without talking to me. And, of course, they fixed it to death.
>
> What I had written was when a Bobby Kennedy–like character gets gunned down, the party, in its cynicism, appoints his wife to fill the unexpired term, thinking she'll be a robot. And she decides to be a person. That's all it was. I brought it to life, and I made it very idealistic. Blake Edwards came to me, and I rewrote it for Julie [Andrews]. Then Berg came to me and said, "No! I've got Mary Tyler Moore." This went on and on, and they never made it. Blake calls me in the middle of the night. He says, "We've got a problem." I said, "What?" He said, "She's got an English accent. There's no way to cover that." I said, "Yes, there is. You'll have a bigot stand up and say, 'How dare you! You've got an English accent!' And she says, 'A hundred and fifty years ago everybody in this chamber had an English accent.'" I was beginning to learn to be a horse thief, but it was too late. Never made it. They never make the good ones. And Berg drove me crazy.

By 1984 Sahl had settled into a routine that kept him productive at the astounding rate of two or three feature scripts a year—fourteen in all. An unabashed classicist, he drew his themes and inspirations from the films of his youth—Hawks, Ford, Huston, Capra, of course. "Whenever I was lost, I'd follow the old stuff," he says. "Because by that time the agents were running the studio and they didn't know anything. I was working at United Artists when it was being run by David Field and Steven Bach, so all I wrote was the old Goldwyn pictures I remembered. They'd say, 'I like this part. It tracks well.' Well, they don't know what the hell tracks well." A kindred spirit was his pal Bob Kaufman, who hated nihilistic movies and had struck gold with his modestly budgeted Dracula parody *Love at First Bite*. "One time, I brought a script in to Kaufman. I said, 'Read this, will ya? Tell me what I can do to tweak it before I hand it in.' He said to me, 'I don't have to read it. I know what it's about. It's about a girl who's crazy until someone loves her, and then she's redeemed.' And it *was*!"

For *Rocky* producer Irwin Winkler, Mort was at work on a story for director Karel Reisz and actress Meryl Streep, the team that delivered *The French Lieutenant's Woman*. "I said, 'What do you want this picture to be about?' Reisz said, 'I don't really care. Just write me a whopping good yarn.' So I wrote a movie about a girl who is so hard that when she becomes pregnant, she gets an abortion without telling the guy because it'll get in the way of work. I wrote a really ruthless girl, and of course Streep loved it." It was, he says, pure Capra, *All About Eve* in a television newsroom, a modern-day fable called *The Last Anchorman*.

Gregory Peck was going to play Edward R. Murrow, and Burt Reynolds would be this kid who's the political cartoonist for the *Washington Post*. Peck says to him, "You can criticize the government, but you want to destroy it." Reynolds says, "Well, that's the right of the press. You wouldn't abridge that, would you Dad?" He says, "No, but when we invade I wouldn't trumpet our schedule to the enemy. You should let the press be the first wave." There was a lot of that in it. [Reynolds' character] could say, "Don't you at long last want to be loved?" And Burt would say, "Mort, people don't talk like that." I really got brave when I was writing those scripts at Tiny Naylor's at night. I really wanted that moment of glory, to soar off the cliff and not have the wings burn up.

I used to sit at those story meetings with Winkler. I'd say, ". . . and they say goodbye." He'd say, "He'll never see her again." I'd say, "No, that's not true. He *has* to see her." "What're you talking about? It's not logical." I'd say, "Because *she loves him*, Irwin. They have to." He'd say, "Oh, my god!" Then there'd be a noise, and the secretary would come in and say, "Is everything all right, Irwin?" He'd say, "It's okay, Janet. It's just that Mort can't contain his narrative."

Mort remained optimistic throughout the development process, telling the press he thought he had finally gotten lucky. "I've got a producer who's made thirty-two pictures, a name director, and a star who's interested. When you put all those things together, it'll start to make sense to the studio." It was Karel Reisz, he says, who drove him out of the job. "He goes to Winkler and says, 'I can rewrite it, but Mort is not a team player. He remains that guy on the stage.' Everybody had agreed to do it, but nobody did it."

Meanwhile, Bob Kaufman's patron, suburban mall tycoon Mel Simon, bought a spec script from Mort, who recalls:

Bob Relyea was Simon's head of production. He said, "I want you to be in this, and don't get nervous. We're going to get somebody seasoned—I think it'll be Natalie Wood. She'll lead you through it; you'll be all right." He called me back and said, "I've talked it over with Mel, and it's too much for you. But, we haven't double-crossed you. You're going to direct it, because you know the material." So I said: "You mean having found that I don't have the talent to be a passenger, you've made me the pilot?"*

I was going to direct, but the directors were on strike. Sydney Pollack said, "Meet me at six. I'll help you." They had the strike meeting at eight. So I went over there, and there was Norman Jewison and Richard Brooks and Sydney. "You got the assignment, we're not going to let you blow it. We'll be right behind you." And that knocked me out. I never heard that from any writer—not like that. They were ready to go to the mat with me, and I knew I was going to get lost as a director, for Christ's sake. I was scared to death. It was one of the most touching things that ever happened to me.

Battered by losses, Simon got out of the movie business before the picture could be made. Then director George Roy Hill called Mort, whom he had known since 1962.

Hill said, "I want to work with Paul and Bob again." [Hill had directed Newman and Redford in *Butch Cassidy and the Sundance Kid* and *The Sting*.] So I wrote this thing. It was a movie about fascism, and I had George C. Scott playing General Haig. I had a deal where I'd put them on a couch and read the script to them. Hill said, "You scare the hell out

---

* In 1965 writer George Axelrod briefly considered making Mort the director of *Lord Love a Duck* before deciding to do the job himself. "I couldn't direct anyone," Mort says today. "I couldn't figure it out myself."

of me." I said, "You? The Marine Major who shot down seven Korean Zeros? You're scared of me?" He said, "You're damned right I am." He turned on me, and I was the guy who walked him through Hollywood when he got *Period of Adjustment*—I took him around, he met everybody. Hill was a Catholic among all these Jewish people, and a non-hipster among all these junkies. I credentialed him, but he backed away. And I knew his sidekick, Pat Kelley. He was his producer at MCA. Soldier at the door; good guy. By that time, it was: "Mort has to go." So that's all right. Turns out I didn't go. *They* went.

Hill directed just one more film, the pallid Chevy Chase comedy *Funny Farm* (1988).

The inauguration of Ronald Reagan in January 1981 put a man in the White House whom Mort Sahl actually considered a friend. (More so than Jack Kennedy who, depending on who Mort was getting it from, was at best a fan and at worst a sworn enemy.) "Ronald Reagan?" he'd say. "We're good friends. He was, after all, the president of my union. Nancy and I have great simpatico."

Mort remembers their initial meeting as taking place in 1973, when Reagan was in his second term as governor of California and deeply unpopular within the entertainment industry. The governor was set to be guest of honor at a benefit dinner for National Jewish Health, and a call had been placed to Barron Hilton when the scheduled emcee for the event backed out. Working the Casino Theater in Las Vegas, Sahl was soon to take up residence in the Vestal Virgin Room, then under construction. Hilton "came in one night and said, 'You have Thursday off. You're appearing at the Beverly Hilton in Los Angeles for the National Jewish Hospital [*sic*]. Goodbye.'"

The way they raise money for these affairs is to honor a man of the year, who is lampooned, and this year the man was Governor Reagan. When I arrived, though, it seemed that a lot of people were canceling, so I went over to the P.R. girl and said, "Where is everybody?" And she said, "Well, they don't like him; they think he's a reactionary. And I agree with them. [I was] for McGovern." Now this seemed strange to me, because they weren't victimizing Reagan; they were victimizing the hospital. But I got up and did a monologue that really savaged him—and which he laughed at by the way—and then at the end of the dinner I said, "You know, there're a lot of people who live about three blocks from here in Beverly Hills and who didn't see fit to come. But the Governor flew here from Sacramento knowing these guys weren't going to show up." So Nancy Reagan came over to me afterwards, thanked me, and invited me to dinner. And I went over there and . . . we just got along. They didn't really talk politics with me; they talked people. Then, later on, when Nancy read my book, she called me up—she was crying—and she said, "You know, Mort, about being out of work—we've been there, too."

Sahl came to admire Reagan's sense of humor, as old school as it tended to be. "He throws a lot of one-liners," he said at the time, "and he'll always stop to tell one. I don't know where he gets 'em, but he's got a million of 'em. He'll stop governing to tell a joke. And some of them are on him. You can practice a lot of damage control if you kid yourself." It impressed China that when she and Mort went through their divorce the following year, the Reagans were the only people who called. "I was over at the [Reagans'] house in Pacific Palisades," Mort said, "and Ronnie sits down with me after dinner and says, 'Mort, sometimes you have to accept divorces. For instance, I'm divorced.' And I said, 'You know, I appreciate the interest, but when you think about it, isn't this high-priced help for marriage counseling?' But I can kid him five ways from Sunday, tell him to forget about politics and we'll produce *Atlas Shrugged* and he'll play John Galt. There's no loyalty oath with the Reagans; if you're their friend, it's in perpetuity."

Once Reagan was in office, Mort considered him fair game. "If they can turn the Democrats around to where they want them to be," he said of the new administration, "the Democrats will trade off and say, 'If you do something for the blacks in Watts, we'll let you bomb the blacks in El Salvador.'" In the act, he described a "bad dream" scenario in which he was haunted by the persistent image of Reagan pulling a ninety-year-old man up out of his wheelchair by the frayed lapels of his bathrobe. "When I was your age," he screamed at the man, "I was working!"

In spite of his frequent whacks at the new president, it took only a few months for Mort to be asked to a state dinner. The event, which took place on September 9, 1981, was given for Israeli prime minister Menachem Begin, who was making his twelfth visit to the United States and meeting Ronald Reagan for the first time. Mort and China were among the ninety-six guests at the White House that night, as were Dinah Shore, David Susskind, advice columnist Ann Landers, and novelist Herman Wouk. How, asked Jeff

Silverman, "Page 2" columnist for the *Los Angeles Herald-Examiner*, could he end up supping with The Powers rather than railing against them? "You have to distinguish between personal friendship and political policy in life just as I do on the stage. You don't attack the man. You attack the policy."

Mort's account of the evening would become a major portion of the act. "They served a kosher dinner," he told a nightclub audience. "We had fillet of sole and Begin had a steak. So Reagan says to him, 'How's the steak?'

"Begin says, 'It's delicious. Is it aged?'

"'We try not to talk about age here.'"

Three years later, Sahl's assessment of the Republican National Convention bordered on rage:

> The complacency was unbelievable. Dentists who make $125,000 a year wearing funny hats and blowing kazoos. It showed us a party of the rich, white, and beautiful. There was no loyal opposition. To voice any opposition at all is to be considered disloyal. That platform! One of the strongest planks was the vote to give Hitler a second chance. And those planks! Reagan is suddenly a born-again conservative, but to paraphrase the old saying, how can you send an old geezer up in a crate like that? You notice that nobody from his cabinet was there. I guess the reasoning was, "You don't need to remind people of reality." When Reagan said, "America moves forward unashamed and unafraid," I was tempted to say, "Yeah, and uninformed."

15

THE LOYAL OPPOSITION

By 1984 Mort Sahl's immersion in screenwriting was so complete that media critic Ron Powers wrote a piece for *GQ* titled "Whatever Happened to Mort Sahl?" That year, Sahl played only a smattering of dates, including a week at a Georgetown jazz club called Charlie's, during which Powers' attempt at an interview went awry. "He had got wind of a question I asked of the nightclub manager—'Did you take a chance booking Sahl?'—and chose to interpret it as a sign of hostility, a reference to what Sahl believes is a general media distortion of him: as washed-up, as has-been, as yesterday's comic on the comeback hustings. (In fact, my question had to do with the strategy of booking a comedian into a club known almost exclusively as a jazz spot.) The demons that fire Sahl's dangerous genius still deny him, perversely, the access he seems to crave."

While movie work played its part in keeping him away from clubs, it also informed the act to the extent that it changed the very nature of it. Less political than sociological, it evolved into a set of lengthy stories in which Mort himself was an observant, if somewhat clueless, character among the Hollywood elite. "And I gave them the lines," he says. "China took great exception to it. When it was over, she'd say, 'Redford didn't say that—Mort did.' But it worked better with him saying it. I'm writing a movie, interacting with the stars. One night a guy said, 'Did that happen?' And I said, 'No, but it could.' And then I took that on to: 'Everything I tell you is true, but this is actual.'"

The form itself dated from Mort's account of a visit to the Johnson White House, a routine that took up the entirety of his 1967 album *Anyway . . . Onward.*

I was looking for examples of social hypocrisy, and I just made use of where I was. Handy illustrations. In other words, a long story I did about going to a [Ted] Kennedy fundraiser at Barbra Streisand's house. Well, they weren't having me to their house, but I found a joke in it. Or I'm walking to my car at Warners, and Norman Lear says, "I'm gonna vote for Jesse Jackson. Oh, I know a black man can't win in a country based on hatred, but I've got to look at this mug in the morning when I shave." So I say, "God bless you." And then I keep running into these stars. They say, "I'm gonna work for Gary Hart. I know he doesn't have a chance, but I have to live with myself." And then finally Newman comes up to me, and he says, "I think the candidate is an opportunist." So he's moved to somebody to the left. He says, "Can you understand working for a guy when you know he can't win?" I say, "Does this have anything to do with when you're shaving?"

I'd put myself in the ignorant role, and then I finally found the joke. I started doing routines where I'd thinly veil it—I'd tell them I wrote *Ordinary People*, then I'd start on Redford. We're behind the camera together. Donald Sutherland says to Mary Tyler Moore, "You're not a very loving person, Beth." And I say to Redford, "How long have they been married? He just found that out?" "Shhhhh! They're rolling." Sutherland says, "I'm leaving you." She says, "Okay." So Redford says, "What do you think, Mort?" I say, "Well, I think she's taking it awfully well. She has no skills in the job market." I make the feminist case. "And then she has no material provision for her immediate future."

He says to me, "Mort, I think you're showing a tremendous insensitivity. Chauvinism." I say, "No. I think they should be everything they want to be." And I make this ornate apology. "I've always been on the side of the women, Bob." A guy trying to keep his job. That's a hard thing for the audience to accept from me, but I wanted to show the corruption that being around it brings you. And he says to me, "Now Mort, I think at heart you're a feminist, but you can't come to terms with it." So I make him pretentious, and I make me deceptive.*

Over the years, I told them I wrote *Regarding Henry*, which I didn't, and I caricatured Mike Nichols and Harrison Ford and the premise of

---

* Mort's old friend Alvin Sargent, who actually *did* write *Ordinary People* (and won an Oscar for it), remembered being in the audience at the Westwood Playhouse one night when Mort went into his account of working on the film. "He did it so well that even I wasn't sure. I thought: 'Well, gee, maybe I didn't write that part.' And my wife was nudging me and saying, 'Did he write that? Did he write that?' I said, 'No.' But he did it so beautifully—and I hope he doesn't do it everywhere—that you just believed that he wrote *Ordinary People* for Bob."

the picture. And I told them I wrote *Sabrina*, which I didn't. I don't think I really came into myself until I started those elaborate stories and I took on the established order. And I let them have the laugh; I was the dumb guy at the party. What I'd try to do is get all of the truth and none of the facts.

Sahl met General Alexander Haig at the White House and immediately incorporated him into the act. At first, Haig was Reagan's gloomy Secretary of State, forever fretting about Russian military strength. Then, as Mort got to know him better, he grew to admire Haig for his quick wit, if not necessarily for his politics. Haig resigned his position as "the vicar of American foreign policy" after repeated conflicts with Defense Secretary Caspar Weinberger and National Security Advisor William Clark. "I'd actually gone to see him when he quit Reagan," Mort remembers. "I said, 'You can't keep quiet now. You have to become the Adlai Stevenson on the right: *I quit because of my conscience*.' And he liked that. I said, 'I'll write it.' By that time, I knew I couldn't work with the Democrats. There *were* no Democrats."

The night before Haig officially began his campaign for president in March 1987, Mort appeared at a dinner honoring the general and raising funds for his candidacy at New York's Waldorf-Astoria. ("He said, 'I appreciate your help.' I said, 'I want a job. I want to head the CIA when you're elected.'") At a press conference the next morning, Haig borrowed a line from him in declaring that he was formally "throwing my helmet in the ring." Then Mort was goaded by China, an arch conservative, into endorsing Haig's candidacy, something he was never comfortable in doing. "I said, 'I have to keep my virginity because of the act.' She said, 'No, no. You really have to support him.'"

During the debate, George Bush said, "I was Reagan's co-pilot. You can't consider any of these other people." And General Haig said, "When Iran-Contra came along, were you his co-pilot or were you sitting back in economy?" I enjoyed all that; I liked the action. The only other celebrity supporting him was Billy Dee Williams. Chris Matthews said, "What's the matter with Mort Sahl? Doesn't he know this guy can't win?" Which, of course, is the final arbitration with these people.

When I worked for NBC in 1978, I drove out to Annapolis with my son. And I thought to myself: What if I had really come here? Then I synthesized it within the act that I'd met Haig at West Point. To the end of his days he was damned with that. He'd say, "I'm tired of being asked what you were like at West Point." They'd ask him, "Was that guy there? Didn't you straighten him out then?" In the act I'd say he was my officer of the day, and that he'd come in for bed check. "And he was so strict that even though I was there on time and in bed, if I had a smile on my face he'd give me demerits." That stuff became folklore. They believed that he and I were contemporaries at West Point—because we couldn't explain our alliance otherwise.

When Mort turned sixty, China threw a birthday party at Ruth's Chris Steak House in Beverly Hills. Mort went around the table and said something funny about each of the guests, but his mind wasn't on age so much as work. Solo shows were all the rage in the legitimate theatre, and with the surprise hit of Jackie Mason's *The World According to Me* in New York, he was convinced the time was right for another run at Broadway. He had taken the first step in March by staging *Mort Sahl 1987* at Hollywood's Henry Fonda Theater, a two-hour dose of his strongest material, debuting his new one-man show as Mason had done in Beverly Hills the previous year. Dick Crenna and Dick Carroll were among those at the opening, but interest proved slight despite glowing reviews.

"I wasn't getting any clubs," Mort says,

and I thought: If I get out there and they see somebody in the clear, it'll be a new incarnation. What happened was the William Morris office signed Al Haig for his book [*Inner Circles: How America Changed the World*] and then Norman Brokaw of the Morris office said, "Don Regan needs a speech. We told him of your gifts. Will you do it for us?" And I said, "Yeah, but you can do something for me." "What do you want?" I said, "I want to go to Broadway." He said, "What's been the response?" I said, "[independent agent] Irvin Arthur is handling it." Norman Brokaw said, "That's the wrong level." The next thing we knew, we had the meeting and we're on our way to Broadway.

Brokaw settled the show with twenty-seven-year-old Morris client James L. Nederlander, scion of the famous theatrical family of owner-producers who, given Jackie Mason's considerable success at the Nederlanders' Brooks Atkinson Theatre, saw little downside to the idea of installing Mort Sahl at one of the organization's other Broadway houses—especially with an election year on the horizon. "They didn't quite see it," Mort acknowl-edged, "but probably Mason's success had a lot to do with the change of mind. But mine is a very different show, and if audiences come looking for the same kind of thing they'll be disappointed."

Buoyed at the prospect of a fall opening in New York, Mort took on an open-ended engagement at Enrico's, the North Beach restaurant-bar that Enrico Banducci owned but nearly lost before Bill Cosby stepped in with a fresh infusion of cash. Over the summer, Mort did what he did best, greas-ing the machinery on a nightly basis, refining his takes on the various can-didates as they came and went. The two front runners, George H. W. Bush and Jesse Jackson, exhibited "the evils of two lessers," while Senator Gary Hart, whom Sahl described as "Jack Kennedy without the batteries," self-destructed in a sex scandal that was actually "a cynical attempt to humanize himself." Bush, he added, "looks like the fourth man in any carpool."

For a while, the old magic of the hungry i was there amid the flesh joints that had overtaken what had once been a prosperous club strip. Mort bridged the years by deftly summarizing three decades of sexual politics: "In the fif-ties, you had to be a Jew to get a girl. In the sixties, you had to be a black to get a girl. In the seventies, you had to be a girl to get a girl." China, who didn't like Banducci, watched the door and counted the house, and on opening night even Herb Caen came, although he rebuffed all efforts at a reconcilia-tion. After a quiet shakedown at clubs in Santa Barbara and Hermosa Beach, Sahl flew to New York, where the Nederlander organization booked him into the Ritz-Carlton. He had a full calendar of media encounters—twenty inter-views in two weeks—and a schedule of five previews commencing October 7. With fistfuls of phone messages to return, Mort was, in the words of his friend Larry Christon, "peevish and drained" in a city he had never really liked. "I'm so disjointed," he complained, "I don't know what I'm doing."

"He was really scared," said Christon, who was there on assignment for the *Los Angeles Times*. "He didn't show it, but he showed it in anger and complaint. Very nervous, and China defended him, took care of him, made sure he got his rest. She did all the things—combination manager, wife, agent, handler—she did *all* that. She really protected him." Strategically, *Mort Sahl on Broadway!* was set for a limited four-week run, with plans to extend it if demand warranted. "I think this may be his time to come back," Eugene McCarthy told *People* magazine. "Mort was too sophisti-cated for the 70s; there wasn't much reflection then. Now people may be more responsive to satire." Mort himself saw the need as acute. "There are more comedians and less relevance than we've ever had before," he said. "Why there's so much information, and why nobody knows anything, is a joke in America."

The *People* profile portrayed him as relentlessly honing his lines: "Reagan's kidding around [during a sound check for a radio address] and says, 'I've just outlawed Russia. We begin bombing in five minutes.' And my friend Al Haig says, 'I hope this isn't another empty campaign promise.'" Or: "All these Democratic campaign staffs are trying to employ me—Gore and Dukakis. They all say the same thing. 'Mort, our man's just like Kennedy. You loved Kennedy, Mort.' So I say, 'Good Lord, isn't there anybody in this Democratic Party who isn't like Jack Kennedy?' And somebody says, 'Ted Kennedy.'" Or: "I've endorsed Al Haig as the least of all evils. He's a really nice guy. Beside, he doesn't promise much, so you can't hold him to much." Or: "[Japanese prime minister] Nakasone is talking to Reagan about the economy and cars. Nakasone says to him, 'Mr. President, we'll acknowledge the economic problem, but what about Hiroshima? We never destroyed one of your cities.' Reagan says, 'What about Detroit?'"

Mort Sahl on Broadway! opened at the 1,362-seat Neil Simon Theatre (formerly the Alvin) on October 11, 1987. At a weekday top of $25, seats were readily available right up until curtain, and the only concession the star made to the size of the room was to wear a body mic, which allowed him to move freely around the stage and gesticulate a little more grandly than usual. He began the show by listing the principal topics of the evening (politics, women, and movies) and then proceeded to warm up the audience with the Gary Hart scandal, smoothly moving to allegations of corruption in the Ed Koch administration. "Donald Trump," he concluded, "is building prison high-rises to house the friends of the mayor." Making his way to a set piece about a state dinner at the White House—this one for Israeli Prime Minister Yitzhak Shamir—he touched on subjects as varied as Joe Biden, Sylvester Stallone, Ronald Reagan ("Washington could not tell a lie, Nixon could not tell the truth, and Reagan cannot tell the difference"), and the gulf between conservatives and liberals. ("The conservative is willing to bear arms to defend his goods, the fascist is willing to bear arms to take your goods, and the liberal wants everyone's goods but feels guilty about it.") Singled out for special abuse was actress Vanessa Redgrave, whom, he confided, it was possible to dislike for herself.

The producers required a show of at least ninety minutes—more than twice the ideal length of a Sahl performance—and in delivering one, sans intermission, he betrayed a certain amount of padding. "At nearly two hours, the show is overlong," judged David Sterritt of the *Christian Science Monitor*, "especially when Sahl indulgently strings out the climax. It's an anecdote—with enough first-person pronouns to qualify as a Spalding Gray monologue—wherein he waltzes (literally) up to President Reagan at a dinner party and warns him the Middle East peace is about to be scuttled by disagreeing dignitaries at the other end of the dance floor." In the main, however, Sterritt liked the show, calling it smart and funny. "Liberals and conservatives will long debate which camp suffers the most losses."

Apart from Thomas M. Disch of *The Nation*, who loathed both the show and its star, *Mort Sahl on Broadway!* was greeted with solid raves, and even Clive Barnes, notoriously difficult to please, filed a lovingly detailed notice for the *New York Post*. Boldface display ads were built from the rapturous quotes, and it would only take audiences willing to follow the praise to keep the show running into the new year. "It did fair business," Mort recalls, "and they wanted to close it. And [agency president] Lee Stevens from William Morris went down to see Nederlander and said, 'Mort doesn't have a history like that. You've got to leave it open and it'll gain its own steam.' It was then I realized the power of the agents. . . . Then Lee Stevens moved to California, and I couldn't get anybody in the office to push it. So they closed the show. It was doing fair business, but they closed it. And then I was back to ground zero again. And because of my roots I went back to Hollywood, where there was nothing happening."

Nineteen eighty-eight was a dismal year, with little work and few prospects. "It's time to go on television," Mort declared in a March feature for *GQ*. "I think we ought to get the politicians in a different setting. I'd like to do the human side of politicians—a half hour of jokes with Mrs. Thatcher, Al Haig, Ronald Reagan, or Gorbachev. People. They're all people." And although he didn't say it, the one bright spot on the horizon that year was a TV film being made by a young documentarian named Robert Weide.

Bob Weide had met Sahl a few years earlier when contemplating a three-part show about him, Lenny Bruce, and Dick Gregory called *Shaping Laughter*. He got some seed money from the Corporation for Public Broadcasting and began filming all three episodes. The funding, however, didn't get him very far, and he decided it would be easier to seek out the dollars for each film individually. Weide was in his twenties, and when he broached the subject of a film exclusively about Mort, China's antenna naturally went up.

Who is this kid? What makes him think he can pull this off? Weide had produced a widely seen film on the Marx Brothers for public television, and had
moved into directing with an HBO documentary called *The Great Standups*.
"She was a little suspicious of me," he admits, "and I *was* a little wet behind
the ears in some ways, in some ways naive—certainly to take on a subject
like Mort. I mean, I had a very steep learning curve. Fortunately, I was able
to take my time with the film and research it as I went."

Working out of pocket, Weide began by filming Mort at San Ysidro in
1986. "I had to go through China to get to Mort initially, and then there
were scheduling problems—things like that. 'He's not going to be available
that week to do that. You'll have to do it some other time.' Then as Mort
trusted me more and we got friendlier, it was fine." In time, Bob Weide was
able to shoot interviews with Enrico Banducci, Steve Allen, Jim Garrison,
Larry Christon, John Hart, and Moo Sciambra. He was still in production
in 1987 when he created a fine-cut of the uncompleted film, which inspired
a new PBS series called *American Masters* to give him the finishing funds.
Assembling the footage would extend into the following year. "I don't think
he knew what I was doing in the editing room," he said of Mort, "although I
think he intrinsically trusted me enough."

A screening of the completed eighty-five-minute film took place before
an invited audience at KCET, the public television station for Los Angeles.
Said Weide:

> I don't think there were more than seventy people there in this small
> screening room, and Mort was there in the audience. What's very
> touching to me now is that he got a standing ovation—and it wasn't
> for me, it was for *him*. I felt very satisfied that this moment was a
> little different from him doing a performance and people applauding.
> They were applauding his whole story, his life, and everything he had
> done. And it was very heartening for me to see this, and for Mort to sit
> there, very humbly, as the room stood up around him and applauded.
> Then, finally, he stood up and sort of gestured toward me, and I got up
> and went over to him and gave him a hug, and he whispered in my ear,
> "You're the first one to get it right." So that was a big triumph for me.
> But aside from him, what I hoped the film, in some small way, would
> do, is that whoever saw it would go, "Wow! Look at what this guy's
> been through. Look at what he did—and nobody talks about him."

Narrated by Richard Crenna, *Mort Sahl: The Loyal Opposition* was televised nationally on September 18, 1989. Reactions in the press were earnest, respectful, at times admiring, the reviews aimed at assessing the film's subject more than the film itself. It came at a time when he needed the exposure, a necessary correction to the ebb and flow of his career based on national election cycles. But there was no flood of offers, no stampede to put the trailblazing father of modern comedy back into clubs and on TV. Nor was there any acknowledgment of the price he paid for his dogged savaging of the Warren Report. ("I thought somebody would come in and say, 'Oh, by the way, a medal arrived for you in the mail—for finding the killers of President Kennedy.' Not at all.") There was talk of a late-night show for Viacom, and there were guest appearances on NBC's *Later with Bob Costas* and the syndicated *Evening at the Improv*. In all, it was an astonishingly meager harvest for an hour and a half of network television that made an eloquent case for one man's impact on American culture. Bewildered, he slogged on.

China left in 1991 and filed for divorce. Approaching fifty, she was convinced Mort had turned their fifteen-year-old son against her—a charge Mort leveled at her as well. "I remember one day, I got a left-handed compliment from her. She was cynical about the world, and she said to everybody in the room, 'It doesn't pay to be good. Look at Mort—he's good. Look at him.' That's the last nice thing she said about me." China entered into a relationship with Jack Van Berg, a Hall of Fame horse trainer who had relocated from Kentucky to Southern California and owned a ranch in Hesperia.

"China always had someone who was in love with her," said her friend Teddy Howard, "but I think that Mort was probably the first one that she was ever in love with. In Mort, she liked that he was an intellectual. She wasn't a frivolous person. I think with Jack it was the horses. China loves horses, China loves to own horses, she loves to race horses, ride horses . . . plus he was a pretty famous trainer. I mean, he had a lot of big wins, and she felt comfortable in that atmosphere. And I think she felt uncomfortable in the entertainment field because she felt the pressures of picking the right thing, of making sure she was keeping Mort on the right path for his career." China was well known around Hollywood, and she was generally quite popular. "In the industry there were the people that liked her," says Mort, "and the people that didn't quite understand her. The people that liked her were great champions of hers—Clint, Sam Peckinpah. They thought she was a straight shooter."

Bob Weide was able to observe the later years of the marriage up close. "Sometimes," he said, "they were the cutest couple you could ever hope to see, and she would sit on his lap and have her arms around him. And he was very affectionate towards her and very loving, truly cared about her. And then other times it was cats and dogs." One time, Mort called Weide, who lived nearby, to ask if it was okay for him and Mort Jr. to stop by. "Hey, pal, let me ask you something else: What size shirts do you wear?" Not only did Mort need a place to stay, Weide realized, but he would also need a change of shirt before going home. Other times, it was Mort who was fuming, and his rage could fill a room. "I didn't have a lot of time with them together," said John Hart, "and the few times I saw them together China was sometimes just the Hollywood wife, and at other times she was astonishingly cruel to him in front of his friend. In the end, I just figured, with my amateur psychology, that she really wanted to *be* him. And that she had some envy that she could not actuate. I wouldn't put myself in the position to judge, because I don't know her that well, but I know that Mort's loyalty is unique in the world. He never forgets his love of anybody."

China had a natural aversion to counseling, yet she had indulged Mort to a surprising degree in the waning days of the marriage. "I didn't want to give up on therapy," Mort says,

and I'd savaged those guys from the beginning. I made fun of the fact that everybody in Beverly Hills was going—then I met them all at Democratic rallies. They were all Democrats; there wasn't one of them who was a fascist. China looked upon it as weakness—to go tell a stranger. And the Chinese thing was that you don't publish your feelings. They're exactly the opposite of the Jews. The family, when anybody was in trouble, they never reached out for any help. They tried to bury their fallibilities. China and I went for a long time to Dr. Rogowski, and he believed in me so much—he died later of a brain tumor—that he told his wife, "The reason I like Mort is that he keeps fighting—no matter what the adversity."

He was a hell of a mensch. He took us on for nothing—just to help. He'd run like four hours at a time, and I've got to say it didn't work for her, oddly enough. At the end of the formulation she said, "That's all wrong. I don't agree with anything you've said." He said, "That's strange, China. I agree with everything you've said." It went over hard up there. She told him he doesn't know how bad I am. And I thought to myself: He knows how bad *everybody* is."

In retrospect, even China allowed as how couples therapy had been somewhat effective. "I left him right after Alex Rogowski died," she said. "I counted on him to help out in the relationship. When he passed away, I knew there was no shot [at reconciliation]."

China was still in the picture when their friend John Hart left NBC to anchor a nightly TV news program produced by the *Christian Science Monitor* and seen twice daily on the Discovery Channel. When Mort learned that the venerable paper's brand would soon extend to an entire cable network, he asked Hart if there might be a place for him on the schedule. And, as it developed, there was. The chairman of Monitor Television, a former business consultant named John H. Hoagland Jr. (who, ironically, had worked at one time for the CIA), was a big Mort Sahl fan and leapt at the chance of making him part of the all-news programming mix on a channel owned by the Church of Christ, Science. "I was very dubious about making the association," Mort cracked, "but the medical benefits are what did it for me."

The announcement that Mort Sahl would host a weekend issues and commentary series for the new Monitor Channel was made in November 1990 at the Western Cable Television Conference and Expo in Anaheim. It would, however, take another five months for nightly programming to debut on the network, and a full year for the first episode of *Mort Sahl Live!* to actually appear. Guiding the series would be a Boston-based producer named Bob Burns, who had only vague memories of the star of his show and faced an immediate challenge from said star's estranged wife. "Jack Hoagland wanted to pay me a larger salary," Mort says, "but didn't think he could get it by the board. Then he got the idea to hire China as producer to give the family more money. So she was *very* territorial when Bob came in."

Burns flew out to Los Angeles to have lunch with Mort and discuss how the show would be structured. "Almost immediately," he recalled,

China attacked me. "What have you ever done? Why did they hire you to do this?" That went on for a while. I got through the lunch, and then I tried to set up a first working meeting with Mort. China was there at the meeting, and she wouldn't let Mort and me talk. She was very concerned about what color was going to be used in the set and what

sweater Mort was going to wear. It was very hard for me to get anywhere. I had to go home at the end of the day and report back, and
I said, "I can't get anything done if China's going to be there all the
time. I have to meet with Mort alone." The show almost got cancelled
because of that. Mort and China tried to get rid of me, but the Monitor
Channel stuck by their guns and said, "Look, you've got to work with
Bob. That's the deal." So finally Mort and I got to spend some time
together, and we hashed out what some of the content of the first show
would be. Mort was very concerned about what music we would use,
but we got some stuff done and our relationship started to get a little
bit better. Still, it was very touch-and-go for the first show.

Mort, Burns observed, wasn't a terribly confrontational guy in private.
So it fell to China to say the negative things that Mort didn't feel he could
say himself. "She was the bad cop in that relationship," he said. "It took me
a while to figure that out." The first show was taped in October 1991 at Merv
Griffin's Resorts International Casino Hotel in Atlantic City. The set in the
intimate Viking Theater was comprised of collapsible flats illustrated as if
by an editorial cartoonist, its principal components a fanciful newsstand
and desk holding a big-screen TV set on which news clips could be shown.
Providing the music was Amy Duncan and the Brass Tacks, a horn-heavy
jazz band in the Kenton tradition (although Sahl made it clear that he would
have preferred the original). The rehearsals were disastrous; Mort seemed
lost and unable to master the physical business Burns had worked out with
him. The executive producer urged him to just let Mort do his standard act,
and Burns threatened to resign on the spot. Then, when tape began to roll,
everything fell beautifully into place. "It was like five percent of his brain
was engaged during rehearsal," Burns said, "and the other ninety-five percent came on line when the curtain came up. He was a different person."

China also saved the day, at last justifying her credit as consulting producer. "The P.R. firm that arranged for the audience had pulled in a bunch of
kids from local community colleges," Burns recalled.

It just was not Mort Sahl's audience. They didn't know who he was.
His things require a little understanding of history—communism and
the Kennedy assassination and the Cold War—and in 1991 kids in the
local community colleges weren't clued into that stuff at all. China recognized that instantly—and this was the day of the show. She just

threw a shit-fit: "This is not going to work!" She pulled all those kids out. ("Sorry, you're not going to be in this audience.") And she went down into the casino, with the help of the now-discredited P.R. firm, and pulled up enough people to fill out the audience. And so, although she was a bit of a pain, that one thing made the show work. That first audience would have killed him. So I have to take my hat off to China in that regard.

The show played out mostly in real time, Mort doing an opening mono-logue, a news review, a chalk talk, and a Critical Issue segment devoted to the war between men and women. "What I'm trying to do," he said, "is when you open up [a magazine like] *Aviation Space and Technology* and they show you a plane in a cutaway, and you see a view you haven't considered before. That's what I'm trying to do with America." He ended with a summary under the title "What Does This All Mean?" because, as he put it, "there's a deluge of information out there, and I suspect none of us know what it all means." Then the credits rolled over tape of Mort and China walking away from the camera holding hands, a privately optimistic little touch that Burns added in the editing room. "A lot of it wasn't resolved for her," Mort says of China. "She tried to be a manager of musicians. She wanted to be an agent. I got her the job producing the Monitor show with a fat salary. Even when she left me, I kept her on. In fact, it would make a good scene in a movie. I got her a great suite at the hotel, and after we taped she came down the hall. She said, 'What are you watching?' I was watching TV. And she stood in the doorway an awfully long time . . . and then she said goodnight."

Mort Sahl Live! had its premiere on November 16, 1991, and drew the best numbers of any show in the brief history of the network. Over the next few months Burns and his crews delivered handsome one-hour episodes from Anaheim, New York City, and Boston featuring guests like Eugene McCarthy and screenwriter Robert Towne, but the church itself was roiled by internal conflicts over the $250 million to $500 million that had been invested in a broadcasting and magazine empire whose crown jewel was supposedly the Monitor Channel. By February 1992, when the fifth and final show was taped, production money had all but dried up, forcing *Mort Sahl Live!* into a tiny studio with a miniscule audience. Within days, the longtime chairman of the church's board of directors was forced out and the network put up for sale. The Monitor Channel officially went dark on April 15, 1992, almost exactly one year to the day from its ambitious start.

⋄ ⋄ ⋄

When the Monitor Channel failed, Mort Sahl went back to screenwriting. "Jon Peters called me up. He bought Gary Sick's book *October Surprise* [about a secret deal between Iran and the Reagan campaign]. So I wrote it, and I wrote it where an investigator for the Senate committee finds out what they're doing to elect Reagan. He's a Republican, middle western religious guy, and he says, 'This is not in your charter. Fend for America.' And they didn't want to do it—the liberals. There's nothing heroic about those guys. As with Goldwater—same thing. All mobilized against the apparent enemy. But the enemy, I think with them, is within."

A few club dates followed, and a 1993 stand at the Improv on Melrose was heralded in the *Hollywood Reporter* as Sahl's first local club appearance in seven years. He said at the time that he was in talks with KCAL-TV (formerly KHJ) to do a locally based version of the Monitor show on Sunday nights, but nothing came of the idea. In 1994, having learned the lesson of working too large a room for *Mort Sahl on Broadway!* he opened at the 300-seat Theatre Four on West 55th Street in another version of the act, this time called *Mort Sahl's America.* Jackie Mason's new show, *Jackie Mason: Politically Incorrect*, opened the same week, meaning the two shows would be inexorably linked in most of the reviews.

The gambit worked: *Mort Sahl's America* ran sixty-four performances— more than all his other Broadway excursions combined—and the title itself would fuel regional bookings for years to come. Its relative success, in fact, may have inspired producer Alexander H. Cohen to package him with juggler Michael Davis and singer Dorothy Loudon in a shapeless vaudeville called *Comedy Tonight*, which played several tryout performances in Stamford, Connecticut in November of that year. "Kander and Ebb wrote a song for it ["Three"] which was horrible. And they wanted me to come out in a tuxedo and sing that with the cast. So I called [producer] Bobby Roberts and said, 'I can't do that.' Roberts said, 'No, this is the way you handle it. Tell 'em you'll do it, then you come out and sing at the rehearsal. Kander and Ebb will say, 'Mort's ruining our song!' and they will relieve you.' And that's exactly what happened." Freed of his vocal responsibilities, Mort dominated the stage in a way that neither Davis nor Loudon could manage. The show was so lopsided in his favor that Cohen added comedienne Joy Behar to the cast prior to its December 18 opening at the 1,500-seat Lunt-Fontanne. Received with genuine bewilderment, *Comedy Tonight* lasted all of eight performances and closed on Christmas Day 1994.

16

WHO THE ENEMY IS

"My kid was like a more human version of me," Mort Sahl once said. Mort Jr. was a miracle baby, the child Mort and China never thought they'd have. "I think that they both took a great deal of pride in him," said Teddy Howard. "He was an unusually bright kid, but he was never a little boy. He was always around adults, and he drew his own conclusions." Mort took his son with him to Canada in 1980, wanting him to meet his grandmother's family. "A terrific, bright little boy," remembered Jack Schwartz, one of Mort's cousins. "He was only four years old when he was here in Montreal. What a terrific little kid. I mean, he was the light of Mort's life. Mort called him 'Little Mort' and 'pal.'" At age six, Mort Jr. was described by Larry Christon in an article for the *Los Angeles Times* as having "the smooth good looks and quiet demeanor of a young career diplomat." He also inherited Mort's way with a line. One night, he was in the kitchen with his mother at San Ysidro. "Go find your father," she said to him, "and tell him dinner is ready." The boy ran off and reappeared moments later. "He's watching the Playboy Channel," he reported, "but only for the articles."

"Oh, he was amazing," said Teddy. "At my wedding to [producer] Peter Kares, Mort and Little Mort were sitting at a table with some other people. You had three things to choose from, and the woman sitting next to him ordered lamb. When she was served the lamb, she noticed he was looking at it and said, 'Would you like a bite?' He goes, 'Baaa . . . Baaa.' And he used to come over when Mort and China went out. Usually he went with them, but sometimes he'd come over and stay when I was married to Alex Trebek. So he'd sleep in the bed with Alex and me. He'd always say, 'Where's Alex? I'm going to Alex's.' He loved Alex."

Early on, China decided that Mort Jr. would attend the prestigious Buckley School in Sherman Oaks, but when the time came there was a waiting list to get in. She got Sydney Pollack to intercede on her son's behalf. "The school was no great shakes," Mort says, "and it couldn't be egalitarian because they were shaking the money out of the stars—Newman, Poitier, Bob Conrad. It led to a joke: 'When I'm rich, I'm going to buy the school and fire the parents.'"

An honor student at Buckley, Little Mort came off as worldlier than other children his age. "He was just *precious*," said Mark Russell. "They would take him everywhere, and he was a perfect little gentleman. And he was funny, just adorable." Bob Weide's first memory of him was when he was chatting with the family at a Christmas party in the mid-eighties. "Somehow the conversation turned to China's background, her biography. I think maybe we were discussing Woody Allen, and she talked about being in *What's Up, Tiger Lily*? because she knew I was interested in him. Anyway, as she was giving me a little bit of her professional background, Mort Jr. turned to her and said, 'Mom, don't forget this!' And he made what looked like a peace sign with two fingers. She looked at him and said, 'Oh yes, and I was a Playboy Bunny for a while.'"

Mort liked to point out that the boy was Chinese and Jewish. "The kid has ten thousand years of culture on his shoulders." A familiar pair, they were clearly devoted to each other. "Whenever I used to come back from the road," Mort remembers, "I would bring him a present. So, when he was sufficiently young, I got him a Rambo machine gun. I said, 'I've got to stick my head in a party and then we'll go to dinner.' So I went to this party at [writer-producer] Bill Froug's house. 'You let your child play with a gun? A gun took the life of Martin Luther King.' I said, 'For Christ's sake, don't be so pious. He's seven years old.' So I walked out of the house and Mort said, 'What's the matter, Dad?' I said, 'Aw, that crowd . . .' He said, 'Didn't like my gun, did they?' I said, 'No.' 'Why didn't they?' I said, 'Because they're liberals.' And he said, 'They're not liberals, Dad. They're your friends.'"

"He was an affectionate kid," said Weide. "Loved his dad. Whenever I'd go to visit Mort, we were always in his bedroom, which is where the big TV was. Mort Jr. would often be in there with us, and Mort Sr. was really sweet with him. Mort Jr. was into Batman at that time. I think they were re-running the old TV series, and so they'd watch that together for kicks. Mort Jr. was very much into comic books, like DC and all the stuff I looked at when I was a kid, and Mort Sr. would indulge all that. But very often they had this kind of casual affection where Mort Jr. would be sitting on the chair next to his dad and would just drape his arm around his dad's shoulders. I remember being very touched by that."

"I think the whole story of your life is finding out who the enemy is," Mort Sahl said in 1990. "When you're young, you think it's the people you work for. When you're out of office, you think it's the people who are in office. The enemy, I have found, is the group. Even if it's your group—if you're lucky enough to find a group. I rarely did, if ever. I think it's the individual versus *the group*. The idea is to keep your state of mind independent, which is a war." When Mort Jr. took up that battle at age fifteen, his father knew the enemy all too clearly: "It's the same old stuff, you know. Does he have any enemies? His friends. It's the peer group."

Bob Weide tried to reassure him:

> I remember Mort really fretting over the right approach to take with Mort Jr. You know—there's the "tough love" mentality, and then there's the totally giving in and being sympathetic on all points and being there for him no matter what. I'm sure he was talking to different experts and different psychiatrists or counselors who were giving him all different kinds of information, but I just remember it being a real struggle for him about what to do. He was really at his wit's end. I guess he discovered that Mort Jr. was smoking pot, and Mort is somehow the one guy who got through the sixties, as far as I know, without taking that route.
>
> This was my sage advice: "Don't worry about it." I said, "You know, I went through that phase." I didn't get into hard stuff, but I was smoking a lot of pot in high school. I personally don't have a very addictive personality, so by the time I was out of high school it was behind me. I mean, *occasionally*, but it wasn't a big part of my life. We did it the way guys would get together and have a beer or whatever, and it was no big deal. And then I came out the other end, and I turned out okay. So I told Mort, basically, "Look, everybody smokes pot. Everybody at a certain age or younger is experimenting. Don't panic and don't worry about it." And then, as in those educational films we saw in high school about pot being the gateway drug . . . it did escalate and it did get into more and more stuff. At that point I had no advice to offer, because this was beyond my pay scale.

"They lived on top of that hill," said Larry Christon, "and there was no place for kids to play. You couldn't skateboard or roller skate or go out and play baseball because the hill was so steep. Where were they going to go? The parents in that neighborhood were all showbiz people, so they were out at night at these galas and soirees and dinners. And their kids were home alone, so they would call taxis, and the taxis would come up and pick them up and take them downtown to get drugs, and they'd pay with credit cards. They'd go back up the hill and get high. And I think that's what happened with Mort Jr.'s world—there was just nothing for those kids to do."

Mort Jr. began cutting classes in his sophomore year at University High School, intent on forming a band. China bought him a piano, and then, once he had his license, a car. "I said, 'Well, we'll see about a car,'" Mort fumed. "They went down one afternoon and bought a new Honda. She did it impulsively, like buying the piano. She didn't consult me. So then he didn't drive to the school; he drove other places." China told Mort that he'd have to hire somebody to live at San Ysidro and supervise the boy. "The car was not a good idea," Mort says. "Then he fell behind in school because he never went. And he was mixed up with the sophistication of the music business." In hindsight, it seems inevitable that Little Mort would progress to heroin. He idolized the hard rock band Guns N' Roses, whose song "Mr. Brownstone" portrayed the cycle of addiction as lived by guitarist Izzy Stradlin and his bandmates. And when he started his own band, he called it Crash Diet after another of GN'R's drug-themed songs.

Mort Sahl had no understanding of the drug culture, other than what he had observed among jazz musicians. He once described using LSD as "like stuffing cotton in your ears instead of changing the orchestra." But he had the horrifying example of friends who had lost children to drugs—Paul Newman, whose only son Scott overdosed in 1978, George Englund and Cloris Leachman, whose son Bryan died in 1986. "I never told anybody," Mort says. "I buttoned it up. I felt like it was a discreditation. It minimized him because he was a lot of other things. He was very gifted musically. And he was loyal to me. He kept saying, 'I'm going to clean up. I'm going to do it, Dad. You have to believe me.'"

Others tried to help, particularly Teddy Howard, who had known the boy since he was a newborn. "I said, 'Little Mort, don't you know what you're doing to yourself?' He said, 'But Teddy, I'm like my dad. I'm in this bubble looking out at people. I don't feel like I can really be a part of it.' I said, 'But Little Mort, you're destroying yourself. I'm so excited to watch you go through life. How can I help you get off these drugs?' He said, 'Heroin is my drug, Teddy, and the horses are my mother's drug. It's the only time I feel I can cope.'" China saw a darker scenario, as if the warm embrace of heroin was a form of self-medication: "My mother was schizophrenic—she heard voices," she said. "She would sit alone arguing with herself. My son started to have the same problem. He started to hear voices coming from the closet."

"It was just rough," said Bob Weide. "I remember Mort Sr. telling me that Mort Jr. took some vintage Rolex watches of his that must have been worth tens of thousands of dollars, and sold them for a hundred bucks (or whatever the figure was). So it got real ugly under that roof, and Mort was really in despair." Mort Jr.'s daily scramble for money gradually destroyed the net worth his father had accrued through years of unlikely investments. "I really got hot about two years after I started with Enrico," Mort says. "So when I went to Switzerland, I went to the watch factories and they all got to know me. Then I'd come back and get them dealers in Beverly Hills. So then they'd give me advance stuff. I had a Patek Philippe—the enamel was all hand done. That watch is worth about $900,000 now. That was one. I had five hundred of them. The watches were a special thing because he liked them too. So I bought him some along the way. And at the end, he didn't have any that I gave him. I gave him Breitlings—pilots' watches. He didn't have any of them. He didn't have any of his clothes. I bought him a lot of sound equipment, and it was gone. It got so bad that I'd stay up with him two or three days, and when I'd go to sleep he'd take my wallet and go down to the ATM. By that time, we were out of a lot of money, and I didn't have any of my stuff. I got cleaned out, but I couldn't call the cops on him."

"Mort," said Larry Christon, "was a little bit afraid of him at that point, because Mort Jr. had threatened him physically, and he had broken things and stolen things, and Mort was almost trapped in his own room. Clearly things were out of control. Mort Jr. was out of control, and when you're sleeping in a house with someone who is crazy or dangerous, you can't sleep. Not that Mort's a great sleeper to begin with, but it was very rough." Mort finally got his eighteen-year-old son into a treatment program at a local hospital, but then he was appalled by what he observed: "There were things I never imagined. They were exchanging stuff in the corridors of the hospital. Everybody had everything."

In the program for only a day or two, Mort Jr. was moved to another hospital in Beverly Hills, a boutique affair. "It was very pricey," said Christon.

"Mort found a way to sneak into the hospital at night and visit Mort Jr. We both sneaked in one night. It was after hours. I think we had to climb over a fence or something, and Mort knew the back way and how to get in some kind of entrance. Mort Jr. didn't look bad; he looked quite good. He'd lost some weight but had the junkie's charm. When he saw me it was: 'Hi Larry. I was just thinking about you.' So you knew it was a lie. He had the patter and was very warm to his dad. He said he was feeling pretty good and was looking forward to getting out, and that everything was fine. He was making progress. All the lies that addicts do. And you could see that was Mort's central concern at that point in his life."

"Mort could not understand what Little Mort needed or what *he* needed to do," said Teddy Howard. "He and China fought over rehabs. China thought that she could just do what her father did to her: 'Don't you dare!' and be angry. That's how she could control the situation—to get angry. And in this instance it just didn't work. . . . I think when she'd get mad and pull away from him, that was tragic to Little Mort. It was worse than any way she could have hit him." Mort Jr. relapsed and ended up living on the streets. Eventually, he found his way to County-USC Medical Center in Boyle Heights, where the psychiatric interns took him in on a 5150—an involuntary seventy-two-hour hold for evaluation.

"When he got out of the hospital," says Mort, "I put him in a sober living house in Van Nuys. And then I found out that all these rehab guys have got their own racket going too. All self-righteous, you know. They'd say to me, 'Get him out of the house. He's got to know there's a penalty and he won't take anything else.' 'When can you take him in?' 'We can take him in the day after tomorrow. But we suggest you bring him to our motel. We own a motel in back of the Galleria.' So I put him in a motel. And who goes over to the motel all night? Guys are going in and out of there, bringing him stuff." In the end, Mort Jr. was too consumed by his addiction to come anywhere close to recovery. "He kept saying to me, 'I'm kickin' it Dad. I'm cuttin' down.' And then this Israeli girl, tall, who's now, by the way, teaching at the University of Judaism, said to me, 'There's no kicking where he is.' She loved him, so when she said it it was very rueful."

Lou Lotorto hadn't seen Little Mort in years when Mort asked one day if he would pick him up. "It was down in Van Nuys," Lou remembered, "and it was a little park. So I drove over there, and I saw Junior sitting on the curb looking really, really wasted. I said, 'Hi, Mort. Get in the car. I'm bringing you home.' He said, 'Oh, okay.' He was just completely out of it. I said,

'Can I get you anything to eat? Would you like a cup of coffee or anything?' He said, 'No, no. That's okay.' So, I drove him home, but it broke my heart seeing him in that condition." New Path, the people who ran the sober living house, recommended a low-cost treatment center operated by the Los Angeles County Department of Health Services, but there was a waiting list to get in. In his desperation, Mort appealed to Nancy Reagan. "She was one of my best friends. It was really full, and I asked her to move him up the list—as a last stroke. Her secretary called me back and said to me, 'If she does this for you, everybody will want something.' I couldn't believe that answer—and that it came by proxy. So I sent a letter right to her home. And I said: 'I now know what Just Say No means.'"

A place finally opened at the Warm Springs Rehabilitation Center, a long-term residential facility in Castaic, about thirty miles north of Beverly Hills. Mort Jr. seemed to be doing well, but there was a chronic dullness to him, as if a light had gone out inside. Lou Lotorto rode out there one day with Mort: "He said, 'The rules are that we're not supposed to talk to him, but I'm bringing him a radio.' Mort Jr. was on the curb when we pulled up, and Mort Sr. did what he was told, not to talk to him, not to make a connection. We brought the radio, left it at the office. As we were driving away, I turned around, and it was like a premonition that I'd never see him again. He looked so sad, standing there, and I waved from the window, and he waved back."

About a week later, Mort had a call from his son. Mort Jr. had run afoul of the rules at Warm Springs and had been expelled. "They told him to stay in the area, and he said he walked up to the top of the hill [in the Angeles National Forest near Castaic Lake] because of the view. With two other guys. So they threw him out. I said to him, 'When can I see you?' He said, 'I'm staying at this guy's house, Dad, but I'm fine. I want you to know I'm fine. I'll see you tomorrow.'"

The next morning, Mort was up early to take a call from Don Imus' New York–based radio show. At about five minutes to six, there was a furious pounding at the front door, as if whoever was there was trying to break it down. It was the police, and they had a question: "Does your son have a tattoo that says 'Sarah' with a saber?"

Mort called China. "I said, 'Sit down. I've got some bad news for you. . . .' She [listened], said, 'Oh, okay.' And she hung up. About two hours later, the phone rings, and it's her again. She said, 'Jack thinks you should come over for some coffee.' They left me in the house with the news from the cops. She didn't say, 'Come over.' Then I went over to her house. She called her family and they all came out. And they all came out to Jack's house. She cooked for everybody, and made sure she never sat with me or talked to me."

One of the first people Mort called that terrible morning was his pal John Hart, who was at his home in Connecticut. "I'll be out on the next airplane I can catch," Hart told him, and he was. Mort, he found, was scarcely functional: "He was sort of spaced out." Gradually, the details of the boy's final hours emerged, and Mort was urged by China's brother, Jefferson Parish Sheriff Harry Lee, to sue the county. "I thought I had them dead to rights because they said, 'This is your medication. And you're not going to be here, so we'll give it to you for three months.' They gave him all that stuff. And then, of course, they couldn't awaken him." Morton Lyon Sahl Jr. had been clean for five weeks. He died on March 27, 1996, in an apartment on South Norton Avenue in the Jefferson Park area of Los Angeles. He was nineteen years old.

"I had a real tough time," says Mort. "I had an attack of vertigo and couldn't get out of the chair. I couldn't even walk to the kitchen, couldn't get my balance back. Hart did a little cooking and got me around. I never went out anywhere." Teddy Howard stepped in and took charge of the arrangements. "China was very upset," she said, "and Mort was like in a daze, like in a walking coma. He didn't know what to do. He couldn't even fathom how it happened, how he got there." Mort decided on burial at Hillside Memorial Park, not because Mort Jr. was half-Jewish, but because the cemetery, just east of the San Diego Freeway in West Los Angeles, was the closest to where China was then living. "China wanted to know if I had a Guns N' Roses t-shirt," Teddy remembered. "I said, 'You're not going to put him in that, are you?' She said, 'I wouldn't acknowledge it or let him do it while he was alive, and he liked them. And I need chains and stuff . . .' She dressed him in what she had *prohibited*. She said, 'Teddy, I have to because he's dead and I want him to be in what he'd want.'"

The funeral took place on March 31, a warm Sunday afternoon. "Mort was standing outside looking a little bewildered, greeting people" said Larry Christon. "That's one thing about Mort. He understands deportment, behavior, manners, courtesy—a lot of the stuff that's gone out of social behavior now." The services were private, but Alvin Sargent was struck by who wasn't there. "Friends of his, like Clint Eastwood and Sydney Pollack—they didn't come. He was hurt by that, I think." Bob Weide flew in from Las Vegas, where a friend of his was getting married. "When I got there, China assumed that I'd gone to the back room and had seen Mort [Jr.], because I guess in the back they had an open casket and I didn't know about it. So I came in and probably saw Larry Christon and a couple of people I knew, and then I came up to China and I gave her a hug. I remember her saying to me, 'That's not him back there.' I said, 'What do you mean?' She said, 'What you saw—that wasn't him. That's not really him.' I didn't know what she meant by that, I literally didn't know what she was talking about, and then I realized . . .'"

A succession of people spoke—Weide, Teddy Howard, some of the young addicts who were part of Mort Jr.'s circle of friends. "They were people he was associated with and went to rehab with," said Teddy. "And the guy that was with him when he died, who OD'ed him, was there. China invited them all to come to the funeral and to the house so that they could *see* and stop using drugs. They got up there like assholes: 'Well, he was a good guy. You know, we are what we are.' That type of thing. I gave them such hell. China wanted to be kind to them, and she spent a lot of time talking to them. She wanted to help them, and that never worked out because they couldn't have cared less. But she insisted that they be allowed to talk, and I said, 'Okay, fine, maybe we'll all learn something.' I wanted to kill them."

John Hart rose to speak. With his anchorman's authority, he brought even the kids from rehab to a respectful, attentive silence. "I bring Mort's voice," he began.

> In the words of a song he wrote two years ago and gave to me. We talked about it two weeks ago, and he quoted some lines from it. When we talked, his voice was strong, clear, lively. I was surprised. Different from his voice two years ago when he gave me the song. He'd just been hiking in the mountains and he said, "It's beautiful." He loved to hike in those mountains. He did it several times since.
>
> I asked him what they did up there, and he said, "Go to meetings. Eat."
>
> "How's the food?"
>
> "Not wonderful."
>
> "Find any pals?"
>
> "Well . . ."
>
> "Anybody to hang out with?"

Then he used a word I've forgotten. I didn't understand it. To explain he said, "Sex Pistols." The kind of pals he hung out with. And I guess he figured I needed more explaining so he said, "Nihilism."

"Kindred spirits," I said to show him I understood.

"Yeah," he said.

Hart's words left the mourners struggling with their emotions. China, who had insisted that Mort sit next to her, turned to him and said, "This is not what he would want. Why don't you get up there and liven this up?" So Mort got up and, in what must have been the most difficult performance of his life, proceeded to regale the mourners with stories of Mort Jr., his outlook, his humor. "I thought it was a very mensch-y thing," said Bob Weide. "He did a very funny eulogy, and it really opened my eyes to what a mitzvah that can be—especially with the death of a kid. My God, it was just awful. He might as well have been murdered or died in a car accident. This made no sense, and everybody was getting tearful. Then Mort got up and had the room laughing. And I thought: God, what a great gift to give on a day when Mort's probably as low as he'll ever be, that he turned it into something light for the benefit of the people in the audience. I never forgot it."

In the days immediately following his son's death, Mort lashed out at those responsible for his care.

I drove up there to the [Warm Springs] facility and I said, "You threw him out!" They said, "He broke the rules." "And you gave him advance medicine!" And the guy who had sent me there runs the facility out in Van Nuys. I said, "You're supposed to be saving lives! Why are you sending people up there?" And China adopted all those kids who were at the reception, gave them money in case they were trying to get sober or something. And, of course, I'm sure she never saw them again.

China came up to the house after the service. Al Sargent was up there, and [screenwriter] Dick Simmons. E. Jack Neuman. She spoke to everybody at the reception, but she didn't speak to me. Didn't say good night to me or anything. So she was pretty mad even then. It's pretty heavy stuff because I can process almost everything, but I can't come to any conclusion about that. And then I got into it with the county coroner. They were ducking me; I couldn't get a call through for weeks.

When the toxicology results finally did come back, the death certificate was amended to show the cause as "Acute Heroin/Morphine Intoxication." It was, the coroner concluded, accidental.

"They gave him three compounds," Mort says of the authorities at Warm Springs, "but I don't know what they were. And then the county coroner says to me, 'We found that he had been using cocaine since he was eight.' Well, don't you think I would have known that? I wanted to get a lawyer, but everyone wanted a huge down payment. And I was broke. China was broke because of the horses [she bought]. So there was not much I could do." He dealt with his grief quietly, talking it over with friends like Larry Christon and visiting the grave on an almost daily basis. "I don't think it will ever go away," he said. "He opened my head up a lot. He was the guy who said, 'Keep your material contemporary.'"

Having not worked since the debacle of *Comedy Tonight*, he decided to revive *Mort Sahl's America* for local audiences. "In L.A. you can really get buried," he says, "so I figured working was the best thing." The initial engagement was limited to three weeks at the ninety-nine-seat Tiffany Theater on Sunset Boulevard, just steps from where the Crescendo and the Interlude once stood. Previews were set to begin on July 17, with regular performances commencing Saturday, July 20. "I speak more from my heart than I used to," he said in an advance interview with the *Orange County Register*. "I've gone through a lot of trauma. I lost my son, who was 19, in March. That doesn't mean I shut my sense of humor down. I speak in more human terms. I was pretty tough in the beginning; I was pretty relentless. I thought I knew who the enemy was. The idea is to make the case, and when the majority decides it's worthwhile, to move on."

On opening night, he came dressed in his trademark sweater, the rolled newspaper in one hand, the volumes of the Warren Report once again arrayed on a table at the back of the stage. The first half of the show centered on politics and foreign affairs, the second half on Hollywood and screenwriting. "Why did we go to Bosnia?" he asked. "Probably so Nike can make tennis shoes there." On the current administration in Washington: "Clinton says he's a new type of Democrat. That's for sure—he's a Republican." And on the subject of the president's unbridled libido: "When did we go from Camelot to Dogpatch?" At the end of the evening, he warmly thanked the audience for forty-two years of support. "I've always treated the audience as if they had a Ph.D., and I've never been disappointed." Then he added: "Is there any group I haven't offended?"

Audiences and critics embraced him, and the SRO engagement at the Tiffany was extended into late September. Then, while more time was being cleared in Los Angeles, he adjourned to San Francisco to play five weeks at the Alcazar Theatre. He wrapped the year with another thirty-six performances at the Tiffany, two of which featured his longtime fan, actor Charlton Heston. During the year 1997, *Mort Sahl's America* would again play New York and Boston's Hasty Pudding Theatre. The show itself would appear as an audiocassette from Dove Entertainment, constituting his twelfth comedy album in a span of forty years.

In the months following their son's death, there was tension between Mort and China but the lines of communication remained open. "China went to the graveyard every day for a long, long time," said Teddy Howard. "She would meet other women there who were visiting and she would become friendly with them. And Mort went all the time. I think that Little Mort's death really destroyed both of them."

Mort held out hope that the relationship could again be repaired, and one night he had a call from China. "She said, 'I have to get out of here.' And I said, 'This will always be your house. Come on over.' I made up the spare room for her. I gentrified it, got her a carton of L&Ms, all the Hershey bars she liked. I went down to Saks and I got the best nightgown I could find, and I put it across her bed. And I put a sign on the bed that said, 'Welcome.' She brought a lot of stuff, like she was going to stay a while and make up her mind about whether to stay in town. She walked all the way to the back of the house, and she just cried and went to bed. The next day she said, 'I'm leaving.' And she left."

Teddy's conviction was that Mort and China belonged together, and she continued to press for a reconciliation long after it had become a lost cause.

Everybody thought—and I thought—well, they'll come back together. They always do. But this time it was different. Mort was part of the Lee family in New Orleans, but China wanted a total cut-off, and I think she had to do that to survive. So when China and he split, Mort lost his family, not just China. She said, "I'm so tired, Teddy. You have to understand, I am so *tired*. I cannot do it anymore. I don't want to talk about it, I don't want you to . . ." I tried many times to get her back with Mort, and then she called me one day out of the blue. I hadn't talked to her for about six months. She said, "Teddy, I know I haven't talked to you. I know you've called, but I really can't talk to you if you mention him. I can't. You always try to get us back together. It's not gonna happen."

During the initial run of *Mort Sahl's America* at the Tiffany Theatre, Mort's friend Judy Balaban attended a performance with actress-writer Shelby Hiatt, a striking blonde in her early fifties. They talked after the show, and Judy called Shelby a few days later to say that Mort had asked for her number. The approach on Mort's behalf was tentative at best. "I really lost a lot of will with [Mort Jr.'s death]," he comments. Trained at the Actors Studio, Shelby had actually appeared on a television panel with Mort some twenty years earlier, but he didn't remember it. They entered into a relationship that lasted two years, and she was briefly with him during the Boston run of *Mort Sahl's America*.

He turned seventy on May 11, 1997, a birthday he shared with Irving Berlin, Margaret Rutherford, Salvador Dalí, and Nation of Islam leader Louis Farrakhan. Three months earlier, Herb Caen had died of lung cancer at the age of eighty. "It's a shame," Mort says. "When he got sick, I tried to get to him and straighten it out, but he wouldn't talk to me. I tried to get to Jerry Bunson, who really wrote the column. He said, 'He won't have anything to do with you. You can't even apologize.' The irony was that there was no great love affair with this girl. The momentary flirtation. And she, like any chick, was trying to survive."

In 1999 Mort wed Kenslea Ann Motter, a Delta flight attendant thirty-three years his junior. Club work was wickedly scarce for seventy-four-year-old comedians, and when Sahl played a four-night stand at Joe's Pub in New York in 2001, it was a booking arranged by Woody Allen and his manager, Jack Rollins. Mort lost the house on San Ysidro in 2004, a particularly grim year for income. Trying to stir up work, he pitched *New Yorker* editor David Remnick about covering the 2004 conventions for the magazine. "I said, 'Instead of all these lily-white liberals, like Jonathan Alter and [Hendrik] Hertzberg, let me go in there.' [Remnick] said, 'We don't give assignments like that.'"

The years of the second Bush administration should have been prime performing years for Mort Sahl. But as his eightieth birthday approached, bookings had dwindled to the point where it looked as if his days as an entertainer were over. An admirer, comedian and motivational speaker Ross Shafer, got the idea of creating a foundation for older comics down on their luck, and with a knowing assist from Bob Weide, it evolved into the Heartland Comedy Foundation and an all-star fundraiser conceived as an eightieth birthday commemoration. Said Weide, "We brought [Improv founder] Budd Friedman and [actor-director] Howard Storm into it, as I recall, because they were always good to help out anyone. We had done the same thing for Lenny Bruce's mother, Sally Marr."

The event, *All Star Sahl-ute: A Tribute to Legendary Comedian Mort Sahl*, was set to take place on June 28, 2007, at UCLA's Wadsworth Theater, with tax-deductible ticket prices ranging from $100 to $200. Larry King agreed to emcee, and names announced for the bill included Jay Leno, Bill Maher, Paula Poundstone, David Steinberg, Albert Brooks, David Brenner, Drew Carey, Jonathan Winters, Shelley Berman, and Richard Lewis. "Hearing that Mort Sahl had turned eighty was the social equivalent of realizing that one's high school sweetheart was now a grandmother," commented *Los Angeles Times* columnist Al Martinez.

As with all such affairs, appearances were "subject to personal availability." Jack Riley was pressed into service when King had to bow out, and both Steinberg and Brenner were no-shows. "Mort Sahl changed the face of comedy," Riley said up front. "Before his, that face was Marty Allen's." The procession of comic talent that night was awe-inspiring. From the guest of honor's generation came Winters, Berman, and the malaproping Norm Crosby. Newer generations were represented by Leno, Lewis, Carey, Maher, Kevin Nealon, satirist Harry Shearer, and, in a surprise appearance, George Carlin. Woody Allen and Don Rickles sent tributes on videotape, and Hugh Hefner, Tommy Chong, Rob Reiner, Larry Gelbart, Fred Willard, Sydney Pollack, and Dick Van Patten were among those in the audience.

By most accounts, the hit of the evening was Albert Brooks. "I'm embarrassed tonight," he began. "And angry. And I'm confused. I don't know the people that produced this show at all, but I would strongly suggest that when they do an event like this again, they spend a little extra money and hire a real publicity firm to disseminate the information correctly. I was told that Mort Sahl passed away. So you can imagine my shock, my dismay, and, quite frankly, my disappointment when I arrived here this evening and saw him standing there . . ." Brooks proceeded to read his carefully written eulogy: "I remember the last time I saw Mort alive. It was at a Starbucks near where I live. And now I wish I'd said the things that I really felt. I wish I'd said how much he influenced all of us here. How brave he was. I wish I'd have told him how much of an innovator he was. I wish I'd have told him how much I loved listening to his records. While he was here. But I didn't. All I think I said that day was, 'Are you gonna finish that latte?'"

When Mort finally took the stage, he was genuinely humbled by the love and respect in the room. "I've been very moved by everybody tonight," he said. "And I had a good time laughing. I want you to know it really did knock me out. And I also want you to know that I'll do it as long as they let me. I didn't want this to be a retirement party, you know. I'm still in business . . ."

Somebody shouted, "Hey Mort! You avoid 9/11 in your act. You always talked about the Warren Commission. You were all over it!"

You hear that? It was something to do with the Warren Commission. Well, you know, that's how I went out of business for about twelve years. But I stuck to my guns, because I remember something [Bobby] Kennedy said: "To all you with the guns out there, you may be able to slay the dreamer, but you haven't slain the dream." I came to this because I really thought I was an American and really had the capacity to dream. You all know that if you watch Turner Classic Movies. That's what the movies were about. It was a dark place where people could fall in love and moral issues could be resolved. My grandfather came from Lithuania, although Lou Dobbs tried to stop him. I dreamed that dream.

When I started this act, although I was just lonesome and looking for a family, in a larger sense I saw it as a rescue mission for America— but believe it more than ever in spite of the odds. That the good guys will win . . . I tried to get to your funny bone and get into your head, but apparently I also got into your heart.

17

MORE COMEDIANS, LESS HUMOR

Concurrent with the announcement of the *All Star Sahl-ute* at the Wadsworth was word that Mort Sahl would be joining the faculty of Claremont McKenna College as a visiting lecturer teaching screenwriting and a course he called *The Revolutionary's Handbook*. The news raised eyebrows, as CMC was a conservative liberal arts campus with a reputation for turning out corporate executives and right-of-center politicians. ("Leaders in the making" was the school's stated mission.) Bringing Sahl into the midst of what many considered enemy territory was the director of the Gould Center for Humanistic Studies, Robert Faggen. "Mort's career has been spent pushing people to rethink their most cherished beliefs," he said in a statement. "To have an innovator of modern American political satire in the classroom is such a rich opportunity for students. We couldn't pass this up."

Initial concerns weren't assuaged by the reading list for *The Revolutionary's Handbook*, which included Stephen Kinzer's *Overthrow: America's Century of Regime Change from Hawaii to Iraq* and Jon Lee Anderson's *Che Guevara: A Revolutionary Life*. "I want to show these young students some real heroes," Mort said, "not the ones they see on cable. I want to teach them about their country's hidden history. There is another America out there that is different from the one the students know." He also proposed to show movies like *Mr. Smith Goes to Washington* and John Sturges' *Marooned*, films about people taking a stand. "Mort has always taken enormous risks," Faggen said admiringly. "That is sometimes what is expected of you. From the beginning of his performing career, he's never done the safe thing." Said Mort: "I hope I can just obfuscate the fact that in school ī was a lousy student."

Sahl taught two years at Claremont McKenna, effectively dividing the student body between those who loved him and those who thought him wholly unsuited to a college classroom. ("They wanted screenwriting," he said. "It's all a facade; I really talk about the same thing.") Not long before the end of the spring 2009 semester, he was reported missing from his Claremont home by his wife of ten years, Kenslea. The police located him several days later in the company of a friend named John Albertson. "He's where he wants to be voluntarily," Claremont Police Lt. Paul Davenport told the press, effectively signaling the acrimonious end of Sahl's marriage to the woman he described in 2004 as the greatest love of his life. "I wish it had worked," Mort said sadly. "When I met her, I had such a devout wish for it all. But that doesn't make it come true. It's very elusive, very elusive."

Two months later, he announced the end of his teaching stint in an interview with the *Berkeley Daily Planet*. He described CMC students as "running around with an Apple under their arm and an i-Phone in their hand, not understanding they're carrying the instruments of divisiveness." Two years, he said, were enough. "Claremont's too isolated. I've had a call from the University of Chicago, another from UCLA. Time to move on, do something else." He added that he had been offered a course on the Holocaust but turned it down. "I want to see first how history judges the event."

By then, he had relocated to Mill Valley, about ten miles north of San Francisco, at the urging of Woody Allen. "Everything was falling apart for me in L.A., professionally and personally, too," he explained. "I lived in the same house in Beverly Hills for forty-three years, but L.A. has gotten out of reach. So I came up here where I could talk to people. It was lucky for me here the first time." In Mill Valley, he played Lucy Mercer's 142 Throckmorton Theatre, both solo and in tandem with Dick Gregory. "Whenever I've had him here, he sells out," Mercer said. "Audiences are very positive. They tend to be people who remember him, and they tend to be pretty intelligent." He also became a regular at the Throckmorton's *Tuesday Night Live!* comedy showcase, although what he observed rarely impressed him. "I was over at the theater last night," he told the *Marin Independent Journal* in 2010, "and it wasn't especially dirty, which I appreciated. But those guys in their Big 5 clothes aren't very adventurous. They're in neutral sociologically. More comedians, less humor."

In 2011 *Mort Sahl at Sunset* was enshrined in the National Recording Registry of the Library of Congress as the first standup comedy recording. (A 1908 wax cylinder of "Take Me Out to the Ball Game" and humpback whale songs captured by biologists in 1970 were among the other inductees.) The same year, Mort took to the Internet and social media with the help of his friend Chris Britt, maintaining a website at www.mortsahlofficial.com and posting frequently on Twitter @mortsahlsays. Enthusiastically embracing the lean 140-character format, he commented on new bookings, world events, and the inevitable passings of his contemporaries.

Some examples:

Our elected officials will do anything to save the country, including destroy it.

and:

Dave Brubeck enlisted every college kid in America to the cause of jazz, with a little help from Bartok.

and:

Detroit has 40,000 feral dogs walking around. So does Wall Street.

and:

My religious preference is Apple.

and:

People called me a communist when I started and now they call me a Republican. They're both wrong. I'm a radical.

and:

Many of you have written and asked what I dream about. I dream about fighting fascism and, if it's a deep sleep, a woman loves me for it.

ACKNOWLEDGMENTS

I thought about this book for maybe a dozen years before I finally proposed it. One reason for my hesitation was that it concerned a living subject, a potential complication I wasn't sure I could handle. Finally, in December 2012, I contacted Lucy Mercer through Mort Sahl's official website and asked the question: Was anyone writing a biography? And if not, would Mr. Sahl be open to cooperating on one? She responded by saying that she'd check with him, and so the long, sometimes rocky process began with a trip to Mill Valley, about ten miles north of San Francisco. Mort was understandably hesitant at first, and my wife remembers my calling her after our first interview session and saying I wasn't sure I was going to able to do this. Gradually, Mort and I established a rapport that enabled us to record some forty hours of conversation. In time, no subjects were off the record, and he responded with a candor I'm not sure I would have gotten had I acted on my original notion back in the year 2000.

Needless to say, this book would not have been possible without the cooperation of Mort Sahl himself. He welcomed me into his home, answered all my questions to the best of his ability, and didn't insist upon reading or passing approval on the resulting manuscript. I am very grateful to him, as I am to Lucy Mercer, proprietor of the 142 Throckmorton Theatre in Mill Valley, who is his friend and confidante, and whose considerable work behind the scenes made this book happen at times when it seemed as if it wouldn't. If there is one person ultimately responsible for bringing it to fruition, it is Lucy; I couldn't have done it without her.

Other friends of Mort Sahl pitched in as well. Robert B. Weide generously shared his memories, as well as unedited transcripts of interviews he shot with Steve Allen, Enrico Banducci, Jim Garrison, and Andrew Sciambra for his 1989 documentary *Mort Sahl: The Loyal Opposition*. Likewise, Lawrence Christon, the influential comedy critic for the *Los Angeles Times*, talked of a personal friendship that extended back to the late 1960s. Larry also read an early draft of this book, offering valuable thoughts and suggestions.

Ben Alba, author of *Inventing Late Night*, a fascinating history of Steve Allen's *Tonight!*, consulted his research files to pinpoint the exact date of Mort Sahl's TV debut. Cari Beauchamp very helpfully put me in touch with her friends Judy Balaban and Nancy Olson. Gerald Nachman, author of *Seriously Funny*, the definitive history of topical comedy in the postwar era, provided contacts and valuable insights. I also appreciate the timely help rendered by Chris Britt, Dan Dion, Debra Green, Kathleen Hahn, Larry Harnisch, Anthony Slide, Gini Tamberi, and Lisa Troland.

A number of libraries and institutions were consulted for this project, and I am grateful to the following librarians and administrators for being so helpful: the Paley Center for Media: Martin Gostanian. Marjorie G. and Carl W. Stern Book Arts and Special Collections Center, San Francisco Public Library: Tom Carey, Tim Wilson. UCLA Film and Television Archive: Mark Quigley. Cinematic Arts Library, University of Southern California: Ned Comstock. Regional History Collection, University of Southern California: Dace Taube.

I am also grateful to the friends and colleagues of Mort Sahl who graciously submitted to interviews for this book: Woody Allen, Judy Balaban, Orson Bean, Shelley and Sarah Berman, Bob Burns, Dick Cavett, the late Yvonne Craig, Dave Dawson, Ann Elder, Megan Flax, Leonard Green, John Hart, Shelby Hiatt, Elaine Trebek Kares, Bob Lally, Lou Lotorto, Elliot Mintz, Nancy Olson, Mark Russell, China Lee Sahl, Alvin Sargent, Jack Schwartz, Maynard Sloate, and John Whiting.

My agent, Neil Olson, was an indefatigable champion of this project through a seemingly endless number of ups and downs. Leila W. Salisbury, in her role as director of the University Press of Mississippi, was instrumental in bringing this project to UPM, and her enthusiasm for it was infectious.

Finally, the faith and conviction of my wife, Kim Geary, helped bring this book into being, and her great affection for its subject, and occasionally its author, has sustained it ever since. As Mort would say: Onward!

James Curtis
Brea
June 2016

SOURCE NOTES

Forty hours of talks between the author and Mort Sahl took place in Mill Valley, California, between March 31, 2012, and March 3, 2014. There were also occasional exchanges via telephone and e-mail. Quotes from these interviews are expressed in the present tense ("Mort says . . .") while quotes from contemporary sources are in the past tense ("Mort said . . .").

PART I: THE NEXT PRESIDENT OF THE UNITED STATES

Chapter 1: I'm Not Geared to Total Acceptance

4   Seated at a table: This performance took place on June 3, 2013.

5   "a meeting place": Maya Angelou, *Singin' and Swingin' and Gettin' Merry Like Christmas* (New York: Random House, 1976), 79.

6   "started to paint": *San Francisco Examiner*, 6/8/71.

6   "relaxed": *New York Times*, 1/5/70.

6   "European": Donald Pippen Oral History, Bancroft Library, UC Berkeley, 2001.

6   "pure genius": *Oakland Tribune*, 11/7/56.

7   "Mort's audition": Robert Rice, "The Fury," *New Yorker*, 7/30/60.

8   "women and behavior": Mort Sahl to the author, Mill Valley, 4/23/13.

8   "horrible": *San Francisco Chronicle*, 2/27/55.

8   "nightclubs": *San Francisco Chronicle*, 4/4/07.

8   "Take the tie off": MS to the author.

9   "a guy from another country": Ken Kelly, "Enrico Banducci: The Best of Broadway," *San Francisco Focus*, March 1987.

9   "Herbert Hoover": *San Francisco Examiner*, 1/11/54.

9   "all to himself": MS to the author.

9   "He never stopped talking": John Whiting, "The Future Lies Behind," posted at www.thankyouoneandall.co.uk.

10   "public domain": Mort Sahl, *Heartland* (New York: Harcourt Brace Jovanovich, 1976), 18.

11   "he was with me": MS to the author.

11   "finish the show": Sahl, *Heartland*, 20.

12   "What's the wall going to be": MS to the author.

12   "lean, bristly": Herb Caen, liner notes, *The Future Lies Ahead* (LP, Verve, 1958).

13   "I observed people": *Oakland Tribune*, 7/31/54.

13   "The room": Kelly, "Enrico Banducci: The Best of Broadway."
13   "really strict": Enrico Banducci audio interview, "Back Story," *San Francisco Chronicle* podcast, 4/4/07.
13   "a coterie": MS to the author.
14   "subterranean": Sahl, *Heartland*, 21.
14   "putting down McCarthy": Kelly, "Enrico Banducci: The Best of Broadway."
14   "too thoughtful": MS to the author.
14   "Comic Mort Sahl": Two reviews by the same writer appeared in *Variety,* 7/28/54 and 8/4/54.
14   "Mort Sahlien technique": Enrico Banducci, "I Remember Mort Sahl," *San Francisco,* November 1976.
14   "all night": *San Francisco Examiner,* 7/21/54.

Chapter 2: I Knew We Were in Trouble

16   "new outfit": MS to the author, via telephone, 9/18/13.
16   "Dr. Arthur Ellen": MS to the author.
16   "made Mort so mad": *San Francisco Examiner,* 8/10/54.
17   "a conversational gale": *Chicago Tribune,* 8/15/54.
17   "Speaking of the 'i'": *San Francisco Chronicle,* 10/2/54.
18   "We got very tight": MS to the author.
18   "shocking": *San Francisco Examiner,* 10/5/54.
18   "stayed with him": Banducci, "I Remember Mort Sahl."
18   "mesmerize": MS to the author.
19   "I liked Mort": Gerald Nachman, *Seriously Funny* (New York: Pantheon, 2003), 59.
20   "His delivery": *Variety,* 12/8/54.
20   "didn't get Jonathan": MS to the author.
20   "lingering disappointments": *Ibid.*
21   "did his act": Kliph Nesteroff, "An Interview with Pat Carroll," posted at www.classic-showbiz.blogspot.com.
21   "write gags": *San Francisco Chronicle,* 2/27/55.
22   "Herb took Ackerman to dinner": MS to the author.
22   "One Saturday night": *San Francisco Chronicle,* 2/27/55.
23   "I'll be your manager": MS to the author.
24   "Enrico fired": *Ibid.*
25   "Do-It-Yourself Show": This concert was recorded by Fantasy Records on June 26, 1955, and released as *Mort Sahl at Sunset* in 1958.
28   "strikingly comparable": *Monterey Peninsula Herald,* 6/27/55.

Chapter 3: I Discovered I Had to Talk

30   "He was estranged": MS to the author.
30   "owned Montreal": *Ibid.*
32   "powers of persuasion": Robert Sklar, *Movie-Made America* (New York: Vintage, 1994), 175.

32   "very secretive": MS to the author.

33   "a better world": Sahl, *Heartland*, 10.

33   "It's all fixed": MS to the author.

33   "easy to decode": *Ibid.*

35   "lived in uniform": *New York Post*, 11/21/65.

37   "West Point": Edward Linn, "The Comic Who'll Never Be In," *Saturday Evening Post*,
        9/19/64.

38   "chopped": Rice, "The Fury."

39   "gas station": MS to the author.

39   "astonishing collection": John Dunning, *On the Air: The Encyclopedia of Old-Time Radio*
        (New York: Oxford, 1998), 316.

39   "being fourteen": MS to the author.

40   "met a guy at Compton": *Ibid.*

41   "met her parents": Sahl, *Heartland*, 8.

41   "very smart": MS to the author.

41   "wanted to be a writer": *Christian Science Monitor*, 10/29/87.

41   "four one-act plays": "Free Association," *New Yorker*, 11/30/57.

42   "He rejected me": *Chicago Tribune*, 2/17/57.

42   "agreeing about much": MS to the author.

42   "lived in a hotel": *Ibid.*

43   "went over fine": *San Francisco Chronicle*, 2/27/55.

43   "dynamics of the orchestra": Mort Sahl, "The Modern Idiom," *The Arts*, February 1953.

43   "bunch of misfits": MS to the author.

43   "Real Bohemia": *Minneapolis Sunday Tribune*, 9/11/60.

44   "very good to me": MS to the author.

44   "the other radicals": *Ibid.*

44   "three shifts": Sahl, *Heartland*, 10.

44   "calling out": *Berkeley Daily Planet*, 12/23/05.

44   "no money": MS to the author.

45   "vague protest": *Los Angeles Mirror News*, 11/19/58.

45   "didn't have the equipment": Sahl, *Heartland*, 12.

Chapter 4: Are There Any Groups We Haven't Offended?

46   "He thought": MS to the author.

47   "Gramercy Park": *Ibid.*

47   "The first time": Steve Allen to Robert B. Weide in interview footage shot for the docu-
        mentary *Mort Sahl: The Loyal Opposition* (1989).

47   "on the stage": MS to the author. Sahl made his television debut on September 29,
        1955, as part of a typically eclectic *Tonight!* lineup: jazz singer Sylvia Syms, a
        Brooklyn baseball fan named Hilda Chester, and an animal act from Graham,
        Texas, billed as Charles Hipp and His Lion. Sahl made a second appearance on
        November 7. (Courtesy Ben Alba)

47   "some comedians": Steve Allen to Robert B. Weide.

48   "very experimental": Ben Alba, *Inventing Late Night* (Amherst, NY: Prometheus, 2005), 17.

48   "Herbert Jacoby": MS to the author.

48   "writer development": Woody Allen to the author, via telephone, 3/4/15.

49   "overstepped": MS to the author.

49   "Can't stay mad": *San Francisco Examiner*, 4/15/56.

50   "oral columnist": *San Francisco News*, 5/2/56.

50   "the first thing": Nachman, *Seriously Funny*, 67.

51   "kind of funny": MS to the author.

52   "young and strong": *Ibid.*

52   "festive and happy": Sahl, *Heartland*, 83.

52   "great gang": MS to the author.

53   "political punch lines": *Oakland Tribune*, 11/7/56.

53   "Lang came up there": MS to the author.

53   "like the car": *Boston Globe*, 12/11/56.

54   "The audience": *Harvard Crimson*, 12/13/56.

54   "I always get attention": *Boston Globe*, 2/11/56.

54   "jazz dentist": Sahl, *Heartland*, 40.

54   "Eisenhower's secretary": MS to the author.

55   "brilliant actor": Janet Coleman, *The Compass* (New York: Alfred A. Knopf, 1990), 200.

55   "tangible": *Chicago Tribune*, 11/15/59.

56   "I have an idea": Jeffrey Sweet, *Something Wonderful Right Away* (New York: Avon, 1978), 129.

56   "pretty soon": Shelley Berman to the author, Bell Canyon, CA, 4/1/14.

57   "I wasn't a comedian": Coleman, *The Compass*, 221.

57   "Seeing Mort": Sarah Berman to the author, Bell Canyon, CA, 4/1/14.

57   "doing fine": Coleman, *The Compass*, 187.

57   "topical humor": *Variety*, 2/20/57.

57   "Young Mr. Sahl": *Daily Review*, 2/25/57.

58   "last five years": *Chicago Tribune*, 2/17/57.

58   "timeline": MS to the author.

58   "found it funny": *Ibid.*

58   "young urban man": "Playbill," *Playboy*, June 1957.

59   "like everybody": Sahl, *Heartland*, 24.

60   "a lot of gin": MS to the author.

61   "It was a restaurant": Shelley Berman to the author.

62   "network of places": Sahl, *Heartland*, 40.

62   "Ciro's": Dominic Priore, *Riot on Sunset Strip* (London: Jawbone Press, 2007), 33.

63   "Lenny was my friend": Maynard Sloate to the author, via telephone, 4/15/14.

64   "60-some-odd hours": *Variety*, 5/20/57.

64   "He was a riot": *Los Angeles Times*, 8/5/66.

64   "The audience": Robert B. Weide to the author, via telephone, 4/25/14.

64   "Hollywood": MS to the author.

64   "Lenny was a product": Sahl, *Heartland*, 22.

65 "I love you": Sahl, *Heartland*, 44.

65 "used to sit there": Sahl, *Heartland*, 61.

65 "Gene Norman hated him": MS to the author.

65 "Maître d'": Maynard Sloate to the author.

66 "durable Blue Note": *Variety*, 7/17/57.

66 "In the beginning": MS to the author.

66 "Sue": MS to the author.

67 "the fever": Sahl, *Heartland*, 67.

67 "very exciting": *Los Angeles Times*, 11/27/81.

67 "People in the business": MS to the author.

68 "*Outlook*": According to records on file at the UCLA Film and TV Archive, this episode aired on 7/28/57.

68 "They first decide": *Boston Globe*, 12/11/56.

69 "the girl you're taking out": MS to the author.

70 "The Crescendo": MS to the author.

70 "Topicality": *Variety*, 8/7/57.

71 "They're afraid": Nat Hentoff, "The Iconoclast in the Night Club," *The Reporter*, 1/9/58.

72 "Rotarians": "Free Association."

72 "never a fan": Nachman, *Seriously Funny*, 78.

72 "losing discipline": "Free Association."

72 "dates ran so long": MS to the author.

73 "political and social questions": Steve Allen to Robert B. Weide.

73 "So far as I know": Hentoff, "The Iconoclast in the Night Club."

74 "Most of the time": MS to the author.

74 "need the therapy": "Free Association."

Chapter 5: You Can't Do Better Than Capacity

75 "supply the public": *Variety*, 6/19/57.

75 "longtime bartender": MS to the author.

76 "reasonable": Details of the Sahl divorce are from *San Francisco Chronicle* 1/20/58 and 1/21/58, and *San Francisco Examiner*, 3/29/58.

76 "nine minutes": *Long Beach Independent Press-Telegram*, 7/4/58.

76 "my idea": *Hutchinson News*, 7/14/58.

76 "prove to them": MS to the author.

77 "improvise": Hentoff, "The Iconoclast in the Night Club."

78 "great dame": MS to the author.

78 "Her father": *Ibid*.

78 "insomnia": Marshall Berges, "Mort and China Sahl," *Home*, 7/11/76.

78 "Bright chicks": Alfred Bester, "Mort Sahl: The Hip Young Man," *Holiday*, September 1958.

78 "Our father": Megan Flax to the author, via telephone, 6/10/14.

79 "more tolerant": *Saturday Review*, 8/2/58.

79 "not accepted": Bester, "Mort Sahl: The Hip Young Man."

79   "liked married women": Doug Ramsey, *Take Five* (Seattle: Parkside Publications, 2005), 150.

79   "one report": Paul Desmond to Mort Sahl, 3/12/58. Paul Desmond Papers, Holt-Atherton Department of Special Collections, University of the Pacific.

79   "social club": Lou Lotorto to the author, Palm Springs, 3/8/14.

81   "Nichols": MS to the author.

82   "a genius": David Allyn, *There Ain't No Such Word as Can't* (Bloomington, IN: Author-House, 2005), 160.

82   "every theatrical convention": Sahl, *Heartland*, 59.

82   "three things happen": *Chicago Tribune*, 4/11/58.

82   "wonderful": "Phyllis Gets the Last Word—Natch," *TV Guide*, 5/31/58.

82   "Pie and coffee": Bester, "Mort Sahl: The Hip Young Man."

83   "NBC": *New York Herald Tribune*, 10/9/58.

83   "always a cinch": *New York Journal American*, May 1958.

83   "The list": *Village Voice*, 3/19/58.

84   "he and Anhalt": Philip Dunne, *Take Two: A Life in Movies and Politics* (New York: McGraw-Hill, 1980), 294.

85   "hepatitis": *Los Angeles Examiner*, 8/14/58.

85   "exhausted": *Variety*, 8/15/58.

86   "beat": *New York Herald Tribune*, 10/9/58.

86   "How old": *San Francisco Chronicle*, 10/20/58.

86   "can't seriously think": "The Plight of the TV Comics," *Esquire*, August 1958.

87   "Beat Generation": *Los Angeles Times*, 9/28/58.

87   "trend": *New York Herald Tribune*, 10/9/58.

88   "didn't get them often": MS to the author.

88   "the reason": Dunne, *Take Two*, 294.

89   "Mort is brilliant": *Los Angeles Mirror News*, 11/20/58.

89   "only man": *Los Angeles Mirror News*, 11/21/58.

89   "Hello": Herbert Mitgang, "Anyway, Onward with Mort Sahl," *New York Times Magazine*, 2/8/59.

90   "like a genius": MS to the author.

91   "My secret": Harvey Kubernik, *Canyon of Dreams: The Magic and Music of Laurel Canyon* (New York: Sterling, 2009), 15.

91   "Stan was the prophet": *Los Angeles Times*, 1/2/58.

92   "whispering of sadness": MS to the author.

92   "start Sahl": *Daily Variety*, 12/9/58.

92   "velvet censorship": *Oxnard Press-Courier*, 2/4/59.

93   "Gimmick City": *Los Angeles Mirror News*, 2/23/59.

93   "snowed": *Ibid.*

93   "first performance": *Los Angeles Times*, 3/2/59.

93   "hanging": MS to the author.

94   "Everybody will know": Shelley Berman to the author.

94   "Ben Webster": Tad Hershorn, *Norman Granz: The Man Who Used Jazz for Justice* (Berkeley: University of California Press, 2011), 256.

95   "eggheads": *Variety*, 3/10/59.

95   "original sicknic": *Time*, 7/13/59.

96   "Lenny Bruce": Shelley Berman to the author.

96   "sick jokes": *New York Times*, 12/7/58.

96   "Whenever anyone paid": MS to the author.

97   "Gisele MacKenzie": *Ibid*.

97   "Sammy Davis": Mitgang, "Anyway, Onward with Mort Sahl."

97   "limited audience": *Variety*, 3/10/59.

97   "Jerry wanted tails": MS to the author.

98   "If it weren't for him": *Los Angeles Mirror News*, 11/21/58.

100 "blockbuster": *Daily Reporter* (Dover, OH), 4/13/59.

101 "Everybody dance": MS to the author.

102 "refreshingly funny": *Boston Globe*, 4/12/59.

102 "lawless, anarchic": MS to the author.

102 "hanging out": Lou Lotorto to the author.

103 "brilliant guy": MS to the author.

104 "glamour of acting": *Los Angeles Times*, 8/17/58.

104 "dressing in the same way": *Los Angeles Examiner*, 5/3/59.

104 "I'm in love": *Chicago Tribune*, 7/9/59.

105 "Vitalis": Sahl, *Heartland*, 25.

105 "Currently": *Chicago Tribune*, 7/28/59.

105 "not too easy": *Boston Globe*, 10/6/59.

106 "prove something": MS to the author.

106 "Popsie Whittaker": *Ibid*.

107 "quite an experience": Tim Taylor, "After Dark," *Cue*, 9/5/59.

Chapter 6: A Pretty Good Exercise

108 "I'm the host": *New York Herald Tribune*, 9/11/59.

109 "remarkably uneventful": Sidney Poitier, *This Life* (New York: Knopf, 1980), 238.

109 "subtlety": MS to the author.

110 "good exercise": MS to the author.

111 "As I traveled": *Boston Globe*, 11/17/59.

111 "Castro": Sahl, *Heartland*, 82.

112 "spontaneous": *New York Times*, 10/8/59.

112 "writing jokes": Woody Allen to the author.

113 "Cates' $225,000 extravaganza": *The Future Lies Ahead* was extraordinarily expensive for a one-hour show populated largely by unknowns. By comparison, a typical Bob Hope special for the same network was budgeted at around $130,000.

113 "modifying": MS to the author.

114 "gets worse": *New York Journal-American*, 1/25/60.

114 "standard variety show": *New York Times*, 1/23/60.

114 "the Pontiac people": *Variety*, 1/27/60.

115 "he was funny": *Lowell Sun*, 1/23/60.

115   "meant a lot": MS to the author.

116   "I knew her": MS to the author.

117   "thought of proposing": *New York Sunday News*, 1/17/60.

117   "Hilarity": Bester, "Mort Sahl: The Hip Young Man."

118   "new kind of humorist": Studs Turkel interview, aired on 2/17/60.

120   "wanted to know everything": MS to the author.

122   "Today's forum": *Beverly Hills Citizen*, 3/28/60.

123   "plush room": *Pacific Stars and Stripes*, 7/31/62.

123   "third partner": Leonard Green to the author, via telephone, 12/22/14.

124   "lot of bickering": *San Francisco Examiner*, 4/27/60.

124   "Sahl rolls along": *Variety*, 5/11/60.

125   "Enrico": Kelly, "Enrico Banducci: The Best of Broadway."

125   "one network's insurance": *New York Herald Tribune*, 4/5/60.

125   "Kennedy": MS to the author.

126   "not my ambition": *New York Times*, 6/2/60.

127   "run for governor": *Oakland Tribune*, 7/11/60.

130   "stunned silence": Details regarding *The Future Lies Ahead* and the Bart Lytton incident
        are from *Oakland Tribune*, 7/11/60; *Los Angeles Times*, 7/12/60 and 7/13/60; *Reno
        Evening Gazette*, 7/14/60; *Pacific Stars & Stripes*, n.d.; and MS to the author.

131   "Kennedy came down": MS to the author.

133   "went to La Scala": MS to the author.

133   "about four people": MS to the author.

133   "the future of Lenny Bruce": *Daily Variety*, 7/25/60.

134   "writing on the wall": MS to the author.

Chapter 7: My Life Has No Dissolves

135   "bailing": *Variety*, 7/27/60.

137   "a lot of guys": 11/19/58.

139   "Mort carries the show": *San Francisco Examiner*, 12/20/60.

141   "Hefner's house": MS to the author.

141   "cars and watches": *Los Angeles Mirror News*, 11/19/58.

142   "understood everything": MS to the author.

143   "Chamber of Commerce": *Pasadena Independent Star-News*, 9/4/60.

143   "political science class": *The Inter Lake*, 10/17/60.

143   "I landed": Details of Sahl's visit to Russia are from *Daily Variety*, 10/7/60 and 10/11/60;
        New York Post, 10/10/60; *San Francisco Examiner* 10/10/60; *Time*, 10/17/60; and MS
        to the author.

145   "grossed more than $45,000": Figures on Sahl's twenty-seven city tour are from *Daily
        Variety*, 9/22/60, and *Variety*, 11/9/60.

145   "One day I did a breakfast": MS to the author.

147   "prickly": Ada (OK) *Evening News*, 12/22/60.

147   "the larger local supper clubs": *Los Angeles Times*, 11/19/60.

148   "Bob should remember": *Variety*, 10/26/60.

148 "He sold his company": *Variety*, 6/20/62.

149 "sold 125,000 units": John McPhee, "The Third Campaign," *Time*, 8/15/60.

149 "Intellectuals": *San Francisco Examiner*, 4/14/61.

152 "Something new and old": *Los Angeles Times*, 4/25/61.

153 "the forerunner": Enrico Banducci to Robert B. Weide, in interview footage shot for the documentary *Mort Sahl: The Loyal Opposition* (1989).

Chapter 8: I'm Still in Business

154 "I attack Kennedy": *New York Times*, 6/7/61.

154 "doing TV": *New York Herald Tribune*, 6/12/61.

156 "effective enough": Critical reaction to *The Mort Sahl Show* is from *New York Times*, 7/20/61; *Los Angeles Times*, 7/21/61; *New York Herald Tribune*, 7/21/61; *Newsweek*, 7/23/61; *Time* 7/28/61; *Altoona Mirror*, 7/29/61; and *San Francisco Examiner*, 8/20/61.

156 "no time flat": *Los Angeles Times*, 7/26/61.

156 "Sinatra": MS to the author.

156 "absolutely fascinating": Nancy Olson to the author, via telephone, 8/12/14. "Bill Harbach said, 'I know a nice girl,'" Mort remembers. "He was right. She had a genuine American thing about her . . . but too healthy for me. I ran for my life. Nobody's gonna make me happy!"

157 "on this trip": Details on Sahl's relationship with Patricia Manley are from *Los Angeles Examiner*, 8/18/61, 8/19/61, and 10/5/61; *Los Angeles Herald Express*, 8/19/61; *Time*, 9/1/61; *Los Angeles Mirror-News*, 10/4/61 and 11/9/61; *Hollywood Citizen-News*, 10/5/61; and *Los Angeles Times*, 10/5/61, 10/7/61, and 10/28/64.

158 "Bunkie Knudsen": MS to the author.

158 "sick business": *Racine Journal-Times*, 11/28/59.

159 "Schweitzer": *Daily Variety*, 11/30/59.

160 "national hero": MS to the author.

162 "around $2,500": Details of the problems with the American Federation of Musicians, Local 47, are from *Hollywood Citizen News*, 11/25/61; *Daily Variety*, 11/29/61; and *San Francisco Examiner*, 12/2/61. Joanie Sommers' live set with the Bob Florence Sextet was recorded on December 9, 1961, at Valley State College, Northridge. It was issued as "The Concert Side" of her 1962 album *For Those Who Think Young*.

162 "knocked hell": *Daily Variety*, 11/29/61.

162 "kind of wild": *Los Angeles Examiner*, 12/3/61.

163 "After that": *Daily Variety*, 10/29/63.

164 "newness": *Ibid.*

165 "He drank": *Ibid.*

165 "When people reject": Sahl, *Heartland*, 85.

165 "I see myself": *New York Times*, 6/2/60.

166 "I could do it": *Hollywood Citizen News*, 1/16/62.

166 "out of my depth": MS to the author.

166 "The presence of Mort Sahl": *Cumberland (MD) Evening Times*, 1/15/62.

167 "capital punishment": *Los Angeles Times*, 1/15/62.

168   "comedy series": *Daily Variety*, 4/10/62.

169   "stunning girl": MS to the author.

170   "Big Colyumists": *Los Angeles Times*, 6/13/61.

170   "flew off to Europe": Lily Valentine married Joe Cates, the producer of Mort's TV
          special *The Future Lies Ahead*. She is the mother of actress Phoebe Cates and the
          mother-in-law of actor Kevin Kline.

170   "The metamorphosis": *San Francisco Chronicle*, 2/2/62.

170   "luxury": MS to the author.

170   "Coldwater Canyon": *Variety*, 2/7/62.

171   "Mort did apologize": *Los Angeles Times*, 3/13/62.

171   "The problem": *New Castle* (PA) *News*, 2/10/62.

Chapter 9: The Meaning of the Word *Loyalty*

173   "Jack Paar": MS to the author.

173   "never liked": *New York Herald Tribune*, 5/30/62.

174   "throwing out the desk": *Cedar Rapids Gazette*, 6/7/62.

174   "It was stunning": Dick Cavett to the author, via telephone, 12/18/14.

175   "Advise and Consent": Preminger cut Mort's scene from the 138-minute picture, but he
          can still be glimpsed in the background of one shot.

175   "He's turned": *Fitchburg* (MA) *Sentinel*, 8/1/62.

176   "no screaming laughs": *New York World-Telegram*, 6/13/62.

176   "Dave Tebet": MS to the author.

177   "You wouldn't believe": *Chicago Tribune*, 11/4/62.

177   "I didn't want to play him": Nachman, *Seriously Funny*, 425.

178   "plainclothes policemen": MS to the author.

178   "I saw his show": Yvonne Craig, *From Ballet to the Batcave and Beyond* (Venice, CA: Kudu
          Press, 2000), 95.

178   "Joan Collins": *San Francisco Chronicle*, 9/19/62.

179   "his type": *Los Angeles Times*, 11/25/62.

179   "*Today* show": Yvonne Craig to the author, via telephone, 8/20/13.

179   "I was with Newman": MS to the author.

180   "I went over": Sahl, *Heartland*, 87.

180   "unpredictable behavior": Yvonne Craig to the author.

182   "eight years": *Bakersfield Californian*, 3/5/63.

182   "Too many firms": *New York Times*, 4/21/61.

184   "By that time": *Variety*, 3/13/63.

184   "proud possessors": *Variety*, 3/20/63.

185   "complete control": *Los Angeles Times*, 11/28/62.

185   "The Morris office": MS to the author.

186   "an hour and a half": *Los Angeles Times*, 9/23/63.

186   "rehearse": MS to the author.

187   "telegram": *Anderson* (IN) *Herald*, 10/4/63.

188   "Tom Moore": MS to the author.

188 "rumors": *Los Angeles Times*, 10/21/63.
189 "Ebbins used to return": Sahl, *Heartland*, 92.
189 "Goodness": *Salt Lake Tribune*, 6/3/62.
189 "Insiders": *Coshocton* (OH) *Tribune*, 7/12/62.
189 "that kind of pressure": Steve Allen to Robert B. Weide.
189 "He did whatever": MS to the author.
190 "call me a lot": Dick Cavett to the author.
190 "I was so busy": Jerry Lewis to David Susskind, n.d.
190 "left Mort's house": Dick Cavett to the author.

PART II: ANYWAY, ONWARD

Chapter 10: The Nation's Conscience

193 "I was shocked": MS to the author.
194 "difficult role": *New York Herald Tribune*, 9/17/64.
194 "never, ever": Woody Allen to the author.
195 "back of my head": Joanne Stang, "Verbal Cartoons," *New York Times Magazine*, 11/3/63.
195 "great jazz player": Woody Allen to the author.
196 "government popular": *Gettysburg Times*, 6/1/64.
196 "less toxic": *Daily Variety*, 5/4/64.
197 "He used to say": Yvonne Craig to the author.
197 "wonderful girl": Fort Pierce (FL) *News Tribune*, 5/1/64.
197 "Mort and I": Fort Pierce (FL) *News Tribune*, 5/13/64.
197 "stoke interest": *Variety*, 3/25/64.
198 "an offer": Yonkers (NY) *Herald Statesman*, 6/17/64.
198 "persistently juvenile": *New York Times*, 6/19/64.
199 "Elizabeth Taylor": Sahl, *Heartland*, 71.
200 "antiauthoritarian": Linn, "The Comic Who'll Never Be In."
200 "If there had been time": Rita Moreno, *Rita Moreno: A Memoir* (New York: Celebra, 2013), 208.
200 "went so well": *New York Herald Tribune*, 9/17/64.
201 "The director": MS to the author.
201 "give him": Yvonne Craig to the author.
202 "Bombay": "Bombay was a crooked guy who kind of moved among the stars," says Mort. "Never did see the guy again. He was always lifting watches and dropping names. Forgetting hotel bills and all."
203 "get to the people": *Los Angeles Times*, 11/23/64.
203 "very down": MS to the author.
204 "Paul Newman": *Ibid.*
205 "invented exaggeration": *Cedar Rapids Gazette*, 1/16/66.
205 "The reason": Sahl, *Heartland*, 111.

206 "more appreciation": *Los Angeles Times*, 8/10/65.

206 "The club thing": *Los Angeles Times*, 8/16/65.

207 "I walked in": Sahl, *Heartland*, 112.

208 "Oswald": *New York Times*, 11/28/65.

208 "workable format": *New York Times*, 11/29/65.

208 "James Farmer": Sahl, *Heartland*, 114.

208 "Hitler": Yvonne Craig to the author. In another account of the incident, a company
     executive remembered a slightly different version of the remark: "The problem
     with Hitler wasn't that he killed six million Jews, but that he missed the ones at
     Metromedia."

Chapter 11: A Vast Spirit of Pessimism

210 "People used to say": Yvonne Craig to the author.

210 "hard knowing me": Sahl, *Heartland*, 21.

210 "intense": Yvonne Craig to the author.

210 "been through so much": Craig, *From Ballet to the Batcave and Beyond*, 95.

211 "Door Bunny": Elaine Trebek Kares to the author, West Hollywood, 4/7/15. (Note:
     Elaine Howard, in her bunny days, went by her middle name, Teddy. Subsequently,
     she was known on Canadian TV as Elaine Callei. For the sake of clarity, she is iden-
     tified as Teddy Howard throughout the text.)

211 "barracuda": Katherine Leigh Scott, *The Bunny Years* (New York: Gallery Books, 2011),
     108.

211 "windmill pitch": "China Doll," *Playboy*, August 1964.

211 "working at Mister Kelly's": MS to the author.

212 "When he called": China Lee Sahl to the author, via telephone, 9/23/13.

212 "back to work": *Ibid*.

213 "really unique": *New York Times*, 6/15/66.

213 "The audience": *Los Angeles Times*, 1/21/66.

213 "call from Jim Gates": Bob Lally to the author, via telephone, 5/24/14.

214 "the Establishment": *Los Angeles Times*, 4/26/66.

216 "Even my agent": *Ibid*.

217 "Ebbins and Lawford": Mike McGrady, "What's Bothering Mort," *Weekend with News-
     day*, 7/16/66.

220 "a vocation": *Los Angeles Times*, 7/8/66.

220 "His area of interest": MS to the author.

220 "working the Crescendo": Maynard Sloate to the author.

221 "completely obsessed": Sally Marr to Robert B. Weide, in *Lenny Bruce: Swear to Tell the
     Truth*, Whyaduck Productions, 1998.

221 "very sick": *Los Angeles Times*, 8/5/66.

221 "kill me": *Pasadena Star News*, 9/11/66.

222 "first book": *New York Times*, 7/6/66.

223 "go up to his house": Ann Elder to the author, via telephone, 1/14/14.

224 "Judging the report": Dwight MacDonald, "Critique of the Warren Report," *Esquire*, March 1965.

225 "I was skeptical": Bob Lally to the author.

225 "a new platform": *Los Angeles Times*, 11/18/66.

225 "not a friend": *Los Angeles Times*, 11/18/66.

226 "vote for anyone": *San Francisco Examiner*, 11/25/66.

226 "knowing nods": *Las Vegas Sun*, 12/22/66.

227 "drastic drop": *Los Angeles Times*, 12/30/66.

227 "honest men": *Ibid*.

227 "dangerous": *Daily Variety*, 12/30/66.

228 "Chuck Young": MS to the author.

228 "It's the movies": *Ibid*.

228 "assassination information": Sahl, *Heartland*, 115.

228 "every major expert": Bob Lally to the author.

228 "Cowan": MS to the author.

229 "zombie-ville": *San Francisco Examiner*, 12/5/66.

231 "unusual": MS to the author.

231 "The decision": *Los Angeles Times*, 4/22/67.

231 "Mort Sahl was fired": *Los Angeles Times*, 6/18/67.

231 "stop talking": MS to the author.

231 "There was a drop": Ann Elder to the author.

231 "We get over there": MS to the author.

232 "The general manager": Bob Lally to the author.

232 "Despite our protests": *Long Beach Press Telegram*, 5/18/67.

233 "intensely embittered": *Los Angeles Times*, 5/31/67.

Chapter 12: Uncontaminated by Reason

234 "Last November": *New York Times*, 2/19/67.

235 "in the cab": MS to the author.

235 "A capacity house": *Daily Variety*, 6/19/67.

236 "Back at Mister Kelly's": *Chicago Tribune*, 7/23/67.

236 "He called me": Yvonne Craig to the author.

236 "Kup": MS to the author.

236 "One afternoon": Ann Elder to the author.

237 "the permanent opposition": *San Francisco Chronicle*, 10/29/67.

237 "lost his touch": *San Francisco Examiner*, 10/4/67.

238 "The first act": Ann Elder to the author.

239 "The script wasn't ready": MS to the author.

239 "hung up": *The Journal* (Flint, MI), 12/2/67.

239 "Here I am": *San Francisco Examiner*, 12/5/67.

240 "he was tremendous": Jim Garrison to Robert B. Weide, in interview footage shot for the documentary *Mort Sahl: The Loyal Opposition* (1989).

240   "Everybody who saw him": Andrew Sciambra to Robert B. Weide, in interview footage
        shot for the documentary *Mort Sahl: The Loyal Opposition* (1989).

241   "expenses": Jim Garrison to Robert B. Weide.

241   "no computers": MS to the author.

241   "my passion": *Tacoma News-Tribune*, 3/23/69.

241   "take all the risk": MS to the author.

241   "Rudy Tellez": *Ibid*.

243   "looked right in his face": *New York Times*, 2/1/68.

244   "Friends of Garrison": *Pocono Record*, 2/1/68.

244   "journalistic dud": *New York Times*, 2/11/68.

244   "nightmare session": *Variety*, 8/12/70.

244   "Carson": MS to the author.

244   "All the things": Woody Allen to the author.

245   "self-pity": MS to the author.

245   "Mark Lane and I": *San Mateo Times*, 3/1/68.

245   "The action": *Variety*, 10/30/68.

245   "where the kids are": *Variety*, 1/8/68.

245   "pressure tactics": *San Francisco Chronicle*, 2/28/68.

245   "worked with this man": *Boston Globe*, 1/2/68.

246   "wanted to close": MS to the author.

246   "Mort": Elliot Mintz to the author, via telephone, 10/18/14.

247   "Movies are finished": *Los Angeles Times*, 6/27/68.

248   "ABC thought": MS to the author.

249   "a performance": *New York Times*, 8/31/68.

249   "It's really funny": *Los Angeles Times*, 12/20/68.

249   "a succinct stating": "Playboy Interview: Mort Sahl," *Playboy*, February 1969.

250   "going to arrest him": MS to the author.

250   "discredit": *New York Times*, 4/20/68.

250   "don't have to prevail": *Tacoma News-Tribune*, 3/23/69.

251   "never all that interested": Elliot Mintz to the author.

251   "Don Gregory": MS to the author.

251   "all that material": It was in New York City that Mort Sahl had his only encounter with
        Jacqueline Kennedy. "Seventy-third and Madison," he remembers. "I walk into an art
        gallery, and she looks at me. And I start to walk toward her. She said, 'I know. I know.'"

252   "old measuring stick": *San Francisco Chronicle*, 3/2/69.

252   "raise the $23,000": *Daily Variety*, 3/19/69.

252   "unable to change": *Ogden Standard-Examiner*, 8/31/69.

252   "very thin thread": *Oakland Tribune*, 1/11/70.

253   "Hefner hired them": MS to the author.

253   "It wasn't just Garrison": Lawrence Christon to the author, via e-mail, 4/6/16.

254   "sex is everything": "Playboy Interview: Mort Sahl."

255   "never on one foot": MS to the author.

255   "My mother": China Lee Sahl to the author.

255   "the usual religious ceremony": *National Enquirer*, 12/20/70.

Chapter 13: I Have Met My Dream Girl

256   "general idea": *Los Angeles Herald-Examiner*, 6/19/69.

257   "big chance": *The Derrick* (Oil City, PA), 4/20/70.

257   "dream girl": *Women's Wear Daily*, 5/8/74.

257   "He asked me": *Arizona Daily Sun*, 8/14/71.

258   "The colonel": MS to the author.

258   "political thing": *Chicago Sun-Times*, 7/25/71.

258   "head through the wall": Bette Midler to David Steinberg, *Inside Comedy*, Season 3, Episode 3, Showtime.

258   "wanted to get married": MS to the author.

259   "I loved Stan Kenton": China Lee Sahl to the author.

260   "She was terrible": MS to the author.

260   "sense of humor": *Daily Tribune* (Mesa, AZ), 1/3/73.

261   "My job": China Lee Sahl to the author.

261   "a bargain": MS to the author.

261   "Mort did a thing": Yvonne Craig to the author.

262   "The Fire Chief": MS to the author.

262   "Among my acquaintances": *Ibid*.

263   "That news came": Mark Russell to the author, via telephone, 11/5/14.

264   "heavy dough": MS to the author.

264   "When Liberace's here": *Long Beach Press-Telegram*, 1/12/75.

264   "What I did": MS to the author.

264   "I thought": China Lee Sahl to the author.

265   "never a Dragon Lady": Elaine Trebek Kares to the author.

265   "continual Vegas thing": MS to the author.

266   "Jokes about the SLA": *Los Angeles Times*, 1/26/74.

266   "She took her time": MS to the author.

267   "far apart": *Variety*, 12/18/74.

267   "stimulating": *Daily Variety*, 1/8/75.

267   "The real trouble": *Los Angeles Times*, 1/11/75.

268   "I kept synthesizing": MS to the author.

268   "Meeting him": Dave Dawson in an e-mail to the author, 9/19/15.

268   "In eight days": Interview with Rudy Tellez by Charles Martin, 10/13/89, Institute of Oral History, University of Texas at El Paso.

268   "Exactly what day": Dave Dawson in an e-mail to the author.

268   "he'd lose his temper": MS to the author.

268   "mock controversy": *Ibid*.

269   "combination of things": MS to the author.

269   "personalities": *Daily Variety*, 2/28/75.

269   "our druthers": *Ibid*.

269   "We went to Rome": MS to the author.

270   "looking forward": *Los Angeles Times*, 7/11/76.

270   "five pounds": MS to the author.

Chapter 14: Why Am I the Only One?

272   "Jovanovich": MS to the author.

273   "disconcerting": *Daily Variety*, 3/22/76.

273   "restore": MS to William Jovanovich, Western Union Mailgram, 4/11/76.

274   "distinct social document": *New York Times Book Review*, 10/3/76.

274   "very likable": *San Francisco Chronicle*, 12/9/76.

274   "certain flamboyance": Sahl, *Heartland*, 19.

274   "He makes me out": Banducci, "I Remember Mort Sahl."

275   "very fearless": MS to the author.

275   "Any time": *Los Angeles Mirror-News*, 11/20/58.

276   "meaningful relationships": *Los Angeles Times*, 12/13/76.

276   "She wanted me": MS to the author.

277   "go to Elaine's": MS to the author.

277   "no quality of life": Ramsey, *Take Five*, 306.

277   "When Paul died": Yvonne Craig to the author.

278   "The Comedy Store": MS to the author.

279   "Kenton said": *Los Angeles Times*, 8/8/77.

279   "Young comedians": *San Diego Evening Tribune*, 10/6/77.

279   "My father": *Variety*, 1/11/78.

280   "I was in L.A.": MS to the author.

280   "One thing": *Washington Post*, 10/15/78.

280   "shake people up": *Christian Science Monitor*, 11/14/78.

281   "talked about the CIA": MS to the author.

281   "working for NBC": John Hart to the author, via telephone, 2/13/15.

281   "Coming from New Orleans": MS to the author.

282   "We'd have a lunch": *Ibid.*

283   "You don't see it": Ed Kaufman, "Free-Associating with Mort Sahl," *Orange Coast*, August 1978.

283   "*The Gauntlet*": MS to the author.

283   "the same script": *Christian Science Monitor*, 11/14/78.

283   "trying to write": Kaufman, "Free-Associating with Mort Sahl."

284   "Stan": MS to the author.

285   "When I got pregnant": China Lee Sahl to the author.

285   "very explosive": MS to the author.

285   "afraid of me": China Lee Sahl to the author.

285   "China felt": Elaine Trebek Kares to the author.

286   "constant refrain": MS to the author.

286   "vagabonds": MS to the author.

286   "Christmas": Elaine Trebek Kares to the author.

287   "great gambler": China Lee Sahl to the author.

287   "I'll get it back": MS to the author.

287   "When I left him": China Lee Sahl to the author.

288 "He has survived": Salley Rayl, "He Didn't Like Ike," *People*, 5/10/82.

288 "Offended": *Ibid*.

288 "We all wrote": MS to the author.

290 "I've got a producer": *Chicago Tribune*, 3/10/85.

291 "He goes to Winkler": MS to the author.

292 "Ronald Reagan?": *Fort Myers News-Press*, 10/2/81.

292 "they raise money": *Chicago Tribune*, 3/10/85.

293 "one-liners": *New York Post*, 10/8/87.

293 "Pacific Palisades": *Chicago Tribune*, 3/10/85.

294 "You have to distinguish": *Los Angeles Herald Examiner*, 9/16/81.

294 "The complacency": *Los Angeles Times*, 9/2/84.

Chapter 15: The Loyal Opposition

295 "got wind": Ron Powers, "The Last Angry Man," *GQ*, August 1984.

295 "gave them the lines": MS to the author.

296 "He did it so well": Alvin Sargent to the author, via telephone, 9/21/13.

297 "gone to see him": MS to the author.

298 "wasn't getting any clubs": *Ibid*.

298 "didn't quite see it": *New York Post*, 10/8/87.

299 "peevish": *Los Angeles Times*, 11/1/87.

299 "really scared": Lawrence Christon to the author, Downey, CA, 2/13/14.

299 "this may be his time": Ken Gross, "Not Going Gentle into That Good Night," *People*, 10/12/87.

300 "more comedians": *Christian Science Monitor*, 10/29/87.

301 "Nearly two hours": *Ibid*.

301 "fair business": MS to the author.

301 "time to go to television": "The Joker Is Riled," *GQ*, March 1988.

302 "suspicious": Robert B. Weide to the author, Studio City, 1/29/14.

303 "somebody would come": MS to the author.

303 "left-handed compliment": MS to the author.

303 "China always had someone": Elaine Trebek Kares to the author.

303 "In the industry": MS to the author.

304 "Sometimes": Robert B. Weide to the author.

304 "didn't have a lot of time": John Hart to the author.

304 "therapy": MS to the author.

305 "I left him": China Lee Sahl to the author.

305 "Jack Hoagland": MS to the author.

305 "Almost immediately": Bob Burns to the author, via telephone, 9/14/15.

307 "Trying to do": Rip Rense, "Sahl and Pepper," *Emmy*, January-February 1992.

307 "wasn't resolved": MS to the author.

308 "Jon Peters": *Ibid*.

308 "Kander and Ebb": MS to the author.

Chapter 16: Who the Enemy Is

309   "My kid": *Spokesman-Review* (Spokane, WA), 7/8/07.

309   "pride": Elaine Trebek Kares to the author.

309   "terrific": Jack Schwartz to the author, via telephone, 9/30/13.

309   "good looks": *Los Angeles Times*, 5/22/83.

309   "amazing": Elaine Trebek Kares to the author.

310   "The school": MS to the author.

310   "take him everywhere": Mark Russell to the author.

310   "the conversation": Robert B. Weide to the author.

310   "The kid": *New York Post*, 10/8/87.

310   "back from the road": MS to the author.

310   "affectionate": Robert B. Weide to the author.

311   "the whole story": *Los Angeles Times*, 11/11/90.

311   "same old stuff": MS to the author.

311   "I remember Mort": Robert B. Weide to the author.

312   "lived on top": Lawrence Christon to the author.

312   "stuffing cotton": *Sandusky Register*, 9/13/67.

312   "never told": MS to the author.

312   "Little Mort": Elaine Trebek Kares to the author.

313   "My mother": China Lee Sahl to the author.

313   "rough": Robert B. Weide to the author.

313   "really got hot": MS to the author.

313   "a little bit afraid": Lawrence Christon to the author.

314   "could not understand": Elaine Trebek Kares to the author.

314   "When he got out": MS to the author.

314   "down in Van Nuys": Lou Lotorto to the author.

315   "one of my best friends": MS to the author.

315   "The rules": Lou Lotorto to the author.

315   "bad news": MS to the author.

316   "China was very upset": Elaine Trebek Kares to the author.

316   "Mort was standing": Lawrence Christon to the author.

316   "Friends of his": Alvin Sargent to the author.

317   "When I got there": Robert B. Weide to the author.

317   "people he was associated with": Elaine Trebek Kares to the author.

317   "Mort's voice": John Hart, Mort Sahl Jr. eulogy. (Courtesy John Hart)

318   "very mensch-y thing": Robert B. Weide to the author.

318   "I drove up there": MS to the author.

319   "don't think it will ever go away": *San Francisco Chronicle*, 9/29/96.

319   "really get buried": MS to the author.

319   "speak more from my heart": *Orange County Register*, 7/15/96.

320   "China went": Elaine Trebek Kares to the author.

320   "get out of here": MS to the author.

320   "Everybody thought": Elaine Trebek Kares to the author.

321   "a shame": MS to the author.

322   "Budd Friedman": Robert B. Weide to the author.

322   "Sahl had turned eighty": *Los Angeles Times*, 5/18/07.

Chapter 17: More Comedians, Less Humor

324   "Mort's career": *Newsroom: Mort Sahl Teaching CMCers About the Other America*, Clare-
       mont McKenna College, Office of Public Affairs and Communications, 10/23/07.

324   "I want to show": *Ibid.*

325   "They wanted screenwriting": *Berkeley Daily Planet*, 7/23/09.

325   "where he wants to be": "Comedian Mort Sahl Found," www.insidesocal.com, 5/9/09.

325   "wish it had worked": *Marin Independent Journal*, 8/9/10.

325   "running around": *Berkeley Daily Planet*, 7/23/09.

325   "falling apart": *Marin Independent Journal*, 8/9/10.

325   "he sells out": *Ibid.*

INDEX